Masterworks from the Musée des Beaux-Arts, Lille

The Musée des Beaux-Arts, Lille, designed by the architects Bérard
and Delmas, which opened to the public a century ago, on
March 6, 1892. The principal façade dates from 1889 to 1892.

Masterworks from the Musée des Beaux-Arts, Lille

THE METROPOLITAN MUSEUM OF ART

DISTRIBUTED BY HARRY N. ABRAMS, INC., NEW YORK

This volume has been published in conjunction with the exhibition
"Masterworks from the Musée des Beaux-Arts, Lille," held at
The Metropolitan Museum of Art, New York, October 27, 1992–
January 17, 1993.

The exhibition is made possible by Crédit Lyonnais.

It has been organized with the cooperation of the Musée des Beaux-
Arts, Lille. An indemnity has been granted by the Federal Council on
the Arts and the Humanities. Additional support for the exhibition
catalogue has been provided by Orcofi.

Published by The Metropolitan Museum of Art, New York
Copyright © 1992 by The Metropolitan Museum of Art
All rights reserved

John P. O'Neill, Editor in Chief
Ellen Shultz, Editor
Malcolm Grear Designers, Designer
Susan Chun, Production
Pamela T. Barr, Bibliographer

Set in Monotype Baskerville by The Sarabande Press, New York
Separations, printing, and binding by Arnoldo Mondadori Editore
    S.p.A., Verona, Italy

Translations from the French by Jean Marie Clarke and Ellen Shultz

Jacket/cover: Francisco de Goya y Lucientes. *Time*. See cat. no. 34

Frontispiece: The Musée des Beaux-Arts, Lille

Library of Congress Cataloging-in-Publication Data

Lille (France). Musée des beaux-arts.
    Masterworks from the Musée des beaux-arts, Lille.
        p.   cm.
    Includes bibliographical references and index.
    ISBN 0-87099-649-5.—ISBN 0-87099-650-9 (pbk.).—ISBN 0-8109-6417-1 (Abrams)
    1. Art, Modern—Exhibitions. 2. Lille (France). Musée des beaux-
arts—Exhibitions. I. Metropolitan Museum of Art (New York, N.Y.)
II. Title.
N6350.L56 1992   92-24688
707'.4'7471—dc20   CIP

Contents

Director's Foreword

In 1974 The Metropolitan Museum of Art signed an important protocol with the Réunion des Musées Nationaux in Paris. Since then, a series of major exhibitions has been organized by the museum in collaboration with the Musée du Louvre or with the Musée d'Orsay that include "Masterpieces of Tapestry from the 14th to the 16th Century" (1974), "Impressionism: A Centenary Exhibition" (1974–75), "French Painting 1774–1830: The Age of Revolution" (1975), "France in the Golden Age" (1982), and monographic celebrations of Manet (1983), Boucher (1986), Zurbarán (1987), Fragonard (1988), Degas (1988–89), and, most recently, Seurat (1991).

Although the museum world of France is highly centralized, some of the greatest works of art in French collections may be found in cities other than Paris. That this should be the case was envisioned by Napoleon, who, in 1801, decreed that fifteen cities outside of Paris were to have museums that would be filled in part with paintings and other objects dispersed by the national government. Among the finest of these institutions is the Musée des Beaux-Arts in Lille. Its splendid building (1885–92), formerly called the Palais des Beaux-Arts, is undergoing renovation until 1994, allowing a selection of the city's treasures to be seen in New York.

Lille was Flemish and then French before it became, by marriage, part of the duchy of Burgundy. In his essay below, entitled "The Birth of the Modern Museum," the distinguished French historian Marc Fumaroli reviews the role of Lille as a city of the Southern Netherlands (one still follows signs to Rijssel, Lille's Flemish name, in many parts of Belgium), and then, after its reconquest by Louis XIV, as a cultural and commercial center of northern France. Numerous Northern European artists found patrons in the city; Rubens's monumental *Descent from the Cross* (cat. no. 1) was, for example, one of several altarpieces sent directly by an Antwerp painter to a church or convent in Lille. Institutional patronage more typical of the nineteenth century was the purchase by the Lille museum of Delacroix's *Medea About to Murder Her Children* (cat. no. 37) and of Courbet's *After Dinner at Ornans* (cat. no. 40)—in both cases at the Salons in which these ambitious paintings were first placed on public view.

The Metropolitan Museum's exhibition, "Masterworks from the Musée des Beaux-Arts, Lille," presents one of several possible cross-sections of the collections of the Musée des Beaux-Arts. The forty-one paintings catalogued here date from about 1600 to 1850, except for Lille's unusual late van Gogh (cat. no. 42). Well-known paintings from before 1600 were excluded on conservation grounds, while those dating from after 1850 were judged too numerous to represent adequately. A few pictures were chosen not as "masterworks" but for their distinctiveness and charm, such as *The Young Draftsman* (cat. no. 6) by Wallerant Vaillant, who was born in Lille, and the casual portrait of a woman by Paul-Ponce-Antoine Robert (cat. no. 22). The full range of the paintings collection in Lille is surveyed in an essay by Walter Liedtke, Curator of European Paintings at the Metropolitan Museum and coordinator of the exhibition.

William M. Griswold, Assistant Curator of Drawings, describes in another essay why Lille has such an extraordinary collection of Old Master drawings, hundreds of which were left to his native city by Jean-Baptiste-Joseph Wicar (see his *Self-Portrait*, cat. no. 29). Nine Raphaels and nine Delacroix are among the forty-nine drawings dating from the late fifteenth to the mid-nineteenth century that were selected for exhibition in New York. Finally, reliefs by Donatello and by David d'Angers merely hint at the quality and scope of the sculpture in the Lille museum, to say nothing of the decorative arts and other areas of the collections.

Throughout the planning and realization of this exhibition the staff of the Metropolitan Museum enjoyed the ardent support and friendly cooperation of Arnauld Brejon de Lavergnée, Chief Curator, in charge of the Musée des Beaux-Arts. His energy and expertise are sensed throughout the catalogue while his words fill many pages, including those on which his essay on the history of the Lille museum appears. William Griswold catalogued most of the drawings, and Walter Liedtke nearly half of the paintings; the other catalogue entries were written by members of the curatorial departments in New York and Lille: Katharine Baetjer, James Draper, Anne Norton, and Susan Stein at the Metropolitan Museum, and Arnauld Brejon de Lavergnée, Barbara Brejon de Lavergnée, and Annie Scottez-De Wambrechies at the Musée des Beaux-Arts. In addition, we wish to thank, at the Musée des Beaux-Arts, Annie Castier, who helped to organize the exhibition, and Odile Liesse, Conservator in the Department of Drawings. We wish to acknowledge support from Orcofi for the catalogue.

As a city museum the Musée des Beaux-Arts depends on the good will and support of the entire community, and above all of the Mayor of Lille and former Prime Minister of France Pierre Mauroy. We are enormously grateful to the Mayor and to the Deputy Mayor for Cultural Affairs, Jacquie Buffin, for their indispensable cooperation. Monina von Opel, their representative in the United States, gracefully coordinated contacts between the city of Lille and the Metropolitan Museum in the earlier stages of the project.

Finally, we are deeply indebted to our corporate sponsor, Crédit Lyonnais, for making the exhibition possible, and we appreciate especially the enthusiasm of Jean-Yves Haberer, Chairman of the Board, and Robert Cohen, Executive Vice President in the United States.

PHILIPPE DE MONTEBELLO
Director
The Metropolitan Museum of Art

Chairman's Statement

Crédit Lyonnais has enjoyed a solid reputation as a patron of the arts since its founding in 1863. Nevertheless, its association with the exhibition "Masterworks from the Musée des Beaux-Arts, Lille" at The Metropolitan Museum of Art in New York marks the first time that Crédit Lyonnais is the sole corporate sponsor of an art exhibition in the United States. The decision was prompted by three important factors:

First of all, there is the singular importance of the occasion itself. As M. Pierre Mauroy has pointed out, this is the first complete collection from a French museum to be presented by The Metropolitan Museum of Art, and the quality of the works makes it one of the most noteworthy international exhibitions in recent years. The Lille collection elicits the deep sense of pride that is sought by any patron.

Secondly, this sponsorship offers us a historic opportunity to acknowledge the relationship we have enjoyed with the United States through the development of increasingly closer connections with leading American companies since our first United States branch opened in New York in 1971. Our network of branches and the large volume of business over the past two decades has enabled Crédit Lyonnais USA to become a veritable American citizen. Thus, it was only appropriate that Crédit Lyonnais USA recognize its citizenship by participating in this prestigious cultural event.

Thirdly, we believe support of the exhibition has a special significance for us because of what it symbolizes. The masterpieces in the Musée des Beaux-Arts in Lille have made it the second most important French museum after the Louvre in Paris. By bringing these major works of art from regional France to New York, we are demonstrating the growing interrelationship among regions, nations, and the world community. This mirrors Crédit Lyonnais's strategy, which is based on regional commitment, national prominence, and international vocation. By sponsoring "Masterworks from the Musée des Beaux-Arts, Lille," Crédit Lyonnais is fulfilling both its cultural commitment and its corporate role.

JEAN-YVES HABERER
Chairman
Crédit Lyonnais

Mayor's Statement

It is no exaggeration to call the presentation of "Masterworks from the Musée des Beaux-Arts, Lille," made possible by the generous sponsorship of Crédit Lyonnais, an international event. Not only is it the first time that the Metropolitan Museum has hosted an exhibition solely of works from the collection of a museum in France; it is also the first time that the citizens of Lille have had to part with their museum's most precious jewels. The city will take advantage of the sojourn abroad of these treasures to begin to renovate and modernize its Palais des Beaux-Arts, and, following this latest renovation project, the Musée des Beaux-Arts will take its place among the finest museums of Europe.

The Musée des Beaux-Arts represents the legacy of four centuries of commissions and collecting by the citizens of Lille. Among its masterpieces are magnificent paintings created by Rubens for the churches and convents of Lille as well as more recently acquired French pictures, such as Jean-Baptiste-Siméon Chardin's *The Silver Cup*. There are examples by important artists of all the major schools of European painting: Spanish (Goya), Italian (Raphael), Flemish (Bouts and Rubens), Dutch (de Witte), and, of course, French.

We hope that our friends in America will come away from this exhibition reassured that the collection of the Musée des Beaux-Arts in Lille is a vital and continuously evolving cultural resource. A number of the paintings shown in New York have been restored; some have even been remounted. Rubens's *Descent from the Cross*, to cite just one picture, has benefited from a splendid remounting, and the unfortunate repaints over the years have finally been removed. Some works of art have been discovered in storage, including David d'Angers's four bas-reliefs depicting the invention of printing in the four corners of the world—superb preparatory studies for the artist's *Gutenberg Monument* in Strasbourg. In addition, the entries in the catalogue to the exhibition bear witness to the extensive and careful research carried out by the curators at the Musée des Beaux-Arts as well as by those at the Metropolitan Museum.

The city of Lille is committed to becoming one of the most influential centers of international business in the Europe of tomorrow. I am convinced, however, that cultural creativity and vitality will also play an essential role in deciding the future of the city. I take great pleasure in inviting our American friends to discover the treasures of Lille's Musée des Beaux-Arts at the Metropolitan Museum and, beginning in 1994, to come to Lille to admire and appreciate them again in our restored museum.

PIERRE MAUROY
Former Prime Minister of France,
Member of Parliament,
and Mayor of Lille

Contributors to the Catalogue

KBB   Katharine B. Baetjer

ABL   Arnauld Brejon de Lavergnée

BBL   Barbara Brejon de Lavergnée

JDD   James David Draper

WMG   William M. Griswold

WL   Walter Liedtke

AN   Anne Norton

AS-DW   Annie Scottez-De Wambrechies

SAS   Susan Alyson Stein

Introductory Essays

The Birth of the Modern Museum

MARC FUMAROLI

Preface

The masterpieces from the Musée des Beaux-Arts in Lille, presented to the American public for the first time at The Metropolitan Museum of Art in New York, were chosen from among the outstanding collections of this French provincial museum. The description might appear paradoxical, but the English language has no equivalent for the distinction made in French between the genitive "*de province*" ("from the provinces") and the adjective "*provincial*" ("provincial"). The works by Goya, Delacroix, Rubens, David, and Chardin that have crossed the Atlantic from Lille are, indeed, worthy of the Metropolitan Museum and of the Louvre, and in no way do they reflect the negative connotations that the designation "provincial museum" shares in both French and English. In order to clarify this seeming paradox, we will retrace the origins and the significance of this French institution. It is rooted in the sweeping political history of Europe, and is inseparable from the history of the very idea of the Museum.

"*Province*" is a word whose usage in French has a long history. It bears witness to the degree to which France identified with Rome, even through its language. While this phenomenon prevailed under the Ancien Régime, it reached its peak during the Revolution and under the Empire, at the same time that the French "*Musées de province*" came into being and the modern concept of the Museum was formulated. "*Province*" is actually a Latin word, employed by the Romans to designate the lands conquered outside of Italy that were subject to Roman law and ruled by Roman governors. The kings of France had applied the term to the vast fiefdoms that were annexed to the Île-de-France over the course of time, although in France "*provinces*" enjoyed a far greater degree of autonomy than those administered by the Roman Empire. France became a Republic "one and indivisible" in 1792, a Consulate in 1799, and an Empire in 1804. The number of "provinces"—this time, in the Roman sense of the term—grew well beyond the traditional French borders. "*Musées de province*," set up by the Consulate and modeled after the Louvre (which had been established by the Convention as the Muséum Central de la République), still exist today in Lille and in Strasbourg, as well as in Geneva, Milan, Brussels, and Mainz. They were the heirs to the "temples of Fine Art" created by the Revolutionary State, and they were meant to symbolize the universality of the laws and the guiding spirit of its Empire. The provincial Museum was as characteristic a product of the French Revolutionary Republic as the temples to Jupiter and the thermae erected in the forums of provincial capitals had been for the Roman Empire.

Lille, by right of conquest, had become a provincial capital in 1668, under Louis XIV, after the signing of the Treaty of Aix-la-Chapelle between France and Spain. In order to affirm the new status of this Flemish city within the realm, the king had a number of monuments built in the Roman style, such as the triumphal arch known as the Porte de Paris (see fig. 1), and the Church of the Madeleine, with its classical façade, at the end of the rue des Carmes. Using Paris as a model, a vast urban renewal project was conceived by the architect Vauban, providing the city with new neighborhoods (Le Beauregard) and streets (the rue Royale, rue de Paris, and rue de la Monnaie), which today still preserve the characteristics of Parisian architecture of the *Grand Siècle*. To maintain its rank, this provincial metropolis called upon its master craftsmen (weavers, goldsmiths, ceramists) to make suitable objects to decorate its churches, convents, and mansions. Architects, painters, and sculptors in Lille, as in Paris, had their own Académie in the eighteenth century. However, the time of the Museum had not yet come—and would not, until the Revolution.

The Musée de Lille, along with the other provincial museums, owes its existence to a decree issued in Paris by the First Consul, Napoleon Bonaparte, on the 14th day of Fructidor in the Year IX (September 1, 1801). This decree, which was based on a report submitted by the Minister of the Interior, Jean-Antoine Chaptal, provided for the establishment of museums in eleven other French cities (see fig. 2): Bordeaux, Caen, Lyons, Strasbourg, Marseilles, Rouen, Nantes, Dijon, Toulouse, Rennes, and Nancy. In addition, Geneva, Brussels, and Mainz—now the capitals of countries, states, or regions outside of France—were to be given paintings collections by the State. These cities had been liberated from despotism and superstition by the French Revolutionary armies and became part of the *Grande Nation*. The museums created in these cities by the consular decree are today the pride of French-speaking Switzerland, Belgium, and the Rhineland-Palatinate area of Germany. At the beginning, though, they were "*Musées de province*" like the one in Lille, and they, too, owed their existence to a decision made in Paris by the French Revolutionary State.

In order to create fifteen museums at once, all of them equally worthy of being called "miniature Louvres," the Revolutionary State had to have prodigious resources of works of art. The decree of 14 Fructidor stated only: "Article II: The paintings will be taken from the reserves of the Louvre and Versailles."

Unlike the great American art patrons of the twentieth century who could fulfill such an ambitious program independently, relying only on the buying power of the dollar and the advice of experts, not on federal law, the French Revolutionary State, although not lacking in art experts, had no financial resources. However, its determination to create museums by law was even stronger than that of the American philanthropists. The Republic, and then the French Empire, considered themselves the executors of the legacy of the Age of Enlightenment. The philosophers of the Enlightenment believed that the political and moral freedom of Man could be effected through education: both through the Arts, the sons of "Genius," and the Sciences, the daughters of "Reason." The initial formulation of these principles may be found in the essays of David Hume (1742): "The only suitable cradle in which to shelter these nobles [the Arts and the Sciences] is a free State; they may, however, be transplanted into any kind of government; a republic is the most favorable for the birth of the Sciences, and a civilized monarchy for that of the more refined Arts." The nascent French Republic therefore not only had to obey its principles by founding polytechnic schools, but it also had to "transplant" the heritage of the Arts from the monarchy by opening museums. It is true that the Republic first had to dispense with the archaic political and religious systems of the Ancien Régime that stood in the way of its program of political renewal. Among the "spoils" of the Ancien Régime, there was more than enough with which to stock the Louvre and the fifteen other museums. It was in the museums that, under the laws of liberty, the seeds of the spirit of the Arts would be cultivated and made to prosper.

In 1801, the Consulate redistributed the property that the Constituante, the Convention, and the Directoire had removed, by law and treaty, from the Church and from former kings and princes. The works of art salvaged from the "shipwrecked" monarchy and the Church henceforth became part of the public patrimony of the Nation. The Empire perfected this policy by widening even more the circle of provincial museums that revolved around the almighty Louvre. Northern Italy—which Napoleon I established as a viceroyalty and entrusted to his son-in-law, Eugène de Beauharnais—was endowed with a museum in Milan, even though its art treasures had been seized unmercifully by the Directoire. Expropriations from private and ecclesiastical collections, however, were abundant enough to fill the Museum's needs. To this day, the collections of the Pinacoteca di Brera are a faithful reflection of this Revolutionary redistribution of art. Louis Bonaparte, made king of Holland by his brother Napoleon I, arranged to have his arrival in Amsterdam on April 21, 1808, coincide with the opening to the public of a museum—the present Rijksmuseum. General Bonaparte had had the cream of the princely collections in Kassel transferred to Paris, which did not prevent his brother Jerome Bonaparte from building and richly endowing a museum in Kassel when he was made king of Westphalia. On December 20, 1809, as Spain was being plundered by French troops, yet another of the emperor's brothers, Joseph, named king of Spain, founded a museum in Madrid—the future Museo del Prado.

This explains the high standing and excellence of the Musée de Lille: It was part of the first generation of European museums—in the modern sense—created by the French Revolution. The institutions that belonged to this first generation defined and established the standards of the Museum, as opposed to the kinds of collections or assemblages of works of art that existed earlier. The Museum was set up as a public institution whose purpose was to educate its public by conserving and exhibiting its collection of masterpieces, which was public patrimony. Over time, the original prototype of the Museum would be interpreted and implemented in many different ways: Acquisitions policies, principles of classification, and criteria may have changed, but the essence of the institution has triumphantly weathered two centuries, and today prevails worldwide.

The Revolutionary State and Works of Art

With the French Revolution having provided the means, Chaptal's report to the First Consul in 1801 fulfilled the dream of a century of philosophers. As Hume or Diderot might have done, Chaptal wrote that museums should be established wherever "acquired knowledge, a large population, and a natural predisposition presage success in the education of students." Museums—as the creations of a state whose aim was education—were repositories of the national heritage; they would use their holdings as a tool with which to educate first the artist and then the general public. The concern of the Revolutionary State for the preservation of its nationalized works of art and for their use in civic education had already been advanced, albeit in more abstract and pressing terms, in the many declarations issued by the Revolutionary Assemblies. On March 20, 1791, the Assemblée Constituante had enacted an *Instruction concernant les châsses, reliquaires et autres pièces d'orfèvrerie provenant du mobilier des maisons ecclésiastiques et destinés à la fonte* (directions concerning shrines, reliquaries, and other goldsmiths' work belonging to ecclesiastical institutions and designated to be melted down), which stipulated that "all monuments dating to before 1300 are to be preserved." Pursuant to a decision made on December 18, 1793, the Convention printed and widely distributed the following spring an *Instruction sur la manière d'inventorier et de conserver dans toute l'étendue de la République tous les objets qui peuvent servir aux arts, aux sciences et à l'enseignement* (directions for cataloguing and preserving objects that could serve the arts, the sciences, and education throughout the Republic). All patriotic citizens in the country were invited to transform themselves into curators of a Museum of France, which, henceforth, was to become a vast public repository of works of art that would bring about a general renewal through education. The forewords to the *Instructions* stipulated that: "The people of France, having accepted a republican constitution, must ensure that it is respected abroad through force, but at home it can be maintained only through the influence of reason. The people should not forget that reason is strengthened only by a sound and proper education. Having been placed within their grasp, education has already become their most powerful means of regeneration and glory."

Like the idea of the Museum, the concept of a national and potentially universal patrimony originated with the Revolution. Paradoxically, Revolutionary enthusiasm was divided between a determination to destroy the Ancien

Régime and all its symbols and a no less firm desire to preserve for the people anything from the past that might further their education and edification. The Ancien Régime had not been conservative. In an exchange with Emperor Francis I, Louis XV received the duchy of Lorraine, which he gave to his father-in-law, Stanislaus I Leczinski. Upon the latter's death in 1766, King Louis XV inherited Lorraine, made it a French province, and immediately had all of the royal furniture and art objects from his father-in-law's residences put up for sale. The Château de Lunéville was converted into a garrison, the Château de Commercy abandoned, and the charming country estates of the last prince of Lorraine were demolished and their furnishings sold at auction. The masterpieces of art and the decorative objects that they contained were destroyed. To understand what the Abbé Grégoire called Revolutionary "vandalism," one must bear in mind these traditional rites of succession. Yet, the notion of a national heritage and of public ownership of works of art, introduced under the Revolution, is a conservative concept of which museums—and, more recently, ecology, which imposes on Nature the role of a museum—are the logical extension.

The decree of 14 Fructidor, Year IX, more restrained than the *Instructions* of the Assemblies, posited the dual principle of a national heritage and a goal of universal education. In creating so many museums, the Consular Republic wanted as complete a collection as possible of State-owned works of art, which could be exhibited in all the major cities where such a collection might further the education of both artists and the general public. Chaptal borrowed the concept of an "educationally useful" collection from eighteenth-century art history. Works of art were to be organized into "schools," following the method established by Vasari and perfected by Luigi Lanzi, the Italian art historian, who had adopted the system at the Galleria degli Uffizi in Florence, as well as in his *Storia pittorica dal Risorgimento delle Belle Arti fin presso al fine del XVII secolo* (1789). At the Uffizi, the arrangement of art works by school was combined with their chronological ordering. The German archaeologist Johann Joachim Winckelmann advocated a similar approach in his *History of Art among the Ancients* (1764). Applied to European art, it led the statesmen of the Revolution to the concept of a panoramic, or encyclopedic, Museum, bringing together characteristic works by the foremost masters of the various "schools" of European art. For the French State, the most comprehensive collection had to be at the center of the Republic itself—at the Louvre. The same principles governed the founding of the National Gallery of Art in Washington, D.C., in 1937—more than a century later. To fill the Louvre and, in addition, fifteen provincial museums, and to make the latter worthy of their Parisian model, Bonaparte and Chaptal had at their disposal, both in Paris and in Versailles, much larger collections as rich in masterpieces as that assembled by Andrew

Mellon—which, however, had its Raphaels, a van Eyck, and a Titian, obtained as a result of another revolution from the collections of the czars.

The Revolutionary Collections

Under the decree of 14 Fructidor, a total of 656 Old Master paintings were equally divided up by the State. Further distributions followed, but at a slower rate, so that by the end of the Empire 1,058 pictures had been dispersed among the provincial museums. The Musée de Lille received forty-six paintings (see fig. 3). The municipality of Lille had appointed a commissioner, the miniaturist Louis Nicolas van Blarenberghe, who was sent to Paris to try to influence the selections; Lallemant's *Adoration of the Magi* (cat. no. 18) and Champaigne's *Nativity* (cat. no. 19) were part of the original group. Rubens's *Ecstasy of Mary Magdalene* (cat. no. 3), which the French armies under the Convention had confiscated from the Convent of the Recollects in Ghent and had had trans-

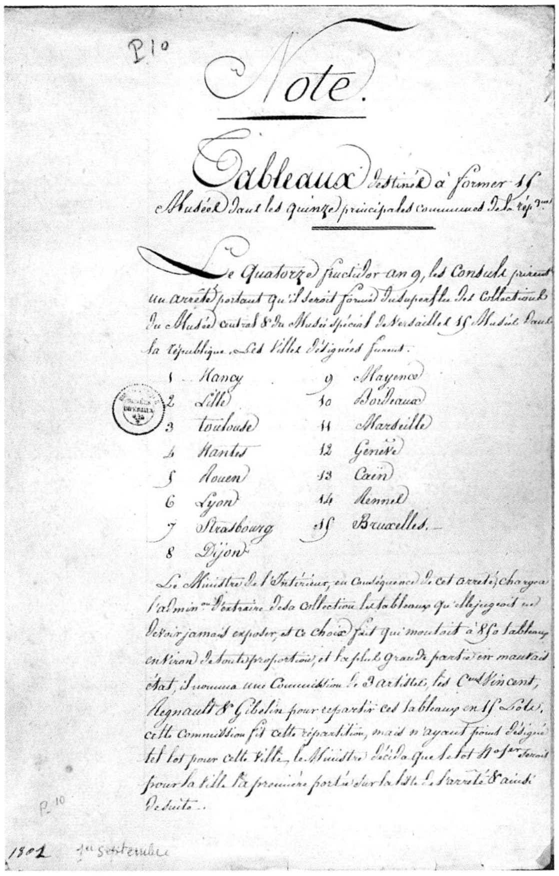

P10

Note.

Tableaux destinés à former 15 Musées dans les quinze principales communes de la Rép.que

Le Quatorze fructidor an 9, les Consuls prirent un arrêté portant qu'il seroit formé du superflu des Collections du Musée central & du Musée spécial de Versailles 15 Musées dans la république. Les villes désignées furent.

1 Nancy 9 Mayence
2 Lille 10 Bordeaux
3 toulouse 11 Marseille
4 Nantes 12 Genève
5 Rouen 13 Caën
6 Lyon 14 Rennes
7 Strasbourg 15 Bruxelles.
8 Dijon

Le Ministre de l'Intérieur, en conséquence de cet arrêté, chargea l'admin.on d'extraire de sa collection les tableaux qu'elle jugeoit ne devoir jamais exposer, et ce choix fait qui montoit à 850 tableaux environ de toute proportion, et la plus grande partie en mauvais état, il nomma une Commission de 3 artistes, les C.ns Vincent, Regnault & Gibelin pour répartir ces tableaux en 15 lots. cette Commission fit cette répartition, mais n'ayant point désigné tel lot pour telle ville, le Ministre décida que le lot N.o 1er seroit pour la ville la première portée sur la liste de l'arrêté & ainsi de suite.

P. 10

1801 1er septembre

FIGURE 2. Decree issued by Napoleon on 14 Fructidor, Year IX (September 1, 1801), providing for museums to be established in eleven French cities. Archives du Louvre, Paris

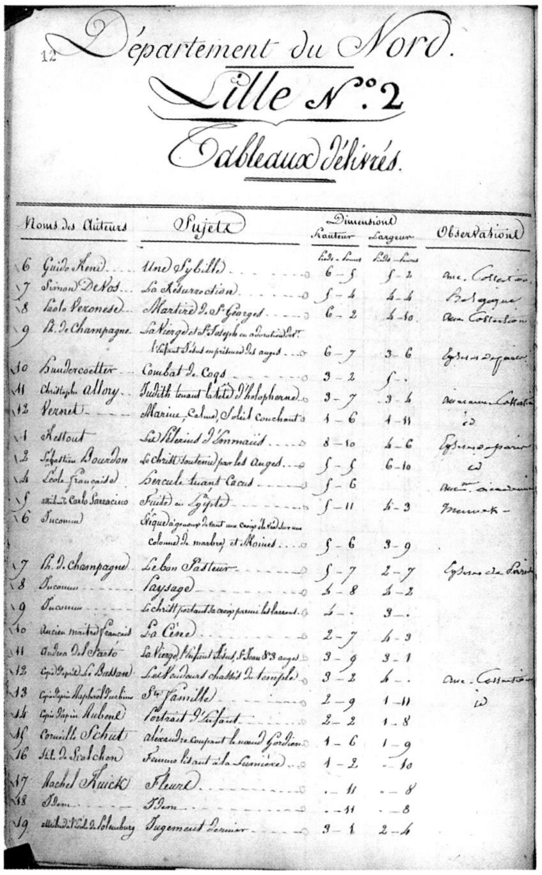

12 Département du Nord.

Lille N.o 2

Tableaux délivrés.

	Noms des Auteurs	Sujets	Dimensions Hauteur (Pieds – Pouces)	Dimensions Largeur (Pieds – Pouces)	Observations
6	Guido Reni	Une Sybille	6 – 5	5 – 2	Anc. Collection
7	Simon De Vos	La Résurrection	5 – 4	4 – 4	Belgique
8	Paolo Veronese	Martire de S.t Georges	6 – 2	4 – 10	Anc. Collection
9	Ph. de Champagne	La Vierge et S.t Joseph en adoration de l'Enfant Jésus environné des anges	6 – 7	3 – 6	[illegible]
10	Hondecoeter	Combat de Coqs	3 – 2	5 – .	
11	Christophe Allory	Judith tenant la tête d'Holopherne	3 – 7	3 – 4	[illegible] Collection
12	Vernet	Marine, Calme, Soleil Couchant	4 – 6	4 – 11	id
1	Restout	Les Pèlerins d'Emmaüs	8 – 10	4 – 6	[illegible]
2	Sébastien Bourdon	Le Christ soutenu par les anges	5 – 5	6 – 10	id
4	École française	Hercule tuant Cacus	5 – 6		[illegible]
5	attribué à Carlo Saracino	Fuite en Egypte	5 – 11	4 – 3	[illegible]
6	Inconnu	Évêque à genoux devant une croix [illegible] colonne de marbre et Moines	5 – 6	3 – 9	
7	Ph. de Champagne	Le bon Pasteur	5 – 7	2 – 7	[illegible]
8	Inconnu	Paysage	4 – 8	4 – 2	
9	Inconnu	Le Christ portant sa croix parmi les larrons	4 – .	3 – .	
10	Ancien maître français	La Cène	2 – 7	4 – 3	
11	Andrea Del Sarto	La Vierge, l'Enfant Jésus, S.t Jean & 3 anges	3 – 9	3 – 1	
12	Copie d'après Le Bassan	Les Vendeurs chassés du temple	3 – 2	4 – .	Anc. Collection
13	Copie d'après Raphaël d'urbin	S.te Famille	2 – 9	1 – 11	id
14	Copie d'après Rubens	Portrait d'Enfant	2 – 2	1 – 8	
15	Corneille Schut	Alexandre coupant le nœud Gordien	1 – 6	1 – 9	
16	H.t de Scalchen	Femme lisant à la lumière	1 – 2	– 10	
17	Rachel Ruisch	Fleurs	– 11	– 8	
18	Idem	Idem	– 11	– 8	
19	attribué à [illegible]	Jugement dernier	3 – 1	2 – 4	

FIGURE 3. Document listing the paintings delivered to the museum in Lille in 1801. Archives du Louvre, Paris

ferred to the Louvre (along with van Eyck's altarpiece of the *Adoration of the Mystic Lamb*, the pride of the Cathedral of Saint Bavo), found its way back north on this occasion as part of the Lille museum's allotment of pictures by the State. In Lille, it joined a *Descent from the Cross* (cat. no. 1) by Rubens that had previously belonged to the Capuchin Convent in Lille and had been in storage since 1791 at the former Convent of the Recollects, along with other paintings seized during the Revolution. The *Descent* had already been requested by Comte d'Angiviller, Surintendant des bâtiments to the king, at the time that d'Angiviller was setting up the Muséum in the Louvre, and was attempting to form a comprehensive royal collection.[1] However, the monks in Lille had politely refused him, and Louis XVI did not insist. Rubens's masterpiece, declared State property by the Assemblée Constituante, would surely have been transferred from Lille to the new Revolutionary depository at the Louvre had it not been for a group of works, seized from churches in Antwerp in 1794–95, which entered the collections of the Muséum Central. Among these pictures was a large *Descent from the Cross* that Rubens painted for Antwerp Cathedral shortly before he began the version in Lille, as well as several other important works by the same artist from the churches of his native city, such as the *Raising of the Cross* from the church of Sint Walburga, and the *Coup de lance* from the Church of the Recollects.

Thus, one has some idea of the upheaval caused by the French Revolution, as the Revolutionary State—through requisition, transfer, removal, regrouping, redistribution, sale, and destruction—gradually became the most formidable collector in history, since the era of Roman conquests in Egypt and Greece. What had transpired in France in the wake of the nationalization of property belonging to the clergy, to émigrés, and to the Crown, soon spread, under pressure from the Revolutionary crusade, throughout continental Europe. From 1791 to 1800, the main depositories in Paris (former convents and royal palaces) received a constant flow of paintings, statues, and art objects that had been removed from their traditional sites, or saved from destruction or looting—victims of the expropriation of the private residences or places of worship that they had once adorned.

Yet, with the exception of a few extreme situations, events were not nearly as chaotic as in the Early Christian period, when pagan idols, temples, and monuments were destroyed by the population, and then by Christian authorities. This time, the emptying of churches and convents, and of homes and palaces—and even their demolition—was carried out under strict legal injunction. The process was accompanied by a stream of bureaucratic activity: Inventories were drawn up, reports were made, and official statements were meticulously transcribed to verify the nature of the goods that were seized and to record their legal transfer from private to national property. French officials,

FIGURE 4. Pierre-Maximilien Delafontaine. *Portrait of Marie-Alexandre Lenoir* (1761–1839). Musée National du Château, Versailles

having inherited the notarial duties of the Ancien Régime, dispassionately executed the often contradictory legislation of the Assemblies, registering each object and keeping its archives in perfect order. The transport of works of art was conducted according to detailed instructions and with ingenious safeguards, especially after the events of Thermidor. The determination to irrevocably uproot the Ancien Régime, and even to remove any reminders of it, was tempered accordingly by a concern to preserve the national treasures and by the desire to save the works of human "genius," which, although removed from their original contexts, would still prove useful for the education of the citizenry. In addition to individual efforts to preserve works of art, such as those for which Alexandre Lenoir is remembered, legal measures were also ordered by the Assemblies; they had been informed of the perils by eminent deputies like the Abbé Grégoire, who had coined the word "vandalism" in this connection in his report on the dangers of such destruction and on the means to prevent it (the *Rapport sur les destructions opérées par le vandalisme et sur les moyens de les réprimer* of August 7, 1794).

These countermeasures could not repair the irreparable. However, the tragic feeling of "nevermore," unknown during the Ancien Régime, appeared only after the fact, when the romantic imaginations of Chateaubriand's and especially Mérimée's contemporaries could assess the full extent of the catastrophe. Works of art that once formed an organic whole with their architectural site often were either damaged, desecrated, or completely destroyed. Those works of art and objects that managed to escape fire, destruction, and the tearing apart of buildings became merely scattered fragments, robbed of their original significance. At first they were stored in makeshift depositories, not unlike the common graves into which the remains of the kings and queens of France, exhumed from the crypt of Saint-Denis, were thrown pell-mell. Only within the protective walls of the Museum could they regain a new, yet altogether different, importance. Alexandre Lenoir (see fig. 4) was among the first to understand this. He transformed the depository of the former Convent of the Petits-Augustins (now the École des Beaux-Arts) into the Musée des Monuments français; the museum was approved by the Convention on October 18, 1792, and opened to the public on August 10, 1793. The five hundred fragments salvaged by Lenoir were arranged in chronological order in rooms that were given an architectural decor suited to the style of each period. Following a historicist approach to museology, which remained viable throughout the nineteenth century, the original flavor of the works *in situ* was replaced by a succession of somewhat melodramatic settings, the effects of which were elucidated by explanatory and literary text panels. The Musée des Monuments français was dissolved in 1815 under the Restoration, but it has an American descendant that is very dear to all New Yorkers. The Cloisters, which John D. Rockefeller, Jr., had built in Fort Tryon Park—and which opened to the public in 1938—incorporates sections of Romanesque and Gothic cloisters acquired in France and in Spain by the sculptor George Grey Barnard. Every effort was made to create a harmonious interplay between the architecture, furnishings, and works of art and the actual site itself, which is protected from encroachment as far as the opposite side of the Hudson River. Together with the church of Saint Bartholomew, The Cloisters is one of the few places in New York that invite quiet reflection and meditation. From 1796 to 1815, however briefly, Lenoir was the first to offer Parisians weary of political revolution a similar kind of oasis.

The development of the Musée du Louvre was slower and more complex. Acting upon an ambitious proposal by the comte d'Angiviller, Louis XVI had decided upon the creation of the museum on March 31, 1788. This royal initiative was ratified by the Assemblée Constituante in a decree of 1791, but this time—the property of the Crown having been seized (save for a few exceptions), in the name of the French Nation—it was stipulated that the royal art collections, now public property, had to be reassembled at the Louvre. A Commission des monuments appointed by the Assemblée replaced the Surintendant des bâtiments du roi. On September 27, 1792, after the abolition of the monarchy, the Convention voted to establish a Muséum Central des Arts. It opened its doors to the public on the same day as the Musée des Monuments français—August 10, 1793—on the anniversary of the "fall of Tyranny" and in the midst of the Reign of Terror. The Muséum Central exhibited 537 paintings and 124 works of art in the Grande Galerie, and, as in Diderot's time, the Salon continued to be held in the Salon Carré. The museum's pedagogical orientation was evident. It was open three days out of ten for the general public, and five days for artists only, with the remaining two days reserved for members of the Commission temporaire des Arts, headed, beginning in July 1793, by Jacques-Louis David.

The Museum of 1793 had been content to draw upon the former royal collections and the depository at the Convent of the Petits-Augustins. A second wave of acquisitions brought to the Louvre some of the greatest masterpieces from churches and princely collections throughout Europe. As early as 1794–95, Paris reveled in the arrival of convoys laden with paintings removed from the churches of Antwerp and Ghent, among which were fine works by Rubens and by van Eyck. In the following years, the armies of the Directoire invaded Italy. As would be the case during General Bonaparte's expedition in Egypt, he invited a committee of scholars to accompany him on his military campaign, and they were joined in Italy by David's pupil from Lille, Jean-Baptiste-Joseph Wicar. It was Wicar who was best able to select from among "the finest art treasures that Italy had to offer," according to the formula adopted by the future emperor from Jean-Baptiste Colbert. Buoyed by its triumphs, the Revolutionary crusade extended throughout Europe, acquiring the where-withal to establish in Paris a "Theater of the arts" that brought together for the education of humanity the most outstanding examples of its artistic genius. This influx of treasures in the storerooms of the Louvre also made possible the creation of the museums in the provinces, so richly endowed was the Muséum Central. Following Napoleon's victories in Northern Europe, masterpieces of the German School took their place alongside those of the Flemish and Italian schools in the capital of the Empire. It was a grandiose plan, to be sure. The dream of the "enlightened despots" of the eighteenth century—to assemble a comprehensive collection of works representing all of the European schools of painting, as well as Antique statuary—was pursued to its absolute extreme. The dream became a reality through a truly enlightened and inspired, but implacable, determination.

The Crisis of 1796 and the Louvre of Vivant-Denon

The climax of the triumph of Reason over centuries of obscurity was the arrival in Paris—the new Rome of the Enlightenment—of the immense convoy trans-porting to the Louvre masterpieces dating from Antiquity and from the Italian Renaissance (see fig. 5). It was a modern version of the triumphal processions of Roman generals on the Capitol. The heavily laden wagons were filled with spoils from Rome, Milan, Venice, Florence, Parma, Modena, and Ravenna,

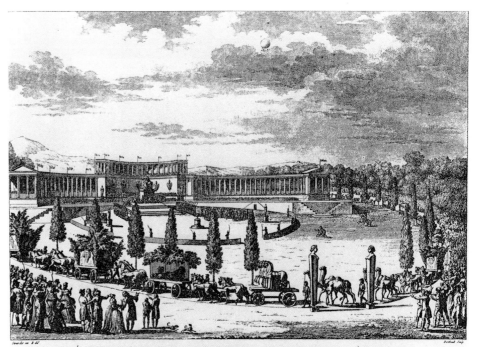

FIGURE 5. *The Triumphal Entry of the Monuments of Science and the Arts into France*. Engraving. Bibliothèque Nationale, Paris

ENTRÉE TRIOMPHALE DES MONUMENTS DES SCIENCES ET ARTS EN FRANCE; FÊTE À CE SUJET. les 9 et 10 Thermidor, An 6.me de la République.

including the sculptures of the *Apollo Belvedere* and the *Laocoön*, works by Raphael and Titian, archives from the Vatican, scientific collections, music manuscripts, rare books, and medallions. Ten boats launched from Marseilles carried their loot along the Rhône and Saône rivers to the Canal du Centre and the Canal de Briare, as far as the Seine. The treasures seized in Italy were intended to "put into government hands a powerful means to promote the principles of philosophy, the creations of science, and the discoveries of genius, and to accelerate the development of the seeds of reason and of prosperity that belong to mankind." They were presented to the Parisian populace in a great procession, against a splendid backdrop of allegories and inscriptions, on July 27, 1798—the anniversary of the start of the Revolution, the fall of Robespierre, and the founding of the Directoire on 9 Thermidor.

The speech made on this occasion by the Minister of the Interior, François de Neufchâteau, on the Champ de Mars, summarized the position of the Directoire, which blamed the excesses of "vandalism" on Robespierre and the Montagnards, whose members ruled France under the Reign of Terror. The spoils from Italy were presented as a just return of the works of genius to their eternal home at the center of the world, in the capital of freedom. They had languished too long under the yoke of tyranny and credulity. "The French nation," Neufchâteau proclaimed, "has not been content to enlighten its contemporaries with the torch of Reason but has also avenged the arts, humbled for too long, and broken the chains of renown of so many famous dead. In the same hour, the French nation crowns the artists of thirty centuries, and thus it is only today that they will actually enter the Temple of Memory."[2]

This thesis had already been outlined by Arnauld Guy de Kersaint on December 15, 1791, in a speech on the subject of public monuments delivered to the Council of the department of Paris. "France," Kersaint had declared, "must one day surpass ancient Rome; but at this moment there is nothing to envy in modern Rome. . . . Let Paris become a new Athens; and may the capital of abuse, inhabited by a race of men regenerated by freedom, become, through our efforts, the capital of the arts." How was this to be accomplished? The doctrine was further clarified on February 13, 1794, when the noted politician Boissy d'Anglas stated before the Convention that "with its demise, despotism has left France a vast and superb heritage." On March 6 of the same year, Jean-Baptiste-Joseph Wicar expanded this appropriately French heritage to include that of Antiquity, of which Italy had been the guardian. Before the Société populaire et républicaine des arts, he declared: "Citizens, I hear the voice of this same Liberty. . . . It shows us where it once worked so many miracles; it commands us to fly thither and to vanquish the monsters that today spoil the blissful land where it once dwelled, and, with this triumphant hand, to carry off what remains of its splendor. It is for us that time has spared [these treasures], have no doubt of it. Yes, Liberty has assured us of it; only we are able to appreciate them, and we shall raise temples in their honor, worthy of them and of their illustrious creators."

Before Bonaparte set off on his Italian campaign, which would fulfill this vow, the French Revolutionary armies invaded Flanders. On September 20, 1794, Jean-Luc Barbier, a painter from Lille and a lieutenant in the Hussars in the Sambre and Meuse army, presented to the Convention the first shipment of paintings confiscated in Antwerp, Ghent, and Brussels: "The fruits of Genius," Barbier declared, "are the heritage of Liberty. For too long these masterpieces were tarnished by their condition of servitude. It is here, in the midst of a free people, that the legacy of famous men should remain. The sorrows of slavery are unworthy of their glory, and the honor of kings disturbs the peace of their graves. The immortal works from the brushes of Rubens and of van Dyck have been deposited in the homeland of Genius and of the Arts, in the land of Liberty and sacred Equality, in the French Republic."

With the arrival of the spoils from Italy, Paris could finally become the "Temple of Memory" for the arts, the site of the universal Museum envisioned by the "patriots." The expression "*Temple de mémoire*," coined by Neufchâteau, is, indeed, the consummate definition of the modern Museum, as it was invented during the French Revolution: the church and school of the new civic religion. Works of genius, kept hidden or else dishonored until then by the forces of tyranny and obscurantism, would at last fulfill their true and glorious purpose, which previously had been stifled: to serve liberty and justice, under the enlightened authority of the State.

This doctrine of the Revolutionary State, however, wound up offending the artists, even those who had supported the Revolution with the most fervor. David, who had never really been interested in the Museum, nevertheless was reconciled to the enrichment of its storerooms with booty from the churches and palaces of France and Flanders. Yet, when it came to applying the same tactics in Rome and elsewhere in Italy, he protested. With a number of other artists, he signed a manifesto requesting that the Directoire renounce this undertaking. There is every reason to believe that he shared the views of Quatremère de Quincy, the most eloquent advocate of this motion to censure, who had defended his position admirably in the *Lettres sur le déplacement des monuments de l'art de l'Italie* (1796).

According to Quatremère, the idea of a Museum—which the Revolution had adopted in order to reconcile its determination to break with the past and its desire to save the finest of the fragments that remained for their social viability—is a concept for the politician and the historian, but it was disastrous for the arts. It would not be stretching a point to compare Quatremère's reasoning with that of Michel Foucault in the latter's *Histoire de la folie* (1976) or his *Surveiller et punir* (1975), where the philosopher, examining the past, expresses indignation at the incarceration of the insane by the leaders of the Revolution, and at their subjection to the cold and objective scrutiny of guards and psychiatrists using panoptical devices. For Quatremère de Quincy, the universal Museum, as defined by the Revolution—which was to provide both a scientific panorama and a methodical display of masterpieces removed from their original environments—was like a vampire that had attacked the real Museum, the truly European Museum, the only one in which the best minds and the finest artists since the Renaissance had found their spiritual home, their inspiration, and their common language: Rome. And along with Rome, Italy. There, far from the administrative and pedagogical disciplines to which the arts were subjected by the Revolution, time and nature had produced a masterpiece in which everything was compatible, spontaneously and harmoniously fitting together, inviting the genius of future artists to create new masterpieces of their own. By uprooting statues and paintings from the organic and pleasing ensemble that Italy as a whole had become—but which this violence had destroyed—the Directoire was committing the supreme and irreparable act of vandalism that it claimed to reject. As long as this vandalism had been confined to France, Quatremère had remained silent, but when Italy suffered the same fate, like David he gave full vent to his anger. In 1789, echoing a sentiment once expressed by Nicolas Poussin in the seventeenth century, David wrote to his pupil Wicar, then in Rome: "In this wretched country [France] I am like a dog that has been tossed into the water in spite of himself, struggling to reach the shore in order to survive, and even so as not to lose the little that I have brought back from Italy."

To plunder Italy, the homeland of ideal Beauty; to despoil Rome, its capital, of its masterpieces; to wrest them away from their natural and architectural settings, was, in Quatremère's opinion, to stifle at their very source the creative principles that had nourished French and European art continuously since the Renaissance. It meant the devastation of the homeland common to all European artists, the places where they sought and found the only truly universal language—that of Beauty. The result of this crime seemed no less fatal to Quatremère: The Museum, to which the fragments brought from Italy would be transported, and in which they would be ensconced, would be merely an abstract and funereal contrivance—a foil for the true perception of the arts. This was the most radical criticism ever leveled at the modern Museum, and at the very moment of its inception, no less. It is comparable to the reactions of ethnologists at the end of the nineteenth century to the gloomy museums in which traditional societies presented their customs and their crafts in a dry and scientific manner. This criticism, as we shall see, anticipated that of Paul Valéry, as well, and it also persuaded Chateaubriand, who was more open than

Quatremère to the tradition of French and Gothic art, to register the same protest in the France of the Ancien Régime in his *Génie du Christianisme* that Quatremère de Quincy had reserved for the Italy of classical Antiquity in his *Lettres*.

The Directoire neither was moved by David's manifesto nor by the eloquence of his friend's *Lettres*. Without deviating from the Revolutionary logic, the Consulat nevertheless took a more moderate stance. Rejecting the temptation to establish a gigantic and unrivaled Louvre, the decree of 14 Fructidor provided for the provincial museums, each endowed with masterpieces of a different school, thus permitting the "comparisons" that Quatremère considered indispensable to the development of taste. Hence, the State's shipment to Lille in 1801 contained paintings by Simon de Vos and Piazzetta, and by Champaigne as well as Cristofano Allori. Although they were removed from their original contexts, which the violence in the name of Reason had destroyed, the policies of the Consulat and of the Empire strove to demonstrate that the new State was not only capable of bringing together these jewels that were so diversified in origin and appearance, but it could also set them into an architectural framework arranged so as to restore a sense of harmony. This became the Empire Style. With an infallible sense of the conjuncture, Bonaparte appointed as Director of Museums one of the opponents to the transfer of monuments from Italy to Paris: Dominique Vivant-Denon. An artist himself as well as a connoisseur, Vivant-Denon, like Talleyrand, was a survivor of the Ancien Régime. He possessed an aesthetic sense that is often lacking in administrators and in soldiers, and he turned the Louvre—until then an abstract idea still in flux—into a veritable work of art itself. In 1803, the museum was renamed the Musée Napoléon. With the help of Visconti, a Roman, and the architect Fontaine (another adversary of the transfer of art to France in 1796), Vivant-Denon managed to transform the long-abandoned royal palace and its fabulous Revolutionary collections into a majestic new ensemble in the Empire Style. The idea of the Museum, which gradually came to fruition amidst the upheavals of the Revolution, took on an irrefutable presence and inevitability. Even when the Empire fell, in 1814, Europe, astonished and intimidated, did not dare touch this sublime palace filled with its spoils, which had been assembled and then extolled according to a grand artistic vision.

It took the Hundred Days and Waterloo for each country to take stock and reclaim its due. However, instead of repairing the rifts caused by the Revolution, the return of the masterpieces to their countries of origin only served to strengthen the rupture for, more often than not, in the interim these masterpieces had been sent to a museum, and had been restored. Concern for the conservation of works of art, inseparable from restoration techniques, was a contribution of the Revolution that the Europe of the Holy Alliance could not deny. A famous example comes to mind. When the French detached Raphael's celebrated *Madonna di Foligno* from the altar of the Umbrian church of Sant'Anna delle Contesse in Foligno for shipment to Paris the painting was in danger of being ruined, and it was carefully restored for display in the Louvre. It was not returned to its original home, where it had suffered damage, but was transferred by the pontifical authorities to the Vatican. The argument in favor of the physical survival and conservation of works of art, more than the educational purpose assigned to them by the Revolution, proved decisive for the Museum. For the most part, the confiscations and appropriations of art works throughout Europe that had led to the creation of numerous public collections no longer occurred. Yet, more museums continued to be created. Nineteenth-century art is an art *of* the museum; twentieth-century art is an art *for* the museum. Because Paris had the Louvre, the original model for this new institution, the city was able to supplant Rome in the nineteenth and the twentieth century as the capital of the arts, contrary to what Quatremère de Quincy had supposed. The Louvre of the nineteenth century was the training ground for students at the École des Beaux-Arts, as well as for those who rebelled against the disciplines of the Académie and the Villa Medici. Since the Revolution, the Museum has become the last source of nourishment left to artists by modern society.

The End of the Ancien Régime of the Arts

Because the Ancien Régime did not acknowledge the Museum, are we to believe that it was an inferno for the arts? On the contrary, as the prodigious crop of masterpieces garnered by the museums of the Revolution attests, under the Ancien Régime the relationship of the monarchy and the Church to the arts was as naturally fertile as that of the apple tree and the apples that it bears— with the accompanying abundance, waste, and indifference that characterize all the traditional societies subject to ethnological scrutiny. At every level, from the top to the bottom of the social scale, craftsmen created masterpieces, while "High" art was reserved for God and for princes. Beauty, whether the modest or the sublime reflection of the Divine, existed consubstantially within a universe whose underlying fabric was divine. The situation only drew to a close during the seventeenth and eighteenth centuries, in the distant wake of human-istic Neoplatonism, when the Christian monarchy established a hierarchy between "High" art—truly advanced art—and craftsmanship. The "artist" came to be considered the equal of the poet, a genius capable of the "*grand genre*," and more respectable than the craftsman, whose "mechanical" skills produced only minor, utilitarian works in the "*petits genres*." This hierarchy, which originated with the humanists, became a dogma of intolerance for David and his pupils. The very modern scorn of these neoclassical artists for craftsmen and for their "*petits genres*" was to explode during the Revolution with a violence unheard of under the Ancien Régime.

To keep the artists satisfied and to disassociate them from craftsmen, the French monarchy had already perfected an intellectual climate of education, emulation, and co-optation. The Académie Royale de Peinture et de Sculpture was created in 1648 and the Académie de France in Rome was founded by Colbert in 1666 in order to train and reward painters, sculptors, engravers, and architects working for the king. Free of the constraints of the crafts guilds, many of them lived in the Louvre; they had status, commissions, and a common language, which, for the most part, they had brought back from Rome. The Salon of the Académie, held every other year since 1725 in the Salon Carré of the Louvre, by permitting comparisons between contemporary paintings and sculpture, was a remarkable instrument for the education of Parisian and European taste. Literati and art lovers partook of a flourishing art market. The public auctions that were held in Paris, accompanied by excellent catalogues, had an impact that was felt throughout Europe. Many private collections, described in published guidebooks, were relatively accessible to travelers, connoisseurs, and artists alike. Churches and innumerable convents—works of art themselves, brimful of works of art—unintentionally were superb museums, and they were usually easy to visit. Engraved reproductions, infinitely more subtle than photographs, permitted inaccessible art works to become known, studied, and understood. One can well imagine the high degree of artistic education that had become current in France by 1789, a fact that also explains the prevalence of so many "experts" during the Revolution. Yet, one can also see that the "Museum impulse" had been weak and somewhat sluggish under the monarchy. The passion to restore and to preserve a cultural heritage could arise only once the feeling of a great loss had become very acute, and for a large public. The same is true today with the passion for ecology, which surfaced only when nature—up to now left to regenerate itself under the care of the farmer—seemed threatened with extinction by industrial pollution. The arts under the Ancien Régime were as rich and as regularly changing as the seasons. Their "style" evolved slowly from reign to reign, without any retrospective anxiety. From the royal palace to the peasant cottage, from the cathedral to the village church, beauty, whether majestic or humble, was the familiar manifestation, over the course of time, of an invisible yet stable order of inanimate objects and living things.

The philosophers of the eighteenth century, abolishing the sacred foundation on which traditional art and crafts relied, concerned themselves instead with isolating the reverence for beautiful things and in focusing on the consid-

FIGURE 6. Joseph-Siffrède Duplessis. *Portrait of Comte d'Angiviller.* Musée National du Château, Versailles

FIGURE 7. Hubert Robert. *The Grande Galerie of the Louvre between 1794 and 1796.* Musée du Louvre, Paris

eration of taste. In 1750, the German philosopher Alexander Baumgarten gave the name "Aesthetics" to this independent discipline, and it became an underlying theme of the Revolutionary debates over the Museum. The Ancien Régime had in no way resisted the inclination, which soon spread throughout Europe, and its leaders gradually came to accept the philosophy of Aesthetics. German and Italian princes, and even Empress Catherine II of Russia, rivaled one another in their fierce and ostentatious passion to own paintings. The Galleria degli Uffizi in Florence was opened to the public as a testament to princely collecting and to the munificence of the last Medici, yet it was perceived as merely the "sport of princes."

Responding to the pamphlets issued in 1747 by Lafont de Saint-Yenne, protesting—in the name of education for both artists and public alike—against the inaccessibility of the king's collections, and their supposed state of neglect, the Surintendance des bâtiments arranged for the exhibition of one hundred paintings from the royal collections at the Palais du Luxembourg on October 14, 1750. (The queen of England recently has done the same, allowing for rotating exhibitions of works from her collection to be held in rooms adjacent to Buckingham Palace.) In the article entitled "Musée" in the *Encyclopédie,* Diderot, in 1765, proposed the transformation of the Louvre into a museum of science and the fine arts, modeled after ancient Alexandria. By 1763, the

FIGURE 8. Henri-Aimé-Charles Demailly. *Portrait of Louis-Joseph Watteau.* Musée de l'Hospice Comtesse, Lille

marquis de Marigny already had construction started and plans made in this regard. His successor, the comte d'Angiviller (see fig. 6), was determined to complete the royal paintings collections (in which the Dutch School had been poorly represented), and repeatedly sought advice with a view to transforming the Grande Galerie of the Louvre (see fig. 7) into a Museum of the Arts. Work had begun in 1789, when the Revolution broke out, under the direction of Hubert Robert, who had been appointed Garde des tableaux du roi (Keeper of the King's Paintings) five years earlier.

What was true for Paris also held true, if on a smaller scale, for the provinces, where the pedagogical beliefs of the Enlightened thinkers had been adopted and their enthusiasm for the fine arts shared. In 1754, a School of Drawing was founded in Lille. It was housed first in the former Hôpital Saint-Louis at 17, rue des Malades (today 248, rue de Paris), before being transferred in 1760 to the "Perche aux draps" in the rue des Récollets, named after the monastery that, forty years later, would become the main depository for works of art confiscated in Lille during the Revolution. The Municipality's decision was fully in keeping with the educational ideals of the time and, as in Paris, with the concern to inspire artistic vocations of a more "enlightened" order than common craftsmanship. The Ordinance stated that: "The artists that the City of Lille has produced, having, more often than not, limited their

FIGURE 9. Attributed to François Watteau. *Self-Portrait*. Musée des Beaux-Arts, Lille

attention to the instruction of a few individuals, always in too small a number to benefit the general public, the Magistrate, ever concerned with the means of spreading useful knowledge, deems that, after due encouragement of the talented, the surest way to accomplish this purpose is to establish free public Drawing lessons of which each one can partake of those best suited to his condition and to his profession.''

In 1762, a School of Architecture was added to the School of Drawing, in 1763 a mathematics course, and in 1765 the institution was renamed the Académie des Arts. The following year, in order to suitably join together and house these flourishing schools, the Municipality erected new buildings in the rue Comtesse, not far from the church of Saint-Pierre. Louis-Joseph Watteau (see fig. 8), a painter of pleasing genre scenes and traditional family subjects, who was from the same Valenciennes family as the famous Antoine, became assistant professor in 1770, and then professor and director of the Académie des Arts from 1778 until 1798. His son François (see fig. 9) was also an artist. François, who painted the *Fête in the Colisée* now in the Musée des Beaux-Arts (see cat. no. 26), became his father's assistant in 1785. Both were to play an important role in the difficult transition from the Ancien Régime to a Revolutionary government in Lille. On February 17, 1792, Louis-Joseph proposed to the district administrators the opening of a museum ''for public

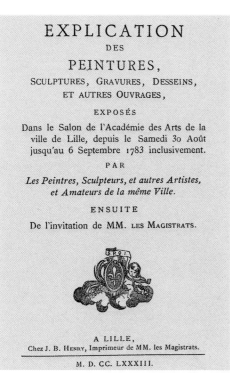

FIGURE 10. Title page of the catalogue of the Salon des Arts in Lille, 1783

instruction." In December 1793, with the permission of the "citizen administrators," he had transferred to the École des Arts five paintings from the Church of the Madeleine, along with twenty others "taken from the chapter of the former Recollects, from various houses and former abbeys." These religious works were assembled in the Grand Salon of the Académie des Arts, where the "reception pieces" of the academicians had always been presented.

Indeed, an Ordinance from the Magistrate in 1775 had endowed Lille with an Académie, an honorific institution that grew out of the pedagogical institution of the same name that had proven its worth for over two decades. It was composed of two "classes," one of painters and the other of sculptors. As academicians, they were "exempted from the performance requirements" of the craftsmen's guilds. This was the same privilege that Parisian artists had sought and obtained in 1648, when the Académie Royale de Peinture et de Sculpture was created. The eight artists named—and then co-opted—as academicians were obliged to offer to the Salon des Arts an autograph work. However, in the future, as at the Académie Royale, their election would depend upon the examination by the academicians of a "reception piece." The Salon des Arts had to preserve and exhibit these "masterpieces" each year (see fig. 10); soon after, they would be supplemented by works from artists who had been sent to Paris on scholarship and were required to submit samples of their progress to the Académie. If we add to this stock of paintings and sculpture (some of which were copy exercises) the group of casts brought to the École des Arts after 1754 for drawing instruction, might it not be said—as some have done—that the beginnings of a museum were already in place? This reserve of paintings and sculpture was seen as an adjunct to, and as an instrument of, the gradually evolving educational institution established by the city. Yet, the idea of a public inheritance that would be of use not just to artists but to all citizens did not surface until 1792. Louis Watteau's initiatives were encouraged by the example set by the Convention, and the art seized during the Revolution gave the director of the Académie the means to turn the annual Salon des Arts into a permanent exhibition, offering visitors a preliminary sampling of the works of the Old Masters along the lines of the Museum in Paris.

The academic plan instituted in Lille between 1754 and 1775 was completed—as before, in imitation of the royal academic system—by the establishment of a contest to be held every three years, with the winner to be awarded an allowance by the city to study in Paris. Engravers such as J.-B. Liénard and Louis-Joseph Masquelier, painters such as François Watteau, and sculptors like Henri Lorthiot benefited from this educational experience, which guaranteed them a position as academician and public and private commissions upon their return to Lille. It is worth noting that the so-called "minor" arts were excluded, in Lille as in Paris, from this system of privileges.

That explains the museological sanctification conferred on sculpture, and especially on painting, during the Revolution, to the detriment of the extraordinarily high-quality craftsmanship that had once been widespread in France, and which suffered a rapid decline in the nineteenth century, with the exception of those luxury goods made in Paris. Today, the hiatus still exists between museums devoted to "High" art and "decorative arts" museums, perpetuating the categories established by the aesthetics of neoclassicism. The abundance of craftsmen during the Ancien Régime explains the singular attitude adopted by artists—and above all by David—during the Revolution. The Académie, under the Ancien Régime, had made them "painters to the king." This liberal institution had sharpened their sense of a hierarchy of genres, but with moderation and flexibility, and without being too finicky. Thus, Antoine Watteau and Jean-Baptiste-Siméon Chardin had both been admitted to the Académie Royale, and flower painters, too, could be accepted.

Winckelmann's doctrine, as well as the cult of ideal Beauty, had narrowed the hierarchy of genres to the point of rendering such indulgences criminal: The new "aesthetic" had no mercy for anything that did not belong to the "*grand genre*" of history *à l'antique*. In England, this would have remained a form of eccentricity, but the doctrinaire spirit and social resentment in France, where all forms of art flourished, led to a terrorist system. Only academic artists endowed with a "great taste" for the Antique and capable of the "*grand genre*" of history painting received the favors of a Revolutionary government that was otherwise so egalitarian. It was also during the French Revolution that the modern cult of "genius" first was formulated and exalted. As early as 1790, a petition had been submitted to the Assemblée Constituante by the Commune des Arts demanding the suppression of crafts guilds and art academies: "Genius of the arts, be totally free. Nature wills it, Reason proclaims it, the Law pronounces it. So soar freely over France, she no longer has any obstacles for you; there are no more organizations, privileges, conditions, or tariffs. The people of France submit all thought, every useful discovery, to the cause of unlimited cooperation. All men are summoned for this sublime show of talent: Genius, take flight, and scatter them with the sparks of your flame." This admonition recalls the section of Rimbaud's *Illuminations* entitled "Génie": "And if Adoration disappears, ring, its promise sounds: Away with these superstitions, these ancient matters, these trappings, and these epochs. It is our time that has failed."

The case of David, the artistic genius during the Revolution, is a very complex one. As artisan and connoisseur, he saw very clearly the pedantic limitations of Winckelmann's theories, yet, like a true master, he was able to recognize the merits of his peers, of Boucher and Fragonard, the Dutch painters, and Caravaggio and Rubens. However, the painter in him, unscathed by ideology in the intimacy of the studio and in discussions with fellow artists, yielded in public life to the temptations of theory, which are also those of absolute power. In the name of ideal Beauty, he could unleash his fury against those "aristocratic" academicians who subscribed to a "French taste" that competed with his own, as well as heap scorn on the "vile" craftsmen who excelled only in the "minor" arts. Such a position, which, while exalting Beauty also served to isolate and to disembody it—first under the Convention, and later during the Empire—gave David the justification to play the role of dictator of the arts and supreme civic guardian of the sublime. This singular, yet typically bourgeois, duplicity manifested itself even more unpleasantly in David's pupil from Lille, Jean-Baptiste-Joseph Wicar. However, Wicar's contribution to the birth of the modern Museum—and, in particular, to the enrichment of the Musée de Lille—deserves pause.

Jean-Baptiste-Joseph Wicar (1762–1834): A Disciple of David

Born in 1762, the son of a poor carpenter in Lille, Wicar benefited from the local branch of the Académie during the Ancien Régime, both in terms of his education and his social advancement. The patronage of an aristocratic alderman from the city enabled the young Wicar to take the course open to the public at the School of Drawing, and thus he escaped the fate of being a mere studio assistant or a craftsman. As a winner of the contest at the Lille Académie, he received a scholarship to study in Paris. In 1781, he was accepted into the studio of David, who—in the latter's own words—was an Académie unto himself. David's "Académie," in the eyes of the master and of his students, as well, was superior to the Académie Royale, for it was unequivocally and unconditionally the Académie of the cult of ideal Beauty. In 1781, David—just returned from Italy, where the taste for the neo-Antique was a complete revelation to him—painted the *Belisarius Begging Alms* (cat. no. 28) in his studio in the Place de Grève. He exhibited the painting with great success at the Salon. The same year, demonstrating his curiosity and the range of his personal tastes, David made a short trip to Lille to study the works by Rubens and other Flemish masters in the collection of another alderman and protector of Wicar, Charles Lenglart. Wicar had begun to send drawings and paintings to the annual Salon in Lille, and these were illustrated in the printed booklets accompanying the exhibition with the proud mention, "Pupil of Monsieur David, painter to the king."

In 1784, David left for Rome once again, and Wicar obtained permission to go along with him, although he had not passed the official examination, received the Prix de Rome, or qualified as a *pensionnaire* at the Palazzo Mancini (then the seat of the Académie de France in Rome). The support of David superseded these other formalities. David went to Rome in search of inspiration to execute the great history painting entitled *The Oath of the Horatii*, which had been commissioned by the comte d'Angiviller, Surintendant des bâtiments du roi. Following in David's footsteps, Wicar discovered Rome and the amazing artistic fervor that pervaded the Eternal City at that time. More than ever before, Rome was the European capital of the Arts, the scene of a new Renaissance. This "return to the Antique" impassioned cultured individuals throughout Europe. The English Society of Dilettanti and the German followers of Mengs and Winckelmann shared the same enthusiasm for Rome (Goethe traveled to Italy in 1787). Together with the Italians, the archaeologists, artists, and those who initiated the excavations at Herculaneum and Pompeii created conditions that fueled this general fever. What an incredible contrast there was between Paris and Rome! In Paris everything had become political, while in Rome aesthetics reigned supreme. Two apparently contradictory abstract concepts were exalted: In the north, people dreamt of a virtuous City, a modern Sparta or Rome, while in the south, their thoughts turned to ideal Beauty, as envisioned by Phidias and Raphael. David felt that in his paintings he could combine both dreams. His *Belisarius*, an homage to the "*grand goût*" of Poussin's and Le Sueur's Roman works, already embodied the noble civic *pathos* championed by Diderot. Overwhelmed by an intense curiosity, David nevertheless painted the *Oath of the Horatii* in seclusion, amidst the impassioned atmosphere of Rome. This pictorial manifesto is a heroic allegory of Rousseau's *Social Contract*, in which the regeneration of art through a return to the Antique coincided with the political and moral regeneration of the City by means of the Contract. The "sublime" as expressed in the painting produced in its spectators a taste for republican government and feelings of noble virtue. With mute eloquence, David's three Horatii already cry out: *Liberty or death!* Their triumph at the Salon of 1786 would prove prophetic.

A dazzled Wicar embraced both the new aesthetic and the political philosophy that David associated with it. Wicar displayed great talent as a draftsman, and especially as a portraitist, and he was also an epigone of history painting, according to David. Upon his return to Paris, Wicar painted a *Judgment of Solomon*, which he sent to the Salon in Lille in 1786. The director of the Académie, Louis Watteau, spread the rumor that the picture was by David and not by Wicar, in order to discredit it. As a consequence, Wicar developed the same loathing for this provincial academy that David bore toward the one in Paris. In 1787, Wicar returned to Italy. During his stay, which lasted until 1793, he often lodged at the Palazzo Mancini when in Rome, and he traveled to Florence, where he made drawn copies of the paintings, statues, and art objects in the Galleria degli Uffizi. Engravings after Wicar's drawings were published in a lavish edition in 1789—yet another demonstration of the new school of painting, the "*grand genre à l'antique*." Quatremère de Quincy wrote an enthusiastic review of the volume, and Wicar became famous. As a respected member of David's circle, he came to be considered—and rightly so—as the leading French expert on Italian art.

In 1793, Wicar hastily departed for Paris. David, a delegate to the Convention, had not only become dictator of the arts but was the official painter of the Jacobins. Through his intervention, Wicar was appointed Curator of the Muséum, and given lodgings at the Louvre, and he was named secretary of the Commission temporaire des Arts, the successor of the Surintendance des bâtiments du roi. Wicar also became a member of the Société républicaine des Arts, a kind of "collective" of Jacobin artists. He proved to be a ruthless informer and purger of fellow members who did not toe the official line of Davidian politics and aesthetics. In April 1794, this merciless investigator accused the celebrated painter Louis-Léopold Boilly of being a "genre painter" of humorous and libertine subjects, persisting in that error even under the Montagnard Convention. Boilly did not allow himself to be intimidated, and invited the judges to visit his studio. There, they found only works that celebrated the heroes and great deeds of the Revolution, among which was an allegorical painting in the "*grand genre*," *The Triumph of Marat* (cat. no. 30), which had been completed in great haste for the occasion. Boilly's presence of mind saved his head, and Wicar began to lose favor.

In his capacity as Curator of the Muséum and member of the Commission des arts, Wicar was able to apply his expertise as a connoisseur, which he had acquired in Italy. He took part in the appraisal of works of art at the Château de Versailles (which at the time contained the richest collection of masterpieces of European art), in the churches of Paris, and in the depository at the Convent of the Petits-Augustins administered by Alexandre Lenoir. He picked the cream of the crop of treasures to fill the galleries of the Muséum. However, the fall of Robespierre and then of David (who was imprisoned for a short time) portended trouble for Wicar. He extricated himself from these difficulties by returning to Italy, where his talents as an art expert soon found a new and still broader outlet. Wicar assisted the committee of scholars entrusted by the Directoire with the selection of works of art seized as war indemnity by Bonaparte and the Republican armies. This time Wicar was able to enrich the holdings of the Muséum on an even grander scale. He went about his task with indefatigable zeal, choosing the rarest and finest masterpieces he could find in private and princely collections, churches, and libraries. His appropriations assumed astonishing proportions in Venice and especially in Rome, where the Vatican, in accordance with the terms of the Treaty of Tolentino, had to surrender to Bonaparte an enormous tribute in works of art.

Under the Consulat and then the Empire, Wicar became the favorite artist of the all-powerful French Embassy in Rome: He received the official commission for a painting to commemorate the signing of the Concordat between Pius VII and France (the painting is now in the pope's summer residence at Castel Gandolfo). On September 29, 1805, he was elected a member of the venerable Accademia di San Luca—of which his friend Canova (a century after Simon Vouet) would become a "Fellow" on January 2, 1811. Wicar himself became director of the Académie in Naples under the ephemeral rule of Joseph Bonaparte. At the peak of his success as a self-made man, the Chevalier Wicar painted the self-portrait now in the Musée des Beaux-Arts in Lille (see cat. no. 29): The rather theatrical vanity of the artist who has "arrived" scarcely masks his cold determination to "survive."

The fall of the Empire did not seriously weaken Wicar's position. In 1814, he signed the appeal made by the academicians at the Accademia di San Luca to the allied sovereigns to force France to return the works of art taken from Italy! When the pontifical government exercised clemency and offered the members of the Bonaparte family sanctuary, Wicar became their official painter. He was even commissioned by Lucien Bonaparte to paint a large portrait of Pope Pius VII. Until his death in 1834, Wicar continued to live peacefully in Rome, making handsome portrait drawings and taking advantage of his expertise to deal in drawings, paintings, and objets d'art. He was thus able to assemble his third art collection (the first had been stolen in Florence in 1800 and the second sold to the great London art dealer Samuel Woodburn in 1823). In his will, Wicar bequeathed this third collection to the Société des sciences, de l'agriculture et des arts in Lille; it included over eight hundred drawings by Italian masters, as well as sculptures, among which were the famous *Head of a Woman* in wax then attributed to Raphael and Donatello's superb bas-relief *The Feast of Herod* (cat. no. 44). The drawings by Raphael included here (see cat. nos. 51–59) provide the best indication of Wicar's excellent taste and of his standards as a collector. Lille was understandably dazzled by the unexpected treasures with which its museum suddenly was filled. Providing additional funds, Wicar charitably endowed two scholarships to send artists from Lille to study in Rome. These scholarships, which have been awarded since 1861 (Carolus-Duran was one of the first two beneficiaries), made Lille—honored by Wicar's bequest—one of the bastions of the Davidian tradition in France in the nineteenth century. To prepare the future recipients, the Société des sciences in Lille continued the practice—interrupted by the Revolution—of public instruction in painting and drawing, not surprisingly calling upon another of David's pupils, François Souchon, to take charge.

A Provincial Museum in the Nineteenth Century

For a long time after the arrival in Lille of the first shipment of art from the State in 1801, the spoils of the Revolution continued to enrich the city's public collections. The European standard of excellence to which Chaptal had wished to hold each of his provincial museums did not cease to serve as the criterion, during the nineteenth century, for their expansion. This was the case particularly in Lille. Only works from the most prestigious private collections in the north were permitted to join—through gift or bequest—this group of masterpieces worthy of the Louvre. The contributions from the State did not depart from the conditions set in 1801: In 1838, Lille received Delacroix's *Medea About to Murder Her Children* (cat. no. 37), and in 1849 Gustave Courbet's *After Dinner at Ornans* (cat. no. 40), a manifesto of Realism; the artist had exhibited the picture at the Salon that same year, at which time the State immediately purchased it and sent it north to Lille. Nor could the Lille museum's own purchases depart from the national and international status that the city's public collections had maintained from the start. From 1841 to 1879, Édouard Reynart, an outstanding curator, had put his talents as a connoisseur, diplomat-administrator, and man of the world at the service of the museum in Lille. Only the best would do for the city. In the tradition of the "*galleria progressiva*" of the Enlightenment—that is, an encyclopedic and chronological anthology of works of human genius—Reynart welcomed Old Master paintings as well as major works by contemporary artists. The number of paintings in the collection rose from eighty-eight in 1841 to seven hundred and fifteen in 1875, and the sculptures increased from four to forty-four. To Reynart, the Musée des Beaux-Arts owes its two Goyas (see cat. nos. 34, 35) and its David—the great *Belisarius* (cat. no. 28). Two exceptional collectors unhesitatingly made bequests to the museum: Alexandre Leleux's collection was acquired in 1873, and several gifts from Antoine Brasseur were received between 1878 and 1885. Two of the finest paintings included here come from these splendid collections: Savery's *A Bouquet of Flowers* (cat. no. 9) was given by Leleux, and Codde's *A Young Scholar in His Study* (cat. no. 13) by Brasseur. Other important paintings entered the Musée des Beaux-Arts during this same period: the large *Allegory of Worldly Vanity* by Pieter Boel (purchased in 1878; see cat. no. 7), a Largillierre portrait, *The Painter Jean-Baptiste Forest* (Gift of the Brame family in 1861; see cat. no. 21), and the wonderful *Study of a Woman* by Paul-Ponce-Antoine Robert (Gift of the art dealer Léon Gauchez; see cat. no. 22).

The rich and abundant collections, augmenting the prestigious Wicar bequest, eventually outgrew their space in the Hôtel de Ville. It became necessary to build a Palais des Beaux-Arts that would state clearly, in architectural terms, that Lille had "the most important Museum in France after those of Paris." This project, in fact, belatedly carried out the stipulation in the decree of 14 Fructidor, Year IX, which made the State's allotment of works of art contingent upon the city providing a "suitable gallery," at the "commune's expense," to receive them. It was anticipated that the future *Palais* would be at the geometric center of the city, which had tripled in size with the annexation of a number of outlying communities, in a vast new square to be christened the "Place de la République." The Palais des Beaux-Arts would face the Hôtel de la Préfecture, the administrative headquarters of the State in the province (see fig. 11).

To meet the enormous costs incurred, Lille organized a public lottery, as the city of Amiens had done several times between 1855 and 1865 to cover the expense of building the Musée de Picardie. The lottery, accompanied by an aggressive publicity campaign that included the press as well, played on the patriotism of the local population. In principle, all the inhabitants of Lille were called upon to finance the new building—and the response was overwhelming.

Every French architect was invited to participate in a contest, with detailed requirements. The composition of the jury, which was determined by the Mayor of Lille, included representatives of the city, the State, and the department, in addition to four well-known architects who were either members of the Institut de France or inspectors of public monuments. All four had been students, and were or had been professors, at the École des Beaux-Arts in Paris, then the leading school of architecture in France, whose influence had spread to America. Thus, the participants in the contest were graduates of the École, as were their contemporaries in the United States: Richard Morris Hunt, a student of Hector-Martin Lefuel and architect of The Metropolitan Museum of Art (1894–1904); Ernest Flagg, a student of Paul Blondel and architect of The Corcoran Gallery of Art in Washington, D.C. (1892–97); and Guy Lowell, a student of Pascal and architect of the Museum of Fine Arts in Boston (1907–15). The winners, unanimously acclaimed by the population of Lille, were the young architects Bérard and Delmas. Theirs was an elaborate project. To satisfy the concerns of the Municipal Council, who feared that the museum would exceed its budget, the Commission of Works declared: "The monument that we are building is not exclusively municipal in nature. It is intended to house treasures that truly are of national importance and of great value. Moreover, it must serve in the instruction and for the intellectual recreation of the people in the surrounding area."

One century had gone by, but the idea of the "*Musée de province*," in the sense in which it was conceived by the Revolutionary State, was more alive than ever under the administration of the Third Republic. The Lille museum had to be another Louvre, a national palace designed for public education through the arts. A new notion had been introduced, that of "intellectual recreation"—the first, modest version of what the French government today refers to as "culture." However, the idea of the Museum, born in 1792, did not only persist in France, where many other fine arts museums were built in the grand "Beaux-Arts" style during the same period as the Musée de Lille: in

FIGURE 11. The Palais des Beaux-Arts, Lille. Principal façade, 1889–92. Designed by Bérard and Delmas

Amiens (1855–65), Marseilles (1862–67), Rouen (1880–88), and Nantes (1893–1900); similar Palais des Beaux-Arts were constructed in Amsterdam (1877), Brussels (1880), Antwerp (1884–90), and Copenhagen, as well. Between 1872 and 1891, in Vienna, Karl von Hasenauer built the superb palace for the Kunsthistorisches Museum, to house the Austrian Imperial collections. The phenomenon was both European and American. In 1885, the subject of the Achille-Leclère contest—established by the Académie des Beaux-Arts for students who had won the Second Prize in Architecture—was "A Museum for a Provincial City." These museums, indeed, belonged to the second generation to have resulted from the French Revolution, and they assumed the monumental guise of royal palaces—in the image of the Louvre—to accommodate their works of art and the public. Like the Louvre, they became the familiar and indispensable landmarks in every modern cityscape, encompassing a geographical area that reached as far as the New World.

The inauguration of the Palais des Beaux-Arts in Lille took place on March 6, 1892. It was a festive occasion for the city, complete with a parade, a marching band, flags, banquets, and speeches. On that first day, ten thousand people visited the museum's brand-new galleries, whose walls were not yet dry. Additional work needed to be done. During this time, Jules Lenglart—a descendant of Wicar's erstwhile protector—pursued an acquisitions policy worthy of that of his predecessor, Édouard Reynart. In 1890, using funds provided by the Brasseur bequest, he purchased the sublime *Choir of the New*

Church in Delft by Emanuel de Witte (cat. no. 16) and in 1900 the *Raising of Lazarus* by Wtewael (cat. no. 11). The acquisitions made throughout the nineteenth century endowed the public collections of Lille with an abundance of riches unrestrained in their luxuriousness (not unlike those of the Louvre of Lefuel) to grace its splendid Palais des Beaux-Arts.

Today, another century has passed and the Musée de Lille is more than ever the pride of the city. It is presently closed in order to undergo extensive yet discreet restoration—which has enabled a selection of its masterpieces to be exhibited at The Metropolitan Museum of Art in the fall of 1992.

1 The following is the text of a letter to the Superior of the Convent of the Recollects in Lille from the comte d'Angiviller in 1785, requesting the transfer of Rubens's *Descent from the Cross* to the Muséum that he was about to open in the Louvre. The letter provides an idea of the civility observed in the procedures undertaken by the administration, under Louis XVI, on the eve of the Revolution:

My Reverend Father, I have submitted to the king the report made by M. Sauvage, painter to His Majesty, on the examination I asked him to make (during a mission in Flanders) of the *Descent from the Cross* painted by Rubens, which is in the possession of your establishment.

M. Sauvage has made clear to you, my Reverend Father, which I myself confirm, the desire of the king and His Majesty's efforts to enrich the already priceless collection that he possesses of paintings of all schools and by all the masters, and which he wants to make, in the capital, the most precious of all monuments devoted to the glory of the arts and to the instruction of artists, for the admiration of the whole of Europe. You will understand, my Reverend Father, that the grand prospect that I have just outlined for you cannot be implemented so long as the works of the greatest masters are dispersed, isolated, and, in fact, practically forgotten in out-of-the-way places like yours, which cannot attract the visits of outsiders; and it happens all too often that a precious painting, which is understandably either unrecognized or undervalued by its ecclesiastical owners, who cannot give it much attention, is lost and perishes, whether through the inevitable effects of time, or through the inadequate, and more often ignorant, care that is provided for its restoration on the part of persons with questionable motives.

It is after these considerations that the king has authorized me to make it known to you, my Reverend Father, that he would be truly grateful to you and to your establishment if he were to be given this painting, which seems worthy of the collection that he wishes to assemble and make available to the public, and if you were to accept in exchange a painting, whose subject your community is free to choose, and which will be executed with the greatest care by the most distinguished artist of the Académie. This manner of proceeding appeared to me to be the most noble, and, consequently, the best one that you could choose in order to provide proof to the king of the sentiments that you expressed so movingly to M. Sauvage, who has made it a special point to communicate them. If you think that I should address myself to your superiors, please be so kind as to let me know, so that I may in no way neglect any means of fulfilling the king's wishes.

I have the honor, my Reverend Father, to be your most humble and most obedient servant,

Signed: D'ANGIVILLER

To the Reverend Father, guardian of the Capuchins of Flanders, in Lille (Lille, Archives, *Affaires générales*, carton 851, *dossier* 32).

2 I have relied a great deal on the excellent work of Édouard Pommier, editor of the *Lettres à Miranda* by Quatremère de Quincy (Paris, 1989). He is also the author of an essay entitled "Naissance des musées de province," published in *Les Lieux de mémoire* (Paris, 1988, IV, pp. 260–79), and of *L'art de la liberté* (Paris, 1991).

See also the Appendix by Marc Fumaroli, "What Does the Future Hold for Museums?," on page 284.

The Development of the Musée des Beaux-Arts, Lille

ARNAULD BREJON DE LAVERGNÉE

Jan van Eyck (about 1390–1441) lived in Lille from 1426 until 1429, when he served as valet de chambre to Philip the Good (1397–1457); Peter Paul Rubens and Anthony van Dyck gave some of their best works to the city's churches and convents; and Jacques-Louis David came to Lille especially to see the art collection of Charles Lenglart. The association of these artists with Lille left an indelible mark on the capital of French Flanders, and set the stage for the flowering of Lille as an art city, with a fine arts museum of its own. Charles Sterling related on more than one occasion how intrigued he was at the discovery of van Eyck's stay in Lille, which was then the seat of the dukes of Burgundy and the favored residence of Philip the Good; the archives contain the record of a meeting of artists attended by Jan van Eyck. Rubens and his pupils profoundly affected the artistic life of the city in the seventeenth century, as did such contemporary artists as Arnould de Vuez, whose work deserves to be reconsidered and given an appropriate place when the museum in Lille is newly reorganized in 1994. As for David, he will forever be remembered in Lille as the master of the city's native son Jean-Baptiste-Joseph Wicar. These illustrious names, among countless others, are responsible for the significance of the Musée des Beaux-Arts today.

Because the roots of the city's artistic heritage run so deep, responses were numerous in favor of the establishment of a museum to house its cultural inheritance. Lille had firmly resisted when the comte d'Angiviller, Surintendant des bâtiments to the king, relentlessly claimed Rubens's *Descent from the Cross* (cat. no. 1) for the royal collections in 1785; one century later, the townspeople of Lille united and overwhelmingly supported the public subscription to build the Palais des Beaux-Arts. The acquisitions made by one of the museum's foremost curators, Édouard Reynart, who was its director from 1841 to 1879, were sometimes more impressive than those of his colleagues at the Louvre. Between 1949 and 1976, Maurice and Denise Masson bequeathed to the museum their collection of Impressionist paintings and of sculptures by Rodin. The foundations of the Musée des Beaux-Arts became even stronger because the artists themselves were directly involved; Gustave Courbet felt the need to visit the museum to see his painting *After Dinner at Ornans* of 1849, completed several years earlier (see cat. no. 40). With Amand Gautier (whose portrait Courbet had painted), François Souchon and Alphonse Colas learned about painting at the museum, studying the canvases of Delacroix and of Courbet. Matisse related how, as a young man, he was often lost in reverie before Goya's *Time* and *The Letter* (cat. nos. 34, 35). In the copy of Marianna Alcaforado's *Lettres portugaises; lithographies originales de Henri Matisse* (Paris, 1946), which Matisse gave to the Musée des Beaux-Arts in March 1947, the artist wrote the following dedication: "In homage to the Musée des Beaux-Arts in Lille, where I felt close to real painting for the first time, half a century ago, in the presence of the *Young Women* and *Old Women* by Goya."

Artists, as well as their families, made prestigious gifts to the Musée des Beaux-Arts: there was, of course, the remarkable bequest by Wicar, but there were also donations of drawings by Puvis de Chavannes and by Mme Fantin-Latour. The museum was not just an elitist reserve of masterpieces for the select few but also inspired the creation of works of art and stimulated artists to develop their talents. If the museum today fulfills its educational and pedagogical roles so well—and not only for artists but also for all who wish to enrich themselves—it is because it has been a great institution for many generations already: It is the remarkable culmination of four to five centuries of creativity, patronage, connoisseurship, and collecting. The museum is also a place for a dialogue between works of art: For example, the *Study of Cows* by Jacob Jordaens was copied by van Gogh (see cat. nos. 5, 42), and the wax *Head of a Woman* formerly attributed to Raphael inspired Paul Bourget and many other distinguished artists at the turn of the century.

These artistic events are, of course, linked to politics. Jacques-Louis David was elected a deputy to the Convention of September 17, 1792, and began his career at the Tribune on October 26, 1792, by requesting that the State compensate the city of Lille, which had just resisted an Austrian invasion; he wanted a monument to be erected commemorating the siege, and he called upon every artist in Lille for suggestions.

If we can mention politics, why should we not add a literary touch? In his *Illuminations* (1873), Arthur Rimbaud recalled nostalgically: "At a party one night, in a northern town, I met all the women of the Old Masters." Young, vagabond poet from Lorraine, when will we find out the name of that city?

The definitive story of the Musée des Beaux-Arts in Lille remains to be written, yet it would be a fabulous institution to study, for the history of this great provincial museum is a metaphor for life itself, with the usual ups and downs. Hervé Oursel, in the third volume of his *Histoire de Lille* (1991), provides a detailed survey of the museum's history from its creation in 1801 until the 1850s, when the museum was still housed in the Hôtel de Ville. Among the most significant events to affect the museum's more recent history was the construction of the Palais des Beaux-Arts, from 1889 to 1892; the tragic aftermaths of the two world wars; the modernization, beginning in the 1960s; and the current renovation campaign. These are unquestionably milestones in the museum's evolution. As for the additions to the collections over the course of the nineteenth and twentieth centuries, these are discussed by Walter Liedtke in the essay that follows.

The Construction of the Palais des Beaux-Arts

Over the years, the museum's collections have expanded at a spectacular rate: The 1856 paintings catalogue listed 285 objects and the 1898 catalogue 1,138. The Commission du musée des peintures (the museum's Paintings Committee, founded in 1845), which became the Commission administrative du musée de peinture in 1862, kept careful lists of new acquisitions; the committee's twenty-two volumes of records, presently being reviewed by Dr. Gérard, bear witness to the institution's extraordinary growth. Great collectors, in the nineteenth-century tradition, bequeathed collections of Oceanic art (such as Moillet, in 1852) and objets d'art (De Vicq, in 1881). At the time, the museum occupied limited space on the second floor of the Hôtel de Ville, in the assembly hall and the chapel of the dukes of Burgundy in the former Palais Rihour.

The actual idea of building a new museum began to take shape when the lack of sufficient space became evident along with general agreement on the necessity of housing the collections in more appropriate surroundings, and problems of security made the town council and government officials anxious. On March 25, 1881, Lille's new mayor, Géry Legrand, designated the Jardin de la République as the site of the future Palais des Beaux-Arts. We know that he lent personal support to the project, which he declared "highly patriotic." In his words, "There is not a citizen of Lille who would not be proud to contribute a stone to the building that will house the second most important art collections after those of Paris." Two years were needed to raise funds, and the contest for the project was made public on April 15, 1884. Architects were invited to submit their plans for a "Palais des Beaux-Arts" to be situated opposite the Préfecture, and the candidates were informed that the people of Lille wanted a monument worthy both of their city and of its artistic riches: The edifice had to live up to its reputation as "the most important museum after those of Paris."

On January 9, 1885, the jury decided in favor of two Parisian architects, Bérard and Delmas; the first was a former student of M. Lisch, Inspecteur général des monuments historiques. The design selected was incontestably the most magnificent and monumental of those submitted, by virtue of the richness of the decoration and the vastness of its scale. Work began on July 20, 1885. However, the opening, slated for 1888—before the municipal elections—had to be postponed. Then, the construction suffered various setbacks, including the resignation of the architect Bérard in March 1889 followed by that of Herlin, curator and vice president of the Commission des Beaux-Arts, one year later.

The inauguration of the new building finally took place just one century ago, on March 6, 1892, a Sunday. It was obvious to all that the adoption of Bérard's and Delmas's project resulted in far more than the creation of a local museum. As a journalist writing for the *Écho du Nord* on January 6, 1885, commented: "It may be said without hesitation that the city graced by the actual stone structure erected from this plaster model will rank among those whose reputations are known throughout Europe." The minutes of the meeting of the Municipal Council held on May 22, 1885, stated: "The monument that we are building is not only municipal in nature. It is designed to house an immensely valuable collection of riches that, indeed, belong to the nation." The idea of the museum had evolved. Erstwhile temple of the Muses, it became a prestigious institution, linked to power. The jury had chosen a plan that embodied excess in its vastness, opulence, and extravagance. At the close of the nineteenth century, there was a tendency to exalt the notion of the palace-museum, an elaborate place of great wealth, containing the artistic heritage of a nation, a region, or even of just a city. To quote Lussien-Maisonneuve, "The concept of a Palais des Beaux-Arts thus seems profoundly rooted in its time, and particularly well suited to the riches and affluence of the city of Lille, the capital of French Flanders. With its two hectares of land and its imposing pair of buildings, the Hôtel de la Préfecture and the Palais des Beaux-Arts, the Place de la République fills the official description of a great modern city, an image that Lille hopes will prevail in the coming twentieth century, vis-à-vis Paris and its illustrious neighbors in northwestern Europe." (This is not the time for a lengthy discussion of the cruel damage wrought by World War I on Lille and its museum, but suffice it to say that their resolve had been broken.) The curator Théodore, who was affiliated with the museum from 1913 to 1937, was instrumental in safeguarding the collections. The museum had scarcely returned to normal when World War II was declared; the building remained open, but was obliged to present exhibitions of Nazi propaganda. Some losses can never be recouped. Homage should also be paid to the curator Pierre Maurois who, from 1938 to 1962, played a major role at the museum.

Renovation in the 1960s

Two curators, Albert Châtelet (1962–69), today Professor of Art History at the University of Strasbourg and a specialist in fourteenth- and fifteenth-century Flemish painting, and Hervé Oursel (1969–87), now Conservateur général du patrimoine in charge of the Musée National de la Renaissance at the Château d'Écouen, brought new life to the Palais des Beaux-Arts.

Châtelet, unassisted, made the museum's collections a known quantity abroad. Masterpieces from the Lille museum were sent to Berlin in 1964, and a selection of the finest Italian drawings from the Wicar bequest were lent to Amsterdam, Brussels, and Florence in 1968–69. The illustrated catalogue published on that occasion was—and still is—an invaluable reference work for students and scholars.

Two landmark exhibitions took place in the 1960s: "Apollinaire et le cubisme" in 1965 and "Au temps du Roi Soleil. Les peintures de Louis XIV (1660–1715)" in 1968; the catalogue accompanying the latter show has become an indispensable research tool, and, in addition, a bibliographical rarity, for, while much is known about the reign of Louis XIII, the period from 1660 to 1715 has been studied relatively little. Châtelet was able to engineer a major acquisition for the museum: the *Entombment* by Pieter Lastman (1583–1633); the painting (see fig. 6, p. 45), signed and dated 1612, is documented in the posthumous inventory of the artist's possessions. It is no exaggeration to state that this *Entombment*, painted by Rembrandt's master, is the most important of our Dutch paintings; with this acquisition, the museum continued the tradition begun by Reynart, who, year after year, bought superb Dutch and French works of art for our collections. Nor has the drawings department been overlooked; many new drawings have been acquired, including a copy by Jacob Jordaens of Rubens's *Descent from the Cross*, also in the museum (see cat. nos. 87, 1). The process of mounting and classifying the drawings was begun, an effort that marked the initial step toward the establishment of the future Cabinet des Dessins. During this period as well, Françoise Viatte prepared the catalogue raisonné (unpublished) of Florentine and Sienese drawings of the fifteenth and sixteenth centuries.

The building itself underwent a careful face-lifting: the roof and all external panes of glass were replaced; the paintings galleries were repainted and electric overhead lighting was installed; a storeroom was created for objects; and studies were begun for the installation of a storeroom for paintings and for the construction of an administration building (the last two projects would be completed somewhat later).

During Hervé Oursel's eighteen-year term as curator, much work was undertaken. The museum's finances were increased and the staff enlarged, enabling it to play a seminal role in the cultural life of the Nord Pas-de-Calais region of France. A detailed description of all of the projects under way would require many pages; instead, only a few of the highlights will be explored, such as the transformation of the building, the enrichment of the collections, and the mounting of important exhibitions, on a continual basis.

The museum has undergone a marked change with the installation of paintings storerooms in the Wicar Gallery and the construction of an annex at the rear of the building. Renovation of the galleries and improvements in the display of works of art have proceeded systematically. Some aspects of the collections were removed from storage and placed on exhibition: ceramics were installed in two galleries on the ground floor, and drawings, in the Wicar Gallery (the Cabinet des Dessins continues to grow as a result of acquisitions, restorations, and scientific studies). Advanced restoration techniques also have enabled many works of art formerly not on display to be exhibited in the paintings and decorative arts galleries.

Remarkable strides have been made in the area of acquisitions, the guiding principle for which was the desire to complete the existing collections, regardless of period or school. Thus, the museum has purchased pictures by Northern painters (Floris, Bril, Jordaens, Lievens, and van der Ast), and artists of the French School (La Hyre, Raoux, Hubert Robert, Vien, and Boilly), as well as drawings, ceramics, examples of goldsmiths' work, and contemporary paintings (by Martin Barré and Ossip Zadkine).

As tangible proof of the success of our acquisitions policy, many of our finest paintings, which are on exhibition at The Metropolitan Museum of Art, entered the Musée des Beaux-Arts through the efforts of my predecessor. The Masson bequest of Impressionist and Post-Impressionist paintings and the Catteaux gift of ceramics have considerably enriched the museum's holdings. In addition, there have been many noteworthy temporary exhibitions, especially those organized by the Association des Conservateurs des Musées du Nord Pas-de-Calais; these have included "Peinture hollandaise" (1972–73), "Peinture française 1770–1830" (1975–76), "La peinture flamande au temps de Rubens" (1977), "La peinture française aux XVIIe et XVIIIe siècles" (1980), "De Carpeaux à Matisse: La sculpture française de 1850 à 1914" (1982), and "Le Nord de la France de Théodose à Charles Martel" (1983), and provided an overview of the artistic riches preserved in the museums of the region. The accompanying catalogues have become invaluable, for they contain exhaustive accounts compiled by the contributing curators of the works of art in their respective museums; countless discoveries have resulted, and numerous art works placed on view.

Other exhibitions adopted a wider scope of inquiry. One of these deserving of special mention is "Au temps de Watteau, Fragonard et Chardin. Les Pays-Bas et les peintres français au XVIIIe siècle," for it offered an unprecedented insight into the Dutch and Flemish sources that nourished French painting of the eighteenth century.

My arrival in Lille in October 1987 as head of the museum coincided with the inception of the renovation project at the Palais des Beaux-Arts. Several weeks earlier, on October 2 to be exact, an agreement had been signed by the Prefect and by the Mayor of the city.

Two clauses established the guidelines for all future construction:

Article 1: The State agrees to place on loan at the Musée des Beaux-Arts nineteen relief models . . . and seven copies.
Article 2: The State and the City of Lille agree to collaborate on the overall restoration of the Musée des Beaux-Arts in order to improve the presentation of its collections and to display the relief models.

The gift of nineteen relief models of French cities, from the Musée des Plans-Reliefs in the Hôtel des Invalides in Paris, was a decisive factor in the current renovation project, as gallery space was needed to accommodate them.

The museum's staff was further expanded: Marie-Hélène Lavallée, Conservateur du Corps d'État, and Barbara Brejon joined Annie Scottez-De Wambrechies and Annie Castier, who had been at the museum for several years. A special program was initiated at the museum, in conjunction with the renovation of the building: Under the direction of Mme Ruel, an architect, and the curators, the museum assisted the Mayor's office in organizing a contest to select an architect for the renovation. The Direction des Musées de France, the Secrétariat d'État aux Grands Travaux, the Direction Régionale des Affaires Culturelles, and the Mayor of Lille—represented by the Cultural Commissioner, Mme Buffin—made the necessary arrangements to ensure that the candidates were highly qualified. And so they were. There were four runners-up: the architects Chemetov, Duhart, Lion, and Jean-Marc Ibos and his associate Myrto Vitart, and in May 1990 the last team was awarded the contract. The work, which is to begin immediately, will enlarge the building and restore much of its former stately appearance. One thousand square meters will be gained on the lower level by excavating below the atrium, and a vast gallery space for temporary exhibitions (750 square meters) will be created under the garden, along the rear façade. An elegant "sliver" building will be constructed at the back of the garden, parallel to the rear façade of the main building, providing 2,500 square meters of space, on five levels; the building will house the Cabinet des Dessins, the restoration studio, offices, and a restaurant. The annex at the back, on the garden side, and the main staircase in the atrium will be removed, making the building lighter and more open, as well as better integrated into the surrounding cityscape. The various departments will be reorganized: On the ground floor, on either side of the atrium, will be two galleries displaying faïence and porcelain, and eighteenth- and nineteenth-century sculpture; the small collection of Mediterranean archaeological objects will be exhibited in the ground-floor gallery on the garden side. The paintings galleries will occupy the first floor, and will be divided into three main areas: Flanders and Holland, France, and Italy and Spain. The lower level will be the domain of three departments: Medieval and Renaissance art, the maquettes of the relief models, and the non-European ethnographical collections. The floor space of the museum will thus be increased from the present 13,000 to 21,000 square meters.

Concurrent with this work in progress, the following special exhibitions—all with accompanying catalogues—have been organized: "Boilly, 1761–1845. Un grand peintre français de la Révolution à la Restauration" (1988–89); "Plans en Relief, villes fortes des anciens Pays-Bas français au XVIIIe siècle" (1989); "Renaissance et Baroque. Dessins italiens du Musée de Lille" (1989–90); "L'Europe de la Faïence, XVIIe et XVIIIe siècles" (1990–91), a selection from the museum's collections; "La Peinture française au XIXe siècle, Le Musée des Beaux-Arts de Lille," which was shown in Japan in 1991; and "Bellezze di Firenzi. Disegni fiorentini del Seicento e del Settecento del Museo di Belle Arti di Lille," held at the Palazzo Pitti in Florence (1991). Our publications program continues with forthcoming summary catalogues of paintings and of Italian drawings, and a guide to the department of Medieval and Renaissance art.

Between 1990 and 1996, twelve million francs will have been spent on the restoration of works of art in the museum.

Lastly, another recent milestone for the Musée des Beaux-Arts has been the acquisition of a painting by Jean-Baptiste-Siméon Chardin, *The Silver Cup* (cat. no. 23).

The curatorial staff is not at a loss for projects. As a result of the renovation campaign, the Musée des Beaux-Arts will resume its rightful place as the second most important museum in France. Once the renovation is brought to a successful completion, we can think ahead to the post-1994 period when the museum will gain a second wind and make up for the time lost when it was closed for restoration.

Our predecessors were not lacking in determination, to be sure. One need only examine as proof the extraordinary building that they had constructed between 1889 and 1892, and the array of masterpieces on exhibition for three months at The Metropolitan Museum of Art in New York. Yes, we will, indeed, need a second wind if we are to pass along to our grandchildren, in perfect condition, these testimonials to the classical history of Europe, preserving them for future generations as they were preserved for us by a handful of our remarkable forebears.

Paintings

The Medea *Drawings*

Sculpture

European Paintings in the Musée des Beaux-Arts, Lille

WALTER LIEDTKE

One of the pleasures gained from repeated visits to a collection is coming to know its character. What at first may have seemed an impressive but—for an old and distinguished city—a somewhat expected assortment of pictures from various schools becomes, for the curious visitor, the unique result of historical moments, some of them fortuitously connected, others linked together by the will of thoughtful individuals or at least by values and traditions distinctive of the place.

There are many museums in Europe that developed along more determined lines and therefore offer a different experience. The Hermitage, the Mauritshuis, the Vatican museums, the collections at Braunschweig and Kassel, and, of course, institutions like the Musée Bonnat in Bayonne are examples of museums created by singular circumstances, and by princes, emperors, empresses, czars, and in the last case a local painter. Most city museums, by contrast, although they were also the heirs of great institutions and individuals, drew upon the far more diversified resources of the indigenous culture and citizenry. The story of these museums is one of directors, curators, and patrons, and it usually begins in the nineteenth century.[1]

How these reflections apply to Lille will be evident from the preceding essays, but may also be seen from a glance at the remarkable range of Northern European pictures in the Musée des Beaux-Arts. The small but interesting group of Early Netherlandish paintings that was on exhibition in the mid-nineteenth century could be described as a consequence, in the broadest view, of Philip the Good's choice of Lille as one of the principal seats of the court of Burgundy (see fig. 1). From the age of Jan van Eyck and Rogier van der Weyden until late in the lifetime of Jacob Jordaens (see cat. nos. 4, 5) Lille was a prominent city of the Netherlands.

The next decision of great significance for this part of the collection was made by a former foundling in the city's care, Antoine Brasseur (1819–1886). He became an art dealer in Cologne and an important collector of early

FIGURE 1. Follower of Rogier van der Weyden. *Portrait of Philip the Good.* Fifteenth century. Oil on wood

German (see figs. 2, 3), sixteenth-century Flemish, and sixteenth- and seventeenth-century Dutch paintings. These were presented to his native city between 1878 and 1886.[2] Brasseur's insightful and occasionally eccentric tastes—the paintings by Barendsz., Blocklandt, van Heemskerck, and the Hungarian Master M.S. come from his collection—did not extend to seventeenth-century Flemish art. However, the oil sketch for one of Lille's greatest treasures, Rubens's *Descent from the Cross* (cat. nos. 1, 2); the large *Christ in the House of Mary and Martha* that Erasmus Quellinus the Younger painted in collaboration with Jan Fyt; and the most entertaining of the museum's several pictures by Jacob Jordaens (cat. no. 4) were purchased with funds from Brasseur's estate.

Lille's exceptional strengths in the area of Rubens, van Dyck, Jordaens, and their contemporaries are the result of forces beyond the control of individuals, whether self made or princely: Most of the works were created in the course of the Counter-Reformation and were confiscated from the Church in the years after the Revolution of 1789. These two movements in the march of Western civilization fall into peculiar harmony when one examines the histories of French, Spanish, and Belgian museums. The Revolution and Napoleon's decree (September 1, 1801) that fifteen provincial cities in France would have museums explain why the Musée des Beaux-Arts might remind visitors, especially those from other countries, of the galleries of paintings in French cities such as Bordeaux, Lyons, and Rouen. In each case, however, the seemingly typical French museum proves to possess a distinctive character, one which reflects that of the city or of the province itself. The museum in Lille is

FIGURE 2. Barthel Bruyn the Elder. *Portrait of a Man.* About 1540. Oil on wood

FIGURE 3. Barthel Bruyn the Elder. *A Skull and Bone in a Stone Niche* (originally the verso of figure 2; now separated). About 1540. Oil on wood

one of the best examples, for it is part of a place that in its history, customs, architecture, and art is French and Flemish, and the sum of individual efforts in ways that can be confused with the culture of no other city in Belgium or France.

Before we turn to a review of the paintings in Lille, and in particular to the many superb pictures that for various reasons could not travel abroad, one more figure should be placed on the pediment where Brasseur and other donors accompany images of History and Geography. Édouard Reynart served the museum for fifty years, first as curator and then, from 1841 to 1879, as director. If the collection of paintings now has breadth and depth as well as concentrated areas, this was achieved in good part by Reynart, who combined taste and learning with such practical assets as energy and *savoir faire*. In this space his legacy must be reduced to statistical terms: The 1841 Lille catalogue records 188 pictures, and that of 1875 lists 715. The later publication includes the 122 mostly Dutch and Flemish paintings that were received as the bequest of Alexandre Leleux (1873).[3] It was a few years later, in 1878, that Reynart went to Cologne and earned the confidence of Antoine Brasseur.

FIGURE 4. Peter Paul Rubens. *The Martyrdom of Saint Catherine.* About 1615. Oil on canvas

Devotees of Goya (see cat. nos. 34, 35) or of Jacques-Louis David (see cat. no. 28) may hold a different opinion, but for many visitors to Lille the museum's greatest painting will be Rubens's *Descent from the Cross* (cat. no. 1). This monumental canvas, painted in 1617 for the Capuchin convent in Lille, is one of a dozen large Flemish altarpieces in the Musée des Beaux-Arts. Altogether four are by Rubens and his workshop; the *Descent* and most of the *Ecstasy of Mary Magdalene* (cat. no. 3) are by Rubens himself. The latter was painted about 1619–20 for the Church of the Recollects in Ghent. *The Martyrdom of Saint Catherine* (fig. 4) dates from about 1615, when Rubens's classicizing style was gradually giving way to a more emotive manner. This epic composition was made for the church of Sainte-Catherine in Lille at the request of a parishioner, Jean de Seur, whom Rubens knew as an adviser to his patrons in Brussels, Archduke Albert and the Infanta Isabella.[4] Other pictures produced in Rubens's workshop for the Capuchin convent in Lille are the *Saint Francis Receiving the Christ Child from the Arms of the Virgin,*[5] which is not well preserved, and full-length paintings of Saints Francis and Bonaventure.

In this context it is almost expected to discover van Dyck as a painter of

FIGURE 5. Anthony van Dyck and Workshop. *Christ on the Cross*. About 1630. Oil on canvas

great altarpieces—a view of the artist one must otherwise seek out in the museum in Antwerp, or in Palermo, or in the Church of Notre-Dame in Kortrijk (Courtrai), just north of Lille. The majestic *Christ on the Cross* (fig. 5) from the Convent of the Recollects in Lille was one of several large religious pictures that were ordered from van Dyck during his second Antwerp period (late 1627 to early 1632).[6] For the same church van Dyck painted *The Miracle of the Mule*, which will be one of Lille's most admired Flemish paintings once restoration allows it to be exhibited.[7]

Conservation projects now in progress will require some recycling of altarpieces in the Flemish galleries. The Revolutionary commission transferred to the museum Jan Cossiers's *Saint Nicholas Delivering Captives* (1660) and Jan Boeckhorst's *Martyrdom of Saint Maurice* (1661), both from the church of Saint-Maurice in the center of Lille;[8] Pieter van Mol's *Annunciation* from a convent in Paris;[9] Gaspar de Crayer's *Miracle of the Fishes* from the church of Saint Peter in Ostend and his so-called *Four Crowned Martyrs* from the church of Sainte-Catherine in Brussels;[10] and Cornelis de Vos's *Resurrection of Christ*.[11] Other large pictures by followers of Rubens and van Dyck, such as Theodoor Boeyermans,[12] Erasmus Quellinus,[13] and Gerard Seghers, round out an imposing survey of religious art from the Southern Netherlands.

More familiar types of Flemish paintings are also numerous in Lille and deserve much closer attention than they can be given here. The inclusion of the picture by Quellinus and Fyt,[14] mentioned above, in the 1992 exhibition at The Metropolitan Museum of Art in New York was sacrificed only for the sake of the extraordinary *vanitas* still life by Pieter Boel (see cat. no. 7), a Reynart acquisition. He also purchased *The Temptation of Saint Anthony* by David Teniers,[15] a delicate work on panel by an artist richly represented in American as well as European museums. Landscapes by Jacques d'Arthois, Paul Bril, Joos de Momper, Jan Siberechts, and Teniers; still lifes by Abraham Brueghel, Jan Fyt(?),[16] Roelant Savery (cat. no. 9), Frans Snyders, and Adriaen van Utrecht;[17] and other Flemish paintings serve as constant reminders that Antwerp, Brussels, and most Belgian cities are now only an hour or two away from Lille.[18]

A painting on panel may be in excellent condition but because of its construction, material, thinness, sheer age, or other factors will not tolerate transport or changes in temperature and humidity. This assessment applies precisely to Pieter Lastman's private altarpiece, *The Entombment* of 1612 (fig. 6),[19] and to Jacob Jordaens's *Temptation of the Magdalene* of about 1618 (fig. 7).[20] The latter picture, one of the artist's most expressive early works, is the first in a remarkable suite of paintings by Jordaens in Lille. *A Huntsman and His Hounds*, dated 1635,[21] like the *Rape of Europa* (cat. no. 4), is set in a lush landscape and is exceeded in celebrity in Lille only by the mythological masterpiece. A fine

FIGURE 6. Pieter Lastman. *The Entombment.*
1612. Oil on wood

Portrait of a Man (of about 1630) and a half-dozen later works by Jordaens and his studio were purchased during or shortly after Reynart's tenure at the museum.

It may seem illogical to mention Early Netherlandish paintings after a review of Rubens and his contemporaries, but this approach at least follows the evolution of taste and of public collections in the late nineteenth and the twentieth century.[22] Lille's greatest treasure of the fifteenth century is a pair of panels by Dieric Bouts, *The Way to Paradise* and *The Fall of the Damned* (figs. 8, 9): The former was purchased by the city of Lille in 1946, while the latter was obtained by exchange with the State in 1957.[23] These extraordinary images are wings of a triptych, the missing center of which probably depicted the Last Judgment.

A long gallery in Lille leads one from Bouts to a survey of Northern European artists of the sixteenth century. The nicely named Master of the Embroidered Foliage, who was probably from Brussels, recalls Gerard David and Hans Memling in his triptych *The Virgin and Child with Angels* (about 1500).[24] The heavenly subject in the center panel is set in a château's exquisite and symbolic garden, which extends into the wings as a continuous scene. Two

FIGURE 7. Jacob Jordaens. *The Temptation of the Magdalene*. About 1618. Oil on wood

triptychs by an artist of the region, Jean Bellegambe (born in nearby Douai about 1470), are from the Abbey of Anchin.[25] Antwerp's sophistication in the next two generations is seen in Jan van Dornicke's triptych, *The Adoration of the Magi* (about 1520?), and in Dirk Vellert's all but outré *Adoration of the Shepherds* (about 1540).[26] Several of Brasseur's donations fit in well with these works, such as the *Mocking of Christ* by a follower of Cranach, *The Adoration of the Magi* by the Master M.S., a *Coronation of the Virgin* from Augsburg (?) of about 1540, and a *Tarquin and Lucretia* (fig. 10) by a stylish follower of Jan Massys.[27] The same collector gave the museum Nicolas Neufchâtel's sensitive *Portrait of the Mathematician Johan Neudorfer and His Son* (painted in Nuremberg in 1561), and the large wing of a triptych of about 1577–79 by Anthonie Blocklandt, which depicts the Baptism of Christ and Saint Philip on the exterior.[28] This powerful panel makes the 1978 purchase of *The Holy Family*, ascribed to Frans Floris, a somewhat surprising supplement,[29] but with Dirck Barendsz.'s small, strange *Dead Rising from Their Graves* (about 1580)[30] and his *Portrait of a Woman*,[31] and Otto van Veen's six oil sketches in grisaille (purchased in 1970), Lille has a fascinating group of pictures representing the post-Floris period in Antwerp and the Northern Netherlands.

FIGURE 8. Dieric Bouts. *The Way to Paradise*. About 1450. Oil on wood

FIGURE 9. Dieric Bouts. *The Fall of the Damned*. About 1450. Oil on wood

A scholar of Dutch paintings would spend an afternoon in the long Dutch gallery in Lille, and then a day in the storerooms, but in this essay our approach must resemble a ten-minute tour of the Rijksmuseum. The peculiar panel by Maerten van Heemskerck, *A Bullfight* (once owned by Brasseur), which is set in a version of the Colosseum (1552),[32] and the works by Barendsz. and by Blocklandt cited above are among the few Dutch pictures to date earlier than Wtewael's important *Raising of Lazarus* (cat. no. 11) and than comparable paintings by the Haarlem Mannerists (Cornelisz. van Haarlem's small painting on copper [cat. no. 12], although a later work, is their representative in Lille). A younger painter from Utrecht, Gerrit van Honthorst, painted the huge and hilarious *Triumph of Silenus* about 1623.[33] Honthorst's highly successful

FIGURE 10. Circle of Jan Massys. *Tarquin and Lucretia.* Second half of the sixteenth century. Oil on wood

career in The Hague from about 1630 onward is reflected in Lille in portraits of women by Willem van Honthorst and by Adriaen Hanneman (both gifts of Brasseur).[34] To say that these artists supplanted the styles of Michiel van Miereveld and Jan van Ravesteyn takes nothing away from the superb pair of Ravesteyn portraits, dated 1620, in the Musée des Beaux-Arts.[35]

Lastman's *Entombment* (fig. 6), purchased in 1962, is one of the finest known works by Rembrandt's teacher.[36] The story of how a young curator just missed out on *The Man in a Golden Helmet*, at the time (1894) a famous Rembrandt, now can be seen in a different light.[37] The hazards of attributing pictures to the Circle of Rembrandt were demonstrated as recently as twelve years ago when Lille acquired its Lievens, *Saint Francis in Ecstasy*, which was rejected by Werner Sumowski a little later on.[38] Lievens's *Head of an Old Man* and his *Moses Stepping on Pharaoh's Crown*, both from the late 1630s, were acquired in 1878 and 1885 and are indisputably autograph works.[39]

The discussion below of Isack Jouderville's *Young Woman with a Candle* (cat. no. 14), one of the finest pictures by an early associate of Rembrandt, takes into account for the first time the artist's close connection with Lievens. It is this sort of revelation that excites the scholar or the *amateur* in Lille: Individual works, unless they are of the most generic kind (and thus have at least local interest), provide insights that are frequently fresher than those one is likely to gain in an afternoon at the Louvre or the Rijksmuseum. For this writer, other Dutch paintings in Lille that invite exclamations in the margins of one's catalogue would include Frans van Mieris's dramatic interpretation (reminiscent of the young Rembrandt's biblical pictures) of a comparatively obscure Old Testament scene (see cat. no. 15); Jacob Gerritsz. Cuyp's large portrait of a

FIGURE 11. Johannes Verspronck. *Portrait of a Young Man.* 1634. Oil on wood

couple and their five children in a landscape, dated 1631, which looks forward to Hals while recalling Thomas de Keyser in Amsterdam;[40] Jacobus Vrel's atmospheric interior scene;[41] Bartholomeus van der Helst's *Venus* (1664), which, like the similar picture now in the Louvre, seems to be too frankly erotic to have remained in the Netherlands;[42] and, of course, Codde's *Young Scholar in His Study* (cat. no. 13).

These paintings also take their place in a collection that admirably represents the variety of the Dutch School. There may be no Hals (the *Malle Babbe* is an old copy) but there are two genre pictures by his brother Dirck; a *Drinker* and a *Young Flutist* attributed to Frans Hals the Younger;[43] and an exceptional *Portrait of a Young Man*, of 1634, by Frans Hals's rival, Johannes Verspronck (fig. 11).[44] The Haarlem tradition is also illustrated by slaughtering scenes by Adriaen and by Isaack van Ostade,[45] a winter view by Isaack,[46] Cornelis Bega's *Smokers*, and impressive landscapes by Jan van Goyen,[47] Salomon van Ruysdael,[48] Gerrit van Hees, and Jacob van Moscher.[49]

There are entirely too many Dutch paintings in Lille to mention more than the best—and then only by category. As Oursel has observed, two sides of Jacob van Ruisdael are seen in his *Mountain Torrent* and *Wheatfields*.[50] Italianate landscapes are represented by Dujardin and Pynacker, and seascapes by Bakhuizen, Dubbels, Allart van Everdingen, and Willem van de Velde the Elder (a splendid grisaille). Two special areas of strength are paintings from Rembrandt's circle (three van den Eeckhouts, a Salomon Koninck, and the works by Jouderville and by Lievens mentioned above),[51] and by artists of the Leiden School (again Jouderville, Lievens, and Frans van Mieris, with genre scenes by Willem van Mieris, Pieter van Slingeland, Godfried Schalcken, and Jan Steen). Much of the history of Dutch portraiture is seen in those works already mentioned as well as in examples by Cornelis van der Voort and Nicolaes Eliasz., van den Eeckhout, van der Helst, Eglon van der Neer, Constantijn Netscher, Anthonie Palamedesz., Jan Victors, and a variety of Vaillants (see also cat. no. 6). Of course, a bare list can convey nothing special, such as how extraordinary an image is Palamedesz.'s portrait of ten adult members of a fashion-conscious family.[52]

Almost all of Lille's Dutch genre paintings have already been cited except for Codde's *Conversation*, Pieter de Hooch's *Young Woman with Her Maid* (of about 1680?), and the usual sprinkling of genre scenes and genre-like history pictures from (in this case) Brakenburg and Brekelenkam to Adriaen van der Werff and Gerrit de Wet. Among the still lifes there are outstanding panels by Savery and van der Ast (see cat. nos. 9, 10), an early van Beyeren,[53] two Jan de Heems,[54] the Brasseur paintings by de Heem's followers Johannes Hannot and Jacob Marrel,[55] a Jan van Huysum of 1716 and pendant flower pictures (of 1747) by Rachel Ruysch. Lille also has fine architectural paintings, which include not only the wonderful de Witte (cat. no. 16) and one of Dirck van Delen's most successful compositions (of 1638), but also late works by both masters and a *Laurenskerk* (of 1669) by Anthonie de Lorme.[56]

The identity of the Musée des Beaux-Arts as the most northern of all great French museums is underscored by the bold strokes of its Dutch, Flemish, and French collections and by the faint lines one can trace through the Italian and Spanish schools. However, there are spectacular exceptions, thanks to thoughtful decisions made by Brasseur, Reynart, and Wicar, the last of whom gave Lille the relief by Donatello (cat. no. 44), as well as his own legendary collection of drawings (see pages 188–91, below). Brasseur's survey of early Northern art was complemented by two Quattrocento paintings, an altarpiece (a *Virgin and Child with Saints*) by the Venetian artist Jacobello del Fiore and the Botticelli-like *Virgin and Child* by Bartolomeo di Giovanni.[57] Another Florentine *Virgin and Child*, by Ghirlandaio's brother-in-law Sebastiano Mainardi, was bought by Reynart in 1874 and is typical of that period's taste.[58] The works assigned to Cosimo Rosselli, Francesco Zaganelli, Bramantino, Andrea del Sarto (certainly a copy), Beccafumi, and a few others reveal a gravitation to the years around 1500, which, compared with the Louvre's holdings in this area, could be described as a malaise of provincial French museums. The altarpiece attributed to Veronese (probably a seventeenth-century copy) in the inventory of the collection of Louis XIV, and a portrait by Tintoretto do not raise one's eyes to a higher plane,[59] but Veronese's *Paradise*, an autograph entry in the competition (won by Tintoretto) for a great mural in the Palazzo Ducale in Venice, is one of the few oil sketches by him that is properly so described.[60] Venetian art is marvelously represented in Lille, considering that, in addition to the Tintoretto, Veronese's *Paradise*, and the paintings cited immediately below, there is a Guardi, and a rare review of the seventeenth century offered by Domenico Fetti, Johann Liss, and Andrea Celesti.

Six non-Italian pictures that reveal the lure of Venice are a *Judith and Holofernes* and a *Noli me tangere* by Lambert Sustris,[61] the sumptuous *Finding of Moses* by Liss (cat. no. 17), two suave scenes of sacrifice by Franz Sigrist (a Viennese of the late eighteenth century),[62] and the *Martyrdom of Saint Stephen*, once thought to be a late Titian but now attributed to Diego Polo (a hypothesis supported mostly by the obscurity of the artist's name).[63]

More assuredly Spanish are Ribera's *Saint Jerome*;[64] El Greco's *Saint Francis* (purchased two years before Picasso was born);[65] and the pendant Goyas (see cat. nos. 34, 35), which, to an even greater degree, exemplify the vision of Reynart.

Why Lille has great French paintings and what all of them are need not and cannot be answered here, yet it should be observed that the collection goes beyond the conventional in good part because of Reynart's acquisitions, and

FIGURE 12. Hubert Robert. *Terrace of a Palace in Rome.* About 1776. Oil on canvas

much more recent purchases. Of the latter, the most remarkable example is the early masterpiece by Chardin (see cat. no. 23), of which ten percent of the price was obtained by public subscription in the fall of 1990.

The centralization of paintings by Poussin, Claude, Vouet, La Tour, and other great French masters at the Louvre is an all but insurmountable policy, one that places Paris before the provinces and, in effect, foreign visitors above local devotees. Considerable compensation is provided in Lille by the surprising *Adoration of the Magi* (cat. no. 18) by Georges Lallemant, who was Vouet's predecessor in Paris and an employer of the young Philippe de Champaigne (see cat. no. 19). Pictures by both artists are found in Lille ultimately because of the suppression of religious orders in Paris, where Lallemant was once the painter to see for an altarpiece.

French Caravaggism can be said to be represented in Lille by Nicolas Régnier's *Soldiers at Cards*, to judge from its style and the fact that the artist was born near Lille, in Maubeuge (Mabuse), France, on the border just south of

FIGURE 13. Luc-Olivier Merson. *The Vision.* 1872. Oil on canvas

Philippe de Champaigne's native Brussels. However, Régnier trained under Abraham Janssen in Antwerp and worked (as Renieri) in Rome and in Venice. Very different aspects of French art of the *Grand Siècle* are Laurent de La Hyre's *Pastoral Landscape* (cat. no. 20), and religious pictures by Eustache Le Sueur and by his exact contemporary Sébastien Bourdon,[66] as well as by Jean-Baptiste de Champaigne (Philippe's nephew). Mythologies by Nicolas Mignard and by Noël Coypel (both from the Palais des Tuileries), and Pierre Mignard's *Fortune* (from the Château de Versailles), descend from the age of Louis XIV, whose successor is glorified in an allegorical canvas by Henri de Favanne.[67] An autograph replica by, and a copy after, that emotional classicist Jouvenet would not both be mentioned were the latter (the *Healing the Sick*) not by his nephew and sympathizer, Jean Restout, whose altarpiece, *The Supper at Emmaus* (of 1735), is also in Lille.[68]

Nearly the entire range of eighteenth-century French painting is represented in the Musée des Beaux-Arts. However, pictures by Jean-François De Troy, Charles-Antoine Coypel, Boucher, and Fragonard; by Noël Hallé, Lagrenée the Elder, and Lépicié (the last three works were royal commissions, ordered by Comte d'Angiviller); and by other familiar names are not always on view.[69] A magnificent mural by Hubert Robert (see fig. 12) was bought in 1981,[70] but the real pleasures in Lille lie in the unexpected—for example, the two kinds of casual portrait by Paul-Ponce-Antoine Robert and by Nicolas de Largillierre (see cat. nos. 21, 22), and Jean Raoux's entertaining if virginal allegories, purchased in 1979 (see cat. nos. 24, 25). In discussing this subject it should be noted that Greuze's *Cupid and Psyche* (cat. no. 27) is anticipated in Lille by Joseph-Marie Vien's scene of the same lovers (of 1761),[71] thus illuminating two species of insincere classicism.

That sentiment could not be revised more dramatically than in David's *Belisarius Begging Alms* (cat. no. 28), which was bought by Reynart in 1863, and in an imposing series of neoclassical and Romantic works: David's *Apelles Painting Campaspe in the Presence of Alexander*,[72] Boilly's *Triumph of Marat* (cat. no. 30; see also cat. nos. 31–33), Gericault's oil sketch of uncontrollable horses (see cat. no. 36), and Delacroix's monumental picture of Medea depraved (see cat. no. 37), which the young Reynart managed to secure in the year of its execution; Reynart performed the same feat when Courbet's *After Dinner at Ornans* (cat. no. 40) appeared at the Salon of 1849.

From Reynart's time to nearly the present the Musée des Beaux-Arts has assembled an exceptional collection of French paintings dating from about 1850 to the early twentieth century. If the exhibition at the Metropolitan Museum excluded paintings from before 1600 for reasons of conservation, those from after 1850 were passed over because conveying their richness was an impossibility. Courbet's *Garden of the Abbey of Loos* was probably painted in 1851 when he visited Lille to see his earlier masterpiece (see cat. no. 40); with these two pictures and three other Courbets the Lille museum has works by the artist dating from regular intervals between 1841 and 1867.[73] All the Barbizon painters are liberally represented, perhaps most picturesquely by Théodore Rousseau's view of the Seine,[74] and there are memorable pictures by Corot, Alphonse Colas (a painter of religious subjects, from Lille), Amaury-Duval, Hippolyte Flandrin, and especially Daubigny, Diaz de la Peña, and Puvis de Chavannes. Luc-Olivier Merson's *The Vision* (fig. 13) of 1872 is one of a number of large canvases in Lille that may frighten young children and inform old hands in the history of art.

A sentimental favorite at the museum is Millet's *La becquée*, which shows a young peasant woman extending a spoon to one of her three little children as if they were tiny birds in a nest.[75] Different aspects of nature are seen in a superb harbor view by Boudin (of 1873),[76] and in (for many visitors) unfamiliar pictures by every Impressionist. The most striking of these are a winter scene by Sisley (of 1876) and two canvases by Monet: *La débâcle* (of 1880), a frigid view of the Seine, and a flamboyant near nocturne of London's Houses of Parliament (of 1904).[77]

The most significant signs of the *fin de siècle* are Toulouse-Lautrec's decorative *Dans l'atelier* (of about 1885), and two still lifes and a portrait by Vuillard.[78] The leading figure in the collection of twentieth-century art at the Musée des Beaux-Arts is Fernand Léger.[79] There are paintings by Félix Vallotton, Derain, and Dufy, and Picassos of the 1920s, and of 1964, but on the whole this section of the collection is slanted toward the Right Bank and various kinds of constructivists.[80] An indigestible Laurencin confirms that the School of Paris is not a school of Lille. The last word may be left to Sonia Delaunay, on the grounds that her *Rythme coloré 1076* of 1939 is an energetic, colorful, critical work by an artist with international experience and appeal.[81] Whether or not the reader would apply these adjectives to this particular composition, they certainly characterize the collections and the city of Lille.

1 See Bazin, 1967, and Haskell, 1976, on European museums.

2 See Lille, 1981, pp. 9–17.

3 See Oursel, 1974.

4 See Paris, 1977–78, no. 121; Vlieghe, 1972, no. 78.

5 See Vlieghe, 1972, no. 95.

6 See Oursel, 1984, no. 15; Larsen, 1988, I, p. 240, fig. 202, II, no. 704. In my view, the faces of John and Mary and most of the figure of Christ are by van Dyck himself. The painting appears to have lost much of its original surface.

7 See Larsen, 1988, I, p. 240, fig. 203, II, no. 655. The picture is also known as *The Miracle of Saint Anthony of Padua*.

8 For the Boeckhorst see Antwerp–Münster, 1990, no. 28.

9 See Oursel, 1984, p. 19, ill. 33 (in Oursel, 1984, "ill." refers to the compendium of black-and-white photographs at the back of the book, while "fig." refers to those in the text).

10 See Vlieghe, 1972, nos. A 36, A 86, plates 41, 87.

11 See Oursel, 1984, p. 18, ill. 24.

12 Boeyermans's *Ecstasy of Saint Rosalie*, purchased in 1886, in my view confirms that van Dyck's so-called *Virgin as Intercessor* in fact represents Saint Rosalie (see Washington, 1990–91, no. 47).

13 See Oursel, 1974, no. 51; not in De Bruyn, 1988 (see his cat. nos. 139–141).

14 See De Bruyn, 1988, no. 67.

15 See Oursel, 1984, no. 25.

16 The *Still Life of Dead Game Guarded by a Dog* (Inv. no. 113) catalogued as "after Jan Fyt" in the Brasseur exhibition (see Lille, 1981, no. 105) is probably by Pieter Boel. The painting should not be confused with Snyders's *Dog in a Kitchen* (Inv. no. 123), purchased in 1882.

17 On the painting attributed to Adriaen van Utrecht in Lille–Calais–Arras, 1977, no. 69, see Sutton, 1990, p. 128 n. 2 (as by Melchior d'Hondecoeter).

18 The so-called *Pomona* (*Ceres?*) attributed to Frans Wouters (Inv. no. 117) is more likely from Rubens's studio, dating to about 1614. Wouters's name is also invoked for the *Prometheus* (Inv. no. 115) after the painting by Rubens and Snyders (Philadelphia Museum of Art).

19 See Paris, 1970–71, no. 132.

20 See Châtelet, 1964, no. 24; Oursel, 1984, no. 16, with further literature.

21 See d'Hulst, 1982, p. 153, fig. 118, colorpl. (see also p. 353 of the Index for paintings by Jordaens in Lille).

22 See my introductory essay in Bauman and Liedtke, 1992.

23 See Oursel, 1984, p. 13, pl. I (opp. p. 16), no. 5. Lille surrendered Piazzetta's magnificent *Assumption of the Virgin* to the Louvre.

24 See Oursel, 1984, p. 14, fig. 7.

25 See Oursel, 1984, pp. 14–15, ill. 18 (*The Trinity* of about 1509–13). The other altarpiece represents *The Mystical Fountain* (see Paris, 1965, no. 41).

26 For the van Dornicke see Oursel, 1984, p. 15, ill. 17; for the Vellert see Paris, 1965, no. 307.

27 See Lille, 1981, nos. 9, 13, 27, 16, respectively.

28 See Lille, 1981, nos. 20, 4, respectively.

29 See Oursel, 1984, no. 9.

30 See Oursel, 1984, p. 24, ill. 41.

31 See Judson, 1970, no. 45; given to the Musée des Beaux-Arts by Brasseur in 1886.

32 See Paris, 1965, no. 161; Lille, 1981, no. 10; Oursel, 1984, p. 24, fig. 14.

33 See Judson, 1959, no. 93, fig. 33; Oursel, 1984, p. 25, ill. 46. The present writer examined the work in the conservation studios in Versailles and must assume that the attribution to Christiaen van Couwenbergh in Amsterdam, 1971, p. 163, is based upon a momentary glance at a photograph.

34 See Lille, 1981, nos. 42, 47.

35 Brasseur's Miereveld (see Lille, 1981, no. 55) is an uncertain attribution. On the Ravesteyns see Ekkart, 1991.

36 See Paris, 1970–71, no. 132; Amsterdam, 1971, no. 1. Compare Lastman's *Resurrection* of 1612 in The J. Paul Getty Museum.

37 Indeed, a light different from that cast by Oursel, 1984, p. 11. See Kelch, 1986, who rightly regards the work as by an anonymous Rembrandt pupil of the 1650s.

38 See Oursel and Scottez, 1979, pp. 382–83; Oursel, 1984, p. 28, fig. 18; Sumowski, 1983, III, no. 1239.

39 See Lille, 1981, no. 53; Sumowski, 1983, III, p. 1784, under no. 1199, and no. 1201.

40 See Slive, 1970–74, II, plates 164, 272 (family portraits of about 1635 and about 1648). Compare the J. G. Cuyp in Lille (see Oursel, 1984, p. 26, ill. 49) to de Keyser's family portrait of the late 1620s in the Schlossmuseum, Gotha (see Robinson, 1979, p. 492, fig. 3), in which there is also a goat cart.

41 See Paris, 1970–71, no. 227; Amsterdam, 1971, no. 50; Oursel, 1984, p. 31, ill. 58.

42 See Oursel, 1984, p. 30, ill. 59. The *Diana* from Brasseur's collection was hastily rejected as a work by van der Helst in Lille, 1981, no. 85, and should be compared with *The Artist's Wife as Granida,*

signed by van der Helst and dated 1660, now on the Paris art market (see Paris, 1991–92-2, no. 22).

43 See Amsterdam, 1971, p. 165; Lille, 1981, nos. 106, 107.

44 See Paris, 1970–71, no. 223; Ekkart, 1979, no. 2; Lille, 1981, no. 70; Oursel, 1984, no. 19.

45 See Amsterdam, 1971, p. 168; Oursel, 1984, no. 21 (Isaack van Ostade's *Interior with a Butchered Pig*).

46 See Lille, 1981, no. 59; Oursel, 1984, p. 25, fig. 16.

47 See Beck, 1972–73, II, no. 74; Oursel, 1984, no. 20.

48 See Stechow, 1975, no. 561 (Leleux bequest).

49 See Lille, 1981, nos. 44, 56.

50 See Oursel, 1984, p. 31, fig. 21, no. 24; Paris, 1970–71, nos. 192, 193.

51 On van den Eeckhout see Oursel, 1984, pp. 29–30, fig. 19, ill. 56; Lille, 1981, no. 40; Berlin–Amsterdam–London, 1991–92, pp. 346–47, fig. 70 C for *The Tribute Money* of 1673.

52 See Lille, 1981, no. 60.

53 See Oursel, 1984, p. 30, pl. II.

54 According to Amsterdam, 1971, p. 164.

55 See Lille, 1981, nos. 43, 54.

56 See Oursel, 1984, p. 27, fig. 17 (van Delen); Amsterdam, 1971, p. 163 (de Lorme); Lille, 1981, no. 23 (Brasseur's late de Witte).

57 See Lille, 1981, nos. 11, 3, respectively; Oursel, 1984, pp. 39–43, for a survey of Lille's Italian pictures.

58 See Oursel, 1984, no. 6.

59 See Oursel, 1984, p. 41, fig. 29, ill. 15; on the *Martyrdom of Saint George* after Veronese see Paris, 1965, no. 311, and Brejon de Lavergnée, 1986, p. 319, no. 294.

60 See Oursel, 1984, no. 10, where, however, the key article—Schulz, 1980—is not cited. The painting is also discussed in detail in Rotterdam–Braunschweig, 1983–84, no. 2.

61 See Paris, 1965, no. 271; Oursel, 1984, p. 41, ill. 14; and Brejon de Lavergnée, 1986, p. 291, no. 252 (for the *Noli me tangere*, which is usually on view), p. 134, no. 56 (for the other canvas by Sustris).

62 See Lille, 1981, nos. 66, 67.

63 See Oursel, 1984, p. 43, fig. 31. Wethey, 1969, pp. 38, 157, no. 136, plates 198–199, praises the "little-known masterpiece at Lille" in almost purple prose (p. 38), none of which seems appropriate before the picture itself.

64 See Oursel, 1984, p. 44, fig. 32; Pérez-Sánchez and Spinosa, 1978, no. 408.

65 That is, in 1879; see Oursel, 1984, no. 11.

66 See Oursel, 1984, p. 46, fig. 35, ill. 66.

67 Oursel, 1984, p. 48, ill. 71, notes the influence of Lebrun.

68 See Oursel, 1984, pp. 48–50, ill. 74 (the *Emmaus*; Oursel records that the *Healing the Sick* was copied in 1724–25 after the original of 1689).

69 See Oursel, 1984, p. 49, fig. 37 (De Troy), no. 29 (Boucher's grisaille, bought by Reynart), pp. 50–51, 223, for the others.

70 See Oursel, 1984, no. 33.

71 See Oursel, 1984, p. 51, ill. 78.

72 See Oursel, 1984, no. 35.

73 See Oursel, 1984, pp. 60, 224, nos. 41, 42; see also Lille, 1981, no. 93.

74 See Oursel, 1984, p. 59 (as about 1845–50), fig. 40, pp. 60–64 (on the works mentioned below).

75 See Oursel, 1984, p. 59, fig. 41.

76 See Oursel, 1984, no. 43.

77 See Oursel, 1984, nos. 44, 45, 47.

78 See Oursel, 1984, no. 46, pp. 67–68, 225, fig. 48, ills. 97, 98 (all three Vuillards are illustrated).

79 See Oursel, 1984, pp. 69, 225, no. 48.

80 See Oursel, 1984, pp. 67–73, 225.

81 See Oursel, 1984, no. 49.

56

PETER PAUL RUBENS

Flemish

Siegen 1577–1640 Antwerp

I   *The Descent from the Cross*

Oil on canvas, 167 3/8 x 116 1/8 in. (425 x 295 cm.)

Inscribed (at the top center), in Hebrew, Greek, and
Latin: "Jesus of Nazareth King of the Jews"

Inv. no. 74

Rubens's monumental *Descent from the Cross* in Lille was
painted in 1616–17 for the chapel of the same city's Capuchin
convent. Cleaning and conservation in 1991 have revealed
that the altarpiece was painted largely by Rubens himself
and that the work is well preserved. These considerations and
an appreciation of the artist's compositional innovations, the
quality of execution, and the depth of feeling in the Lille
Descent allow one to describe it as possibly the most important
painting by Rubens in France.

The canvas is also one of the most memorable interpretations of the subject to date from the seventeenth century,
second only to Rubens's famous *Descent from the Cross* of 1611–
12 (see fig. 1) in Antwerp Cathedral. The Lille painting
appears to initiate a series of four or five large representations
of the *Descent* (or *Deposition*) made by Rubens and his workshop between 1616 and about 1620, all of which depart from
the heroic type of Christ and the graceful rhythms of the
Antwerp panel; instead, they introduce more pitiable figures
of Christ, a stronger sense of pathos in the main protagonists,
and angular patterns of action. To some extent these characteristics may be considered a revival of Late Gothic emotionalism, which was familiar to Rubens from Flemish and
German altarpieces, carved *Andachtsbilder*, and prints;[1] it was
especially in the subjects of Christ's Passion that Rubens's
Northern heritage influenced his interpretation of religious
themes. The more immediate reason for Rubens's development in this direction after 1615 was his close association
with the leading religious orders of the Counter-
Reformation, such as the Jesuits, Franciscans, Capuchins,
and Recollects (see the discussion of Rubens's *Ecstasy of Mary
Magdalene*, cat. no. 3).

Rubens's earlier *Descent from the Cross* (fig. 1) was commissioned in September 1611 by the Guild of Harquebusiers
(*Kolveniers*) to redecorate their altar in Antwerp Cathedral.
Nine wealthy citizens were exempted from "various onerous
civic duties" in exchange for substantial donations in support
of the project.[2] The fact that Rubens was working for prominent men of commerce and government, including his great
patron Nicolaes Rockox, is relevant to the style of the Antwerp altarpiece. The *Descent* of 1611–12 has always been
considered as Rubens's first major work to break with the
aggressive Early Baroque style of the *Capture of Samson* of
1609 (London, National Gallery) and of the *Raising of the Cross*
of 1610–11 (painted for the church of Sint Walburga, Antwerp, but now in the cathedral) in favor of the classicizing
manner that the artist employed between 1612 and 1615.
References to ancient art (the figure of Christ in the Antwerp
Descent is modeled on that of the *Laocoön* in the Hellenistic
sculpture group, but in reverse), relief-like figure groups
arranged with an eye to free-flowing contours and a subtle
counterpoise, and heroic types such as the muscular Christ
and Saint John appealed to Rubens's sophisticated circle in
Antwerp during the period about 1610–15.[3] The understated
emotion of the Antwerp *Descent* and the intellectual conceit of
the "Christ-bearing" theme, which is maintained throughout the triptych's interior and exterior (the wings of the
altarpiece were finally delivered in the spring of 1614), are
entirely in keeping with the taste of Rubens's private patrons
and with the spirit of his contemporary paintings of Roman
mythological subjects.[4]

An index of the classicizing qualities introduced by
Rubens in the Antwerp *Descent* of 1611–12 is provided by his
earlier drawing of the subject in the Hermitage in Saint
Petersburg.[5] The composition, which probably dates from
about 1600–1602, when Rubens was in Rome, combines a
complex design inspired by Daniele da Volterra's wall painting of the same subject (1541) in the Roman church of San-
tissima Trinità de' Monti with purposeful gestures and a
dramatic concentration recalling contemporary paintings by
Caravaggio.[6] The drawing's expressive style was intensified
in early Antwerp works such as the *Raising of the Cross*, but
calmed in the *Descent*, as if Rubens in the second altarpiece
traced Daniele's roots back to Michelangelo.

These antecedents of the Antwerp *Descent* are directly
relevant to the altarpiece in Lille and to Rubens's subsequent
representations of the *Descent* because some of his early Roman stylistic qualities were revived in his Passion paintings of
about 1615–20, along with the Gothic characteristics mentioned above. The Lille *Descent* and the later ones adopt the
shallow zone of space introduced in the Antwerp altarpiece
but they restore a disjunctive pattern of bent torsos and
thrusting limbs that ultimately derives from Daniele. Similarly, the hands and faces in the present painting—for exam-

1: detail

1: detail

FIGURE 1. Peter Paul Rubens. *The Descent from the Cross* (center panel of triptych). 1611–12. Oil on wood. Cathedral of Notre-Dame, Antwerp

similar old shepherdess does in Rubens's Fermo *Adoration* of 1608.[9] The man on the ladder to the right in Antwerp takes on the identity of Nicodemus in Lille (Nicodemus is at the left in Antwerp); he turns around on the ladder, abandoning the ineffectual pose derived from one of Laocoön's sons in order to lower Christ's body in the shroud. All these formal transformations were explored by Rubens in an oil sketch also in Lille (see cat. no. 2), which has almost as its sole purpose the testing of the new design.

Rubens's "reversal of motifs" is discussed by Białostocki in some surprisingly confused pages devoted to the Antwerp and the Lille *Descent*.[10] His analysis is almost entirely stylistic, and fails on this score also by advancing Rubens's drawing in Rennes as an intermediary composition. Julius Held cogently describes the "elongated and elegantly arranged" figure of Christ in the Rennes drawing as "possibly a *prima idea*" for the Antwerp *Descent*, and as having "nothing in common with the stark realism of the Christ" in the Lille picture.[11]

This distinction is of interest not merely for the dating of the drawing in Rennes but for an understanding of how the Lille painting differs from the Antwerp altarpiece in expressive terms. In the earlier composition the body of Christ is idealized, suspended as if in a monstrance and framed with figures all at arm's length, not only because of the classical sources cited above (for Rubens, they were means to an end) but also and especially because Christ's physical form represents "the *Corpus Christi*, i.e., the Eucharist."[12] Recognizing this, Białostocki notes the comparatively unimportant role of the Virgin in the Antwerp *Descent*; the receptive pose of Mary Magdalene; and the action of Saint John, who "does not so much support as receive Christ's body." However, the same scholar sees none of this as very different in Rubens's work for the Capuchin convent in Lille, concluding that "the Lille picture ends one line of development."[13]

On the contrary, the Lille *Descent* is the first of Rubens's interpretations of the subject as a realistic event: the removal of a lifeless body from the cross. No longer staged as a ritual, this *Descent* instead emphasizes Christ's suffering and the sorrow of his mother and friends. The main reason for reversing the central figures of the Antwerp composition was to bring Christ into close contact with the Virgin and thus evoke the Lamentation, which immediately follows the Descent.[14] Rubens painted several impressive versions of the Lamentation between about 1612 and 1617; the one in Liechtenstein demonstrates how closely the proximity of the Virgin's face to that of Christ in the present picture corre-

ple, the limp and bloodied left hand of Christ supported by that of a powerful young man; the wounded right hand pressed against the face of Mary Magdalene; and the tragic juxtaposition of Christ's face and that of the Virgin—are reminiscent of motifs in the paintings of Caravaggio, whose Vatican *Entombment* is paraphrased by Rubens's panel (of about 1613–15?) in Ottawa,[7] which led to the more poignant *modello* for an *Entombment* in the Seilern Collection (London, Courtauld Institute Galleries).[8]

Rubens arrived at the present composition by reversing the figures of Christ, Saint John, and the two topmost figures in the Antwerp *Descent* and then modifying the poses of Christ and Saint John to express the dead weight of the Savior's body. The three women to the lower left in the Antwerp version—the Virgin, Mary Cleophas, and the Magdalene—remain to the left in the Lille canvas, where they are joined by an old woman gesturing operatically, as the

sponds to that tragic encounter after Christ's body had been lowered onto the ground.[15]

Eucharistic symbolism may be assumed for any *Descent from the Cross* by Rubens.[16] In the Lille painting, Mary Magdalene's embrace of the Savior's arm, with her lips pressed against the trail of blood, reminds one that sinners are redeemed by the Sacrament of Communion. The same significance is surely found in the juxtaposition of Saint John's face with the wounded side of Christ. However, Counter-Reformation doctrine is now conveyed in a more visceral manner than in the Antwerp version. The more conspicuous placement of the bloody nails and the crown of thorns is a comparable adjustment.

Shortly before or after the Lille painting was completed (spring 1617 ?),[17] Rubens explored yet another reversal of the main figures, in a drawing (of about 1617–18) formerly in the Wrangham collection.[18] Christ's pose becomes more nearly vertical, as in the *Descent* (of 1617–18) in Saint Petersburg, which is largely by Rubens's assistants.[19] Then, in two apparently subsequent versions, Christ's legs are vertical, and for the first time his torso falls forward from the waist rather than slumping backward. In one of these compositions (employed in a painting by Rubens's workshop in the church of Saint-Jean-Baptiste, Arras, and another formerly in the church of Saint Nicholas, Kalisz, Poland) this precarious position occurs because Christ's right arm is shown still held high at the arm of the cross,[20] and in the other composition (the altarpiece in the Musée des Beaux-Arts, Valenciennes, by Rubens and his workshop) Christ's left arm is seen nailed to the cross but just about to be released.[21] These later paintings of about 1618–20 place the Virgin prominently among the figures receiving—almost catching—the body of Christ, but her role is reduced from that in the Lille picture. In the later works, where attention is focused even more strongly on the physical fact of Christ's suffering, Rubens seems more a Northern artist than he had appeared for nearly twenty years.

WL

1 See, for example, Białostocki, 1964, figs. 16, 17. A more awkward version of Christ's pose (nearly the same as that of Rubens's figure from the waist up) is found in Geertgen tot Sint Jans's *Deposition* of 1495, in the Diocesan Museum in Pelplin, Pomerania (Poland); ill. in Thomas Tuohy, "Found and Lost: Tracking Down Art in Polish Museums," *Apollo*, CXXXIII (May 1991), p. 338, fig. 3. There are many comparable images (Descents and Lamentations) in Late Gothic painting and sculpture. *Andachtsbilder* are devotional images, usually depicting the Descent, the Lamentation, or the Pietà, which invite sympathy through realistic descriptions of sorrow and pain.

2 The quote is from Held, 1980, I, p. 488, about the Antwerp *Descent*.

3 See Morford, 1991, on Rubens's intellectual circle in Antwerp. Morford, 1991, p. 193, notes that after 1615 "the influence of Lipsius' Stoic ethics waned, as Rubens turned increasingly to the public concerns of church and state."

4 See Baudouin, 1977, pp. 76–87, and sources cited, especially Martin, 1969.

5 See Held, 1959, no. 3, pl. 4; Białostocki, 1964, p. 512, fig. 2; Held, 1980, I, p. 490.

6 On Rubens's interest in Daniele's *Descent* see Białostocki, 1964, pp. 512–13, fig. 3; Martin, 1969, p. 44, fig. 23; Held, 1980, I, pp. 490, 496.

7 This date was suggested in Antwerp, 1977, under no. 32. Held, 1980, I, p. 499, implies a somewhat earlier date.

8 See Held, 1980, II, no. 365, pl. 359 (as about 1615–16); Braham, 1981, no. 71, colorpl. XII (as about 1616–18).

9 Pinacoteca Comunale, Fermo. See Antwerp, 1977, no. 17; Baudouin, 1977, pp. 68, 72–74, 129–31, fig. 68.

10 See Białostocki, 1964, pp. 514–16.

11 See Held, 1980, I, pp. 496–97, on the drawing in Rennes (Białostocki, 1964, fig. 7).

12 See Białostocki, 1964, p. 54. See also Held, 1980, I, p. 496.

13 See Białostocki, 1964, p. 517.

14 Rubens anticipated the Lamentation differently in the early drawing of the Descent in Saint Petersburg, as noted by Held, 1959, p. 64.

15 See Baumstark, in New York, 1985, no. 202.

16 See Glen, 1977, pp. 86–87.

17 See Białostocki, 1964, p. 516; Held, 1980, I, p. 496.

18 See Held, 1959, no. 42, pl. 39; Białostocki, 1964, fig. 12. The drawing is now in the collection of Eugene V. Thaw, New York (see Held, 1986, no. 121, pl. 121).

19 See Białostocki, 1964, fig. 13; see Held, 1959, p. 111, on the dating, and Held, 1986, no. 122, pl. 122, for another related drawing now in the Museum of Fine Arts, Boston.

20 See Białostocki, 1964, figs. 17, 19; Held, 1980, I, p. 638.

21 See Białostocki, 1964, fig. 23; Baudouin, 1977, p. 103, fig. 51.

PROVENANCE

Painted by Rubens for the Capuchin convent in Lille; transferred to the Musée des Beaux-Arts, 1803.

EXHIBITION

Lille, 1970, no. 31.

LITERATURE

Białostocki, 1964, pp. 516–17, fig. 10; Châtelet, 1970-1, p. 78, no. 31; Baudouin, 1977, pp. 98, 103; Glen, 1977, pp. 85–87, 277–78; Held, 1980, I, pp. 495–97, 611; Oursel, 1984, no. 13.

PETER PAUL RUBENS

Flemish

Siegen 1577–1640 Antwerp

---

2   *The Descent from the Cross*

Oil on canvas, attached to panel (transferred from wood?), 21 1/2 x 16 in. (54.5 x 40.5 cm.)

Inv. no. 66

This oil sketch is a compositional study by Rubens for the *Descent from the Cross* of 1616–17 in Lille (see cat. no. 1). The role of the sketch in rearranging motifs derived from Rubens's *Descent from the Cross* of 1611–12 in Antwerp Cathedral (see fig. 1 in cat. no. 1), and from the oil sketch for that altarpiece in the Seilern Collection (London, Courtauld Institute Galleries), is considered in the text of catalogue number 1 above, and by Julius Held in his detailed discussion of the present work.[1] Among the changes described by Held, and before him by Białostocki,[2] are the reversal of Christ, Saint John, and the two topmost figures; the different actions of the Virgin and Mary Magdalene; and the use of two rather than four ladders, which rationalizes the less densely and less gracefully grouped figures in the oil sketch and the altarpiece in Lille. The latter follows the oil sketch closely, but the artist added an old woman at the left and an inscription above, and modified the figure of Mary Cleophas and the basin and towel on the ground. The final painting is also taller in format; the angle of Christ's arm and other diagonal elements were adjusted accordingly.

This kind of oil sketch, which employs a restricted palette of browns and grays to economically explore the potential of a freshly conceived composition, is especially common in Rubens's oeuvre dating from about 1615–20. The most comparable oil sketches include the one in the National Gallery, London, for the *Coup de lance*,[3] and a number of oil sketches (not the *modelli*) for the ceiling paintings of the Jesuit church in Antwerp.[4] Van Dyck worked on the latter project and painted oil sketches of a similar kind. Perhaps this connection between Rubens and van Dyck broadly accounts for Horst Gerson's suggestion that "the so-called Rubens sketch of a *Descent from the Cross* at Lille (1101) could in my opinion be by van Dyck."[5] This surprising conjecture resulted in Oursel's ambivalent attribution ("Rubens?") in 1977,[6] and encouraged Foucart to reject the Lille oil sketch and to propose that it was made by someone in

Rubens's studio ("van Dyck?") for an engraving by Pieter Clouwet (who, inconveniently, was not born until about 1629).[7] However, Foucart's conclusion depended principally upon a direct comparison of the Lille sketch with a small panel by Rubens, *The Resurrection*, in the Musée des Beaux-Arts, Marseilles, which was shown (like the present work) in the Paris exhibition "Le siècle de Rubens" in 1977–78.[8] The Marseilles panel, from a predella, is a finished painting (67 x 102 cm.) made about 1617–19 for an altarpiece in the Janskerk, Mechelen (Malines), and thus represents the opposite end of Rubens's creative process from the study in Lille.[9]

WL

1   See Held, 1980, I, pp. 489–91, II, no. 355, pl. 351 (London sketch), and pp. 495–97, no. 360 (Lille sketch).

2   See Białostocki, 1964, p. 516, fig. 9.

3   See Held, 1980, II, no. 352, pl. 347.

4   See Held, 1980, I, pp. 33–62, II, plates 8, 12, 16–18, 24, 29, 30, 36, 37.

5   See Gerson, in Gerson and ter Kuile, 1960, p. 189 n. 5 (note to p. 110, where van Dyck's work on the Jesuit church project is discussed). On Gerson's idea see Białostocki, 1964, p. 516 n. 18.

6   See Paris, 1977–78, no. 153. Châtelet, 1970-1, no. 32, had already considered the oil sketch to be "after Rubens," based on the reservations of Gerson and a few other scholars.

7   Jacques Foucart, in a letter to Hervé Oursel dated November 10, 1977, in the Lille museum files. On the engraving see Bodart, 1977, no. 338.

8   See Paris, 1977–78, no. 127.

9   In his voluminous catalogue of oil sketches by Rubens, Held (1980, I, pp. 495–97) does not mention the question of authorship, although Gerson's (and earlier, Baudouin's) doubts are recorded under "Literature." Held omitted any reference to Baudouin's acceptance of the picture in 1977 (see Literature below).

PROVENANCE

The twelfth duke of Hamilton; sale of the Hamilton collection, London, Christie's, July 8, 1882, no. 1014; Charles Sedelmeyer, Paris, 1882–93; purchased from Sedelmeyer by the Musée des Beaux-Arts, with funds from the Brasseur Foundation, 1893.

EXHIBITIONS

Brussels, 1910, no. 333; Valenciennes, 1918, no. 307; Helsinki–Brussels, 1952–53, no. 4; Berlin, 1964, no. 38; Lille–Calais–Arras, 1977, no. 47; Paris, 1977–78, no. 153.

LITERATURE

Benoit, 1909, I, p. 67; Held, 1959, I, p. 111; Gerson and ter Kuile, 1960, p. 189 n. 5; Białostocki, 1964, p. 516, fig. 9; Châtelet, 1970-1, pp. 101–3, no. 64; Baudouin, 1977, pp. 98, 103, fig. 50; Oursel, in Lille–Calais–Arras, 1977, pp. 106–8, no. 47; Oursel, in Paris, 1977–78, pp. 201–2, no. 153; Held, 1980, I, pp. 495–97, II, no. 360, pl. 350.

63

PETER PAUL RUBENS

Flemish

Siegen 1577–1640 Antwerp

---

3   *The Ecstasy of Mary Magdalene*

Oil on canvas, 116 1/8 x 86 5/8 in. (295 x 220 cm.)

Inv. no. 64

This important altarpiece by Rubens was painted, perhaps with some help from assistants, about 1619–20 for the Church of the Recollects in Ghent.[1] The picture was seized by the French Revolutionary commission in 1794, sent to Paris, and in 1801 assigned to the new museum in Lille.

Until recently the painting's restrained palette, which has been described as predominantly grayish and silvery in tone,[2] encouraged most authors to place the work in Rubens's last decade, the 1630s.[3] Without cleaning and removal of old restorations the picture's original appearance cannot be appreciated,[4] but it is clear nonetheless that the painting never had the luminosity (which justifies the term *silvery*) of Rubens's late altarpieces, such as *The Crowning of Saint Catherine* in the Toledo Museum of Art.[5] In his late religious pictures Rubens's use of radiant coloring usually corresponds with the beatific mood of the figures, whereas in the Lille painting and in some similarly emotional images of about 1618–20—for example, *The Trinity*, the *Christ à la paille*, and *The Last Communion of Saint Francis of Assisi* (all in the Koninklijk Museum voor Schone Kunsten, Antwerp)—the browns, grays, bluish grays, and whites contribute to the expression of more somber themes. In hindsight one might almost describe this (for Rubens) understated palette as Franciscan—a poetic license excused by the fact that from 1618 to 1620 Rubens worked for the Minorites (Recollects) in Antwerp (for whom he painted *The Last Communion* just mentioned and the *Coup de lance*) and for other Franciscan patrons, including the Recollects in Ghent.[6]

As Frans Baudouin discovered, *The Ecstasy of Mary Magdalene* is cited as in the Church of the Recollects in Anthony Sanderus's history of Ghent published in 1627.[7] Baudouin convincingly associates the commission with renovations and embellishments to the choir of the church that date from about 1619–20, following the reform of the Franciscan order in Ghent in 1618. Sanderus refers to the reform as happening "a few years ago," which may indicate that his book was published a few years after it was written. The dating of the Lille canvas is of considerable interest for an understanding of Rubens's style about 1620, and, as suggested below, perhaps also for that of van Dyck, who was once thought to have been partly responsible for the execution of the painting.[8]

Any discussion of Rubens's style must take into account not only what is known of a picture's history but also its subject and the impression it was expected to make on viewers of the time (Sanderus describes the church's decoration as "appropriate to the devotions of the faithful"; the renovated choir was supported by and entirely accessible to the general public).[9] The painting does not represent, as commentators before Rooses (1888) thought,[10] the death of the Magdalene (who is identified by the ointment jar and skull), but an episode derived from *The Golden Legend* by Jacobus de Voragine. The medieval author relates that the saint, in order to contemplate celestial matters, retired to a mountain grotto, which had been prepared by angels. For thirty years the Magdalene did without food and water, but each day angels carried her heavenward, where she heard their music, after which she descended to the grotto "sated by this delicious repast."[11]

Rubens's interpretation of this event departs from early-seventeenth-century examples that represent the Magdalene borne aloft, as in the Assumption of the Virgin.[12] The Lille painting is one of the first examples from the period to represent the saint's experience as a mystical trance, comparable to that of Bernini's *Ecstasy of Saint Teresa*, which was begun twenty-five years later.[13] It seems very likely that, as Baudouin maintains, Rubens referred to Saint Teresa of Avila's *Life* (1562), in which states of spiritual ecstasy are vividly described: eyes that do not see, or see "almost nothing"; hands that can barely be lifted; the suspension of all outward force, as interior strength increases and the soul achieves a mystical union with God.[14] In a later chapter Saint Teresa observes that in moments such as these the body gradually grows colder, loses its natural color, and resembles that of someone who has just passed away.[15]

In a broader view, the conception arrived at by Rubens and by his patrons corresponds with the Counter-Reformation's emphasis on miracles and mystical experience, which one scholar suggests is combined in this case with a reference to the Real Presence in the Eucharist.[16] While these questions and the phenomenon of the cult of the Magdalene go beyond our subject here, it should be noted that the Observant order of the Franciscans, the reformed order of the Discalced (Barefoot) Carmelites, and the founder of the latter order, Saint Teresa of Avila, were complexly interrelated interests of Rubens in the second decade of the seventeenth century.[17] He painted the *Transverberation of Saint Teresa* for the Church of the Discalced Carmelites in Brussels in 1615,[18] and he certainly would have known the editions of the saint's writings and the books and prints devoted to her story that appeared in Antwerp and Brussels between 1610 and 1613.[19] Despite the fact that the visionary painting in Lille represents a different female saint, it can be considered as another contribution to the campaign that led to Saint Teresa's canonization in 1622. Saints Francis Xavier and Ignatius Loyola were canonized in the same year and had likewise been celebrated for their miracles in Rubens's great altarpieces of 1616–18 (both painted for the Jesuit church in

Antwerp, and now in the Kunsthistorisches Museum, Vienna).[20]

The evolution of Rubens's style in the period from about 1616 to 1620 has not been studied with particular attention to the religious orders that were his great patrons in those years. The emotionalism or pathos that he imparted to figures such as the Magdalene, Christ (see cat. no. 1), the Virgin, and Saint John the Evangelist (see fig. 1) is achieved partly through undulating contours, attenuated limbs, and colors that seem to pale or blend together with the irrepressible flow of feelings. That this dimension of Rubens's religious art has been somewhat neglected is seen in such isolated instances as the misdating of the present picture, and

3: detail

FIGURE 1. Peter Paul Rubens. *Le Coup de lance* (detail). About 1619–20. Oil on wood. Koninklijk Museum voor Schone Kunsten, Antwerp

in the earlier perception here, and in the most comparable section of the *Coup de lance*, of van Dyck's collaboration. Rubens's formation of this figure style began about 1615 and progressed rapidly—with appropriate subjects—in the paintings for the Jesuit church and in other religious pictures dating to about 1616–19.[21] As Rubens's assistant, van Dyck did not invent or influence Rubens's figure type as embodied by the Magdalene and the gesturing angel in the Lille painting. However, it is of great interest for van Dyck's style that he joined Rubens's studio when Rubens himself was painting a number of his most intense and moving works.

WL

1 On the commission, see Baudouin, 1981, revising Vlieghe, 1973, no. 131.

2 See Baudouin, 1981, p. 483.

3 Rooses, 1886–92, II, p. 326, no. 474, identifies it as a workshop product of the 1630s with revisions by Rubens; Vlieghe, 1973, p. 121, no. 131, as from the mid-1630s; Oursel, in Paris, 1977–78, no. 143, as from the 1630s. As noted in Baudouin, 1981, p. 483, Michel, 1900, and Oldenbourg, 1921-2, favored a date somewhere in the early to mid-1620s.

4 Earlier attempts at conservation may account for weaknesses such as the face of the angel to the left or the other angel's lower leg.

5 See Toledo, 1976, pp. 146–47, colorpl. VI; see also David Freedberg's discussion in Bauman and Liedtke, 1992, no. 64.

6 See Baudouin, 1981, p. 483, on the Saint Francis altarpieces in the museums of Brussels and Ghent; Vlieghe, 1972, nos. 88, 92, 100.

7 See Baudouin, 1981, p. 485.

8 See Valenciennes, 1918, no. 309.

9 See Sanderus, 1627, p. 432; Baudouin, 1981, p. 485 notes 16, 17. Descamps, 1769, p. 243, describes "l'Autel, en entrant [the choir?], à la gauche."

10 Including Sanderus, 1627, p. 432, who identified the subject as "Magdalenam exhibet morientem" (quoted by Baudouin, 1981, p. 485; see also Baudouin, 1980, p. 166). Baudouin, 1981, p. 486, credits Rooses, 1886–92, II, p. 326, no. 474, with proposing the correct title.

11 Baudouin, 1980 (expanding on the discussion published only later in Baudouin, 1981), pp. 168–69, quotes from a French edition of *The Golden Legend* (see his note 17).

12 See Baudouin, 1980, pp. 167–68.

13 However, see Baudouin, 1980, p. 170, fig. 2, who proposes (too strongly) a possible source in Caravaggio. There may have been intermediary works.

14 Baudouin, 1980, pp. 168–69, quoting from Saint Teresa, *Life*, chap. XVIII.

15 Saint Teresa, *Life*, chap. XX, quoted by Baudouin, 1980, p. 169.

16 See Oursel, in Paris, 1977–78, p. 192; Oursel, 1984, p. 144. The notion of spiritual sustenance in the story recalls Old Testament prefigurations of the Sacrament such as the Gathering of Manna and the Prophet Elijah Fed by an Angel (see Held, 1980, pp. 139–50). Regarding the Magdalene and the Eucharist, see also catalogue number 1.

17 See Glen, 1977; Baudouin, 1980, pp. 170, 175 n. 53.

18 See Vlieghe, 1973, no. 150.

19 These are cited in Baudouin, 1980, p. 170 notes 44–46.

20 On the date of the two Jesuit altarpieces see Baudouin, 1977, chap. 8.

21 For example, see Baudouin, 1981, p. 485, figs. 2 (an engraving after Rubens's *Mater Dolorosa* of 1615), 3 (the epileptic woman in *The Miracles of Saint Ignatius Loyola*).

PROVENANCE

Painted for the Franciscan Church of the Recollects, Ghent, and installed about 1620; French Revolutionary commission, Paris, 1794–1801; assigned to the Musée des Beaux-Arts, Lille, 1801.

EXHIBITIONS

Valenciennes, 1918, no. 309; Lille, 1970, no. 33; Paris, 1977–78, no. 143.

LITERATURE

Sanderus, 1627, p. 432; Descamps, 1769, p. 243; Michel, 1771, pp. 192–93; Spruyt, 1777, p. 149; Spruyt, 1789, p. 195; Rooses, 1886–92, II, p. 326, ill., no. 474; Benoit, 1909, I, pp. 73–74, no. 16; Oldenbourg, 1921-2, p. 273; Vlieghe, 1973, p. 121, no. 131; Baudouin, 1980; Baudouin, 1981; Oursel, 1984, no. 14; Delenda and Melnotte, 1985, no. 160.

JACOB JORDAENS

Flemish

Antwerp 1593–1678 Antwerp

---

4   *The Rape of Europa*

Oil on canvas, 67 3/4 x 74 3/4 in. (172.1 x 190 cm.)

Signed and dated (at the bottom left): J. Jord:ns· Fec. 1643.

Inv. no. 76

The Rape of Europa (Ovid, *Metamorphoses*, II: 836–75) is a subject well known from such great works of art as Titian's painting in the Isabella Stewart Gardner Museum, Boston, and Rembrandt's early panel (1632) in a private collection (on long-term loan to the Metropolitan Museum).[1] These pictures, the illustrated editions of Ovid that flourished from 1557 onward,[2] and a youthful treatment of the story by Jordaens himself (about 1615–16, in a panel formerly in Malmö) show the familiar, climactic scene in Ovid's second chapter when Jupiter (Jove) suddenly abducts the helpless young princess Europa over the sea.[3] A version of the Malmö picture that was probably painted in Jordaens's studio during the 1630s (see fig. 1) redefines the space so that it becomes an expansive outdoor setting typical of Jordaens's mature compositions.[4] Another early invention by Jordaens, the large canvas of about 1615 formerly in Stockholm (and later in Hereford, England),[5] illustrates the moment when Jupiter, having won Europa's trust and her gift of a flower garland (shown here on the ground), slowly draws away from her companions, setting "his borrowed hoofs in the shallow water."[6]

The colorful painting in Lille takes the story one step further back in time, when the fair maiden, attracted by the bull's hide, "white as the untrodden snow," and by his other handsome features, "even dares to sit upon his back, little knowing upon whom she rests." The bull's expression and the involuntary reaction of his tongue suggest satisfaction with the course of events, which required Jupiter's uncharacteristic patience ("he could scarce restrain his passion"). His outthrust foreleg is a sign, familiar to any farmer, that the animal is about to stand up. It will not be long before Jupiter and his latest lover are resting in the fields of Crete (Ovid, *Metamorphoses*, III: 1).[7]

Jordaens's experience as a tapestry designer probably encouraged his inclination to stage mythological subjects against decorative backdrops and with an ample cast of

FIGURE 1. Workshop of Jacob Jordaens. *The Rape of Europa*. 1630s. Oil on canvas. Herzog Anton Ulrich-Museum, Braunschweig

characters.[8] Jupiter's son Mercury, to the right, was sent down to the land of Sidon with instructions to drive King Agenor's cattle from the mountain slopes to the shore. As if reflecting the Roman social circles in which Ovid played a witty part, Mercury was not informed of his father's real interests, which were Europa and "the young girls of Tyre" who used to frolic together on the sands. The only woman who has not removed her clothes must be meant as the beach party's chaperone, but she is oblivious to Cupid riding Jupiter's eagle and brandishing thunderbolts and a flaming heart.

When Jordaens painted this picture in 1643 his two great rivals in the Flemish art world, Rubens and van Dyck, had recently died. He had just built a grand house for himself in Antwerp and received a prestigious commission to decorate the Queen's House in Greenwich. In the 1640s Jordaens was one of the most successful artists in Northern Europe and in many ways was Rubens's successor, but not as an interpreter of classical literature. He never went to Italy and was intellectually less in harmony with Rubens and his learned circle than with the Netherlandish tradition descending from Pieter Bruegel the Elder to Adriaen Brouwer and to Jan Steen. For Jordaens, a profound affection for Ovid could coexist easily with barnyard humor and with a courtier's dream of a princess and ladies-in-waiting wearing nothing but jewels.

As noted by several authors, a drawing possibly for the bull in the center is in the Louvre,[9] and a drawing of a bullock in the van Eeghen collection, Amsterdam, compares closely with the animal in profile behind Mercury.[10] The messenger-

4: detail

4: detail

god himself, but not the superb passage of his rippling back, recalls Jordaens's drawing of a contemporary statuette, which was based, in turn, on a Rubens design.[11]

WL

1 See Hendy, 1974, pp. 257–60, for the Titian, and Bruyn, 1982, II, no. A 47, for the Rembrandt.

2 See Henkel, 1930, especially pp. 77 ff.

3 See d'Hulst, 1982, pp. 52–53, fig. 20.

4 This assessment of the Braunschweig canvas concurs with that of d'Hulst, 1982, p. 330 n. 15. Jaffé, 1968, no. 13, considered the painting to be an authentic early work and made no mention of the Malmö version. On Jaffé's many controversial attributions in the Ottawa exhibition see Held, 1969.

5 See d'Hulst, 1982, p. 49, fig. 16, p. 330 n. 14.

6 Ovid, 1944–46, I, p. 121.

7 See Ovid, 1944–46, I, pp. 119–25, for the translations quoted in this paragraph, with the original text *en face*.

8 See d'Hulst, 1982, chap. IX, for a discussion of Jordaens as a tapestry designer. Jordaens's *Diana and Callisto* in a private collection in New York, and *Marsyas Ill-treated by the Muses* in the Mauritshuis, The Hague (see Jaffé, 1968, nos. 77, 78), which appear to slightly anticipate the Lille picture in date, depict wooded landscapes similarly overrun by naked young women.

9 See d'Hulst, 1974, I, no. A 121 (fig. 132), who dates it to about 1635–40, citing the Lille picture.

10 See d'Hulst, 1974, I, no. A 122 (fig. 133).

11 See d'Hulst, 1974, I, no. A 53 (fig. 60): In the drawing (Paris, Private collection) Mercury's shoulders and most of his back are covered by drapery. The ivory statuette and another representing Venus were in Rubens's estate and are now in the Hermitage, Saint Petersburg. The sculptor may be Artus Quellinus the Elder and the work datable to about 1640 (see d'Hulst's entry, which mistakenly refers to Artus Quellinus the Younger).

PROVENANCE

Said to have been in the collection of the comte de Beysse, Amiens; purchased in Paris by Édouard Boyer; sale of the Boyer collection, Lille, June 7–11, 1880, to "Boudet"; purchased with funds from the Antoine Brasseur Gift, 1908.

EXHIBITIONS

Valenciennes, 1918, no. 178; Lille, 1970, no. 38; Lille–Calais–Arras, 1977, no. 30; Paris, 1977–78, no. 73; Lille, 1981, no. 48.

LITERATURE

Van Puyvelde, 1953, pp. 41, 174–75; d'Hulst, 1974, I, pp. 77, 215, II, p. 390; d'Hulst, 1982, pp. 188, 208, 212, fig. 157.

JACOB JORDAENS

Flemish

Antwerp 1593–1678 Antwerp

5 *Study of Cows*

Oil on canvas, 26 x 32 1/4 in. (66 x 82 cm.)

Strips of canvas added to the original support at some later date were removed during conservation in 1975.

Inv. no. 112

From at least the early sixteenth century onward, Netherlandish and German artists made drawings from life of animals. The carefully finished watercolors of Albrecht Dürer and Hans Hoffmann (died 1591?) are the best known, but simple drawings of animals in different poses also survive.[1] By the early seventeenth century artists such as Pieter Bruegel the Elder, Joris Hoefnagel, Roelant Savery, and Jacob de Gheyn the Younger had established the drawing of animals and other forms of natural life as a great Netherlandish tradition, which in some cases was closely linked to the scientific studies of the time. Jordaens's oil sketch of cows recalls works of biological interest (for example, de Gheyn's *Four Studies of a Frog* in the Rijksprentenkabinet, Amsterdam)[2] only in that one animal—or a pair, in the Lille painting—is rendered repeatedly, and in his effort, admired by several writers and artists (see cat. nos. 42, 43), to complete the composition as a work of art.[3]

This virtue is often found in Flemish oil sketches, which became a common form of preparatory work for finished pictures. Rubens, van Dyck, Jordaens, and other painters (mostly Antwerp artists in their circle) made oil sketches of individual figures and of entire compositions (see cat. no. 2); the oil sketches, while sometimes connected with a particular commission, usually remained in the workshop for adaptation in later designs. Notwithstanding its bovine rather than human theme, Jordaens's painting in Lille, the only known example of its kind in his oeuvre,[4] is closely consistent in style and technique with oil sketches by him such as *Two Studies of a Man's Head* (Karlsruhe, Staatliche Kunsthalle) and *Two Studies of Women's Heads and the Torso of a Warrior* (Antwerp, Koninklijk Museum voor Schone Kunsten).[5] These comparisons with his painted studies of the early 1630s suggest that the *Study of Cows* might date from the same period rather than from about 1620–25, the dating usually proposed.[6]

FIGURE 1. Pieter Boel. *Study of Birds*. Oil on canvas. Musée des Beaux-Arts, Lille

FIGURE 2. Pieter Boel. *Study of Lions*. Oil on canvas. Musée des Beaux-Arts, Lille

Oil sketches of animals, birds, and fish were painted by a number of Flemish artists including not Rubens and van Dyck but Jan Brueghel the Elder,[7] Jan van Kessel the Elder,[8] and Pieter Boel (the Lille museum has two attractive examples: see figs. 1, 2). However, most of these pictures illustrate numerous specimens on a smaller scale than in Jordaens's painting, which, like some of his drawings (see cat. no. 88), depicts a few cows intended for use in paintings of religious, mythological, or pastoral themes (see cat. no. 4).[9] A review of Jordaens's oeuvre reveals that "cows, the peaceful denizens

of luxuriant Flemish meadows,"[10] might turn up almost anywhere, and suggests that many more studies by Jordaens of this preeminently Dutch subject (in the view of Dutch scholars) are no longer known.[11]

Thus, it is hazardous to associate the Lille canvas directly with finished paintings by Jordaens. A previous reference to the *Diogenes Searching for an Honest Man* of 1642 (Dresden, Gemäldegalerie) is irrelevant,[12] while a connection to the *Mercury and Argus* of the early 1620s (Lyons, Musée des Beaux-Arts) is nearly so, although it provides another instance of Jordaens favoring cows seen in three-quarter view from the rear.[13] A different cow drawn in this way is found in the undated but late *Prodigal Son* (Brussels, Musées Royaux d'Art et d'Histoire) and in the *Christ Driving the Money Changers from the Temple* of about 1657 (The Hague, Dienst Verspreide Kunstvoorwerpen).[14] It is only in the *Moses Striking Water from the Rock* of about 1660 (Kassel, Staatliche Kunstsammlungen) that Jordaens appears to have repeated part of the painting in Lille: namely, the three cows at the top, although with heads in different positions. The conclusion one might draw from this reference dating from decades later is not that the Lille canvas languished unattended in the studio, but that virtually every time Jordaens approached the motif of a cow or a bull he was inspired to treat it afresh.

WL

1 For example, four sketches of a donkey on the verso of a life drawing entitled *Draftsman among Ruins* of about 1535 (Oxford, University of Oxford, Christ Church), by a Dutch artist (see Washington–New York, 1986–87, no. 5, p. 52, fig. 1).

2 See Washington–New York, 1986–87, p. 141, fig. 1, where this drawing is compared with the delicately composed *Three Studies of a Dragonfly* (no. 48).

3 Oursel and Nonne, in Lille–Calais–Arras, 1977, p. 79, devote a paragraph of praise to the "heureux effet de diversité, accentué par un groupement dissymétrique," and they quote two writers of the 1870s who responded similarly.

4 As noted by d'Hulst, 1982, p. 106.

5 See d'Hulst, 1982, figs. 103, 112; see also Jaffé, 1968, nos. 24–26, 51.

6 By Jaffé, 1968, p. 140, and by d'Hulst, 1974, I, p. 215, which is said to "fait aussi l'unanimité" in Lille–Calais–Arras, 1977, p. 79.

7 See Haverkamp-Begemann, 1971, pp. 72–73, with reproductions of two oil sketches on panels in the Kunsthistorisches Museum, Vienna.

8 See Krempel, 1983; Paris, 1977–78, nos. 79, 82; Welu, 1983, pp. 82–85, no. 21.

9 For Jordaens's drawings of cows see d'Hulst, 1974, I, nos. A 121, A 122, II, C 72, C 74, C 75; see also those drawings cited under catalogue number 88, below. Compare also Jordaens's drawings of pigs, dogs, goats, and other animals, some of which are reproduced in d'Hulst, 1982, figs. 106, 134, 135, 215.

10 See d'Hulst, 1982, p. 106.

11 On Dutch examples see Spicer, 1983.

12 See Lille–Calais–Arras, 1977, p. 79.

13 See Lille–Calais–Arras, 1977, p. 79; d'Hulst, 1982, p. 106, figs. 74, 188 (for a later version).

14 See Jaffé, 1968, nos. 112, for the latter, and also 141 (the *Offering to Ceres*, a drawing in the Courtauld Institute Galleries, London).

PROVENANCE
Purchased, 1837.

EXHIBITION
Lille–Calais–Arras, 1977, no. 29.

LITERATURE
Benoit, 1909, I, pp. 101–2, no. 29; Jaffé, 1968, p. 115; d'Hulst, 1974, I, p. 215; d'Hulst, 1982, pp. 106, 108, fig. 75; Buijs and van Berge-Gerbaud, 1991, p. 74, fig. 25 a (ill. before added strips of canvas were removed).

WALLERANT VAILLANT

Flemish

Lille 1623–1677 Amsterdam

6 *The Young Draftsman*

Oil on canvas, 46 x 35 1/4 in. (117 x 89.5 cm.)

Signed (at the lower left): W . . . . . ant

Inv. no. 202

Wallerant Vaillant, a native of Lille, came from a family of linen manufacturers. His father, Jean, had three sons, all artists, by his first marriage: Wallerant, Jacques, and Jean, born May 30, 1623, about 1625, and in 1627, respectively. A second marriage about 1630 produced at least eight children, of which four boys and a girl were baptized as Catholics in Lille between 1631 and 1641. Nonetheless, the Vaillant family had a history of Protestant sympathy, which was almost certainly why Jean Vaillant, Claire Bouchout, and their eight children moved to Amsterdam in 1643; they joined the city's Walloon church on March 31 of that year.[1]

It is now known that Wallerant Vaillant enrolled as a pupil in the Antwerp studio of the painter Erasmus Quellinus on September 17, 1639.[2] Vaillant was then sixteen-and-a-half years old, which may suggest that he had had some rudimentary training elsewhere.[3] He joined the Guild of Saint Luke in Middelburg in January 1647, at which time Vaillant was described as a painter and draftsman.[4] In 1649 he painted a portrait of Jan Six, and several portraits of preachers date from the following year. Vaillant appears to have become a successful portrait painter and engraver by the mid-1650s, but his painted portraits of this first Amsterdam period remain confused with attributions to Bartholomeus van der Helst and to other contemporary artists also in fashion.[5]

Much more well known today is Vaillant's role as a pioneer in mezzotint engraving. In a broad view, the medium (in which rich contrasts of light and dark are achieved by scraping the image on a uniformly roughened plate) would seem closely related to the style of Rembrandt and his followers during the 1650s. However, Vaillant learned the mezzotint technique from the young Prince Rupert (Ruprecht von der Pfalz) in Frankfurt, where Vaillant went, no doubt in search of commissions, to attend the election of Emperor Leopold I (1658). The prince and Vaillant traveled to London together, after which the artist settled in Paris and worked mainly as a portrait painter until 1665. It was only then, when the peripatetic bachelor moved back to Amsterdam, that he started to produce scores of outstanding mezzotints—both original prints and vivid reproductions of paintings by a wide range of Dutch and Flemish artists and by a considerable number of sixteenth- and seventeenth-century Italian painters as well.[6]

Apart from portraits, which he continued to paint throughout the last decade of his life (he was buried in Amsterdam on September 2, 1677), Vaillant produced a few trompe-l'oeil still lifes of the "letter-rack" type (as did Edwaert Collier, Samuel van Hoogstraten, and other Dutch artists of the time),[7] and paintings of young artists in studios. The last, of which the Lille canvas is one of the best examples, have in common with the letter-rack pictures and a few of Vaillant's self-portraits a celebration of artists and artistic means. The self-conscious theme of creativity, very much *au courant* in the 1660s, is certainly appropriate to Vaillant, whose inventiveness as a printmaker contrasts with what he probably considered the steady job of portrait painting.

The Lille picture shows a boy seated on a small chair and drawing with chalk. To judge from other paintings with this theme, including different compositions by Vaillant, there can be no doubt that the boy is sketching one of the three casts of classical sculpture on the table (there are two heads, one of them tipped over to reveal its hollow interior). The portfolio in the lower left corner probably contains

6

engravings. An oil painting of Pan and Syrinx stands on the easel,[8] behind which is a larger canvas turned to the wall.

The motif of a young artist sketching sculpture can be traced back through a wide variety of images to at least the late sixteenth century. An engraving by Theodoor Galle (1571–1633) (fig. 1) after a work by the prolific draftsman Johannes Stradanus shows a painter's studio with three apprentices in the foreground. To the right, a boy practices drawing eyes. The rendering of anatomical parts and the copying of two-dimensional models were steps followed in the course of training by drawing from three-dimensional objects and especially from sculpture, which was usually found in artists' studios in the form of plaster casts.[9] This stage of instruction is represented by the boy in the foreground to the left in Stradanus's composition and by Vaillant's young man. The next step involved the preparation of the painter's materials and then the imitation of and collaboration on the master's work. Vaillant may be alluding to these three phases of development with the portfolio, the sculpture, and the painting on the easel. In any case, he is certainly expressing the usual view that the art of drawing is fundamental to the pictorial arts, and that classical sculpture provides appropriate models. He probably expected the viewer to appreciate the point that the rendering of Pan or any nude male figure in painting benefited from the study of anatomy in a sculpture like the Praxitelean statuette, and that Syrinx's expression could be traced back to such dignified classical models as the large female head.

One need not review the history of art academies to realize that Vaillant's subject involves a few of the key issues in the seventeenth century—in particular, the importance of classical sculpture. The theme is familiar from such different examples as Rubens's drawings,[10] Goltzius's set of engravings after great statues in Rome (that of the *Apollo Belvedere* shows an earnest draftsman),[11] and van Dyck's *Portrait of a Man, probably Lucas van Uffel* (New York, The Metropolitan Museum of Art), the last of which includes among the objects symbolic of learning, on the table, the amateur's drawing of an antique head and the sculpted head itself.[12] In slightly later images the education of artists becomes a distinct theme, as in Rembrandt's etching *A Youth Drawing from a Cast by Candlelight* of 1641,[13] Dou's didactic images of studious draftsmen,[14] and Steen's *The Drawing Lesson* (Malibu, The J. Paul Getty Museum), in which a boy competes with a comely young lady for their teacher's attention.

The closest comparisons with Vaillant are found in paintings by Michiel Sweerts (1618–1664), who obtained

FIGURE 1. Theodoor Galle, after Johannes Stradanus. *Color Olivi* (*The Invention of Oil Painting*). About 1580. Engraving. Rijksprentenkabinet, Amsterdam

FIGURE 2. Michiel Sweerts. *Boy Drawing a Bust of Emperor Vitellius*. About 1660. Oil on canvas. The Minneapolis Institute of Arts. The Walter H. and Valborg P. Ude Memorial Fund

permission from the city of Brussels to open a drawing academy in 1656 and worked in Amsterdam in 1660–61.[15] It was surely after Vaillant returned to Amsterdam in 1665 that he made a mezzotint after the painting by Sweerts that is most reminiscent of the Lille picture: the *Boy Drawing a Bust of Emperor Vitellius* of about 1660 (fig. 2).[16] If, as seems likely, Sweerts inspired Vaillant's interest in the theme, then the *Young Draftsman* in Lille would date from the second half of the 1660s, and his similar painting of an older draftsman, in the Bonnefantenmuseum, Maastricht, which is signed and dated *W. Vaillant f 16 [?]8*, would date from 1668.[17] On stylistic grounds one would place Vaillant's so-called *Young Sculptor* (recently sold at auction)[18] and the *Young Draftsman* in the Musée du Louvre, Paris, in the same period.[19] In the Louvre picture, the plaster casts include the head of Vitellius borrowed from Sweerts and the figure of the Christ Child from Michelangelo's *Bruges Madonna*. A cast of the latter was recorded in the 1656 inventory of Amsterdam's greatest art teacher, Rembrandt,[20] after whose work Vaillant made engravings.[21]

WL

1 For these and other biographical details see Vandalle, 1937, pp. 7–12.

2 See De Bruyn, 1988, p. 24, who cites van den Branden, 1883, pp. 790–91; Vandalle, 1937, p. 13, misread the date as 1637 and considered fourteen too young an age for such an apprenticeship (see note 3, below).

3 As noted in Providence, 1984, p. 29, apprentices were commonly twelve to fourteen years old.

4 See Paris, 1991, no. 35, for a portrait drawing of a woman, signed and dated 1648.

5 Vaillant's so-called *Portrait of a Soldier* in Hannover would date from this period—not to about 1645 as suggested in Hannover, 1980, p. 77, colorpl. 17.

6 Vaillant is thought to have made at least 230 mezzotints: see Wessely, 1865; Hind, 1933; Alexander, 1976; and London, 1981 (reviewed by Antony Griffiths in "Current and Forthcoming Exhibitions," *The Burlington Magazine*, CXXIII [July 1981], p. 431).

7 An example by Vaillant was sold in New York at Sotheby's, January 10, 1991, no. 43, ill.

8 Lille–Dunkirk–Valenciennes, 1980, p. 72, reports that "G. Diss [in a personal communication] y a reconnu le *Pan et Syrinx* du peintre flamand Cornelis van der Voort" but the picture is not in that Amsterdam portraitist's style. The composition is commonplace and the immediate model, if any, is more likely Flemish, from about 1630–45. For seventeenth-century artists who treated the subject see Pigler, 1974, II, pp. 200–201.

9 See Gabriele Bleeke-Byrne, "The Education of the Painter in the Workshop," in Providence, 1984, pp. 28–39, especially p. 35 n. 48.

10 See especially Stechow, 1968.

11 See Strauss, 1977, II, nos. 312–314.

12 See Liedtke, 1984, I, p. 58.

13 On this print see Chapman, 1990, p. 65, fig. 100.

14 See Martin, 1913, pp. 17 (the *Self-Portrait* in Dresden), 147 (the *Painter with an Oil Lamp* of about 1653 in Brussels). See also Emmens, 1963, and Amsterdam, 1976, no. 17, on the broader theme of educating children, as treated in a triptych by Dou.

15 See Kultzen, 1958, nos. 38, 39; Bloch, 1968, plates 11, 12, 27; and Held, 1982, pp. 113–15, for Sweerts's pictures of artists at study.

16 Waddingham, 1976–77, reasonably dates the painting to Sweerts's Amsterdam period because of its obvious resemblance to works by Gerard ter Borch. On the print see Ackley, 1980, no. 190, and on the painting see Providence, 1984, p. 35, fig. 20 and cover.

17 It is possible to read the date as 1658 or 1668 (Maclaren and Brown, I, 1991, p. 440, simply cite the date as 1658), but the picture's style is more consistent with a date in the late 1660s.

18 Sotheby's, Monaco, December 6, 1987, no. 35; now in a private collection (a photograph and information were kindly provided by Julien Stock of Sotheby's, London).

19 On the Louvre picture see Paris, 1979, p. 142, Inv. no. R.F. 2562; Schneider and Ekkart, 1973, p. 327, no. 129 (as not by Lievens); Maclaren and Brown, I, 1991, pp. 439–40, on the version, probably an old copy, in the National Gallery, London. Could the London canvas be by one of Vaillant's brothers? Another work close to Vaillant is *An Artist's Studio*, "attributed to Matthieu Le Nain," in the Art Gallery, Vassar College, Poughkeepsie, New York (see Providence, 1984, p. 33, fig. 17). The two boys sketching plaster casts in Vaillant's paintings in the Musée Fabre, Montpellier, and in the Musée de Louviers appear to be portraits, perhaps of Vaillant's younger brothers. Vandalle, 1937, p. 349, identifies André Vaillant (born 1655) in the Lille painting but this is rightly doubted by Oursel in Lille–Dunkirk–Valenciennes, 1980, p. 72. The boy here does not resemble either figure in Montpellier and Louviers and is more likely a type derived from the young man in the Minneapolis Sweerts (fig. 2).

20 Noted first in connection with Vaillant by Goldscheider, 1967, p. 11 n. 8. Vaillant's painting in the Louvre suggests that Strauss and van der Meulen, 1979, p. 385, no. 345, were wrong to propose that "Een kindeken van Michael Angelo Bonalotti" may have been "a cast or even the original of Michelangelo's 'Sleeping Cupid.'"

21 See Wessely, 1865, nos. 78, 132, 153.

PROVENANCE
Said to have been acquired from A. W. Thibaudeau, London, 1888.

EXHIBITIONS
Valenciennes, 1918, no. 349; Berlin, 1964, no. 45; Lille, 1970, no. 55; Lille–Dunkirk–Valenciennes, 1980, no. 28.

LITERATURE
Benoit, 1909, I, pp. 131–32, no. 42, pl. 31; Vandalle, 1937, p. 15.

PIETER BOEL

Flemish

Antwerp 1622–1674 Paris

---

7   *An Allegory of Worldly Vanity*

Oil on canvas, 81 1/2 x 102 3/8 in. (207 x 260 cm.)

Signed (at the center left, near the corner of the sarcophagus): PETRUS · BOEL A. 1663 ·

Inscribed (on the side of the sarcophagus): VANITATI · S ·

Inv. no. 78

Vanitas still lifes and other allegories of vanity were exceedingly common in the seventeenth century,[1] but few of them are so grand and so memorable as Pieter Boel's painting in Lille. The artist was a native of Antwerp, where his father, Jan Boel, and his brother Quirin were active as printmakers. The contemporary Flemish biographer of artists Cornelis de Bie records that Boel spent time in Rome and in other Italian cities;[2] Raffaele Soprani's book on artists in Genoa (1674) mentions Boel's residence there and his frequent visits to the studio of his uncle the painter and dealer Cornelis de Wael.[3] Boel was a pupil of Frans Snyders and then of Jan Fyt, according to Erasmus Quellinus's notation in his copy of de Bie.[4] The information is almost certainly reliable since the engraved portrait of Boel in de Bie is after Quellinus,[5] who was Boel's (and Fyt's) occasional collaborator.[6] Furthermore, Boel's paintings of dead game (especially birds) and of live animals are often mistaken for works by Fyt.[7]

The Lille canvas of 1663 must have been painted in Antwerp, where Boel joined the guild in 1650–51 and was last cited in October 1668. Shortly thereafter he was working for Charles Le Brun in Paris and was named *Peintre ordinaire du roi* in the year of his death (1674).

It was probably also in the 1660s that Boel painted another large *vanitas* picture (Brussels, Musées Royaux d'Art et d'Histoire) in collaboration with Jacob Jordaens, who contributed the winged figure of Time, two putti (one blowing bubbles), a parrot, and a skull.[8] The present picture, by contrast, is hauntingly inanimate, and by Boel alone. Part of a ruined palace, with mournful marble statues under broken vaults, is seen in strong foreshortening behind a stone sarcophagus and a curtained entranceway. These strangely juxtaposed structures, each of them, evidently, a threshold at which all life's treasures must be left behind, are now strewn with luxurious objects, some of them attributes of the highest ranks of man. In front of the globe are a king's jeweled crown;

a bishop's miter, staff, and cushion; and a papal tiara. Above the globe are a crowned turban and a silk brocaded robe with an ermine border. The skull next to the turban is also crowned, but with laurel leaves—a tribute to the final victory of death.[9]

The many other objects in the picture have been discussed at length by de Mirimonde, who sees them as representing three different kinds of human activity, the *vita contemplativa*, the *vita voluptuaria*, and the *vita practica*.[10] Apart from the problem that the last two categories are not well-established subdivisions of the *vita activa*, de Mirimonde's interpretation may be doubted because the objects do not fall into groups visually; some of them escape classification; and their abundance allows several readings, but is most convincing simply as an encyclopedic treatment of the theme of "worldly vanity." Boel's composition is inspired not only by earlier *vanitas* still lifes and literature but also by Flemish paintings of collectors' cabinets (for example, by Jan Brueghel the Elder and by Frans Francken II);[11] by "Merry Company" scenes with musical instruments, wine coolers (like the copper one on the right), and lavish tableware;[12] and perhaps by guardroom scenes or other pictorial sources, with regard to the arms and armor.[13] These comparisons encourage the observation that, notwithstanding Boel's consistent references to the *vanitas* theme in this painting, it remains an extravagantly decorative invention, which probably played a prominent role in the embellishment of a splendid home.

Boel's choice of motifs, accordingly, was very much determined by their aesthetic appeal and associative values, that is, not the vanity but the refinements of sophisticated life. Musical instruments, for example, are sensual and temporal objects, unlike the simple iron ring to the far right, a symbol of eternity. Making this point in no way required Boel's representation of the five emphatically different stringed instruments that are assembled around the chair: the violin and bow on the seat; an archlute (with two tuning heads) and sheet music below, both of which imply the singing of songs; the little *pochette* (a "pocket" fiddle), which, like the tambourine, suggests dancing of the most popular kind; a viola da gamba, for serious chamber music; and the tall *tromba marina* ("trumpet marine"), which was played by mariners, middle-class amateurs of both sexes, and nuns—the last because bowing the long instrument at the neck did not interfere with a lady's skirt.[14]

The fine arts are represented by architecture; by sculpture, in a variety of sizes and materials; and by painting, which may seem insufficiently acknowledged by the palette

7

and brushes and by the portrait miniature in the foreground (resting on what appears to be a mirror frame), although the Roman statue of a female figure in a niche in the background at the left wears a diadem bearing an eye, which identifies her as Pictura (the same allegorical figure occurs in Poussin's *Self-Portrait* of 1650 in the Louvre).[15]

The decorative arts and the martial arts would not have been distinguished in these terms during the seventeenth century. De Mirimonde regards the arms and armor, the bust of a Roman emperor alongside the sarcophagus, and the princely and ecclesiastical headgear as attributes of the *vita practica*,[16] but these motifs are more likely to refer to the Stations of Man (as in Jost Amman's and Hans Sachs's *Ständebuch*), which are made equal by death.[17] The saber and the quiver are contemporary in date and Eastern European in origin, but based on Turkish designs. The parade helmet probably dates from the mid-sixteenth century, and the fluted breastplate from about 1510–35.[18]

For de Mirimonde, the *vita contemplativa* is symbolized by the books in the lower right corner and by the terrestrial globe, although these objects are entirely expected in such compositions. The globe refers to worldliness in general (as in the allegorical figure of "Lady World"),[19] with the vanity of learning a common theme for genre and still-life painters in the Netherlands.[20] On the other hand, the globe and books, along with many of the other objects, may be seen simply as the attributes of a well-rounded gentleman.[21]

Variety for its own sake was probably Boel's reason for including some of the sculptures, the porcelain, the silver and silver-gilt vessels (including the tall guild cup near the palette), and the superb Antwerp cabinet of ebony, mahogany, silver, and gold. A few of these luxuries may have had an additional significance that is either obvious or too obscure to consider in detail. On top of the Antwerp cabinet is a bust of a contemporary ruler, a gilt cupid, a bust of a crying boy, and a statuette of a tragic antique heroine, possibly Cleopatra.[22] At the right the splendid sculpture of Diana on a stag—perhaps a reminder of the hapless Actaeon or even of Time[23]—is actually a covered drinking cup made in sixteenth-century Augsburg. Here, and in the other vessels, gold and silver suffice to suggest worldly vanity. The large platter, which is Flemish or French, shows Adonis, who, despite the entreaties of Venus, hurries off to meet a boar and death.[24]

Finally, at the bottom right are letters or documents (one with a great wax seal), two letter openers, classicizing sculpture (of another emperor), and exotic shells. The inscription on the tomb, VANITATI · S[ACRIFICIUM] · ("The Sacrifice to Vanity"), and the skull emphasize that every object in the pyramid of collectibles represents an idle pursuit. That Boel and his contemporaries nonetheless were fascinated by such exquisite things is a paradox typical of the period, and one that marks a fleeting moment between medieval and modern times.

WL

1 See Tapié, 1990, with extensive bibliography.

2 See de Bie, 1661, p. 364.

3 See Soprani, 1768, p. 466, cited by Greindl, 1983, p. 116.

4 See Levin, 1888, p. 133.

5 See De Bruyn, 1988, no. 209.

6 See De Bruyn, 1988, pp. 40, 243, no. 203, colorpl. 5; see also pp. 144, under no. 67, 313 (document no. 18), nos. 68 a, 167, 168.

7 See Greindl, 1956, p. 152, Greindl, 1983, p. 340, for corrected attributions. *A Hound Guarding Dead Game*, a painting in Lille attributed to Fyt (Inv. no. 113) (see Greindl, 1956, p. 165; Lille, 1981, no. 105, as After Jan Fyt), is in my view by Boel.

8 See Greindl, 1956, fig. 78; de Mirimonde, 1964, pp. 114–19, fig. 4; d'Hulst, 1982, p. 181.

9 Compare this motif in Dutch pictures such as Edwaert Collier's *Vanitas Still Life* in the Rheinisches Landesmuseum, Bonn (see Amsterdam, 1976, no. 14).

10 See de Mirimonde, 1964, p. 119.

11 See Speth-Holterhoff, 1957, and Filipczak, 1987, on Flemish paintings of this type.

12 See Legrand, 1963, chaps. II, III.

13 See Klinge, 1991, nos. 21, 25, for examples by Teniers, who frequently included stacks of arms and armor in the foreground. See also Rodee, 1967, on Rubens's depiction of armor: He often favored older examples, as in the helmet and breastplate here.

14 Compare de Mirimonde, 1964, pp. 119–23. Laurence Libin, the Metropolitan Museum's Frederick P. Rose Curator of Musical Instruments, kindly discussed these details with this writer.

15 See de Mirimonde, 1964, p. 123, fig. 10, for this comparison and a detail of the Poussin. The statue is based on a Roman sculpture in the Giustiniani collection in Rome (or some closely related work), which was thought to represent Memory (see Reinach, 1897, I, p. 256). The nude male figure in the background at the left is very similar to the Antinous type; Antinous's early death may have prompted the figure's inclusion in Boel's composition. Joan Mertens, curator in the Metropolitan Museum's department of Greek and Roman Art, kindly helped with these identifications.

16 See de Mirimonde, 1964, p. 125 (who takes an odd view of the clergy).

17 See Amman and Sachs, 1568, which opens with woodcuts of a pope, a cardinal, a bishop, and three other churchmen; then an emperor, a king, and a prince; and after "One hundred persons and fourteen/In jobs, professions, Church and State," ends with injunctions against idleness and wealth (p. 125).

18 Stuart Pyhrr, the Metropolitan Museum's curator of Arms and Armor, provided these identifications.

19 See Amsterdam, 1976, no. 43.

7: detail

20 See Eikemeier, 1984, and Jochen Becker, in Münster–Baden-Baden, 1979–80, pp. 448–78 ("Das Buch im Stilleben—Das Stilleben im Buch").

21 See the discussion of van Dyck's *Portrait of a Man, probably Lucas van Uffel*, in Liedtke, 1984, I, pp. 56–64.

22 These sculptures, apparently bronzes, all date from the late sixteenth or early seventeenth century and are common types, according to James Draper, curator in the Metropolitan Museum's department of European Sculpture and Decorative Arts. De Mirimonde, 1964, p. 123, implausibly discerns a "Vénus pudique" and a "tête de la Niobide" here.

23 The stag, which draws the chariot of Diana or of Time, is a common symbol of Diana. De Mirimonde, 1964, p. 125, correctly attributes the sculpture but wonders whether Diana is Nemesis.

24 De Mirimonde, 1964, pp. 123–25, sees instead the obscure subject of Artemis and Orion.

PROVENANCE

Jacomo de Wit; sale of the de Wit collection, Antwerp, May 15 ff., 1741; Constant Troyon (1810–1865); sale of the contents of Troyon's studio, Paris, January 22–February 1, 1866; Édouard Fould; acquired from Édouard Fould, 1878.

EXHIBITIONS

Brussels, 1965, no. 13; Lille, 1970, no. 41; Paris, 1977–78, no. 8.

LITERATURE

Greindl, 1956, pp. 123, 151; Gerson and ter Kuile, 1960, p. 161, pl. 148 B; de Mirimonde, 1964, pp. 119–27, figs. 6, 7; Braunschweig, 1978, p. 176; Konečnỳ, 1983, p. 129; Oursel, 1984, no. 26.

JORIS HOEFNAGEL

Flemish

Antwerp 1542–1601? Vienna?

8 *Allegory of Life's Brevity* (*Diptych with Flowers and Insects*)

Watercolor on parchment, glued to panel, each, 4 7/8 x 7 1/8 in. (12.3 x 18 cm.)

Each signed and dated (at the bottom center): G.H./F/·1·5·91·

Inscribed (on panel A): (above) ROSĀ[M]QVÆ PRÆTER/IERİT NE QVÆ/RAS İTERV̄[M]., (below left) *Homo sicut fœnum dies / eius, tanquā[m] flos agri/ sic efflorebit. psal. 102.*, (below right) *Omnis caro fœnum, / Et omnis gloria eius/quasi flos agri· Isa.42.*; (on panel B): (above) İPSA DİES APERİT/CONFİCIT/İPSA DİES., (below left) *Florete flores, quasi / Lilium, et date odorem, / Et frondete in gratia[m]:/* (below right) *Et collaudate canticum, / Et benedicite Dominum / In operibus suis. Ecc: 38.*

Inv. no. 732

Among the rarest and least-often exhibited treasures of the Lille museum is this diptych, or pair, of watercolor miniatures on parchment, probably painted in 1591 by the Fleming Joris Hoefnagel for Emperor Rudolf II in Prague.[1] This type of work was always intended for private contemplation in a collector's cabinet, but Roelant Savery (see cat. no. 9) was able to study Hoefnagel's miniatures in Prague, and they were made more widely known through the collection of engraved plates, *Archetypa studiaque*, which Hoefnagel's son Jacob (1575–about 1630) produced after his father's designs and published in Frankfurt in 1592.[2]

The son of an Antwerp diamond dealer, Joris (or Georg) Hoefnagel described himself as an autodidact, but van Mander records that he studied with Hans Bol.[3] When in his twenties Hoefnagel traveled in France, spent four years in Spain (1563–67), and then went to England before settling in Antwerp, where he married in 1571. His career as a miniaturist depended upon court patronage, which Hoefnagel had no trouble finding once he left Antwerp (about 1576–77). Hans Fugger in Augsburg recommended the artist to Duke Albrecht V of Bavaria, in whose service Hoefnagel remained while visiting Italy (with Abraham Ortelius) before returning to Munich. During this period he made city views that were later published in Georg Braun's and Frans Hogenberg's *Civitates orbis terrarum* (Cologne, 1572–1618). Between 1582 and 1590 Hoefnagel worked on illuminations for the famous *Missale romanum* (Vienna, Österreichische Nationalbibliothek) for Archduke Ferdinand II of the Tirol, and in April 1590 he negotiated to enter the service of Rudolf II. The artist probably visited Rudolf's capital, Prague, in 1590 or 1591 and in 1594, but in these years he lived mostly in Frankfurt. At Rudolf's request Hoefnagel painted numerous miniatures (mostly of flowers, with some animals and insects in decorative arrangements) in two *Schriftmusterbücher*— calligraphic masterpieces composed a generation earlier by Georg Bocskay, who had been secretary to Rudolf's paternal grandfather, Emperor Ferdinand I.[4] Hoefnagel's independent miniatures date from the same years and from 1595 until his death in September 1601. During the last five years of his life Hoefnagel lived mostly in Vienna but he visited Prague in 1598.

The Lille diptych is one of the artist's earliest independent works and may have been painted in Prague, Munich, or Frankfurt. In any event, the miniatures were made while he was in Rudolf II's service and reflect a few of the emperor's sophisticated interests, such as species of natural life, exquisite works of art, and clever allegories. The two miniatures have many elements in common but are distinguished

8

IPSA DIES APERIT
CONFICIT

IPSA DIES

Florete flores, quasi
Lilium, et date odorem,
Et frondete in gratia:

Et collaudate canticum,
Et benedicite Dominum
In operibus suis. Ecc:38.

8

especially by the central motif of an angel's head or a skull. These refer to life and death, or to the soul and death, respectively, and together indicate that the miniatures form an allegory of life's brevity. As will be seen, this theme carries through the two panels; it cannot be said that one panel is an allegory of death and the other an allegory of life. The angel's and bat's wings, in conjunction with the hourglass, may also suggest the passage of days and nights. Both panels are rich in reminders of time: time as fleeting, life as precious, and death as inevitable.

Hoefnagel's miniatures anticipate many features of the earliest Dutch and Flemish still-life paintings (see cat. no. 9): for example, their depiction of flowers that briefly blossom (lilies predominate on one panel, roses on the other) and that attract the gastronomic attention of various insects. One of them, the butterfly, symbolizes the soul, since its metamorphosis from the caterpillar may be seen as a resurrection from an earthbound to a heaven-bound state. In the Lille diptych Hoefnagel presents two butterflies and four different kinds of caterpillars in heraldic arrangements that may be considered central to the meaning of the images.

The composition of each miniature obeys peculiar laws of physics that pertain equally to the second and third dimensions, as these laws had since their formulation in the borders of fourteenth-century illuminated manuscripts. The scroll-shaped cartouches and brackets, which conform to the Antwerp manner of architectural embellishment known as the Floris style,[5] are joined by the continuous borders of the miniatures as if by a thin brass frame. At the sides, cut flowers are secured in metal clamps. Similarly, the brackets attached to the upper borders support small urns from which either bright flames or gloomy puffs of smoke ascend. These commonplace reminders of life's brief flame complement the symbolism of the angel and the skull (compare the vase in figure 3, catalogue number 14).

Rudolf II and his artistic entourage had no need of helpful quotations to comprehend Hoefnagel's iconography. The Latin inscriptions were provided by the artist (or a scholarly collaborator) as another level of learning, one that confirms a basic tenet of the time: that the scientific study of nature and age-old moral wisdom coexist in complete accord.

In the "nocturnal" miniature, the inscription above (ROSA̅[M] . . . İTERV̅[M]·) is from Erasmus's compendium of *Adages* (II, VI, XL) and may be translated as, "The rose that has gone by, do not look for it again." At the lower left is a line from Psalm 102 (Vulgate; 103: 15 in King James), "As

for man, his days are as grass: as a flower of the field, so he flourisheth." The theme is continued at the right with a passage from Isaiah 40: 6, "All flesh is grass, and all the goodliness thereof is as the flower of the field." Rudolf II could have continued reading in his Bible (Isaiah 40: 7–8), "The grass withers, the flower fades, when the breath of the Lord blows upon it; surely the people is grass. The grass withers, the flower fades; but the word of our God will stand for ever."

The "diurnal" miniature provides a classical source for Erasmus's reference to the rose in a quotation ("İPSA DİES . . .") from the fourth-century Roman poet Ausonius's *Rosae edyllium*, IV: 40: "The day itself opens [the blossom]; the same day finishes [it]." However, a happier thought is offered by the continuous lines at the bottom of the composition (*Florete . . . operibus suis*). The Ecc: 38. refers not to Ecclesiastes but to the Vulgate book of Ecclesiasticus 39: 19 (Ecclus. 39: 14 in King James): "And give ye a sweet savour as frankincense, and flourish as a lily, send forth a smell, and sing a song of praise, bless the Lord in all his works."

This last line supersedes the others and Hoefnagel's *vanitas* theme to convey the essential message of the miniatures.[6]　　　　　　　　　　　　　　　　　　　WL

1 See Kaufmann, 1988, p. 204, no. 9.2, a, b.

2 See Edinburgh, 1991, no. 42. See also Bergström, 1985; Kaufmann, 1988, pp. 211–14.

3 See the biography compiled by Kaufmann (1988, p. 202).

4 These manuscripts are in the Kunsthistorisches Museum, Vienna, and in the J. Paul Getty Museum, Malibu; see Kaufmann, 1988, p. 9, figs. 7, 8 (with Hoefnagel's views of Prague), pp. 207–8, no. 9.9, pl. 9, and pp. 13–14 on the patrons. See also Bergström, 1985, figs. 2, 3.

5 See Hedicke, 1913.

6 My discussions of both the motifs and the inscriptions in the Lille diptych are indebted to Hoefnagel's premier interpreter, Dr. Thea Vignau-Wilberg (see Literature, below) of the Staatliche Graphische Sammlung, Munich (letter dated October 26, 1991). The biblical sources were properly identified and all the inscriptions translated with great kindness by John McMahon, master of Latin at the Harvey School, Katonah, New York.

PROVENANCE
Probably Emperor Rudolf II, from about 1591 to his death in 1612; Auguste Ozenfant; Gift of Auguste Ozenfant, 1894.

EXHIBITIONS
Brussels, 1963, no. 136; Paris, 1965–66, no. 167.

LITERATURE
Bergström, 1956, pp. 33–36, figs. 30, 31; Bergström, 1963, p. 66, colorpl. p. 6; Foucart, in Paris, 1965–66, pp. 132–33, no. 167; Wilberg Vignau-Schuurman, 1969, I, pp. 220–21, 226–27, II, p. 117, no. 9, figs. 75–76; Hairs, 1985, p. 481; Vignau-Wilberg, 1986–87, pp. 148–49, figs. 158–159; Kaufmann, 1988, p. 204, no. 9.2.

ROELANT SAVERY

Flemish

Kortrijk 1576–1639 Utrecht

_____

9   *A Bouquet of Flowers*

Oil on wood, 10 1/2 x 7 1/4 in. (26.6 x 18.4 cm.), with additions on four sides; original dimensions, 9 3/8 x 6 1/8 in. (23.7 x 15.5 cm.)

Signed (at the lower left): R. SAVERY FE.

Inv. no. 1036

This small, exquisite flower painting is one of some two dozen known still lifes by Roelant Savery, who was from Kortrijk (Courtrai), just north of Lille. His flower pictures comprise about ten percent of his oeuvre (which consists mostly of landscapes with animals) and date from 1603 to the late 1620s. The Lille panel is not dated but has been assigned convincingly to about 1611–12.[1] The few earlier examples are dated 1603 (New York, Private collection, and Utrecht, Centraal Museum), 1609 (Whereabouts unknown), and 1610 (Kortrijk, Museum voor Schone Kunsten);[2] these also depict a bouquet of flowers set in a green glass (*roemer*), but the arrangement is taller and is framed by a shallow stone niche. The Lille composition differs as well in its subtle asymmetry, with a lower massing of the larger flowers and a tracery of delicate forms above, and a dark background that is consistent with the more shadowy and atmospheric appearance of the work overall.[3] These qualities first appear in Savery's still lifes of about 1612,[4] and continue in the mostly more elaborate examples dating from 1615 onward. Savery achieved extraordinary variety with a subject that, with only one or two exceptions, may be described simply as flowers in a glass on a shelf with a few flying and crawling creatures. Through 1615, the remarkably small scale of the Lille painting was the artist's norm.

The dating of the present work deserves close attention because it places the picture at the end of Savery's stay in Prague, where he served Emperor Rudolf II until the latter's death on January 22, 1612. Savery continued as court painter to Emperor Matthias, but moved to Amsterdam in 1613. He had been trained not in Flanders but in Haarlem, where his family lived from about 1685. His older brother, Jacob, was his teacher, and Roelant probably went with him to Amsterdam in 1591, remaining there until Jacob's death in 1603. Savery may have arrived in Prague during the fall of that year; his two flower still lifes dated 1603 (which are virtually

identical in composition) have been associated with Rudolf II's reputation—according to the botanist Emanuel Sweerts in 1612—as the "greatest and most enthusiastic admirer of such things [real flowers] in the world, as well as of the arts."[5]

Savery's brother Jacob appears to have preceded him both as a painter of flowers (see fig. 1) and as a painter of animals—specifically, of "Paradise" landscapes teeming with exotic menageries.[6] Roelant's own interest in these subjects was surely more sophisticated, and it seems likely that Rudolf II, who set up his own zoo in 1576, accepted Savery into his service as a naturalist as well as an artist.[7] Savery never repeated the same view of a particular flower in different compositions, as did his contemporaries—for example, Jan Brueghel the Elder and Ambrosius Bosschaert the Elder; he omitted flowers that they routinely depicted, and he introduced some species not found in their works.[8] As many as one hundred and fifty varieties of flowers and seventy kinds

FIGURE 1. After Jacob Savery. *Vase of Flowers with a Parrot and a Peacock*. Engraving. The Metropolitan Museum of Art, New York. The Elisha Whittelsey Collection. The Elisha Whittelsey Fund, 1949

9

FIGURE 2. Diagram by Sam Segal (1991) of catalogue number 9:

1	Borage	*Borago officinalis* L.
2	Columbine (foliage)	*Aquilegia vulgaris* L.
3	Rute (foliage)	*Ruta graveolens* L.
4	Superb Pink	*Dianthus superbus* L.
5	grass (foliage)	*Poaceae*
6	Pheasant's Eye	*Adonis flammea* L.
7	Pansy	*Viola tricolor* L. var. *hortensis* DC.
8	Love-in-a-Mist	*Nigella damascena* L. *granda*
9	Forget-me-not	*Myosotis scorpioides* L.
10	Pot Marigold	*Calendula officinalis* L.
11	Red Martagon Lily	*Lilium chalcedonicum* L.
12	White Rose	*Rosa x alba* L.
13	Larkspur	*Consolida ambigua* (L.) Ball & Heyw. *rosea*
14	Love-in-a-Mist	*Nigella damascena* L. *semiplena*
15	Reed-grass (foliage)	*Phalaris arundinacea* L. *picta*
16	Rosemary (foliage)	*Rosmarinus officinalis* L.
17	Wallflower	*Cheiranthus cheiri* L.
18	Red German Catchfly	*Lychnis viscaria* L.
19	Maltese Cross	*Lychnis chalcedonica* L.
20	Columbine	*Aquilegia vulgaris* L.
21	Columbine	*Aquilegia vulgaris* L. *rosea-alba*
22	African Marigold	*Tagetes patula* L.
23	Lesser Celandine	*Chelidonium majus* L.
24	Apothecary's Rose	*Rosa gallica* L. cv. *Officinalis*
25	Damask Rose hybrid	*Rosa x damascena* Mill. x *R. gallica* L.
a	Poplar Hawk moth	*Laothoe populi* (L.)
b	Elephant Hawk moth	*Deilephila elpenor* (L.)
c	Small tortoiseshell	*Aglais urticae* (L.)
d	House Fly	*Musca domestica* (L.)
f	Blow Fly	*Sarcophaga carnaria* (L.)
g	Earth Bumble Bee	*Bombus terrestris* L.
e	not identifiable	

of insects and little animals have been counted in Savery's intimate oeuvre of still-life paintings.[9] His botanical sources must have included actual specimens as well as drawings, prints, and miniatures by older artists. Perhaps most important for Savery's still lifes were the watercolor miniatures painted during the 1590s by Joris Hoefnagel, whom, in effect, Savery succeeded at Rudolf II's court. The connection is illustrated clearly by the pair of Hoefnagel miniatures in Lille (see cat. no. 8).[10]

Hoefnagel described himself as an *inventor hieroglyphicus* and, indeed, his watercolors overflow with emblematic conceits.[11] The extent to which Savery conceived his compositions along similar intellectual lines has been a matter of debate;[12] in the Lille painting he was probably content with the commonplace *vanitas* theme. Flowers of different seasons (fig. 2) briefly blossom, then wither and fall, all of which suggests, like the buzz of busy insects, the passage of time and of life itself. The butterfly, however, matures through a sort of resurrection, and thus symbolizes the soul.[13] The red rose above the butterfly may refer to the love or the Passion of Christ. Rudolf II and his circle delighted in the discovery of philosophical and occult niceties (and proofs of the emperor's learning) in their encyclopedic surveys of the natural world.[14] To his patrons Savery's still lifes were like *Kunst- und Wunderkabinette* in miniature.[15]

WL

1 Kaufmann, 1988, p. 244, no. 19.54, suggests "c. 1611, or slightly before," refining the dating of about 1606–12 proposed in Spicer, 1979. Müllenmeister, 1988, p. 341, no. 291, follows Sam Segal's verbal advice that the Lille painting dates from about 1612.

2 See Kaufmann, 1988, nos. 19.1, 19.2, 19.38; Müllenmeister, 1988, nos. 269–271, 290; Cologne–Utrecht, 1985–86, no. 2, for the 1603 Utrecht picture.

3 In New York, 1985, p. 289, no. 184, the writer related these qualities to Savery's experience as a landscape painter. The composition here should be compared also with an earlier (1607) panel by Bosschaert in a private collection (see Bergström, 1982, p. 178, fig. 4), where a butterfly is placed similarly in the foreground.

4 See, for example, Müllenmeister, 1988, nos. 274, 275.

5 Kaufmann, 1988, p. 229, quoting from Emanuel Sweerts, *Florilegium*, Frankfurt, 1612. See also Kaufmann, 1988, pp. 65, 126 n. 65. Segal, 1982, p. 311, felt that the 1603 still life in Utrecht "must have been painted in Amsterdam"; he reinforced this view in Cologne–Utrecht, 1985–86, pp. 62, 64 n. 20, while allowing that Savery may have painted a second version to show Rudolf II in Prague. Compare Spicer, 1979, p. 257, and Kaufmann, 1988, pp. 228–29, nos. 19.1, 19.2.

6 See Segal, in Cologne–Utrecht, 1985–86, pp. 55–57 (flowers); Roelofsz, 1980; Anne-Caroline Buysschaert, "Roelant Savery als Tiermaler," in Cologne–Utrecht, 1985–86, pp. 51–54. Two "Para-

dise" landscapes by Jacob Savery are catalogued in Cologne–Utrecht, 1985–86, nos. 93, 94 (both in private collections).

7 See Kaufmann, 1988, pp. 228–29, and pp. 74–89 for a general survey of these interests in Prague.

8 See Segal, 1982.

9 See Segal, in Cologne–Utrecht, 1985–86, p. 61.

10 See Kaufmann, 1988, p. 204, no. 9.2; Wilberg Vignau-Schuurman, 1969, I, pp. 226–27, II, figs. 75–76.

11 See Wilberg Vignau-Schuurman, 1969; Kaufmann, 1988, pp. 202–10.

12 See, for example, Kaufmann, 1988, p. 229, under no. 19.1; New York, 1985, p. 292, under no. 184, for my own interpretation of one of Savery's most sophisticated still lifes (the 1612 panel in Vaduz, also catalogued in Kaufmann, 1988, as no. 19.59).

13 See Segal, 1982, p. 329; Segal, 1983, pp. 31, 53, 55; Wilberg Vignau-Schuurman, 1969, I, pp. 285–86, 306, on Hoefnagel's use of the butterfly for various meanings—in particular, to represent an individual's faith.

14 See Evans, 1973.

15 Kaufmann, 1988, pp. 293–94, lists about twenty studies of Rudolf II's *Kunstkammer*. See also Gisela Luther, "Stilleben als Bilder der Sammelleidenschaft," in Münster–Baden-Baden, 1979–80, pp. 88–128.

PROVENANCE

Alexandre Leleux (1812–1873), Lille; Gift of Alexandre Leleux, 1873.

EXHIBITIONS

Ghent, 1954, no. 40; Lille–Arras–Dunkirk, 1972–73, no. 51; Lille, 1974, no. 54; Kortrijk, 1976, no. 11.

LITERATURE

Erasmus, 1908, no. 88; Segal, 1982, p. 335 n. 14; Hairs, 1985, pp. 218, 490; Kaufmann, 1988, p. 244, no. 19.54, ill.; Müllenmeister, 1988, pp. 340–41, no. 291.

BALTHASAR VAN DER AST

Dutch

Middelburg 1593/94–1657 Delft

10   *Still Life with Fruit, Flowers, and Shells*

Oil on wood, 14 1/2 x 25 1/2 in. (37 x 65 cm.)

Signed (at the bottom center): ·B· *vander* · A*st* · *fẽ* · 1623 ·

Inv. no. 1937

With his brother-in-law, Ambrosius Bosschaert the Elder (1573–1621), Balthasar van der Ast was one of the most important pioneers of still-life painting in the Netherlands (see

also cat. no. 9, by Roelant Savery). He was a generation younger than Bosschaert and surely his pupil in Middelburg. Modern biographies often give the romanticized impression that "the orphan Van der Ast" was taken in by Bosschaert and married his sister.[1] When van der Ast was ten years old his sister married Bosschaert, whose family had fled Antwerp fifteen or twenty years earlier.[2] Thus, Bosschaert joined the family of the wealthy Middelburg merchant Hans van der Ast, whose six children sold off the widower's real estate (at least five houses) in 1609.[3] Van der Ast lent his guardians fifty Flemish pounds (at seven percent interest) when he was seventeen;[4] that he and his elder brother, Hans (whose painting of a "flower pot" was retouched by Bosschaert in 1615),[5] lived and studied with Bosschaert is well established, but the older painter did not save the van der Asts from the streets.

This point is of interest in part because the imported fruits, rare flowers, exotic shells, and Chinese porcelain (in this case a Wan-li plate of about 1600–1610)[6] depicted in the Lille panel were the appointments of distinctly patrician homes. The same may be said for this kind of painting (Bosschaert's family could easily live on the proceeds of three or four small still lifes per year),[7] while a knowledge of natural curiosities—species of insects, lizards, and flowers, and types of shells—was likewise suggestive of gentility.[8] In the early seventeenth century Middelburg was still a prominent city and Zeeland rivaled Amsterdam in shipping and trade.[9] The port also gave merchants firsthand exposure to the kind of objects that are depicted here.

In 1615 Bosschaert and van der Ast moved to Bergen op Zoom; Bosschaert became a citizen of Utrecht in 1616 and van der Ast may have gone there at the same time or shortly thereafter. He joined the painters' guild in Utrecht in 1619 and painted his first known still lifes between then and 1632, when he settled in Delft. The Lille panel, dated 1623, thus was painted in Utrecht not Middelburg.

It was also in 1619 that Bosschaert moved to Breda (he died in 1621 while delivering a still life to Prince Maurice at The Hague) and that the guild in Utrecht admitted Roelant Savery (see cat. no. 9). Savery's depiction of lizards and the trompe-l'oeil carving of his name in a stone ledge, as well as other motifs, were adopted by van der Ast from the formerly Rudolphine artist, whose style to some extent must also account for the rich sense of texture and atmosphere in van der Ast's mature work. Compared with those of Bosschaert, van der Ast's paintings are stronger in modeling, sense of rhythm, and sensual qualities in general; his compositions

are eccentric,[10] his subjects are teeming not still, and in some works he conveys a contemplative, even brooding mood. Van der Ast's distinctive personality was evidently drawn out by Savery and by his own change of scene, which exposed him to one of the most imaginative schools of painting in Northern Europe at that time.

The painting in Lille has been interpreted energetically as a "Christian meditation on human destiny."[11] Fruits, flowers, and shells figure in contemporary emblem books and other sources as earthly things; the various signs of decay in this still life surely serve as reminders of mortality in the midst of the sensual world.[12] It has been suggested further that the apple signifies the Fall, the grapes Redemption, and the red and white roses "blood, sacrifice and love" as well as "purity and grace."[13] The serpent would fit nicely in this religious allegory as the antipode of Christ, but the shells and other elements remain no more than attractive little vanities—as is the painting itself. In the case of such a luxury object one should probably not press the spiritual interpretation, which in any event may have been for van der Ast's patrons an essentially literary exercise. Moralizing books and pictures were a form of refined entertainment by which their owners might also claim to be edified.

It was the aesthetic achievement of this kind of picture that brought princely sums. Among the painting's subtler effects are its transitions from dark to light colors, and the handling of hard and soft surfaces, with a range that extends from a stone ledge and porcelain to seashells,[14] leaves, butterfly wings, and the backs of bugs. Van der Ast frequently placed shells from Indo-Pacific waters next to Chinese plates and bowls—a comparison that may be traced back at least as far as Marco Polo's use of the same word, *porcelain*, for both of these decorative commodities.[15]

WL

1 See Gaskell, 1989, p. 48. The best biography remains Bol, 1960, pp. 36–40 (pp. 14–33 on Bosschaert).

2 His status as an immigrant qualifies Bosschaert and his entire entourage for discussion in Briels, 1987, pp. 239–57.

3 See Bol, 1960, p. 102 notes 51, 52, citing Bredius, 1913.

4 See Bol, 1960, pp. 36, 102 n. 77.

5 See Bol, 1960, p. 27. On Hans (Johannes) van der Ast see Amsterdam, 1984, pp. 42–44, 136–37, no. 10; Grimm, 1988, pp. 101–2, pl. 47.

6 Compare Amsterdam, 1982, sections 1.1.2, 1.1.3 ("Plates with flattened rims"), especially p. 64, no. 2026, ill.

7 See Bol, 1960, pp. 26, 29.

8 On shells see Gaskell, 1989, p. 50; Jost, 1968. See Bol, 1960, pp. 15–18, on Middelburg flower enthusiasts and their contacts with learned botanists.

9 On Middelburg see Unger, 1954; Amsterdam, 1984, p. 25; Haak, 1984, p. 204.

10 The present design, however, was used by various Dutch and Flemish painters of the period and remains indebted to Bosschaert, as shown by Bergström, 1983.

11 See Oursel and Scottez, 1979, p. 381; see also Oursel, 1984, p. 152.

12 See "The Symbolic Meaning of Fruits," in Segal, 1983, pp. 14–43, and also pp. 53–55 on fruit still lifes by van der Ast in which similar readings are proposed; butterflies and dragonflies represent "heavenly" symbols opposed to all "earthly" ones (pp. 40, 53, 55); rare shells are seen as an example of human vanity (p. 55); the lizard is regarded as a symbol of deceit and sin (p. 55).

13 See Oursel, 1984, p. 152.

14 The five shells at the bottom center are, from left to right, a West Indian Top (*cittarium pica*) from the Caribbean; an Episcopal Miter (*mitra mitra*) and a long Spindle Tibia (*tibia fusus*), both Indo-Pacific; a Cuban Tree Snail (*polymita picta*) from the Caribbean; and a Lollipop Murex (*haustellum haustellum*), also Indo-Pacific. Van der Ast is known for several paintings of shells alone: for example, the late panel in the Museum Boymans-van Beuningen, Rotterdam (see Meijer, 1989, pp. 52–53, no. 2).

15 See Olschki, 1960, p. 160 n., pp. 168–69. Marco Polo's journal was first published in Nuremberg in 1477, and then in Venice in 1496. My thanks to Clare Le Corbeiller of the Metropolitan Museum's department of European Sculpture and Decorative Arts, who provided this reference and cautionary words about the origin of the term *porcelain*.

PROVENANCE
Purchased, 1977.

LITERATURE
Oursel and Scottez, 1979, pp. 380–82, fig. 2; Oursel, 1984, pp. 152–53, no. 18.

JOACHIM WTEWAEL

Dutch

Utrecht 1566–1638 Utrecht

11 *The Raising of Lazarus*

Oil on canvas, 62 1/4 x 81 7/8 in. (158 x 208 cm.)

Inv. no. 150

This spectacular picture, one of Wtewael's major essays on a religious theme, was purchased by the Musée des Beaux-Arts in 1900 as a work by Bartholomeus Spranger (1546–1611). That flamboyant Flemish artist was extremely influential in the formation of Wtewael's Mannerist style. However, the

Lille painting dates from a period when he had already responded to the most "Sprangeresque" inventions of the Haarlem artists Hendrick Goltzius (1558–1616) and Cornelisz. van Haarlem, as well as of his near contemporary in Utrecht, Abraham Bloemaert (1564–1651), and had achieved his own distinctive and somewhat more tempered style. Accordingly, Jacques Foucart rejected Lindeman's view that the canvas may have been painted during Wtewael's early residence in France (about 1590–92), and placed the picture in the mid-1590s, "en pleine période maniériste."[1] Anne Lowenthal concurred but more cautiously proposed a dating to about 1595–1600, in part because Wtewael appears to have been inspired by Bloemaert's *Raising of Lazarus* of the mid-1590s (known from Jan Muller's engraving; see fig. 1), and perhaps by the naked man with a hat in the center of Bloemaert's *Baptism of Christ* (fig. 2) "from the mid-to-late 1590s" (compare this figure with the one to the extreme left in figure 1).[2] As discussed below, the present writer would strongly favor a date of about 1599–1601 on the basis of comparisons with Wtewael's other works.

The question of dating is worth pursuing here if only to illustrate the point that Dutch Mannerist pictures of the 1590s were the products of immensely fertile imaginations and were composed by painters closely acquainted with each other's activity. Many of their ideas circulated through engravings, to which the Haarlem and Utrecht artists devoted exceptional attention as inventors and undoubtedly also as collectors. Wtewael's relationship to Bloemaert in the 1590s was the most sustained; they had both been pupils of the Utrecht painter Joos de Beer, and Bloemaert—following his stay in France (about 1580–83) and a period in Amsterdam (1591–93)—became one of Utrecht's most prominent artists and teachers. In his history of Utrecht, written in 1592, Aernout van Buchell refers to "two growing talents in the prime of life, to whom the judgment of time will give still greater fame: Abraham Bloemaert and Joachim Wtewael . . . ."[3]

Lille is fortunate to have Wtewael's drawing of very nearly the same composition (see cat. no. 86 and fig. 3). Lowenthal describes the sheet as a preparatory drawing, which would not exclude its possible function as a *modello* to be submitted for a patron's approval. In the painting Wtewael modifies the composition of the drawing, which seems distinctly closer in style to Bloemaert's elaborate designs of the mid-1590s (see fig. 2). The figure in the left foreground in the drawing is even more prominent, and his angular contrapposto more extreme than that of his coun-

FIGURE 1. Jan Muller, after Abraham Bloemaert. *The Raising of Lazarus.* Engraving. Los Angeles County Museum of Art. Purchased with funds provided by Mary Ruiz and The Ahmanson Foundation

FIGURE 2. Abraham Bloemaert. *The Baptism of Christ.* Oil on canvas. Ham House, Surrey, England

terpart in the painting, where the figures of Christ and Lazarus become more central to the crowd's and the viewer's attention. Christ's head is raised and strongly set off by three columns in the background, which are part of an extensive revision of the more distracting architectural setting in the sketch. Most of the figures to the far left have been newly posed so that the focus is shifted toward the center of the picture; the circular patterns of gestures and glances here and to the immediate left of Lazarus are displaced by straightened arms, heads more nearly in profile, and other adjustments that favor the key protagonists. On the whole, space is clarified and the figures are more tightly grouped

II

along diagonal lines that converge toward Christ's commanding gesture and Lazarus's raised face.

Wtewael's shift away from the convoluted surface effects in his work of the mid-1590s (one might also compare Bloemaert's *Moses Striking the Rock* of 1596 in The Metropolitan Museum of Art in New York)[4] is accompanied by a tendency toward more realistic anatomy and figure types. The small heads, long thighs, and other elegant distortions found in the drawing are less exaggerated in the painting, where Christ, Lazarus, the woman supporting him, and the male figures at the left frame might be described as tentative participants in the international reform of art of about 1600—at least as it was witnessed in Haarlem and Antwerp. The bright coloring and many Mannerist conceits (ranging from splayed fingers to exotic headgear) are counterbalanced by the strong use of light and shade to study anatomy (as in the workman with a spade in the right foreground) and by the incipient classicism of the principal figure. Similar qualities are evident in Wtewael's *Martyrdom of Saint Sebastian*, dated 1600, in the Nelson-Atkins Museum of Art, Kansas City.[5] The Lille painting appears to mark an important moment in Wtewael's development about 1600 and in several respects is more advanced than almost anything else painted in Utrecht at that time.

The subject of the Raising of Lazarus (John 11: 1–44) received frequent attention from Flemish and especially from Dutch artists during the late sixteenth and the early seventeenth century, in part because the miracle was a dramatic example of salvation through grace alone—a central Protestant doctrine. Lazarus had not performed good works or otherwise earned redemption; thus his resurrection, which prefigured that of Christ and of Christian souls at the Last Judgment, was a powerful rebuttal to the Catholic church's granting (and, in the late Middle Ages, selling) of indulgences, which had been prohibited by Pius V in 1567 but remained a sensitive point in Wtewael's day. In his sermon of 1518 Luther—who with Erasmus and other Reformers joins the crowd in Lucas Cranach the Elder's *Raising of Lazarus* (Nordhausen, Blasiuskirche)—passed over Jesus' close friendship with the brother of Martha and Mary, and proclaimed that "Lazarus, finally, signifies those who are so entangled in sin that they go beyond all bounds . . . they stink and are buried in sin."[6] The same image is more gently sketched in the Latin inscription on Muller's engraving after Bloemaert (see fig. 1).[7]

Another aspect of the story that appealed to Protestant theologians was its insistence on the power of individual

FIGURE 3. Joachim Wtewael. *The Raising of Lazarus*. Pen and brown ink, with wash. Musée des Beaux-Arts, Lille (see cat. no. 86)

belief. Christ said to Martha (who is probably the woman to the left of Lazarus in Wtewael's picture): "And whosoever liveth and believeth in me shall never die. Believest thou this?" (John 11: 26). In Netherlandish paintings and engravings dating from the mid-sixteenth to the early seventeenth century (culminating in Rembrandt's theatrical painting of this subject, of 1630–31, in the Los Angeles County Museum of Art) there is a broad development away from a ritualistic staging of the story toward an increasingly emotionalistic interpretation, which emphasizes Christ's gesture, Lazarus's reaction, and the responses of the witnesses. In this sense also Wtewael's painting is a transitional work.[8]

It may seem to modern viewers that the aesthetic affectations of Netherlandish Mannerism were inconsistent with such serious subject matter. It is true that the style appealed principally to sophisticated private patrons in two or three Dutch cities during a comparatively brief period,[9] and that many of its most successful moments were devoted to an urbane interest in classical mythology.[10] However, there is no doubt that, in an age of firm belief, religious subjects such as the Raising of Lazarus were valued as more than mere vehicles for artistic display. That the very same subject was soon to be rendered in profoundly different ways by artists such as Rembrandt and Rubens is an index of how important meaning is in the Lille picture—which in turn suggests that Wtewael's style, however fashionable, was hardly inaccessible to patrons in Utrecht about 1600.

WL

11: detail

1 See Foucart, in Paris, 1965–66, no. 325.

2 See Lowenthal, 1986, pp. 87–88, no. A-10 (quote from p. 88).

3 See Lowenthal, 1986, pp. 62 (English translation), 184 (original Latin), for the passage from Aernout van Buchell, "Familiae Traiectenses tam nobilium et patriciorum quam plebeorum 1594 collectae," an unpublished manuscript (Utrecht, Bibliotheek der Rijksuniversiteit, no. 1658); this extract was previously published in Muller, 1906, p. 256.

4 See The Hague–San Francisco, 1990–91, no. 8.

5 See Lowenthal, 1986, no. A-14, pl. 21; The Hague–San Francisco, 1990–91, no. 73.

6 See Halewood, 1982, p. 41; chap. 3 on the subject; and pp. 36–37, fig. 12, for Cranach's painting.

7 A German translation of the Latin inscription is given by Guratzsch, 1980, I, p. 132.

8 In addition to Guratzsch, 1980, and Halewood, 1982, chap. 3, see Washington–Detroit–Amsterdam, 1980–81, pp. 123–25; Hamburg, 1983, no. 209; and Rand, 1991, on Rembrandt's painting in Los Angeles.

9 For some brief remarks on Wtewael's patronage see Lowenthal, 1986, chap. 1.

10 This is made clear by Sluijter, 1986.

PROVENANCE

Purchased from the Parisian dealer van Hassel (as a work by Spranger), 1900.

EXHIBITIONS

Valenciennes, 1918, no. 333; Recklinghausen–Utrecht, 1962, no. 24; Berlin, 1964, no. 44; Paris, 1965–66, no. 325; Lille, 1970, no. 27.

LITERATURE

Lindeman, 1929, pp. 17, 63, 98–100, 253, no. 36, pl. 25; Guratzsch, 1980, I, pp. 130–31, 133, II, p. 351, no. 211, fig. 103 (about 1590); Oursel, 1984, pp. 140–41, no. 12, colorpl.; Lowenthal, 1986, pp. 45, 87–88, no. A-10, pl. 14 (about 1595–1600).

CORNELIS CORNELISZ. VAN HAARLEM

Dutch

Haarlem 1562–1638 Haarlem

---

12   *Venus, Cupid, Bacchus, and Ceres ("Sine Cerere et Baccho friget Venus")*

Oil on copper, 8 1/2 x 9 1/2 in. (21.5 x 24.1 cm.)

Signed (at the lower right): CvH [monogram] 1624

Inv. no. 1680

In this endearing depiction of a familiar mythological theme, the Haarlem painter Cornelisz. van Haarlem achieves re-markable monumentality on a miniature scale. The skillfully poised composition, reminiscent of sculpted metopes, conveys the mood of the classical subject with refreshing sensitivity, given the number of times Dutch and Flemish artists, including Cornelis, had already visualized it before this date (1624).[1]

The subject was adopted from *Eunuchus*, a comedy of 161 B.C. by the Roman playwright Terence (IV: verse 732): *Sine Cerere et Libero [Bacchus] friget Venus* ("Without Ceres and Bacchus, Venus will freeze"), meaning that love will not flourish without the help of food and drink. The adage is a perfect blend of folk wisdom, humanistic learning, and dinner conversation, and in pictorial form was enjoyed principally in cultivated art centers such as Antwerp and Prague.[2] The popularity of this and other mythological themes in Cornelis's native Haarlem owed a great deal to his well-traveled colleagues Carel van Mander and Hendrick Goltzius. Many of the trio's subjects were vehicles for their interest in drawing from life, in antique and Renaissance sculpture (Cornelis's estate included numerous plaster casts and bronze or wax statuettes),[3] and in classical literature, especially love stories (such as those of Venus and Adonis and Diana and Actaeon) taken from Ovid's *Metamorphoses*.[4] The fables and particularly the adages occasionally were drawn upon for philosophical or moral edification, with the encounter of Venus, Bacchus, and Ceres seen by some contemporary writers as a warning against sensuality in general and, more pragmatically, against drinking too much.[5]

Cornelis, by contrast, seems to have shared the hedonistic sentiments of Spranger and Goltzius, both in the Lille painting and in an earlier and much larger picture in Dresden (see fig. 1).[6] At the same time, comparisons with previous interpretations and with the Dresden composition make the tender mood of the Lille picture all the more impressive, not least because of its intimate scale. Venus, a plain Dutch beauty, modestly takes an apple from Ceres' cornucopia, while Cupid, with his arm almost protectively around his mother, reaches for Bacchus's bunch of grapes. The god smiles as would a kindly uncle treating the boy to his first glass of wine. Ceres, identified by the stalks of wheat in her hair, is a passive figure whose solid pose expresses her close connection, as the goddess of grain or "cereals," with Mother Earth (*Tellus Mater*). The broadly balanced way she sits is an expressive counterpoint to Venus's tightly perched position, which suggests the coolness in the air. The detail of one foot rubbing the other is probably Cornelis's independent observation but it recalls the barefoot John the Baptist

12

98

seated in a chilly wilderness in Geertgen tot Sint Jans's painting in Berlin (Staatliche Museen Preussischer Kulturbesitz).

There are many similar figures in Cornelis's work of the preceding twenty years; to recount them all would be merely to illustrate the ease with which he adopted and modified nude figures in different contexts. Venus and Cupid in the Dresden picture (fig. 1) are very similar to the two lovers at a table in *The Golden Age*, also dated 1614 (Budapest, Szépmüvészeti Múzeum),[7] in which there is a male drinker who resembles Ceres. The Lille painting is a thorough revision of the Dresden design.[8] The result, a sort of "Two Graces" with male attendants, centered on the multicolored still life of fruit, is one of the artist's most exquisite achievements, to which the copper support lends an appropriate warmth.

WL

FIGURE 1. Cornelis Cornelisz. van Haarlem. *Venus, Cupid, Bacchus, and Ceres*. 1614. Oil on canvas. Staatliche Kunstsammlungen, Dresden

1 See Pigler, 1974, II, pp. 51–52, for a list of paintings and engravings dating mostly to about 1590–1620.

2 On this theme in Rubens's circle see Renger, 1981. For examples painted in Prague see Kaufmann, 1988, nos. 1.39 (*Bacchus, Ceres, and Cupid*, by Hans von Aachen), 6.7 (by Mattäus Grundelach), 20.48, 20.49 (by Bartholomeus Spranger).

3 See van Thiel, 1965, p. 128.

4 See Sluijter, 1985; Sluijter, 1986.

5 See Sluijter, 1986, pp. 261, 344 (n. 11-1, citing the foreword to D. D. Pers, *Den Gulden Winckel*, 1613). See also Sluijter's essay in

Washington–Detroit–Amsterdam, 1980–81, "Depiction of Mythological Themes," especially pp. 56–59.

6 See de Bosque, 1985, pp. 176–79, for examples by Spranger, Goltzius, and Carel van Mander; on Goltzius's famous drawing of the subject in the British Museum see Hirschmann, 1915, and Reznicek, 1961, I, pp. 284–88.

7 See Lowenthal, 1986, fig. 36.

8 The relief-like composition bears comparison with Rubens's celebrated painting of the subject (of about 1612–14) in Kassel, but there the figures openly refer to ancient sculpture and perhaps to Michelangelo, and the Epicurean theme is treated with almost Stoic gravity. See Stechow, 1968, pp. 48–49, on the Rubens painting, in which the figure of Venus recalls the artist's early drawing of Michelangelo's *Night* (Paris, Fondation Custodia; see Jaffé, 1977, fig. 20).

PROVENANCE
Gift of G. Herlin, 1928.

EXHIBITION
Lille–Arras–Dunkirk, 1972–73, no. 13.

LITERATURE
De Bosque, 1985, p. 92, colorpl.; Sluijter, 1986, p. 386 n. 46-6.

PIETER CODDE

Dutch

Amsterdam 1599–1678 Amsterdam

13   *A Young Scholar in His Study*

About 1630–33

Oil on wood, 18 1/8 x 13 3/8 in. (46 x 34 cm.)

Signed (at the bottom center of the desk) in monogram: CP

Inv. no. 240

This frequently published picture is certainly the most familiar seventeenth-century Dutch painting in Lille. The Amsterdam artist is seen at perhaps his finest moment in this small work, but its appeal cannot be explained solely in terms of art history and connoisseurship. The viewer's encounter with the subject is remarkable for its immediacy; as in Vermeer's interior views of about thirty years later, one has the misleading impression that Codde has merely recorded a scene staged in his studio. However, the theme and motifs are conventions, and the figure's expression was of course not captured in a moment but likewise was invented by Codde. The young scholar seems at once accessible and yet psycho-

13

logically distant; his thoughts, whatever they might be, reveal that there is more to everyday experience than the bare facts of one's physical environment or the knowledge acquired from large and learned tomes.

The exceptional nature of the picture is apparent from comparisons with other genre paintings by Codde and by artists in his circle, and with Dutch pictures similar in theme. From the late 1620s onward, Codde, Willem Duyster, and Simon Kick painted elegant companies in interiors and guardroom scenes that are broadly related to Haarlem views of high life by artists such as Willem Buytewech and Dirck Hals.[1] Many of Codde's works are multi-figure compositions set in what might be called a shoe-box space,[2] but from about 1630 to 1635 he, Dirck Hals, and a few other artists in the Haarlem-Amsterdam area also depicted solitary figures in simplified settings, often with only a wall in the background to delimit the space.[3] That these compositions owe something to the single-figure genre paintings of Hendrick ter Brugghen and other Utrecht painters is suggested by the Haarlem artist Judith Leyster's response to those examples, and by the closer attention to qualities of light and atmosphere that is usually found in works of this type.[4] It should be mentioned, however, that Dutch genre painting in general was moving in this direction and that a number of small-scale portraits—for example, the full-length figures by Hendrick de Keyser—exhibit some of the same formal qualities.[5] This connection with portraiture is of special interest with regard to Codde, since he was also a portraitist and Amsterdam portraits in general are perhaps the most subtly nuanced in their expression of thought and mood.

It may not be surprising, then, that modern critics have had difficulty in discerning the meaning of Codde's painting in Lille: The scholar is alternately dejected,[6] "contented with little,"[7] or ambivalent about the *vita contemplativa (ma non troppo*, in his case).[8] Literary interpretations that assign symbolism to the casually held pipe[9] or identify the figure as a personification of melancholy[10] trivialize the picture, which, unlike an emblem, was meant not for momentary edification but to be enjoyed repeatedly for its intriguing subject and as a visual experience. Thus, Chapman's reference to the fashionability of this theme—the affliction or affectation of melancholy as the appropriate mood of scholars, artists, poets, philosophers, and all others who are creatively inclined—comes closer than conventional iconographical analysis to an understanding of how this work was appreciated in its own day.[11] Rembrandt's self-portraits of the early 1630s, Jan Lievens's portrait of Constantijn Huygens (fig. 1), and Jan

FIGURE 1. Jan Lievens. *Portrait of Constantijn Huygens*. 1628. Oil on wood. Rijksmuseum, Amsterdam, on loan from the Musée de Douai, La Chartreuse (since 1962)

Davidsz. de Heem's early painting of a somber scholar in his study (with which the present picture is routinely compared)[12] are among the numerous contemporary explorations of melancholy or of creative and contemplative temperaments. By 1633 Codde was a published poet, and he surely would have been familiar with this theme.[13]

Codde's delicate treatment of textures and tones recalls the "monochrome" still lifes of precisely this period, one of which may have inspired the trompe-l'oeil motif of a nail in the undecorated but far from featureless wall.[14] The temptation to identify this plane with that of the picture lends life to the volume of space claimed by the abruptly receding floor. The latter and the jutting pipe accent the figure's impatiently settled pose, which contrasts with the desk's inertia. This scholar's mood is not the dark melancholy of Dürer or Huygens but the familiar frustration of youth.

The picture's style and the figure's costume suggest a date of about 1631–33.[15] It was in about the mid-1630s that Codde's paintings first came to the attention of the teenaged Gerard ter Borch. WL

1 See Sutton, in Philadelphia–Berlin–London, 1984, pp. XXXII–XXXIII; Liedtke, 1988, p. 100.

2 For example, see Philadelphia–Berlin–London, 1984, nos. 28, 29, and some of the paintings reproduced in Torresan, 1975.

3 Compare the Lille picture with Codde's *Self-Portrait* in the Museum Boymans-van Beuningen, Rotterdam (see Chapman, 1990, fig. 31); Dirck Hals's *Seated Woman with a Letter* of 1633 in the Philadelphia Museum of Art (see Philadelphia–Berlin–London, 1984, no. 46; see also comparative figures 1, 2 in that entry); and with various works by Judith Leyster (Hofrichter, 1989, plates 16–18, 26, 38 ff.).

4 See Hofrichter, 1989, pp. 24, 26.

5 De Keyser's *A Musician and His Daughter* of 1629 (New York, The Metropolitan Museum of Art) is a composition that sets the Lille picture in a broader context and at the same time underscores Codde's command of naturalistic effects.

6 See Playter, 1972, p. 89.

7 See Bauch, 1960, p. 246. This familiar Dutch notion was adopted as a title for the painting ("Le contentement de peu"): See Châtelet, 1970, no. 44; Paris, 1970–71, no. 40.

8 See Sutton, in Philadelphia–Berlin–London, 1984, p. 175, in the main following Oursel, in Lille, 1981, no. 37.

9 See de Mirimonde, 1970, p. 266 n. 37, who claims that the pipe is in the picture solely to emphasize that the vanity of human learning is nothing but smoke (which is, however, absent here).

10 See Lille, 1981, no. 37; Oursel, 1984, p. 25, fig. 15.

11 See Chapman, 1990, pp. 26–29.

12 See Brown, 1976, p. 50; Oursel, in Lille, 1981, p. 68; Sutton, in Philadelphia–Berlin–London, 1984, p. 175, fig. 1; Chapman, 1990, p. 28, fig. 29. On the de Heem see also van Gelder, 1950, no. 34; Meijer, 1988, p. 35.

13 See the biography in Philadelphia–Berlin–London, 1984, p. 174.

14 Jan de Heem employed the same motif in a *vanitas* still life of books, dated 1629, in Liberec, Czechoslovakia (letter from S. Segal dated October 8, 1991), and in the kitchen still life of 1631 in the Stedelijk Museum "De Lakenhal," Leiden (see Segal, 1991, no. 5, and see p. 35 on the illusionistic nail).

15 Sutton, in Philadelphia–Berlin–London, 1984, no. 27, dates the painting "c. 1628–30." The composition may be compared with interiors depicted by Dirck Hals in 1631 (see Liedtke, 1988, figs. 5–13) and 1633 (see note 3, above).

PROVENANCE

Private collection, Utrecht; Antoine Brasseur (1819–1886), Cologne; Gift of Antoine Brasseur, 1885.

EXHIBITIONS

Valenciennes, 1918, no. 62; Berlin, 1964, no. 8; Paris, 1965, no. 17; Paris, 1970–71, no. 40; Amsterdam, 1971, no. 16; Lille, 1981, no. 37; Philadelphia–Berlin–London, 1984, no. 27.

LITERATURE

Benoit, 1909, II, no. 84, pl. 60; Martin, 1925, p. 44, fig. 2; Plietzsch, 1956, p. 196, fig. 153; Bauch, 1960, pp. 245–46, fig. 217; Plietzsch, 1960, p. 30, fig. 20; Rosenberg, Slive, and ter Kuile, 1966, p. 109, pl. 79 A; de Mirimonde, 1970, p. 266, no. 37, fig. 19; Playter, 1972, pp. 89, 92–93; Brown, 1976, p. 50; Chapman, 1990, p. 28, fig. 30; Smith, 1990, p. 154, fig. 16.

ISACK JOUDERVILLE

Dutch

Leiden, about 1612–1645/48 Amsterdam

---

14   *Young Woman with a Candle*

Oil on wood, 26 x 20 in. (66 x 50.7 cm.)

Signed (at the lower right): Joud . . . [?]

Inv. no. 1786

This well-preserved painting represents a pretty young woman with a songbook in her left hand, which is strongly silhouetted by the flame from a single candlestick to her right. As in other Dutch genre paintings, a lute on the table suggests a romantic duet—a notion that the woman's expression, with lips parted in song, and a fancy dress that enhances her swelling bosom would have reinforced in the contemporary male viewer's imagination. As discussed below, the sky-blue gown with gold brocade and the magnificent baroque pearl earring may indicate that the figure is allegorical, but in any case her dress differs delightfully from what was considered proper attire at the time. These and other points of visual excitement emerge from the surrounding darkness in a private corner of space (the woman's shadow falls on a wall to the right) to evoke an evening's entertainment of the kind Samuel Pepys confided to his diary and Jacob Cats decried in his moralizing tracts.[1]

Isack Jouderville has lately become one of the most attentively studied pupils of Rembrandt, whereas a decade ago he was almost unknown.[2] In 1629 or 1630, when the twenty-three-year-old Rembrandt was closely associated with the slightly younger Jan Lievens, and had been Gerard Dou's teacher for less than a year, the newly orphaned Jouderville became an apprentice in his studio. Jouderville's guardians paid Rembrandt a fee covering the years 1630 and 1631, and they financed the pupil's two known trips to Amsterdam shortly after his apprenticeship ended in November 1631. It has been proposed that Jouderville may have served as Rembrandt's assistant in Amsterdam and that he had a hand in Rembrandt's portraits of patrician patrons painted about 1632–33.[3] However, Jouderville retained a residence in Leiden and enrolled in the city's celebrated university in April 1632. He married an Amsterdam woman in Leiden in February 1636 and appears to have remained there until the couple moved to Deventer in 1641. In 1643 he was in Amsterdam, where he died sometime between 1645 and 1648.

FIGURE 1. Jan Lievens. *Portrait of a Boy in Persian Dress*. 1631. Oil on wood. Formerly Private collection, England

FIGURE 2. Jan Lievens. *Bathsheba Receiving David's Letter*. About 1631. Oil on canvas. Formerly, art market, Los Angeles (now, Private collection)

All of the pictures plausibly attributed to Jouderville— there are only about sixteen—may be dated to the period from about 1631 to 1635. Other Dutch artists gave up painting as their main profession when they married; perhaps this was the case with Jouderville. His wife, Maria Lefevre, appears to have been active as a lace merchant, which was a flourishing trade in those years.[4]

On the grounds of quality alone the *Young Woman with a Candle* should be central to any discussion of Jouderville, which on the contrary has focused on his hypothetical role in Rembrandt's Amsterdam studio.[5] The painting has been dated to the mid-1630s but may be from 1632–33, to judge from its almost certain source of inspiration in works painted by Jan Lievens in or about 1631.[6]

Lievens left Leiden for London in 1632.[7] From 1631 to 1632 he painted several pictures of exotically clad young men and women who are theatrically lit from the side, as here. The most familiar example is the *Portrait of a Young Man in a Gold Robe (Self-Portrait?)* in the National Gallery of Scotland,

Edinburgh,[8] but the *Portrait of a Boy in Persian Dress* of 1631 (fig. 1) is more like the Lille painting, in part because of the similarity of support (panel) and size. A related type of young woman in fancy dress and with analogous silhouetting effects (which Lievens appears to have derived from the Utrecht painter Gerard Honthorst) is found in the *Fortune Teller* in the Staatliche Museen Preussischer Kulturbesitz, Berlin; the *Bathsheba Receiving David's Letter* (fig. 2) formerly in Los Angeles; and the *Young Woman with an Old Woman* formerly in Berlin; all are datable to about 1631.[9] Like Jouderville's woman, Lievens's figures are smoothly modeled, with crisp contours and sharp divisions between areas of light and shade. Both artists favor bright colors, especially in the costumes; in this and in their shallow spaces and comparatively slight attention to subtle effects of light and atmosphere these paintings by Jouderville and Lievens differ from those that Rembrandt painted in Leiden about 1631. Other single-figure paintings by Jouderville deserve close comparison with the last works Lievens painted in Leiden,[10] which is not to say that Rembrandt's influence was not strongly felt by Jouderville (as it was by Lievens) at the same time. However, in the genre-like paintings by Lievens mentioned above, it seems that Jouderville discovered models more sympathetic to his own abilities and manner than were the Rembrandt portraits on which almost all of his earlier efforts were based. One might summarize Jouderville's highly dependent development in very broad terms by suggesting that after his apprenticeship to Rembrandt (1630–31) Jouderville turned to the example of Lievens in Leiden, and then, about 1633 or 1634, to that of Dou.[11] Thus, the *Young Woman with a Candle*, which, to judge from the files at the Lille museum, once appeared to have come out of nowhere,[12] can be placed precisely in the context of Rembrandt and Lievens, about 1631–32. In this regard, the painting's anticipation of Dou and of later Leiden artists such as Godfried Schalcken seems almost inevitable.

The picture's meaning was clarified when a painted *cartellino* bearing a moralizing inscription disappeared during cleaning in 1977, thus removing a misleading element.[13] Music connotes sensual pleasure and, by its measured progress, underscores the temporal nature of worldly things. This commonplace theme is treated with textbook lucidity in the frontispiece to an actual lute book, Georg Leopold Fuhrmann's collection of European compositions, published in 1615 (see fig. 3):[14] Next to a lute and a songbook are plucked flowers of particular fragility—a quality they share

FIGURE 3. Georg Leopold Fuhrmann. *Testudo Gallo-Germanica.* Nuremberg, 1615. Frontispiece. Bayerische Staatsbibliothek, Munich

with human beauty and youth.[15] A hand in the sky assists slow-witted viewers by drawing attention to the urn in a niche: The vessel is composed of a death's-head from which serpents and a somber cloud emerge.[16] Burning candles frequently symbolize mortality in Dutch paintings with *vanitas* themes, and here the frame of the niche is inscribed *Vanitas Vanitatum et omnia Vanitas* ("Vanity of vanities; all is vanity").[17]

The allegorical nature of Jouderville's painting would have been evident to his contemporaries not only from its still-life motifs but also from the woman's unusual dress. The same sort of stage costume occurs in Rembrandt's *Musical Allegory* of 1626 (Amsterdam, Rijksmuseum).[18] The pearls, an attribute of Venus,[19] and, of course, the lady herself recall music's intimate relationship with love.[20] That warm emotion, not the moral lessons for which Leiden artists are known, is at the heart of Jouderville's vision by candlelight. For a brief moment, this young artist had something in common with Rembrandt, beyond his immature understanding of Rembrandt's style.

WL

1 On Pepys's diary and Dutch genre painting see Liedtke, 1991, pp. 234–37. An appropriate comparison in Cats, not least for the lady's dress and abundant pearls, is emblem XLVII in the "Mirror of Olden and Modern Times," which illustrates Cats's characteristic complaint that "a woman without shame is like a lamp with no light" (Jacob Cats, *Spiegel van den ouden ende nieuwen tijdt*, The Hague, 1632, p. 141: The emblem is reproduced and compared with Rembrandt's *Musical Allegory* of 1626, in Schwartz, 1985, pp. 42–43, figs. 23, 25).

2 See Amsterdam–Groningen, 1983, pp. 59–69, 178–81; Bruyn, 1982, II, pp. 76–88, III, pp. 31–34; Sumowski, 1983, II, pp. 1434–52, V, pp. 3104–5, 3241–45; Berlin–Amsterdam–London, 1991–92, pp. 308–13.

3 Bruyn, 1982, II, pp. 78–88, nos. C 68–69, III, pp. 31–34. This view is debated in Liedtke, 1989, and is doubted by Brown, in Berlin–Amsterdam–London, 1991–92, p. 308.

4 See van de Wetering, in Amsterdam–Groningen, 1983, p. 60, citing Bredius, 1915–22, pp. 1963, 1969. The name *Lefevre* might indicate that the family came from the Southern Netherlands, where lace manufacture was a specialty of several towns. In the same paragraph van de Wetering cites the first (and last) mention of Jouderville as an independent painter: in 1641 a shoemaker asked for the return of his lace collar, which Jouderville had reportedly used when painting the man's portrait and which got mixed up with items in Maria Lefevre's inventory. Of course, the portrait, now unknown, could have dated from sometime between Jouderville's marriage in 1636 (or even earlier) and 1641. Bruyn, 1982, III, p. 31, notes that "Jouderville did, during his later career in Leiden after 1636, paint portraits and may thus have been involved in earlier years in Rembrandt's studio production in this field." Thus, the shoemaker's collar serves as a lifesaver for Bruyn's "workshop hypothesis" (on which see Liedtke, 1989; Liedtke, 1992).

5 See note 3, above. The 1992–93 exhibition of works from Lille at The Metropolitan Museum of Art, New York, will allow this securely attributed work to be compared directly with two paintings that Josua Bruyn has credited largely to Jouderville: the "Van Beresteyn" pendant portraits, which are each signed "RHL van Rijn" and dated 1632 (see Bruyn, 1982, II, nos. C 68–69).

6 Sumowski, 1983, II, p. 1437, proposed the mid-1630s date. To my knowledge the connection between Jouderville and Lievens has never been considered before.

7 See Brown, 1983-1, especially p. 670.

8 See Braunschweig, 1979, no. 31, cover ill.; Sumowski, 1983, III, no. 1264.

9 See Sumowski, 1983, III, nos. 1187, 1189, 1188, respectively. Compare such Caravaggesque pictures as Hendrick ter Brugghen's *Songstress* in Basel, and Jan van Bijlert's *Girl with a Lute* and Honthorst's *Soldier with a Girl* both in Braunschweig; all were exhibited in Utrecht–Braunschweig, 1986–87, nos. 28, 43, 62.

10 For example, Jouderville's *Young Woman* in Augsburg, the *Standing Woman in Fancy Dress* and the *Flora* (see Sumowski, 1983, II, nos. 943–945), and the *Young Woman in Profile* (Sumowski, 1983, V, no. 2104 a), which might be compared with works by Lievens published in Braunschweig, 1979, and in Sumowski, 1983, III. One should also compare such seemingly Rembrandtesque exercises as Jouderville's *Young Woman* in Helsinki (Sumowski, 1983, II, no. 942) with Lievens's *Portrait of the Young Rembrandt* (Sumowski, 1983, III, no. 1260): The scheme of lighting in the face and the drapery's relationship to the body, two areas in which Jouderville is said to reveal his hand (see Christopher Brown's quote from van de Wetering in Berlin–Amsterdam–London, 1991–92, pp. 308–10), are possibly dependent on the example of Lievens. Works by Lievens and Rembrandt were already confused in the early 1630s and an artist of Jouderville's discrimination would have found the two painters equally inspiring.

11 The main evidence for Jouderville's "Anschluss an Dou" (Sumowski, 1983, II, p. 1434) is the *Violinist in a Painter's Studio* formerly in Berlin (Sumowski's no. 951; see also no. 952).

12 Or everywhere: a variety of well-known scholars have proposed attributions to Willem de Poorter, Hendrick Pot, Pieter de Grebber, Pieter Potter, Johannes Verspronck, Gerbrand van den Eeckhout, Godfried Schalcken, Arnold Boonen, and Jan Rutgers van Niwael.

13 Compare Lille–Arras–Dunkirk, 1972–73, no. 75, and Sumowski, 1983, II, p. 1437, under no. 946.

14 See Fischer, 1975, pp. 52–54, on this book and the engraving, where the letters at the frets express the intended function of the book as a whole: to present music in the French-Netherlandish tablature.

15 There are numerous seventeenth-century paintings and prints in which cut flowers and musical instruments are combined in the context of a *vanitas* theme: see, for example, Leiden, 1970, nos. 1, 8, 13, 17, 20.

16 Fischer, 1975, p. 54, quotes the verse from Psalms 102: 3–4, which is cited in almost every study of *vanitas* painting: "For my days are consumed like smoke, and my bones are burned like an hearth."

17 The phrase is from the opening lines of Ecclesiastes 1: 2. See Louis Marin, "Les traverses de la vanité," in Tapié, 1990, p. 21.

18 See note 1, above, and Bruyn, 1982, I, no. A 7 (see p. 120 on the costumes).

19 See de Jongh, 1975–76.

20 See Fischer, 1975, chap. V.

PROVENANCE

Recovered in Germany by the French government, after 1945; Dépôt de l'État, 1953.

EXHIBITION

Lille–Arras–Dunkirk, 1972–73, no. 75.

LITERATURE

Sumowski, 1983, II, pp. 1437, 1445, no. 946.

FRANS VAN MIERIS THE ELDER

Dutch

Leiden 1635–1681 Leiden

---

15 *The Wife of Jeroboam with the Prophet Ahijah*

Oil on wood, 9 1/2 x 7 7/8 in. (24 x 20 cm.)

Signed and dated (at the bottom right): *F. van Mieris. fec A° 1671*

Inv. no. 293

During his short career the Leiden painter Frans van Mieris, whom Gerard Dou considered "the prince of his pupils,"[1] produced dozens of highly finished genre scenes and less numerous but equally refined portraits and history pictures. The small panel in Lille may be counted among van Mieris's least familiar compositions; it has just undergone its first cleaning in many years.

In several respects the painting contributes to the view that van Mieris was one of the more eccentric artists of his time. This assessment is supported not only by a number of peculiar paintings but also by inconsistent details of the artist's biography. The high quality of his works, beginning with the earliest, earned van Mieris the admiration of his colleagues in the Leiden painters' guild and the patronage of Grand Duke Cosimo III de' Medici and of Archduke Leopold Wilhelm. Nonetheless, van Mieris was constantly in debt.[2] His family life and steady production contrast with the biographer Arnold Houbraken's image of the artist as a drunkard, which appears to be confirmed by documents. However, the strongest sense of an unusual personality derives from van Mieris's painted cast of characters, who often contribute an element of the unexpected to conventional scenes of everyday life, let alone to subjects like the present one. Van Mieris favored figures characterized by demonstra-

tive gestures and strong, sometimes grimacing expressions; the impression that the artist saw his genre and history paintings as similar to scenes staged in the contemporary theater is more striking than in the oeuvre of any other Dutch painter with the exception of the very different work of Jan Steen.[3] Finally, a few examples of obscure subject matter (*Gyges Spying on the Wife of Candaulus* in the Staatliches Museum in Schwerin) and of new twists on familiar themes (*The Dead Lucretia Discovered by Her Maid* in a private collection in Sweden; and the nearly unrecognizable *Bathsheba* in the Gemäldegalerie in Dresden) add to the distinctive flavor of van Mieris's inventions.[4] Their self-consciously sophisticated style and themes introduce a note of courtly decadence into the domestic worlds represented by the artist's contemporaries such as Metsu and Vermeer.

Jeroboam was the first king of Israel after the Lord "tore the kingdom away from the house of David" (I Kings 14: 8; 14: 1–20 for the full account). When the son of Jeroboam fell sick, the king told his unnamed wife to disguise herself, go to Shiloh, and see the prophet Ahijah, who had predicted Jeroboam's rule. With the queen, Jeroboam sent "ten loaves, some cakes, and a jar of honey." (In the painting, the baked goods are borne by the servant in the background at the right.) God had already instructed Ahijah to advise Jeroboam that unlike David he had made himself "other gods, and melted images, to provoke me to anger," and that when his wife arrived at the threshold of Jeroboam's house their son would die. This bitter news is told by Ahijah in van Mieris's picture; the prophet, who in any event could not see "by reason of his age," knew the identity of his veiled visitor as soon as he heard her steps. With her satin dress, her large but tapered body, and her familiar features (which resemble those of the artist's wife),[5] Jeroboam's queen is a typical van Mieris figure, but the blind old man with his staff, his faithful dog (not mentioned in the Bible), and his emotive behavior seems like a character borrowed from the Leiden works of Rembrandt, or, rather, from his Leiden circle, which included the young Dou.[6]

The biblical subject is rare even by the contemporary standards of the Rembrandt school in Amsterdam, although its obscurity might reflect the intellectual climate of an important university town such as Leiden.[7] As noted by Otto Naumann, however, episodes from the story of Jeroboam, if not this one, were depicted by several Dutch artists.[8] An example not cited previously in connection with the Lille picture is Willem de Poorter's painting of the 1640s, *Jeroboam's Idol Worship Rebuked* (fig. 1), in the Bob Jones Uni-

FIGURE 1. Willem de Poorter. *Jeroboam's Idol Worship Rebuked.* About 1640–45. Oil on canvas. Bob Jones University Collection of Sacred Art, Greenville, South Carolina

versity Collection of Sacred Art, Greenville, South Carolina.[9]

Stories of idolaters and their inevitable downfall had been popular with Dutch painters, writers, and, undoubtedly, preachers since the late sixteenth century. The theme, which usually featured autocratic and superstitious royalty, was for the officially Calvinist Republic of the United Netherlands an ideal analogy for the Roman Catholic Church and its oppressive patron, the Spanish crown. Van Mieris conforms to this widely held viewpoint but he presents it in unconventional terms: Instead of the usual crowd scene he employs two figures, in a private confrontation, to tell a tale of personal tragedy. A regretful prophet informs the misguided mother what her husband's folly will cost.

One measure of van Mieris's maturity in this work is the coherence—or, one might say, integrity—of his pictorial and expressive effects. For example, the immediate contrast of the woman's finery with the prophet's coarse robe is an aesthetic touch that also goes to the heart of the matter, which is the conflict between material and spiritual values, or, more topically, aristocratic luxury compared with the humble virtues of what looks like a modest Dutch home (with archaizing architectural elements to the right). The old man's heartfelt expression and the declarative stroke of his hand are similarly set off by the queen's graceful gesture and pose, and by the well-bred reserve with which she receives a devastating prediction. This reading suggests that the artist painted a gourd—Ahijah's water jug—hanging from a nail in the wall not only because it enriches the composition with a virtuoso passage of still-life painting, but also as a rebuttal to the woman's stylish honey jar. The latter is intended as ancient earthenware but its resemblance to a contemporary Dutch or Flemish silver vessel is one of several hints in the picture that its message is relevant to van Mieris's time.

WL

1 Quoted in Philadelphia–Berlin–London, 1984, p. 256, without referring to the source, which is Houbraken, 1718–21, III, p. 1.

2 See Naumann, 1981-2, especially p. 653.

3 Steen was also from Leiden and is well known for his connections with the comic stage (Gudlaugsson, 1975). However, Plietzsch, 1960, p. 54, pl. 72, overestimates the importance of Steen for the Lille painting.

4 See Naumann, 1981-1, II, nos. 84, 116, 87, respectively.

5 Compare Naumann, 1981-1, II, no. 30.

6 Compare Bruyn, 1982, I, nos. A 3, A 11–A 13, A 36, C 2, C 3.

7 At the same time it should be noted that about 1660 Jacob Jordaens designed an unrealized series of tapestries devoted to the history of Jeroboam that included the present scene (see d'Hulst, 1974, II, nos. A 369–A 373, figs. 390, 388–389, 391–392, respectively; d'Hulst, 1982, p. 307).

8 See Naumann, 1981-1, I, p. 89 n. 11.

9 See Bader, 1976, no. 47.

PROVENANCE

Probably sale of the comte de Watteville collection, Paris, July 12, 1779, no. 11; probably sale of the Duruey collection, Paris, June 21, 1797, no. 10; sale of the Messchert van Vollenhoven collection, Amsterdam, March 29, 1892, no. 5; Joseph Ruston, Lincoln, England; sale of the Ruston collection, London, Christie's, May 21 and 23, 1898, no. 88; purchased, 1899.

EXHIBITIONS

Valenciennes, 1918, no. 232; Paris, 1970–71, no. 147; Amsterdam, 1971, no. 62.

LITERATURE

Phillips, 1894, p. 25; Benoit, 1909, II, pp. 343–44, no. 127; Naumann, 1978, p. 15, fig. 21, p. 22, no. 40; Naumann, 1981-1, I, pp. 89–90, II, pp. 97–98, no. 85, pl. 85.

EMANUEL DE WITTE

Dutch

Alkmaar, about 1617–1692 Amsterdam

16 *The Choir of the New Church in Delft, with the Tomb of William the Silent*

Oil on canvas, 38 1/4 x 33 1/2 in. (97 x 85 cm.)

Signed and dated (at the lower left): E. de Witte / Ao 1656

Inv. no. 236

This picture by Emanuel de Witte, one of the artist's most admired works, is an ideal example of his distinctive interests and style as an architectural painter. In subject and composition, this view of the Dutch republic's most important national monument depends upon de Witte's close association in Delft with two other representatives of the genre, Gerard Houckgeest (about 1600–1661) and Hendrick van Vliet (1611/12–1675). However, this canvas dates from about four years after de Witte moved to Amsterdam, by which time his unusual approach to the theme of the church interior had fully matured.

There is little here to remind one that views of church interiors had been a perspectivist's specialty for about fifty years, or that the composition derives ultimately from one of Houckgeest's most complex perspective constructions—that employed in a painting dated 1650 (fig. 1) and in an expanded version of the same view dated 1651 (The Hague, Mauritshuis).[1] The earlier of Houckgeest's two pictures includes almost all of the elements found in de Witte's painting: the tomb of William the Silent, surrounded by the choir's easternmost columns and the ambulatory; a view of the choir's balcony (or triforium), with Spanish pennants hung as war trophies above; various escutcheons with family crests, which memorialize members of the congregation buried beneath the stone floor; and visitors to the monument, including a couple in the foreground (the man gestures toward the tomb in both pictures), a young girl, a boy with a greyhound, and one or two other dogs.

Despite his obvious debt to Houckgeest, whose example gave the younger artist his start in the genre about 1650–51,[2] de Witte's painting reveals an extraordinary shift in emphasis. Houckgeest, like a draftsman working for an architect, depicts every part of the choir visible from his station point in the ambulatory—a position that seems to have been selected in order to present a side and a rear view of the tomb.

16

The view encompasses the choir's clerestory, a bit of its wooden barrel vault, the ribbed vaulting of the ambulatory almost directly overhead, and much more of the floor in the foreground and to the sides. The checkered pattern of floor tiles did not extend throughout the choir and ambulatory of the actual church but is arbitrarily introduced by Houckgeest to articulate space: Columns and figures are placed on the floor like pieces on a chessboard. De Witte restores a realistic stone floor to the church, brings the view in much closer to the monument, and in doing so moves leftward, so that the viewer, with the figures in the foreground, approaches the tomb from the side. The gesture of the man in the striking red cloak (and the arrangement of all the figures near him) draws attention to the two effigies of William I: the seated warrior in bronze, and the recumbent martyr in marble. A monument that enshrines political independence and heroic sacrifice appears to be of topographical interest to Houckgeest, but of human interest to de Witte. The latter's view seems quieter, the visitors more attentive to the tomb, and the act of charity, a motif common in paintings of church interiors but enacted here with exceptional tenderness, becomes linked with the national character of the Dutch.

The sense of stillness in the Lille painting is found in many pictures by de Witte and in good part depends upon his attention to light. For this artist the interior of a church had less to do with architectural elements than with the feeling of open and ascending space, where light and shade make solid forms visible and immaterial at once. Diaphanous views through windows and white walls rendered as luminous veils give de Witte's interiors a sense of continuity with everything under heaven and with heaven itself. De Witte in Amsterdam remained a Delft painter insofar as this designation calls for comparisons with Carel Fabritius, Pieter de Hooch, and Jan Vermeer.[3] The meaningful analogy to Vermeer, however, is that for him and for de Witte the most interesting aspects of the visual world were its intangible qualities: Experience was always subjective, and reality something more than words could describe.

WL

1 See Liedtke, 1982, figs. 23, 23 a, 24, for both paintings and a perspective scheme of the Mauritshuis picture.

2 Their relationship is the subject of Liedtke, 1982, chap. 1.

3 See Liedtke, 1982, pp. 84–96, on de Witte in Amsterdam.

PROVENANCE

Probably sale of the Daniel Marsbag collection, Amsterdam, October 30, 1775, no. 123; probably sale of the Luchtmans collection, Rotter-

FIGURE 1. Gerard Houckgeest. *The New Church in Delft, with the Tomb of William the Silent.* 1650. Oil on wood. Christie's, London, July 8, 1977

dam, April 20, 1816, no. 167; Count Schönborn, Pommersfelden (1857 cat., no. 230); sale of the Schönborn collection, Paris, May 17, 1867, no. 133; Gustave Rothan, Paris; sale of the Rothan collection, Paris, May 29–31, 1890, no. 119; Morhange, Paris, 1890; purchased by the Musée des Beaux-Arts with funds from the Antoine Brasseur Gift, 1890.

EXHIBITIONS

Valenciennes, 1918, no. 406; Berlin, 1964, no. 52; Paris, 1967–1, no. 306; Lille, 1970, no. 53; Paris, 1970–71, no. 237; Amsterdam, 1971, no. 43; Lille, 1981, no. 78; Rotterdam, 1991, no. 38.

LITERATURE

Benoit, 1909, II, no. 104; Jantzen, 1910, pp. 119–20, 175, no. 617; Manke, 1963, no. 27, fig. 35; Liedtke, 1982, p. 88; Oursel, 1984, no. 23; Schama, 1988, pp. 565–66, fig. 293.

JOHANN LISS

German

Holstein 1595/97–1631 Verona

---

17   *The Finding of Moses*

Oil on canvas, 61 x 41 3/4 in. (155 x 106 cm.)

Inv. no. 22

This superb painting depicts the finding of Moses in the bulrushes by Pharaoh's daughter, who took pity on the Hebrew infant and entrusted him to the care of her own mother, shown here in the background looking on. This Old Testament subject (Exodus 2: 5–6) served as the pretext for representing a sumptuous outdoor scene, filled with emotion and exotic richness, and was a favorite theme in Venetian painting. The celebrated—and much copied—canvas by Veronese in the Museo del Prado, Madrid, was surely Liss's point of departure when he began the present work. At the same time, Liss achieved a new and strikingly modern composition by eccentrically placing the figure group of three women to the left, their faces in *profil perdu*. His Northern European origins and early experience in genre painting afforded the German artist a special facility for rendering genuine feelings, such as, here, the instinctive tenderness of the women toward the abandoned baby.

Liss dispenses with the haughty nobility of Veronese's heroines in favor of a more intimate and sensual female figure type. In describing the fleshy back of the servant, the seductive décolletage of Pharaoh's daughter and her full lips, and the plump form of the little Moses, Liss was inspired by the female figures of Hendrick ter Brugghen and the anatomical studies by Jacob Jordaens. Steinbart (1959) noted the influence on Liss of such works as Jordaens's *Temptation of the Magdalene* of 1618–20, also in Lille (see fig. 7, p. 46): Jordaens's Magdalene, with eyes downcast and her face half hidden in the shadows of her veil, is almost identical to the female figure in the background of Liss's painting.

This blend of European culture—with elements borrowed from the Venetian Renaissance and from the later Caravaggesque painters in the North—enabled Liss to execute this masterful composition in a cadenced style of light and color: The last rays of sunlight glowing in a twilight sky are reflected in the golden highlights of the exquisite yellow gown, in the drapery's translucent whiteness, and in the shimmering blue fabric in the foreground. Such a natural and poetic description of the setting sun looks forward to Claude

Lorrain, while the old women standing at the right anticipate Piazzetta, and the sensual ripeness of the younger women offers a foretaste of Fragonard.

The painting deservedly may be considered one of the first examples of the Venetian Baroque style; indeed, Rodolfo Palluchini, in 1950, even cited the *Finding of Moses* as the most important work of the seventeenth-century Venetian School. At this point in his career Liss had completely adopted an Italian manner and had forsaken the more minutely descriptive approach favored by his Northern colleagues. The Lille picture is a prelude to the grand religious compositions of Liss's late career. Dating the work precisely is difficult, but scholars such as Safarik and Klessmann have concurred in placing it after 1625; Klessmann considers the picture close to Liss's *David* in the Palazzo Reale, Naples. Whether the *Moses* was in the Algarotti collection in Venice in the eighteenth century remains unconfirmed.[1]

Unfortunately, the picture is somewhat abraded, as in the drapery of the figure at the far right, the face of the second figure from the right, and the foliage. However, the *Finding of Moses* remains a masterwork in a collection rich in paintings of the Venetian School of the sixteenth (Veronese) through the eighteenth century (Guardi). With respect to Liss's country of origin, painting and sculpture from Germany is amply represented in examples dating from about 1400 to the artist's own time.

ABL

1 See the excellent entry by Tzeutschler-Lurie in Augsburg–Cleveland, 1975–76. Among related works, there is a drawn copy (pen and brown ink, brush, paint) attributed to a late-seventeenth-century follower of Castiglione, and a reduced replica that is the pendant to the *David and Saul* listed in the 1674 inventory of the collection of Giovan Maria Viscardi.

PROVENANCE

Possibly in the Algarotti collection, Venice, in the eighteenth century; sale of the Camille Rogier collection, Paris, Hôtel Drouot, May 26–28, 1896, no. 27, ill. (as by Strozzi); acquired at that sale by the Musée des Beaux-Arts.

EXHIBITIONS

Valenciennes, 1918, no. 212; Ghent, 1950, no. 29; Berlin, 1964, no. 28; Berlin, 1966, no. 48; Augsburg–Cleveland, 1975–76, no. A-30; Strasbourg, 1987, no. 70; Paris–Milan, 1988–89, no. 95.

LITERATURE

Lenglart, 1893, suppl. 3, no. 1139 (as Strozzi); Oldenbourg, 1914, p. 159, fig. 13; Oldenbourg, 1915, p. 57; von Bode, 1920, p. 176; Gavelle and Turpin, 1920, p. 12; Oldenbourg, 1921-1, pp. 11, 16, pl. XIX; Posse, 1925–26, p. 27; Pevsner and Grautoff, 1928, p. 157; Fiocco, 1929, p. II; Peltzer, in Thieme-Becker, XXIII, 1929, p. 286; Hind, 1931, p. 151;

Leblanc, 1932, p. 27 (as Strozzi); Pallucchini, 1934, p. 15; Steinbart, 1940, p. 178; Ghent, 1950, no. 29, pl. XXIV; Pallucchini, 1950, p. 179; Bloch, 1955, p. 324, fig. 24; Delogu, 1958, p. 277; Berlin, 1964, no. 28, ill.; Bloch, 1966, p. 544, fig. 84, p. 546; Donzelli and Pilo, 1967, pp. 241–42, fig. 261, colorpl. V; Ewald, 1967, p. 10; Châtelet, 1970-1, p. 47, no. 29, ill. p. 75; Klessmann, 1970, pp. 292–93; Tzeutschler-Lurie, in Augsburg–Cleveland, 1975–76, pp. 103–4, no. A-30, fig. 30, colorpl. VI; Adriani, in *Petit Larousse*, 1979, p. 1036; Pallucchini, 1981, I, p. 148; Oursel, 1984, p. 38, fig. 26; Klessmann, 1986, pp. 192–93; Roy, in Strasbourg, 1987, no. 70, color ill.; Volle, in Paris–Milan, 1988–89, no. 95; Brejon de Lavergnée, 1989-1, p. 554, fig. 840 (color).

GEORGES LALLEMANT

French

Nancy, about 1575–1636 Paris

---

18 *The Adoration of the Magi*

Oil on canvas, 74 1/2 x 124 in. (189 x 315 cm.)

Inv. no. 322

Lallemant was one of the most successful and influential painters working in Paris during the first third of the seventeenth century. His obscurity in modern times began in effect with the French Revolution, when many canvases he had supplied to churches were seized and dispersed. This change in critical fortune is virtually symbolized by the Lille *Adoration*, since in 1801 it was sent by the government to the Musée des Beaux-Arts as a work of the Venetian School. From 1810 until 1937, when Charles Sterling suggested Lallemant's authorship, the painting was attributed to Claude Vignon (1593–1670).[1]

The arrival from Italy of Lallemant's chief competitor, Simon Vouet, in 1627, is treated as another revolution in some surveys of French art, but Lallemant's altarpieces and tapestries for Notre-Dame and the six large paintings for Sainte-Geneviève-du-Mont in Paris, as well as other commissions dating from 1630 to his death in 1636 suggest that the artist's reputation was still on the rise in these years.[2] For at least brief periods Philippe de Champaigne (see cat. no. 19), Laurent de La Hyre (see cat. no. 20), and Poussin were Lallemant's pupils.[3]

When Lallemant established himself in Paris about 1601 the dominant painters were Ambroise Dubois, Toussaint Dubreuil, and Martin Fréminet—the "Second School of Fontainebleau." Their activity, especially after the death of Dubreuil in 1602, has been described as a "state of general mediocrity," in contrast to the situation in Lallemant's home-

land, the duchy of Lorraine.[4] Among Lallemant's contemporaries from his native Nancy were the painter Claude Deruet, the celebrated etcher Jacques Callot, and the sophisticated Mannerist engraver Jacques Bellange. Only Bellange, who may have been Lallemant's teacher, was older than Lallemant and a likely influence on his work.

Lallemant's earliest known painting is the group portrait *The Lord Mayor and Aldermen of Paris* (Paris, Musée Carnavalet), which was commissioned in 1611.[5] The portraits strongly recall those by Frans Pourbus the Younger, who was active in France from 1609 to 1622. The Virgin and saints set in niches in the background, however, are reminiscent of Bellange's elegantly attenuated religious figures. This combination of Flemish realism and a distinctly non-Parisian Mannerism—which, itself, had Netherlandish roots—could be described as the foundation of Lallemant's eclectic style. The one Fontainebleau artist with whom he bears comparison is Dubois, who came from Antwerp and for whom Frans Floris, Spranger, and Stradanus were stronger influences than Primaticcio or Dubois's other predecessors at Fontainebleau. As in Dubois's oeuvre, Lallemant's Mannerism is more restrained than that of Bellange or of the Spranger-inspired works of Goltzius, Cornelisz. van Haarlem, and Wtewael (see cat. no. 11); this is evident even in pictures less mature than the Lille *Adoration*, such as the cut-down canvas of the same subject in the Hermitage in Saint Petersburg.[6] However, Lallemant's work shares with that of his colleagues from Lorraine evocations of Late Gothic painting and sculpture, which are sensed in the present picture not only in the proportions and rhythmic arrangement of the figures but also in their realism—in the case of the two standing kings, Balthasar and Caspar—their angularity, their sharply defined drapery folds, and in the strong colors and rich ornamentation of their costumes. This may explain why the Lille painting, with the exception of the fashionable entourage on the right, seems surprisingly like Hugo van der Goes's *Adoration of the Magi* (the Monforte Altarpiece in the Staatliche Museen Preussischer Kulturbesitz, Berlin) brought up-to-date.

To judge from what is known of Lallemant's oeuvre and from works by other artists in Paris, this picture probably was painted about the time that he was appointed *Peintre ordinaire du roi*—that is, 1626—or within two or three years later. The kneeling king (Melchior) recalls the work of Vignon (who had returned from Rome about 1624) in the conspicuous splay of fingers and a few other flourishing effects.[7] The same figure's head and the type of the Virgin

18: detail

and Child appear indebted, by contrast, to Vouet, whose Madonnas of the 1620s may be traced, in turn, to Guido Reni and Domenichino.[8] Lallemant's figure of the Virgin maintains a Roman reserve (if not quite down to her fingertips) in the midst of a courtly Parisian crowd.

In many ways Lallemant's *Adoration* looks outmoded when compared with contemporary religious paintings in Antwerp or Utrecht (however, Abraham Bloemaert, who was a decade older than Lallemant, employed a similar palette and spatial effects in the 1620s). Nonetheless, in Paris this was the *pénultième cri*, and the more exotic details were very much in vogue at the same time in Holland and Flanders. The turbans and plumed berets echo contemporary costumes in imaginary portraits by Rembrandt and by Lievens, while the three gifts of the Magi are recent Flemish or German table decorations in silver gilt, with decidedly secular motifs. Rubens and his followers painted pictures of the Adoration in the 1620s that are equally filled with receding ranks of exotic figures, not to mention the ox and the ass, and fragments of classical architecture. These comparisons reveal that the painting in Lille, despite its busy surface and entertaining details, is also a strongly structured and concentrated composition in which the Savior and the act of adoration are emphasized. Perhaps, for Lallemant, style and content were somewhat separate concerns, but his command of both made him the artist to see in Paris for an important altarpiece.[9]

WL

1 See Sterling, 1937, fig. 7.

2 See Millar, 1967, pp. 158–59 ff., for the eyewitness records of Lallemant's paintings made by Richard Symonds in 1649. See also Blunt, I, 1967, p. 16.

3 On Poussin's relationship to Lallemant see Blunt, 1967, I, pp. 16–19.

4 See Blunt, 1970, p. 106.

5 See Blunt, 1967, I, pp. 16–18, fig. 12.

6 See Ramade, in Meaux, 1988–89, p. 120, ill.

7 Compare Vignon's *Adoration of the Magi* of 1624 in the church of Saint-Gervais–Saint-Protais in Paris (see Meaux, 1988–89, no. 37).

8 Compare the following paintings by Vouet in Thuillier, 1990: nos. 17 (*The Apparition of the Virgin to Saint Bruno* of 1626), 18 (*The Holy Family with the Infant Saint John the Baptist* of 1626), 26 (*Portrait of Gaucher de Châtillon* of about 1633).

9 Accordingly, Ramade's remark in Meaux, 1988–89, p. 119, that the costumes, jewels, and so on "constituent le véritable sujet du tableau," can be considered a cliché less in tune with Lallemant than with outdated books on Mannerism.

PROVENANCE

Said to have come from a church in Paris; assigned by the Revolutionary commission to the Musée des Beaux-Arts, 1801.

EXHIBITIONS

Lille–Dunkirk–Valenciennes, 1980, no. 11; Meaux, 1988–89, no. 28.

LITERATURE

Reynart, 1856, no. 214 (as by Vignon); Gonse, 1874, p. 142; Benoit, 1909, III, p. 393; Leblanc, 1932, p. 18; Sterling, 1937, fig. 7; Oursel, 1984, p. 45; Ramade, in Meaux, 1988–89, pp. 119–20, no. 28.

PHILIPPE DE CHAMPAIGNE

French

Brussels 1602–1674 Paris

19 *The Nativity*

Oil on canvas (with arched top), 81 1/2 x 45 5/8 in. (207 x 116 cm.)

Inv. no. 162

The patron who commissioned this picture, Jacques Tubeuf, as well as the institution for which it was made, the Maison de l'Oratoire, enjoyed considerable importance in mid-seventeenth-century Parisian society. Tubeuf, the son of Simon Tubeuf and Marie Talon, became director of the Exchequer in 1636, president of the Chamber of Finance in

FIGURE 1. Philippe de Champaigne. *Portrait of Jacques Tubeuf.* Musée des Beaux-Arts, Vienne

1643, and intendant, comptroller general of finances, and commissioner of buildings to Anne of Austria in 1645.[1] The recently discovered posthumous inventory of Tubeuf's estate, drawn up in August 1670, indicates that he owned a number of paintings, including Simon Vouet's *Death of Dido* (Dôle, Musée Municipal) and a work by Pieter Brueghel the Younger.[2] Tubeuf also had his portrait painted by Philippe de Champaigne (see fig. 1).[3] He engaged the distinguished architects Pierre Le Muet (1591–1669) and François Mansart (1598–1666) to build him a house in Paris, the Hôtel de Chevry (now part of the Bibliothèque Nationale), which Tubeuf was obliged to sell to Cardinal Mazarin in 1643.[4]

The Maison de l'Oratoire, in the rue Saint-Honoré, housed one of the most famous religious orders in France: the Oratoire de Jésus et Marie. It was founded in Paris on November 11, 1621, by Pierre de Bérulle (1575–1629), who believed in the necessity of training the clergy according to the doctrines advanced by the Council of Trent. However, the Congregation remained open to a wide variety of intellectual currents, as Viard's recent account observes: "In the house in the rue Saint-Honoré, about 1670 to 1675, one could find inhabitants as diverse as Father Quesnel, the apologist of Jansenius and Arnauld; outspoken anti-Jansenists like Father Amelote; and independent-minded theologians such as Father Nicolas de Malebranche. The intellectual achievements of the order further served to attract such men as Massillon and Richard Simon, contributing significantly to its widespread influence."[5]

Félibien[6] and Guillet de Saint-Georges relate that, about 1643–44, Philippe de Champaigne decorated the Tubeuf (or Tuboeuf) Chapel in the Church of the Oratoire. (Among the paintings in the Church of the Oratoire seized during the French Revolution—in addition to the works by Champaigne discussed below—were Simon Vouet's *Temptation of Saint Anthony* [Grenoble, Musée des Beaux-Arts], painted about 1639–40 for the Aubray Chapel, and canvases by Vignon, Poerson, Challes, and Cazes.)[7] We know from Dézallier d'Argenville that the principal altarpiece, *The Nativity* in Lille, was flanked by a *Visitation* (oil on canvas, 112 x 98 cm.; Pasadena, Norton Simon Museum of Art)[8] and a *Dream of Joseph* (presumed lost). Above *The Nativity* there was an *Assumption of the Virgin* (140 x 108 cm.; see fig. 2),[9] one of the few such pictures by Champaigne. Thus, the Lille *Nativity* was the central element of the ensemble in the Tubeuf Chapel of the Church of the Oratoire.

Bernard Dorival, the Champaigne scholar, notes correctly that the Nativity is a rare theme in the artist's oeuvre.[10]

FIGURE 2. Philippe de Champaigne. *The Assumption of the Virgin.* Oil on wood. Musée Thomas Henry, Cherbourg

For Tubeuf's commission Champaigne followed traditional Medieval iconography, representing Mary and Joseph alone and in prayer, beside the Christ Child, instead of the more current convention that combined the Nativity proper with the Adoration of the Shepherds. As Émile Mâle has shown, in the seventeenth century the birth of the Savior was associated with his recognition by others—that is, conversion—which reflected the notion of the Church Triumphant promulgated by the Council of Trent. In the background of the Lille picture Champaigne included the annunciation of Christ's birth to the shepherds. According to Dorival, "The artist would have been familiar with this iconography from engravings, which, throughout the sixteenth century, upheld this tradition in the Spanish Netherlands."[11] In fact, Champaigne himself depicted the Adoration of the Shepherds in a number of paintings—as, for example, those in the Wallace Collection, London, and in the Musée des Beaux-Arts, Lyons—but the Nativity only once.[12]

In his religious pictures Champaigne always adhered closely to the Scriptures. Unlike most of his contemporaries, who portrayed the Christ Child naked on a bed of straw,

19

Champaigne presents him in swaddling clothes, in accordance with the Gospel of Saint Luke (2: 7): "And she brought forth her firstborn son, and wrapped him in swaddling clothes, and laid him in a manger." Likewise, the artist, subscribing to the teachings of the theologian Molanus, represented the Virgin kneeling by her son, and Joseph not as elderly but in the prime of life.[13]

In this composition of calculated simplicity Champaigne emphasized Mary and Joseph's devout contemplation of the Christ Child. Only the head of the ox, whose breath warms the infant, could distract the focus of the faithful from the Holy Family. The picture is harmonious, spare, and without affectation, with a deep spirituality radiating from all of the faces: Mary's is reflective and tender; Joseph's, intense and contemplative; and the Child's, ringed with a halo of light. The execution is precise, except in the foreground, where the brisk and fluid handling suggests something of the style of Luca Giordano. The colors are flatly applied and the light serene.

The execution of the *Nativity* for the Tubeuf Chapel came at a critical moment in the artist's career (1643–44). Between 1642 and 1646, three major events changed the course of his life: the death of his son Claude (1642); the arrival in Paris of his nephew Jean-Baptiste, whom he had invited to come and work with him (1643); and the beginning of his contacts with the circle of theologians associated with the Jansenist abbey of Port-Royal. The same years saw the deaths of Cardinal Richelieu (1642) and of Louis XIII (1643)—two patrons who had frequently requested Philippe de Champaigne's services. According to Dorival, the major turning point in the artist's style, "his passage from a modified Baroque to a classical manner," also dates to this period (1642–43),[14] so that the Lille *Nativity* may be rightly considered as one of the first compositions in Champaigne's classical style.

ABL

1 Tubeuf generally is not mentioned in the major historical dictionaries, such as those by Bonaffé or Bluche.

2 See Thuillier, in Paris, 1990–91, under no. 56, p. 322.

3 The portrait (see Dorival, 1976, II, no. 401) preserved in the museum in Vienne, France, appears to be an old copy of a lost original; two engravings after the original portrait were made: by Jean Morin (1600–1650) and by Michel Lasne (1590–1667).

4 See Roger-Armand Weigert, "Du Palais Mazarin à la Bibliothèque Nationale," in *Mazarin 1602–1661* (exhib. cat.), Paris, 1961, p. VI.

5 See G. Viard, "Oratoire de France," in *Dictionnaire du grand siècle*, compiled by F. Bluche, Paris, 1991, p. 1122.

6 Félibien noted (1688) that in 1643 Champaigne "lived on the Isle

Notre-Dame, where he had a house. The first paintings he did there were those for the chapel of Tubeuf at the Pères de l'Oratoire. . . ."

7 See Paris, 1990–91, no. 49; and *Inventaire général des richesses d'art de la France. Archives du Musée des Monuments français*, part two, 1886, pp. 272, 347.

8 See Dorival, 1976, II, no. 30.

9 See Dorival, 1976, II, no. 85.

10 See Dorival, 1976, II, p. 34.

11 See Dorival, 1976, II, p. 24.

12 Among other paintings of the Nativity by Champaigne is the one that he gave to the Abbaye de Saint-Cyran, in the Berry (see Dorival, 1976, II, no. 476), but this might actually have been intended as an Adoration of the Shepherds; in the literature and in inventories from the seventeenth through the nineteenth century these two subjects were confused.

13 See Molanus, *De picturis et imaginibus sacris*, Louvain, 1570, pp. 45–47, 114–15.

14 See Dorival, 1976, I, p. 159.

PROVENANCE

Commissioned by Jacques Tubeuf for the third chapel on the left in the church of the Maison de l'Oratoire, rue Saint-Honoré, Paris, about 1643, where it remained until the French Revolution; transferred to the depository at the Petits-Augustins;* selected for the Muséum Central des Arts, and turned over to Naigeon, curator of the rue de Beaune depository, December 1797 (Nivôse, Year VI); assigned by the state to the Musée de Lille (pursuant to the Decree of 14 Fructidor, Year IX).

* See Lenoir, 1886.

EXHIBITIONS

Valenciennes, 1918, no. 59; Berlin, 1964, no. 7; Lille–Dunkirk–Valenciennes, 1980, no. 5; Moscow–Saint-Petersburg, 1987, no. 2.

LITERATURE

Félibien, 1688, p. 174; Florent Le Comte, 1699–1700, III, p. 114; Piganiol de la Force, 1742, I, p. 214; Dézallier d'Argenville, 1745, III, p. 373; Dézallier d'Argenville, 1749, p. 52; Descamps, 1753, II, p. 67; Dulaure, 1786, II, pp. 451, 556; Thiery, 1787, I, p. 323, II, p. 541; Guillet de Saint-Georges, 1854, I, p. 243; Clément de Ris, 1859, I, p. 323; Clément de Ris, 1872, pp. 92, 475, 476; Gonse, 1874, p. 142; Reynart, 1875, no. 112; Ingold, 1886, p. 48; Lenoir, 1886, II, p. 272, no. 704, p. 342, no. 28, p. 347; Lenglart, 1893, no. 163; de Poncheville, 1953, pp. 43–44; Vergnet-Ruiz and Laclotte, 1962, p. 229; Châtelet, 1970–1, no. 60, p. 136; Dorival, 1976, II, p. 24, no. 34, pl. 34; Oursel, 1984, pp. 5, 45–46; Allden and Beresford, 1989, p. 402, fig. 24.

LAURENT DE LA HYRE

French

Paris 1606–1656 Paris

20 *Pastoral Landscape*

Oil on canvas, 42 1/8 x 52 in. (107 x 132 cm.)

Inv. no. 1877

The bucolic Arcadian landscape of the imagination, which was inspired by the Roman countryside with its antique ruins, and by the Latin poetry of Virgil, is characteristic of seventeenth-century French painting. Its primary exponents were Poussin (1594–1665), Claude Lorrain (1600–1682), and Gaspard Dughet (1615–1675), who lived in Rome; Laurent de La Hyre and Pierre Patel the Elder (1605–1676), neither of whom seems ever to have left France; and Sébastien Bourdon (1616–1671), the only one who worked both in the Roman *campagna* and in Paris. Their landscape paintings are marked by a consonance of style that is reflective of the cosmopolitan environment in which they worked, and by the prevailing taste of the time.

La Hyre, like Poussin, was primarily a history painter. Born in 1606, the son of an artist, La Hyre studied at Fontainebleau and with Georges Lallemant (1575/76–1636), emerging, while still in his teens, as a precocious painter, draftsman, and printmaker. Sixteen twenty-seven is the probable date of La Hyre's *Martyrdom of Saint Bartholomew*, a large and brilliantly complex Caravaggesque composition: This canvas, intended for public display, was received with acclaim. Among La Hyre's most celebrated Parisian works from the succeeding decade are two altarpieces for the cathedral of Notre-Dame, and altarpieces for the Capuchin churches of the Marais and the rue Saint-Honoré, all painted between 1635 and 1637, and three mythologies commissioned by Cardinal de Richelieu (died 1642) for the Guardroom of the Palais-Royal. The classical revival is embodied in La Hyre's later work, the allegories of the arts, of 1649 and 1650, and the altarpieces for the Carmelite church in the Faubourg Saint-Jacques and, in the year of his death, for the Grande Chartreuse near Grenoble. La Hyre had been awarded the title *peintre du roi* at an early age, and he was among the founding members of the Académie Royale de Peinture et de Sculpture, established in 1648.

Successful and in comfortable circumstances, La Hyre married in 1639. Not long thereafter, toward his fortieth year, he fell gravely ill with debilitating maladies from which his recovery was slow, and which recurred in the early 1650s, resulting in his untimely death in 1656. Among his landscapes, and they are few, are canvases dated 1647, 1648, and 1654. It seems likely that these landscapes were painted when his health did not permit him to work on the very large scale to which he was accustomed. La Hyre's emergence as a landscape painter was not, however, as sudden as it might seem. Although only one pure landscape drawing by him is at present known (Rouen, Musée des Beaux-Arts), some of his earliest mythological drawings have delicately evocative landscape backgrounds. A painting in the Flemish taste (Arras, Musée Saint-Vaast), of 1632, represents two hunting dogs in a naturalistic park-like setting, and there are seven landscape etchings, of which six constitute a set dating from 1640.

Typically, the pastoral landscape in Lille is gentle in mood, timeless in narrative content, and expressive of La Hyre's appreciation of nature. It differs from his other landscapes in that it is proportionately larger, the figures are smaller, and, except for the musician's costume, reference to the antique is absent. The canvas, a recent discovery, is not signed, which is unusual for La Hyre, and may be only tentatively dated, in the opinion of Pierre Rosenberg and Jacques Thuillier, to about 1650.

By the late 1630s La Hyre must have been familiar with the work of his contemporaries in Rome, and with the Roman landscape tradition. Bourdon—with La Hyre among the founders of the Académie—had worked there, and Poussin was summoned from Rome by Louis XIII, spending several years in Paris at the beginning of the 1640s. A number of early Claudes were commissioned for Parisian clients: There were, for example, two inscribed in the artist's record book, the *Liber veritatis*, as belonging to Roger du Plessis de Liancourt, whose distinguished collection coincidentally included paintings by both Poussin and Paul Bril.[1] The planar landscape of the Lille picture, the lucid aerial perspective, and the flute-playing shepherd inevitably evoke Claude, while the diffuse woodland light under the tightly painted canopy of foliage is reminiscent of the work of Bril, born in Antwerp but active in Rome from the last quarter of the sixteenth century until his death in 1626. In a general way, and in the contrast between a barren tree and trees in full leaf, the painting recalls La Hyre's etching of a pool, of 1640.

KBB

1 See Marcel Röthlisberger, *Claude Lorrain: The Paintings*, New Haven, 1961, I, p. 228; Edmond Bonnaffé, *Dictionnaire des amateurs français au XVIIe siècle*, Paris, 1884, pp. 185–86.

PROVENANCE
Purchased, 1973.

EXHIBITIONS
Lille–Dunkirk–Valenciennes, 1980, no. 10; Grenoble–Rennes–Bordeaux, 1988–89, no. 241.

LITERATURE
Oursel, in Lille–Dunkirk–Valenciennes, 1980, pp. 40–42, no. 10, colorpl.; Oursel, 1984, pp. 46, 160–61, no. 22, colorpl.; Rosenberg and Thuillier, 1988, pp. 277–78, no. 241, colorpl.

NICOLAS DE LARGILLIERRE

French

Paris 1656–1746 Paris

---

21 *The Painter Jean-Baptiste Forest*

Oil on canvas, 50 3/4 x 37 3/4 in. (129 x 96 cm.)

Inv. no. 328

Nicolas de Largillierre was the epitome of the successful French painter, flourishing at a time—the first third of the eighteenth century—when the skills of a gifted and cosmopolitan portraitist were much in demand. Born in Paris in 1656, he moved with his family to Antwerp at an early age and remained there until he was eighteen, serving as an apprentice to a local artist, Antoon Goubau (1616–1698), and as a master painter and a member of the Guild of Saint Luke. He visited England from 1665 to 1666, for several years beginning in 1675, and briefly in the mid-1680s. Largillierre returned to Paris in 1679, and in 1686 was awarded membership in the Académie Royale de Peinture et de Sculpture, serving from 1705 as full professor, and subsequently as rector, chancellor, and director. When he died, in 1746, his oeuvre numbered well over one thousand portraits.

Largillierre painted still lifes, landscapes, and religious and commemorative historical subjects, but his fame—and his income—he owed to his highly successful practice as a portraitist. For the most part he painted his sitters' features from life, depending for the hands, costumes, furnishings, and backgrounds upon sketches, models, and studio properties. Very few of his drawings survive, and these are of the sort known as *académies*: studies from the nude that he used in connection with his teaching as a professor of painting. He was not a printmaker himself, but relied upon specialists, whose engravings after his portraits circulated widely. Largillierre is known to have restored, and to have traded in, Old Master paintings. He had a large shop, and numbered among his pupils the still-life painter Jean-Baptiste Oudry (1686–1755). Largillierre's colleague and friend Hyacinthe Rigaud (1659–1743) was a court artist, whereas by preference Largillierre worked for the *haute bourgeoisie*, and his sitters were the wealthy and prominent from Paris and the provinces. His portraits of members of the French and English royal families and their attendants are few in number by comparison with those representing financiers, military officers, and his fellow artists.

The year 1699 was a turning point for Largillierre: His mature style was fully formed and he exhibited no less than thirteen paintings at the Salon, he was elected assistant professor at the Académie, and he married Marguerite-Élisabeth, daughter of the painter Jean-Baptiste Forest (1635–1712). Largillierre's father-in-law had studied history and landscape painting in Rome with Pier Francesco Mola. Admitted to the Académie in 1674, Forest was for a time barred because he was a Protestant, but he was readmitted in 1699. He is said to have been a gifted painter, specializing in depicting extraordinary effects of light and the qualities of untrammeled nature. Forest is known to have worked also as a dealer, and to have formed a collection of his own, which included paintings by or after Titian, Correggio, and Domenichino. It is not surprising, therefore, that he should have been on friendly terms with his son-in-law, with whom he had much in common and for whom, within several years of his daughter's marriage, he sat for a portrait.

During the reigns of Louis XIV and Louis XV the ordained style for official portraits was formal, rhetorical, and extremely artificial—characteristics that tend now to inhibit appreciation of the inherent quality of the works. Largillierre's handling of paint is often quite brilliant. In the present portrait, more exceptionally, he also conveys with a degree of sympathy and humor a sense of the character of the sitter, an individual he knew well. There may be no better example of his talents than this painting of Jean-Baptiste Forest, which is sober and direct, relatively informal, and suggests the degree of intimacy between artist and sitter. Forest reportedly wore this rather eccentric costume, the bonnet and houppelande, or loose coat, when painting. The absence of a wig brings his features, the wrinkles at the bridge of the nose, the ruddy skin, and the gray shadow of the beard more sharply into focus against the soft, supple texture of fur and fabric. His palette, brushes, and mahlstick are unpretentiously incorporated, as is an oval landscape upon an easel, of the sort he must have painted, showing the changing effects of light at sunset. In the harmonious design and subtle coloration of this artist's portrait, Largillierre acknowledges his debt to the Northern painters Rembrandt, Rubens, and van Dyck.

The Lille portrait is of such finesse that it must be Largillierre's primary version, and thus may be identified with the portrait of Forest exhibited at the Salon of 1704 and presented in 1715 by Largillierre to the Académie together with sheets of the engraving by Pierre Drevet (1663–1738) made after Forest's death and bearing a suitably honorific

21

inscription. Another portrait by Largillierre of Forest, either alone or together with his wife, was bequeathed by her to her son-in-law in 1717, but this is unlikely to be the replica, now ascribed to a studio assistant, belonging to the Staatliche Museen Preussischer Kulturbesitz in Berlin. Forest's immortality lies with Largillierre: Of his own oeuvre only one attributed work, a landscape in the Musée des Beaux-Arts, Tours, is at present known.

KBB

PROVENANCE
Jules Brame; Gift of Jules Brame, 1861.

EXHIBITIONS
Paris, Salon of 1704; Lille–Dunkirk–Valenciennes, 1980, no. 60; Montreal, 1980, no. 46.

LITERATURE
De Lastic, 1979, pp. 20–21; Oursel, in Lille–Dunkirk–Valenciennes, 1980, pp. 115–17, no. 60, colorpl.; Rosenfeld, 1980, pp. 34, 36, 222, 231–34, no. 46, ill.; Oursel, 1984, pp. 8, 45, 48, 170–71, no. 27, colorpl.

PAUL-PONCE-ANTOINE ROBERT

French

Séry-en-Porcien 1686–1733 Paris

22 *Study of a Woman*

Oil on canvas, 28 x 22 7/8 in. (71 x 58 cm.)

Signed and dated (at the lower left): P. P. Robert 1722

Inv. no. 347

P.-P.-A. Robert emerges from obscurity as the painter of this exceptionally interesting study of a woman, in half length, before a landscape background. Robert was born in Séry-en-Porcien, a village in the Ardennes, to the north of Reims. He studied with Jean Tisserand (1660–1737), who was a native of Reims, and in Paris with Jean Jouvenet (1644–1717), and, although he was without means, made his way to Rome as early as 1706 to complete his training. There he lived—according to the critic and collector Pierre-Jean Mariette (1694–1774), who knew him—happily but in poverty, painting, making prints, and trading in works of art. Robert is also known to have visited Venice and Parma before 1724, when he returned to Paris in the service of Armand-Gaston, Cardinal de Rohan. Robert twice applied to the Académie

Royale de Peinture et de Sculpture—as a painter and as a sculptor—and was rejected, numbering among his detractors two powerful figures in the academic establishment, Jean-François De Troy (1679–1752) and the younger of the Coustou brothers, Guillaume (1677–1748). He was engaged by the connoisseur and collector Pierre Crozat (1661–1740) to supervise the work on the second volume of his publication on the most famous paintings and drawings in French collections, the so-called *Cabinet Crozat*, but Robert died of consumption in 1733, before the project was completed, leaving some prints, and a few pictures painted for the Capuchins—notably, an altarpiece representing the Martyrdom of Saint Fidelis. There are few canvases by Robert in French public collections; among them is the *Review of Musketeers*, signed and dated 1729, belonging to the Musée National du Château de Versailles.[1]

The present picture, fully signed and dated, was also the subject of an etching by the artist that is inscribed in the left margin *P.P.A. Robert de Seri fec. Rom. 1723*.[2] The existence of the print identifies the picture as a work to which Robert attached importance, perhaps as a souvenir of his life in Rome—from which he was to depart the following year. Strictly speaking, it may not be a portrait. The ample Rubensian form, indifferent expression, and casual pose of the woman betoken the model, as do the styleless simplicity and negligence of her dress. The background is evocative: a flush of light against a screen of foliage and tall, slender tree trunks, a miniature fête galante—a troubadour in a tricorne hat playing to Italian peasant women—and a marble wall with a garden sculpture and a balustrade, reminiscent of the Serliana in the gardens of the Villa Medici in Rome. The informality of the composition; the startling palette of black, white, and red; and the rather broad handling have been seen as incipiently modern: Robert has been compared with Manet and Renoir. Looking rather to his own time, Robert responded to a current of naturalism that was present in both northern and southern Baroque painting, and it was perhaps this aspect of his art that was antithetical to Parisian taste of the 1720s. The poetic, elegiac undertone is, however, in harmony with Watteau, Robert's near contemporary, and Robert also anticipates the brilliant landscapes and figure studies that Fragonard would later draw while visiting Rome and Naples.

KBB

1 See Claire Constans, *Musée national du château de Versailles: Catalogue des peintures*, Paris, 1980, p. 115; Eric M. Zafran, *The Rococo Age: French Masterpieces of the Eighteenth Century* (exhib. cat.), Atlanta, 1983,

22

pp. 112–13, no. 45, colorpl. Robert's small surviving oeuvre comprises mostly religious paintings, and these show the influence, primarily, of Correggio and Barocci.

2 See A.-P.-F. Robert-Dumesnil, *Le Peintre-graveur français*, Paris, 1835, I, p. 280, no. 5.

PROVENANCE

Paul Leroi (pseudonym of the dealer Léon Gauchez); Gift of Paul Leroi, 1883.

EXHIBITION

Lille–Dunkirk–Valenciennes, 1980, no. 66.

LITERATURE

Bourin, 1907, p. 146, no. 2; Châtelet, 1970-1, p. 144, no. 64, colorpl. p. 145; Scottez, in Lille–Dunkirk–Valenciennes, 1980, pp. 124–26, no. 66, colorpl.; Oursel, 1984, p. 48, ill. p. 49.

JEAN-BAPTISTE-SIMÉON CHARDIN

French

Paris 1699–1779 Paris

---

23   *The Silver Cup* (*Les apprêts d'un déjeuner*)

Oil on canvas, 31 7/8 x 25 3/8 in. (81 x 64.5 cm.)

Signed (at the lower left, on the ledge): *chardin*

Inv. no. 1998

The *Silver Cup* is dated by Chardin scholars to about 1730, when the artist was approximately thirty years old. At this early point in his career Chardin was in the habit of developing his compositions very carefully, as is evident from a radiograph of the Lille painting (fig. 1) made at the Laboratoire des Musées de France.[1] The radiograph reveals major revisions in what began as a completely different design; there was once a rather large cabbage behind the knife and a citrus fruit of some kind situated to the left of the goblet. The painter ultimately omitted the fruit and vegetable in order to achieve a more severe and well-balanced "composition"—a term applied to such pictures by P.-J. Mariette. The same writer recorded Chardin's own words, which come to mind when one contemplates this spare table setting: "I have to forget everything that I've seen, and even the manner in which others have depicted these objects. . . . I must set them at a certain distance, so that I no longer see the details. I have to concern myself above all with faithfully imitating, with

the utmost truth, the overall masses of the forms, the values of the color, the volumes, and the effects of light and shade."[2]

Early in his career, the young painter's repertoire consisted mostly of such elements as fruit, dead game, and various animals. The Lille picture stands apart from this category of still life "showing a talent for animals and fruit,"[3] yet, prominently displayed here is the silver footed cup that Chardin so often featured in his paintings of fruit. This silver cup is the subject of a famous anecdote. In March 1759 the cup, which Chardin had used all his life, was stolen by "an unemployed servant," one François Renaud, who had found the door to the artist's lodgings in the Louvre unlocked. The thief sold the cup to a flower vendor along the Pont-Neuf, but it was eventually returned to its rightful owner. Perhaps this is why the artist delighted in including this "motif" in his compositions throughout his career. In his 1983 monograph on Chardin, Pierre Rosenberg catalogued thirteen pictures in which the cup is represented; seven of them are early works and the others date from about 1750 or later.[4] Some of these paintings are also entitled *The Silver Cup* (as, for example, one in the Musée du Louvre, Inv. no. M.I. 1042), but the particular combination of objects in the Lille picture—the cup, a loaf of bread, and a slice of ham on a pewter plate—is not found in any other work by Chardin. Another, almost identical, version (oil on canvas, 63 x 57 cm.; cut down at the top and on either side), once owned by the couturier Jacques Doucet (1853–1929) and later by the Metropolitan Museum (until 1973), is now attributed to a pupil or assistant of Chardin and is on the art market in England.[5]

The Lille *Silver Cup* is outstanding for its quality, its large scale, and its state of preservation. Chardin artfully considered the proportions of the objects in relation to the size of the niche; no incidental details impede the impression of monumentality sought by the artist. The knife projects almost violently toward the spectator and acts as a foil to the insistent verticality of the bottle, the cup, and the sides of the niche. Depth is subtly conveyed by the two ledges and by the placement of the objects in space. One's attention is drawn to such exquisite passages as the bread crumbs casually scattered on the ledge, the striking reflection of the spoon, and the wine just barely visible in the cup. The painting is austere and disciplined, sensual and intellectual all at once—intellectual because it is serene, almost abstract, and thus difficult, and sensual because of the pleasure one derives from admiring the execution, the rich, thick, and textured quality of the paint, the almost Rembrandtesque light on the stone surfaces of the ledges and the niche, and the virtually monochromatic,

23

FIGURE 1. Radiograph of catalogue number 23

warm, richly nuanced browns offset by subtle accents of color. Chardin adopted a restricted range of tonal values, and, apart from any chiaroscuro effect, he used light to blend the varied passages of local color into a balanced harmony.

The acquisition of the *Silver Cup* was a major event for the Musée des Beaux-Arts; rarely can a museum in the provinces afford such a costly work. The purchase depended on two criteria: the exceptional quality of the picture and the desire to strengthen the collections of eighteenth-century art. Besides, the addition of a picture by Chardin has been long overdue at the museum in Lille; the two paintings attributed to the artist in Lenglart's catalogue of 1893, the *Singe savant* and the *Portrait of a Woman*, have been rejected as, respectively, a copy and an eighteenth-century work by an unknown painter. A footnote to this story is that Chardin was often inspired by the Flemish master Pieter Boel, whose splendid *Allegory of Worldly Vanity* (cat. no. 7) is also in the museum in Lille.

ABL

1 I wish to thank the Laboratoire des Musées de France and its former director, Jack Ligot, for their generous cooperation.

2 See P.-J. Mariette, "Chardin," in *Abecedario de P. J. Mariette . . .* , reprinted in Ph. de Chennevières and A. de Montaiglon, *Archives de l'art français*, 1851–53, I, pp. 355–60.

3 It was in these terms that the category in which Chardin was admitted into the Académie in 1728 was described.

4 See Rosenberg, 1983.

5 See Charles Sterling, *The Metropolitan Museum of Art: A Catalogue of French Paintings, XV–XVIII Centuries*, Cambridge, 1955, pp. 127–28, ill. (as Workshop of Chardin); on the sale by the Metropolitan Museum, see *The Metropolitan Museum of Art, Report on Art Transactions, 1971–1973*, Appendix II, p. 2.

PROVENANCE

Possibly one of the two paintings listed under no. 15 in the sale of the Sylvestre collection, Paris, February 28–March 25, 1811: "Two paintings in which two dead birds, a ham, and other inanimate objects are represented, arranged on shelves"; one of four works by Chardin sold in two lots at the sale of the Gounod collection, Paris, February 23, 1824; the opera singer Barroilhet; sale of the Barroilhet collection, Paris, March 10, 1856, no. 18, April 2 and 3, 1860, no. 102, March 15 and 16, 1872, no. 3; Baronne Nathaniel de Rothschild, before 1876; Henry, then James de Rothschild; Anonymous sale, Paris, Galerie Charpentier, May 23, 1951, no. 23, ill.; Victor Lyon, Geneva; Private collection; Purchased, 1990.*

The *Silver Cup* was seized by customs agents in Paris on February 7, 1990, and purchased by the Musée des Beaux-Arts, Lille, on October 15, 1990, after the French Ministry of Culture declared the picture nonexportable (on June 14, 1990). The museum could not have acquired the painting without support from various sources: the Fonds National du Patrimoine (which contributed 52 percent of the financing), the Fonds Régional d'Acquisitions pour les Musées du Nord Pas-de-Calais, the Conseil Régional, the Conseil Général, The White Public Relation Ltd (a Tokyo-based Japanese group), the city of Lille, and a public subscription in which one thousand donors participated.

A French eighteenth-century frame was recently obtained for the painting with the generous assistance of the Banque Scalbert-Dupont and Christie's, France.**

* Most of this information is taken from the entry in Rosenberg, 1979, no. 9, p. 119.
** See A. Brejon, "Quelques encadrements de tableaux au Musée des Beaux-Arts de Lille," *Amis des Musées de Lille*, January 1992, no. 34.

EXHIBITIONS

Paris, 1860, no. 360; Paris, 1907, no. 57; Amsterdam, 1926, no. 17; Paris, 1929, no. 42; Paris, 1956-2, no. 21; Paris–Cleveland–Boston, 1979, no. 9.

LITERATURE

Bocher, 1876, p. 103; de Goncourt, 1880–84, I, p. 130; Dayot and Vaillat, 1907, no. 52, ill.; Guiffrey, 1908, p. 88, no. 202; de Goncourt, 1909, I, pp. 191–92; Furst, 1911, p. 129; Quintin, 1929, ill.; Pascal and Gaucheron, 1931, pp. 139–40; Wildenstein, 1933, no. 1062, fig. 134 (and no. 751 ?); Barrelet, 1959, p. 308; Wildenstein, 1963, no. 24, colorpl. 2 (and no. 286 ?); Rosenberg, 1983, no. 15; Brejon de Lavergnée, 1990-1, pp. 96–97; Brejon de Lavergnée, 1990-2, pp. 353–55.

JEAN RAOUX

French

Montpellier 1677–1734 Paris

___

24 *Vierges antiques*

Oil on canvas, 36 1/4 x 28 1/2 in. (92 x 72.5 cm.)

Signed and dated (at the lower right): I Raoux F^t 1727

Inv. no. 1947

25 *Vierges modernes*

Oil on canvas, 36 1/4 x 28 1/2 in. (92 x 72.5 cm.)

Signed and dated (at the lower left): I Raoux F^t 1728

Inv. no. 1948

The work of Jean Raoux exemplifies an aspect of eighteenth-century French taste and sensibility that now seems alien: His pictures were sought after for their frivolous grace and gentle eroticism, and for their artfulness. In the absence of a serious subject, or, indeed, of any subject at all beyond that which was pleasing, this was an elegant form of art for art's sake, where naturalism might be eschewed but technical virtuosity counted for a great deal. Raoux was highly trained, very skillful, and responsive to the pleasure-loving and cosmopolitan Parisian environment, and he thus enjoyed several brilliant decades—particularly that of the 1720s—as a genre and portrait painter.

Born in 1677 in Montpellier, Raoux was at first placed with a local painter named Antoine Ranc (1634–1716) and then sent to Paris, where he studied with Bon Boullongne (1649–1717). He won the Prix de Rome in 1704, and spent three years in that city as a pensioner, visiting also Florence, Padua, and, for a longer period, Venice. His paintings came to the attention of the Grand Prior of the Order of Malta, Philippe de Vendôme, under whose auspices Raoux returned to Paris in 1714, and was provided with lodging and an income. In 1717 he was accepted into the Académie Royale de Peinture et de Sculpture in the most sought-after category, that of history painter, and in 1720 he made a visit of eight months to England, possibly in the company of Antoine Watteau (1684–1721). He did not find it necessary to exhibit regularly, nor did the artist sustain his association with the Académie, but under the protection of Vendôme and the succeeding grand prior he remained in Paris, where his work, until the last several years of his life, was always in fashion.[1]

Biblical and mythological paintings by Raoux are recorded, as well as portraits, and scenes of bourgeois and low life that must have been inspired by seventeenth-century Dutch painting. The names of Caspar Netscher (1639–1684) and Godfried Schalcken (1643–1706) are often invoked, and, indeed, Dutch "fine painting" on a small scale was widely admired by French artists and connoisseurs in succeeding generations. As a portraitist, Raoux was among the first to present his sitters—aristocrats, actresses, and other ladies of fashion—in allegorical guise. He mined the classicizing vein in Italian art, furnishing costumes and interiors with a delicate and nostalgic neoclassical veneer. As a genre painter, too, young women were his primary subject: alone or in twos and threes, seen as gardeners, shepherdesses, and particularly as vestal virgins.

The earlier of this pair of paintings, the one called *Vierges antiques*, depicts the servants of Vesta, the Roman household goddess and guardian of the hearth. Raoux accurately represents the six young maidens in bridal dress in a rotunda, tending a fire that burned perpetually upon an altar, but he strays from classical sources, including a statue of the goddess in her sanctuary. Raoux's picture was very popular, and the two more prominent figures at the left of the altar were repeated in half length, as a much-enlarged horizontal composition, in no fewer than two and probably many more variants. One of these is in Schloss Sanssouci in Potsdam and another, signed and dated 1730, belongs to the Herzog Anton Ulrich-Museum in Braunschweig. Many single-figure compositions by Raoux, upright, horizontal, and oval in format, are also recorded: In these the younger woman wearing the garland bears, instead of wood for the fire, a flaming basin. A good example of the type is in Montpellier. Raoux invents the *Vierges modernes* as a suitable pendant, without historical or other precedent. By contrast with their ancient sisters, they inhabit a luxurious classicizing interior, furnished with a gilt-wood table, objects of vermeil, and baskets of fruit and flowers in the Flemish taste. Through malachite columns with gilded Ionic capitals there is an oblique view of a colonnade—its ceiling a frescoed vault representing Apollo with his lyre—opening into an informal English garden.

Raoux combined aspects of the two pictures in the near-contemporary *Marie-Françoise Perdrigeon (1716–1734), Dame Boucher*, a portrait of an important lady at court, the wife of the king's secretary. The first, full-scale version of this portrait, destroyed by fire in the nineteenth century, is known to have been signed and dated 1728. A replica, of 1733,

25

belongs to the Musée National du Château de Versailles.[2] The picture offers an interesting comparison not only because it incorporates material from both of the paintings in Lille—the altar, the ewer garlanded with flowers, and a view of a distant landscape—but also since it casts the sitter, who died a young bride, as a modern virgin.

Under the influence of the Dutch "candlelight" masters, Raoux evolved complex light effects, *à contre-jour* and from hidden sources, bringing into sharp relief precious objects and the swan-like necks and delicate pink toes of his beautiful models. He deploys his gift for painting fine textiles to excellent effect, and, typically, shows a preference for ivory reflecting a pale green and a delicate silver. He also acknowledges his debt to Italian painting, in the person of the Bolognese seventeenth-century master Guercino (1591–1666), who must have inspired the turbaned figure with the ewer and basin. It may be imagined that subjects emblematic of chastity, in a historical and modern guise, would have had a piquant appeal to Raoux's cultivated and notably immodest clientele, and are in every respect characteristic of what we know of his art.

KBB

1 See Dézallier d'Argenville, 1745, III, pp. 259–67; Georges Bataille, "Raoux: 1677 à 1734," in Louis Dimier, ed., *Les Peintres français du XVIIIᵉ siècle*, Paris and Brussels, 1930, II, pp. 267–82.

2 See Claire Constans, *Musée national du château de Versailles: Catalogue des peintures*, Paris, 1980, p. 110.

PROVENANCE
Princesse Emmanuelle de Croy; Cailleux, Paris, 1979; purchased, 1979.

LITERATURE
Oursel, 1984, pp. 49, 172–73, no. 28, colorpl., p. 223, ill. no. 72.

FRANÇOIS WATTEAU DE LILLE

French
Valenciennes 1758–1823 Lille

26   *A Fête in the Colisée*

Oil on canvas, 29 1/2 x 35 7/8 in. (75 x 91 cm.)
Inv. no. 352

The Watteaus of Lille were a dynasty of painters—collateral relations of Antoine Watteau (1684–1721)—established in Lille, but originally from Valenciennes, a smaller town, which is also near the Flemish border. Louis-Joseph Watteau de Lille (1731–1798), nephew of Antoine, was trained in Paris at the Académie Royale de Peinture et de Sculpture, and is recorded in Lille in 1755, attached to the local Académie as professor of drawing. From 1773 he organized the Salons, which were held regularly in Lille until the onset of the Revolution. In 1792 Louis-Joseph first proposed the establishment of a museum; in 1795 he inventoried works of art seized from émigrés and from churches in the surrounding area, and by 1797 had gathered together some sixty paintings, the nucleus of a civic collection. He thus anticipated by ten years the founding of the Musée des Beaux-Arts in Lille, one of the first of the provincial museums. François (see fig. 9, p. 20), the son of Louis-Joseph, also studied in Paris, with Durameau, from 1775, eventually returning to Lille as his father's assistant about 1786. He succeeded his father as professor at the Académie, and Bellier de La Chavignerie credits him also with a role in the foundation of the museum.[1]

The Watteaus were Walloons, and thus culturally at one with the people of southern Flanders. Louis-Joseph particularly was as much influenced by such seventeenth-century Flemish painters as the younger David Teniers (1610–1690) as he was by Watteau and by Jean-Baptiste-Joseph Pater (1695–1736). A sometime painter of contemporary historical events, Louis-Joseph specialized in military genre and peasant subjects. François, while influenced by his father, was longer resident in Paris, where he made designs for engravings of the latest and most extravagant Louis XVI fashions, which were published between 1778 and 1787 as *La Gallerie des modes et costumes français*.[2] His style is polished, and he was less the regional artist and more the painter of late-eighteenth-century fêtes galantes. His sentiments were nevertheless appropriately republican, and he also chronicled local and national historical events, revolutionary and imperial. The museums of northern France are rich in the work of both painters.

In the *Fête in the Colisée*, François Watteau represents a view of a pavilion in a stylish pleasure garden on the outskirts of Lille, near the Porte de Canteleu. Designs for the Colisée were commissioned in 1786 from François Verly (1760–1822), a local architect, recently returned from a sojourn in Paris as a student at the Académie Royale d'Architecture. The Colisée, opened in June 1787, was a place of entertainment that comprised ballrooms, pavilions, and tents, arranged amid lawns and woods ornamented with rocks and fountains, and it was much frequented by society. The archi-

26

tect and the painter were near contemporaries, similarly trained in the more cosmopolitan Parisian environment. Thus it was inevitable that this milieu would have appealed to François Watteau, who would have remembered with nostalgia his sketching expeditions in Paris, in the fashionable gardens of the Palais-Royal. In this painting *le tout Lille* is represented—including children and lapdogs—eating and drinking, playing and gaming, generally two by two, in the afternoon sunlight. The costume of the lady with the fan in profile at the center reflects François Watteau's designs for the *Gallerie des modes*—particularly plates 283 and 305—published in the early 1780s.[3] François Watteau's colorful canvas evokes the frantic gaiety of the Revolutionary period. The picture is neither signed nor dated, which is unusual, but is likely to have been painted not long before 1792, when the Colisée was destroyed to make way for the defenses erected at Lille against the siege of the Austrian army. The tricolor cockade, an ornament whose usage was obligatory after July 1789, is much in evidence.

De Poncheville records the existence of two autograph replicas of the picture, evidence that this topical subject was, quite understandably, a favorite.

KBB

1 See Émile Bellier de La Chavignerie, *Dictionnaire général des artistes de l'école française depuis l'origine des arts du dessin jusqu'à nos jours*, Paris, 1885, II, p. 717.

2 Information from Gaëtane Maës.

3 See note 2, above.

PROVENANCE
A. and J. Delannoy; Gift of A. and J. Delannoy, 1861.

EXHIBITION
Lille–Calais–Arras–Douai, 1975–76, no. 66.

LITERATURE
Marmottan, 1889, pp. 51, 53–55, 57–58; de Poncheville, 1926, p. 228; de Poncheville, 1928, pp. 75, 82, 107, no. 8, pp. 108–9; Oursel, in Lille–Calais–Arras–Douai, 1975–76, pp. 127–29, no. 66, ill.; Oursel, 1984, pp. 52, 223, ill. no. 80.

JEAN-BAPTISTE GREUZE

French

Tournus 1725–1805 Paris

27 *Cupid and Psyche*
Oil on canvas, 57 7/8 x 70 7/8 in. (147 x 180 cm.)
Inv. no. 389

Largely self taught, and a brilliantly inventive painter and draftsman, Greuze specialized in a sort of moralizing pictorial drama that lay outside the traditional eighteenth-century system of academic categorization. He was—but did not wish to be thought of as—a genre painter, and he was equally accomplished as a portraitist. Greuze, a countryman, settled in Paris when he was in his mid-twenties. In 1755 he was accorded associate membership in the Académie Royale de Peinture et de Sculpture, and in the autumn of the same year he set out on an extended journey through Italy, the final stage of prescribed artistic training. Greuze participated in each of the Salons held in alternate years from 1755 until 1765, exhibiting in all over seventy-five paintings and drawings—subject pictures, portraits, and studies of human expression. Many of the latter were engraved, and published in 1766 as a volume entitled *Têtes de différents caractères*. Greuze, meanwhile, received commissions on behalf of the king's mistress Mme de Pompadour, and secured the patronage of some of the most distinguished collectors of his time, Lalive de Jully (1725–1779) and Jean de Jullienne (1686–1766) included: At the age of forty he was among the most successful painters in Paris.

In 1767 Greuze was advised that because of his failure to submit a reception piece to the Académie he would be barred from exhibiting at the forthcoming Salon. Outspokenly embittered, he nevertheless set to work on his chosen subject—*Septimius Severus Reproaching Caracalla* (Paris, Musée du Louvre)—an obscure episode from Roman history symbolic of the virtue of filial piety. The painting was accepted by the Académie in 1769, and Greuze was admitted to full membership, but not as a history painter, the highest category, to which he had aspired. The critics remarked that the painting lacked feeling, and that Greuze's talents were ill suited to the austerity of the neoclassical style. This was the greatest tragedy of the artist's professional life. Unhappily married—indeed, victimized by a promiscuous and greedy wife, and with two daughters to support—he nevertheless withdrew from official circles, and from the 1770s showed

27

privately, in his studio. He enjoyed considerable success with engravings of his subject pictures, and he turned increasingly to *têtes d'expression*, the beautifully painted but languid and sentimental studies of young women that were then much in demand. When the Salon was reinaugurated in 1800, his submissions, once again, were greeted with enthusiasm, and he continued to exhibit in his final years, dying at the age of eighty, much honored, in 1805.

Only a small number of Greuze's drawings, and even fewer of his paintings, were devoted to classical subjects, and many of these are of roughly the same date as his *morceau de réception*. At the Salon of 1769 Greuze exhibited the *Votive Offering to Cupid* (London, Wallace Collection), which he had completed two years previously, and for which there is a study of a river-god in The Metropolitan Museum of Art, New York. Wishing to join the Académie as a history painter, and as the equal of Poussin, he seems to have explored various themes from antiquity before deciding upon Septimius Severus. There are two drawings that apparently represent the Roman heroine Pero, who nursed her father, Cimon, when he was under sentence of death by starvation, and there are several drawings of nudes that may be associated with history paintings, such as the study for the central figure in the so-called *Aegina Visited by Jupiter*, also in the Metropolitan Museum. Most of these works were not exhibited in Greuze's lifetime, coming on the market only after the death of his daughter Caroline in 1842.

Such was also the case with the *Cupid and Psyche*: Its existence was unrecorded until the picture appeared in the posthumous sale of the collection of Caroline Greuze, who had retained the contents of her father's studio as a memorial to him.[1] The *Cupid and Psyche* evades interpretation. The ambiguous subject of this impressive but admittedly difficult picture was the artist's own invention, for it does not depend on any narrative source, and neither the patron, if there was one, nor the date is known. What seems certain, however, is that after a decade or more, the 1780s witnessed the revival on Greuze's part of aspirations crushed in 1769 by the Académie. Shortly before 1786, in the last years of the Ancien Régime, Greuze received a commission from the comte d'Artois for what was to be the largest and most ambitious of his history paintings, *Innocence Carried Off by Cupid* (Paris, Musée du Louvre)—a complex, many-figured composition arranged as a frieze against an elaborately articulated landscape and architectural background. Many preparatory studies for the canvas are recorded, as well as small, single-figure pictures deriving from it, and at the same time Greuze

began again to explore more broadly mythological and biblical subject matter.

The *Cupid and Psyche* has been variously dated between about 1785 and 1790, and would thus have been painted on the eve, or at the outset, of the French Revolution. After a recent cleaning it is apparent that while the figures are complete, the background and accessories are not: Apparently, then, Greuze abandoned the work, either because he realized that he would be unable to find a buyer, or because the subject, symbolic of bliss and constancy, was too painful. The picture had been carefully prepared—many drawings connected with it are recorded—and reflects the influence of the Salon entries of Joseph-Marie Vien (1716–1809) and of the elder Lagrenée, Louis-Jean-François (1724–1805), as well as contemporaneously of those of Jacques-Louis David. It is a work of transition, evocative, and beautifully painted, but weighed down by an atmosphere of nerveless sensuality and lassitude. As a draftsman and genre painter, on the other hand, Greuze rose to the heights to which he had long aspired—the rigorous purity of form and nobility of sentiment that are the hallmarks of the neoclassical style.

KBB

1 See Munhall, 1976. I am indebted to Edgar Munhall, who, with his customary generosity, made available all of the material from his file on the Lille picture, and to Colin Bailey, who kindly supplied his English text prior to the publication of the catalogue referenced below.

PROVENANCE

By descent to the artist's daughter Caroline Greuze (died 1842); posthumous sale of the Caroline Greuze collection, Paris, January 25–26, 1843, no. 1; Meffre; sale of the Meffre collection, Paris, November 25–26, 1845, no. 33; comte de Morny; sale of the comte de Morny collection, Paris, May 24, 1852, no. 8; Alexandre Leleux (1812–1873), Lille; Bequest of Alexandre Leleux, 1873.

EXHIBITIONS

Lille, 1974, no. 28; Paris–Philadelphia–Fort Worth, 1991–92, no. 65.

LITERATURE

Oursel, 1974-1, pp. 11, 45–47, no. 28, ill.; Bailey, 1991, pp. 521–27, colorplates pp. 520 (detail), 523.

JACQUES-LOUIS DAVID

French

Paris 1748–1825 Brussels

---

28 *Belisarius Begging Alms (Bélisaire demandant l'aumône)*

1781

Oil on canvas, 113 3/8 x 122 5/8 in. (288 x 312 cm.)

Signed and dated (at the bottom left): *L. David faciebat/ anno 1781 Lutetiae* [?]

Inv. no. 436

Belisarius (about 505–565), one of the most famous generals of the later Roman Empire, loyally served under Justinian I, the Great (483–565). His successful campaigns are fully recorded by Procopius of Caesarea (Belisarius's secretary) in the *History of the Wars* and the *Secret History*. In 562, Belisarius was unjustly implicated in a plot against the emperor and was disgraced, but he recovered favor a year after. According to a later legend, when Justinian learned about the alleged treachery of Belisarius he summarily ordered that he be blinded and dispossessed, reducing Belisarius to a life of begging. This unfounded story first became current in the tenth century and it was circulated in the twelfth century by the Byzantine writer John Tzetges. It resurfaced sporadically throughout the centuries—for example, in a tragic play by Jean de Rotrou (1609–1650) of 1643, and in a painting by Salvator Rosa (1615–1673) of about 1651[1] and one by Luciano Borzone (1590–1645) of about 1620, the latter once attributed to van Dyck.[2] However, it was in eighteenth-century pre-Revolutionary France that the Belisarius legend gained momentum with Jean-François Marmontel's *Bélisaire* of 1767. According to his *Mémoires*, Marmontel had been inspired to write his moralizing novel upon seeing an engraving after Luciano Borzone's painting,[3] and he based his account on those of Procopius and Tzetges. The moral of Marmontel's Belisarius legend—the easy reversal of fortune and the ingratitude of the emperor—was, indeed, a virulent criticism of the monarchy, and it was applauded by the enlightened *"philosophes."*[4] Marmontel's novel influenced David to paint the *Belisarius Begging Alms*.

While in Rome, from 1775 to 1780, David was given a copy of Marmontel's book by Jean-François-Pierre Peyron (1744–1814), a fellow artist, who himself was at work on a painting of Belisarius for the Abbé de Bernis. David would execute a half-length painting of Belisarius and a child[5] and in 1779 the highly finished drawing *Belisarius Recognized by a*

Soldier (Palaiseau, École Polytechnique),[6] both of which seem to have been inspired by the novel. Back in France, in August or September 1780, David set his mind to work on a painting of Belisarius, intending to submit it to the Académie as his *"agrément,"* in lieu of the *Saint Roch* of 1780 (Marseilles, Musée des Beaux-Arts), which had just been refused by the Académie. There is no doubt that David was well aware of earlier pictorial renditions of Belisarius, among them the engraving after Borzone's painting and the illustrations by Hubert-François Gravelot (1699–1773) for Marmontel's *Bélisaire*,[7] as well as the paintings by Nicolas-René Jollain (1732–1804), Louis-Jean-Jacques Durameau (1733–1796), François-André Vincent (1746–1816), and Peyron.[8] Of these last four artists' renditions that by Jollain is closest to David's composition; only these two works treat the moment when the begging Belisarius is recognized by a soldier. Jollain's painting has been known to scholars solely from Diderot's description.[9] A comparison between Jollain's sketch for his *Belisarius* (see fig. 1)[10] and David's painting yields striking, albeit superficial, similarities. Both works feature a bearded Belisarius in the right foreground, seated against an architectural structure. The former general's blindness is alluded to by the stick leaning against the stone block and by the young boy who holds out a helmet for alms. Also common to both pictures is the soldier in the middle ground, who throws up his arms in dismay upon recognizing the general. Whereas Jollain's *Belisarius* is steeped in rococo sentimentalism, David's portrayal is painted in the crisper neoclassical style for which he became famous. David focuses on the four principal charac-

FIGURE 1. Nicolas-René Jollain. *Belisarius.* Oil on canvas. Galerie Charles et André Bailly, Paris

ters, and places them in a theatrical setting under dramatic Caravaggesque light—surely a legacy of the artist's Roman sojourn.

David's choice of Belisarius as the subject for his "*agrément*" was not unusual. Episodes from Marmontel's *Bélisaire* served as the theme of three works exhibited at the Salon, before David's painting of 1781 was shown: Jollain's entry, at the Salon of 1767 (no. 153); Durameau's, at the Salon of 1775 (no. 130); and Vincent's, at the Salon of 1777 (no. 189). It was common knowledge that the comte d'Angiviller, one of the most influential individuals in the French art world,[11] looked favorably on the Belisarius legend: In 1767 he had come to Marmontel's defense when the author's opus was censured by the Sorbonne,[12] and he owned Durameau's Salon painting as well as Peyron's *Belisarius* sketch (most likely the one that now belongs to the Graphische Sammlung Albertina in Vienna).[13]

The thirty-two-year-old David was "*agréé*" on August 24, 1781, upon the receipt by the Académie of the *Belisarius Begging Alms*.[14] In a letter written three days later, the artist announced to his mother, "I did not receive one blackball from the Académie, which is most unusual" ("L'Académie m'a reçu d'une manière peu commune puisque j'ai été reçu tout blanc, c'est-à-dire sans aucune fève noire").[15] The day after his "*agrément*," David sent the *Belisarius Begging Alms*, along with some ten other works, to the Salon of 1781, where it favorably impressed Diderot: "This man shows great style in his work, he has spirit, the faces of his figures are expressive without affectation, their poses are natural and noble, he can draw, and he knows how to render drapery handsomely" ("Ce jeune homme montre de la grande manière dans la conduite de son ouvrage, il a de l'âme, ses têtes ont de l'expression sans affectation, ses attitudes sont nobles et naturelles, il dessine, il sait jetter [*sic*] une draperie et faire de beaux plis").[16] The critic for the *Année littéraire* agreed: "He would do honor to the greatest of artists . . ." ("Il ferait honneur aux plus célèbres artistes . . .").[17] Still, the young painter was criticized for a certain coldness, as well as for his use of a muted palette. Diderot commented, "His color is good without being striking . . ." ("Sa couleur est belle sans être brillante . . .").[18] Harsher criticism came from a writer for *Le Pourquoi*, who found the painting too dark and lacking in harmony or chiaroscuro.[19] As recent scholars have pointed out, the perspective of the work is jarring—most notably, in the flagstones and in the awkward placement of the soldier. This was resolved by David in the smaller *Belisarius Begging Alms* of 1784 (Paris, Musée du Louvre, Inv. no. 3694), commissioned by the comte d'Angiviller.[20]

The success of the *Belisarius Begging Alms* as David's "*agrément*," and its favorable reception at the Salon of 1781, were surely turning points in the artist's career. In the course of the next three years David was fully accepted into the Académie with *La douleur d'Andromaque* of 1783,[21] he received d'Angiviller's commission for the smaller version of the *Belisarius Begging Alms* in 1784, and he was given free lodging by Louis XVI in the Louvre.[22]

AN

1 Rosa's *Belisarius* is owned by the Sitwell Estate, Renishaw Hall, Stafford, Derbyshire, England (see Salerno, 1975, no. 110).

2 The Borzone is in the collection of the duke of Devonshire; see Fried, 1980, pp. 145 ff., 235–36 n. 82.

3 See Paris–Detroit–New York, 1974–75, p. 564.

4 See Crow, 1985, pp. 198 ff.

5 Sold, London, Sotheby's, June 21, 1983, no. 30 (now in Japan, Private collection).

6 See Paris–Versailles, 1989–90, no. 48.

7 For the importance of Gravelot's influence on late-eighteenth-century artists see Boime, 1980, pp. 87 ff., figs. 45–48.

8 Jollain's *Belisarius* (Whereabouts unknown) showed Belisarius receiving alms and being recognized by a soldier. Durameau's *Bélisaire, Général des Armées de l'Empereur Justinien, après avoir illustré le règne de ce Prince, tomba dans sa disgrâce, il lui fit crever les yeux dans un âge fort avancé: c'est le moment de retour dans sa famille*, sold in 1970 in Versailles (see Schnapper, in Paris–Versailles, 1989–90, p. 132), depicts Belisarius's return home after his long exile, as recounted in chapter VI of Marmontel's *Belisarius* (London, 1767; reprinted, New York and London, 1975). Vincent's *Bélisaire, réduit à la mendicité, secouru par un officier des troupes de l'Empereur Justinien* of 1776 (Montpellier, Musée Fabre) portrays a soldier giving alms to Belisarius. Peyron's *Bélisaire recevant l'hospitalité d'un paysan qui avait servi sous lui* of 1779 (Toulouse, Musée des Augustins) represents the moment when the elderly father of one of Belisarius's ex-soldiers, now a peasant, presents the general to his household, as occurs in chapter IV, pp. 28–31, of Marmontel's *Belisarius*, as cited above.

9 See Diderot, 1975–83, III, pp. 285–86.

10 The location of Jollain's *Belisarius* sketch is given in a letter dated November 28, 1989, from Jacques Foucart to Arnauld Brejon de Lavergnée (Lille, Archives of the Musée des Beaux-Arts).

11 Charles-Claude de Flahaut de la Billarderie, Comte d'Angiviller, Surintendant des bâtiments du roi from August 24, 1774, controlled government policy and expenditures for the arts.

12 See Boime, 1980, p. 85.

13 See Paris–Detroit–New York, 1974–75, no. 139.

14 The Académie was divided into three levels: *élèves*, *agrées*, and *académiciens*. David was an *élève* of the Académie by September 1766 (see Wildenstein, 1973, p. 4, no. 13). Eight years later David won the Grand Prix de Peinture for the *Antiochus and Stratonice* of 1774 (Paris, École Nationale Supérieure des Beaux-Arts, Inv. no. 2914), enabling him to attend the Académie de France in Rome. On his return to France, David submitted the Lille *Belisarius* to the Académie and was "*agréé*" on August 24, 1781 (see Wildenstein, 1973, p. 11, no. 87). Not until August 22, 1783, with *La douleur d'Andromaque* completed

that year (Paris, École Nationale Supérieure des Beaux-Arts, on deposit at the Musée du Louvre, Inv. no. 8642), did David become a full member of the Académie: an *académicien*. (On the Académie see Albert Boime, *The Academy and French Painting in the Nineteenth Century*, London, 1971.)

15 See Wildenstein, 1973, p. 11, no. 87.

16 See Diderot, 1957–67, IV, p. 377.

17 See Diderot, 1957–67, IV, p. 351.

18 See Diderot, 1957–67, IV, p. 377.

19 See Diderot, 1957–67, IV, p. 351.

20 This was the first in a number of repetitions of his pictures that David painted, with the help of his students, during his long career. In effect, David supervised the artist François-Xavier Fabre, and possibly also Anne-Louis Girodet-Trioson, retouched the painting, and then signed it himself (see Rosenblum, 1965, pp. 473 ff.).

21 See note 13, above.

22 See Wildenstein, 1973, p. 13, no. 94.

PROVENANCE*

The artist, until 1786; sold for 2,000 ecus to the prince elector of Trier, Clemens Wenzeslaus de Saxe, Coblenz, October 1786, until March 1793; sale of Duke Albert of Saxe-Teschen's seized goods, March 1793;** purchased by Louis Vollant (died 1794); seized December 3, 1794, and stored in the rue de Beaune, Paris; restored to the heirs of Louis Vollant, March 1796; House sale, April 1796, for FFr 8,000; Fould, Saint-Morice, Savalète sale, April 4, 1799, no. 112;*** Claude Tolozan sale, February 23–26, 1801, *hors catalogue*, no. 87;**** purchased for FFr 4,800 by Mr. Simon for Cardinal Fesch, until 1802; Lucien Bonaparte (1775–1840), by 1802; to his mother, Mme Marie-Letitia Bonaparte (1750–1836), at an unknown date, until 1829; purchased by John, Sixteenth Earl of Shrewsbury, 1829, until 1852; to his cousin Bertram Arthur, Seventeenth Earl of Shrewsbury; Posthumous sale, by Messrs. Christie & Manson, *Catalogue of the Magnificent Contents of Alton Towers, The Princely Seat of The Earls of Shrewsbury*, July 6–August 8, 1857, no. 18; purchased by Pott of Nottinghamshire (?) for 126 pounds; John, Second Lord Northwick (1770–1859), Cheltenham; Posthumous sale by Mr. Phillips, *Catalogue of the Late Lord Northwick's Extensive and Magnificent Collection . . . , at Thirlestane House, Cheltenham*, July 26–August 30, 1859, no. 457; purchased by art dealer M. Meffre for 105 gns.; sale, Paris, Hôtel des Commissaires-Priseurs, *Tableaux anciens, Collection de M. Meffre: Vente aux Enchères Publiques pour Cause de Cessation d'Affaires*, March 9–10, 1863, no. 15, bought in for FFr 7,150; sold to the Musée des Beaux-Arts, 1863.

* Most of the information for the provenance comes from Paris–Versailles, 1989–90, no. 47, p. 130.
** By 1789 Clemens Wenzeslaus de Saxe wanted to replace David's *Belisarius* with a painting of Pyrrhus by Vincent. The work was sold in March 1793, either through an intermediary or by Clemens Wenzeslaus de Saxe's own brother Albert (see Seelig, 1990, pp. 52 ff.).
*** Lugt 5891.
**** Lugt 6204.

EXHIBITIONS

Paris, 1781, no. 311; Paris, 1860, no. 116; Paris, 1913, no. 15; Valenciennes, 1918, no. 91; London, 1972, no. 60; Paris–Detroit–New York, 1974–75, no. 30; Rome, 1981–82, no. 30; Paris–Versailles, 1989–90, no. 47.

LITERATURE

Oursel, 1984, pp. 184–85, no. 34, colorpl.; Schnapper, in Paris–Versailles, 1989–90, pp. 130–33, no. 47, colorpl.; Carroll, 1990, p. 200, colorpl.; Rosenblum, 1990, p. 193; Seelig, 1990, pp. 52–58.

JEAN-BAPTISTE-JOSEPH WICAR

French

Lille 1762–1834 Rome

29 *Self-Portrait in Spanish Costume*
Oil on canvas, 39 x 29 5/8 in. (99.1 x 75.3 cm.)
Inv. no. 887

Jean-Baptiste-Joseph Wicar—painter, draftsman, and printmaker—is known primarily as the owner of an immense and distinguished collection of Italian Old Master drawings, including many by Raphael (see cat. nos. 51–59), which he bequeathed to his native city, Lille, at his death in 1834. Born in 1762, in the most humble circumstances, he was the recipient of various gifts and grants in support of his early training. He studied history painting, entering the Paris workshop of Jacques-Louis David in 1781, the year in which his master exhibited the *Belisarius Begging Alms* (cat. no. 28) at the Salon. Wicar, intermittently resident in Italy from 1784, first came to the notice of the French art world upon the publication, in 1789, of the first of four volumes of the *Galerie de Florence*, a compendium of engravings after his line drawings of paintings and sculpture in the collection of the grand duke of Tuscany.

Wicar's career was shaped amid the violence and uncertainty of the French Revolution and the Napoleonic Wars. He seems to have been an opportunist, and, although there were difficult moments, he emerged not only as a successful artist but also as a collector and connoisseur. Returning to Paris in 1794 as a protégé of David, Wicar was appointed curator of antiquities at the Louvre, which opened as a public museum the same year, and he joined the Société Républicaine des Arts and the newly formed art commission. An ardent revolutionary, he denounced several of his fellow artists, and was himself denounced and briefly imprisoned in 1795. After Wicar was released he returned to Italy, and, rehabilitated, served from 1797 as a member of the commission requisitioning Italian works of art for France, to be exhibited in the Musée Napoléon.

Wicar settled more or less permanently in Rome in 1801 and, despite his prior activities, was for a time one of the

29

most celebrated painters in the city. From 1803 to 1804 he painted a portrait of Pius VII ratifying the Concordat; in 1807 the royal family of Naples, Joseph Bonaparte and his wife and children; and in the 1820s altarpieces for the cathedrals of Perugia and Foligno. In 1805 he had been admitted to the prestigious Accademia di San Luca in Rome, and he was a member also of the academy in Bologna and, briefly, director of the academy in Naples. Wicar's pure but rather bloodless late neoclassical style—as exemplified by his most important work, the *Raising of the Son of the Widow of Nain* (Lille, Musée des Beaux-Arts)—testifies to the artist's technical proficiency and knowledge of Old Masters. His small portrait drawings, on the other hand, are fresh and direct, and capture the independence of mind and the republican spirit of the new age.

Wicar's self-portraits are variations on two models, dating, respectively, from 1795 and 1805, showing the artist as republican patriot and as academician. The primary version of the first self-portrait was reportedly given to the artist's sister in the summer of 1795: It is a small tondo representing a man in early middle age, with a sharp, intelligent face, wearing a rather colorless bourgeois costume and a black hat with a tricolor cockade.[1]

Subsequent to his election to the Accademia di San Luca, and prior to his departure for Naples, Wicar seems to have given to the academy in Rome the first version of the second portrait of himself, which was exhibited in 1806. By the terms of his will, this first version—since lost—was withdrawn, and another was provided in its place. The portrait here catalogued is the third version. It shows Wicar in the ennobling guise of an academician, wearing a sumptuous costume complete with cape and starched cuffs—which the artist described as in the Spanish style.[2] The pose and costume are intentionally reminiscent of seventeenth-century art—more specifically, of portraits by Frans Hals and self-portraits by van Dyck. Wicar stands before a curtain, drawn back to reveal the aforementioned painting, the *Raising of the Son of the Widow of Nain*. He worked on that picture from 1806 until 1816; it measures no less than five meters by nine, includes some twenty life-size figures and yet another self-portrait, and was intended as the ultimate statement of the artist's ambitions as a history painter. Unfortunately, the presence of this picture within the picture provides only the most approximate of chronological parameters. Wicar's age at the time—given the fact that he seems to have flattered himself—cannot be determined, but it should be noted that he was forty-four when he began the *Raising of*

the Son of the Widow of Nain and fifty-four when he finished it. Quite certainly, he wished to be remembered thus: The portrait, the *Raising of the Son of the Widow of Nain*, and several of his *académies* constituted part of his bequest to his native city—to which he also left funds to benefit young artists from Lille wishing to study as pensioners in Rome.

KBB

1 Musée des Beaux-Arts, Lille, Inv. no. 666; Fernand Beaucamp (1939) records versions left to one of Wicar's pupils, as well as in the Badaloni collection, Rome. Another is on the Paris art market.

2 The version withdrawn from the Accademia di San Luca was given to the Accademia dei Virtuosi, and reportedly showed Wicar's painting of the Concordat in the background. The second version, still in Rome, includes the *Raising of the Son of the Widow of Nain* in the background. Two other versions are recorded by Beaucamp: one bequeathed to another of Wicar's pupils, and a second in a private collection in Lille.

PROVENANCE

The artist; Bequest of Jean-Baptiste-Joseph Wicar, 1834.

EXHIBITION

Lille, 1984, no. 9.

LITERATURE

Beaucamp, 1939, II, pp. 390, 582–83, 590, 634, no. 39, p. 684; Oursel, 1984, pp. 29–30, no. 9, colorpl. cover (detail).

LOUIS-LÉOPOLD BOILLY

French

La Bassée 1761–1845 Paris

30 *The Triumph of Marat*

1794

Oil on paper (seven sheets), mounted on canvas,
31 1/2 x 47 1/4 in. (80 x 120 cm.)

Inv. no. 395

The subject of this painting is a famous event in the French Revolution: Accused by the Convention Nationale of being hostile to the Girondists, Jean-Paul Marat (1743–1793), a doctor and pamphleteer known as "L'Ami du Peuple" (the "Friend of the People"), was acquitted by the Revolutionary Tribunal on April 24, 1793. Boilly depicts a cheering crowd carrying Marat in triumph through the Salle des Pas-Perdus of the Palais de Justice in Paris. A few months later Marat would be assassinated by Charlotte Corday, the Girondists would fall from power, and the Reign of Terror would begin.

30

A large, virtually finished preparatory drawing for this composition is preserved in the Musée Lambinet in Versailles.[1] It differs from the painting in its broader architectural space, smaller-scale figures, and in the addition of three onlookers in the right foreground.

This *Triumph of Marat* was one of Boilly's most popular works. Tradition has it that the painting played an important role at a critical moment in the artist's career,[2] serving to vindicate him from the violent anti-Republican accusations made against him by his compatriot the painter Jean-Baptiste-Joseph Wicar. On April 22, 1794, speaking before the Société Républicaine des Arts, Wicar denounced Boilly for creating "works of a shocking obscenity that offended Republican morality, and which must be burned at the foot of the Tree of Liberty." Warned by one of his colleagues— either Baron Gérard or Anne-Louis Girodet-Trioson— Boilly is said to have improvised this Revolutionary subject as his defense in record time. Not only did the *Triumph of Marat* absolve him of the accusations, but the picture so convinced the Société Républicaine des Arts that they accepted him as one of their members a month later, on May 18, 1794.

Although the painter's son Julien-Léopold Boilly (1796–1874) was known to uphold this legend, in 1828 he acknowledged his father's silence about the incident: "The only thing that I remember him saying is that he was considered suspect, and that he had been denounced as a *corrupter of morals* because of the sometimes frank subjects he had depicted, engravings of which can be seen everywhere."[3] Had there been any real danger? Indeed, in her introduction to the catalogue of the 1988–89 Boilly exhibition in Lille, Susan Siegfried, assisted by the work of W. Olander and Udo van de Sandt, questioned the actual circumstances behind the genesis of *The Triumph of Marat*.[4] Wicar's violent denunciation actually preceded by two days the announcement by the Revolutionary government of a national painting contest to commemorate Marat's successful acquittal exactly one year before. Boilly decided to participate in the competition out of financial considerations (the Revolution having deprived him of his well-to-do clientele under the Ancien Régime) as well as political opportunism. His inspired choice of Marat as a subject came at a time when the cult of this martyr of the Revolution began to take shape. No one before him had undertaken to portray an episode from the hero's life. If Boilly chose the moment of Marat's triumph, it was as much for the opportunity to depict a historical and especially propagandistic event as for the emotional impact of the

scene: an enthusiastic crowd bearing a "fine-featured, dreamy-eyed Marat, of graceful bearing, extending his hand in a benevolent gesture of greeting."[5]

Yet, with the end of the Terror on July 27, 1794, Boilly left the painting unfinished—a fact much deplored in 1847 by Dinaux: "This painting . . . has remained only *a study*; when the danger passed, the *painter of the Graces* did not have the heart to finish his *Triumph of Marat*. This was no doubt a loss for Art, for it would have been a superb picture if the painter had consented to finish it." In a note he explains that, "This large *study*, one of Boilly's finest, is today in the possession of M. *Jules Boilly*, his son, a painter in Paris."[6] Somewhat later, in 1898, Harrisse reported that the Musée de Lille owned "a sketch on separate sheets, mounted on canvas," adding the comment: "Was retouched by Julien Boilly, much to the family's regret."[7] According to Susan Siegfried, Julien's decision to alter the picture was governed by commercial reasons, filial piety, and probably also stemmed from a complex vis-à-vis his father's artistic talents.[8] If Julien did not assemble and then mount the separate sheets on canvas, he did, at the very least, finish painting the composition with the help of the sketch preserved in the Musée Lambinet. This is confirmed in a letter to the future owner, Charles Vatel, a scholar at the Library of Versailles, informing him that the picture was now at his disposal, Julien having finished "adding to the painted figures."[9]

Julien Boilly's additions to the painting may be seen primarily in the awkwardly drawn figures in the shadows at the left and right sides of the canvas. However, this reworking in no way detracts from the picture's intrinsic quality, nor does the fact that the monumental architectural setting and the effect of a "crowd overflowing with optimism and charged with emotion" seem to have been inspired by David's important project of 1791, the *Oath of the Jeu de Paume* (Versailles, Musée National du Château), also never completed.[10]

With his characteristically keen observation and smooth and supple technique, Boilly juxtaposed the isolated figure of Marat against a teeming crowd, with assorted figures frozen in mid-action, as if caught by a camera. Julien Boilly merely put the finishing touches on his talented father's ambitious composition—the first in a series of history paintings that the elder Boilly continued to produce under the First Empire.[11]

A S - D W

1 Pen and black ink, with gray and brown wash, heightened with white gouache and watercolor, on beige paper, 66.5 x 80.7 cm.;

inscribed in pencil in the margin of the mount, at the lower right: *24 avril*. See Lille, 1988–89, no. 13, ill.

2 See Dinaux, 1847, pp. 200–201; Harrisse, 1898, pp. 13–16; Marmottan, 1913, pp. 45–57; de Poncheville, 1931, p. 60.

3 See Benisovitch, 1958, p. 371.

4 For a reconsideration of Boilly's *Marat* see Siegfried, in Lille, 1988–89, pp. 6–13.

5 See Siegfried, in Lille, 1988–89, pp. 8–9.

6 See Dinaux, 1847, p. 200.

7 See Harrisse, 1898, p. 14.

8 See Siegfried, in Lille, 1988–89, p. 6.

9 See Gendre, 1981, p. 13; this was in about 1862, the year Vatel purchased the drawing from Julien Boilly.

10 See Siegfried's remarks and analysis in Lille, 1988–89, p. 9.

11 For example, *The Conscripts of 1807 Marching before the Saint-Denis Gate* of 1808 (Paris, Musée Carnavalet) and the drawing *Napoleon Decorating the Sculptor Cartellier at the Salon of 1808* (Paris, Musée National de la Légion d'Honneur).

PROVENANCE

Collection Julien Boilly; sold for FFr 4,000 to the Musée des Beaux-Arts, 1865.

EXHIBITIONS

Lille, 1889; Valenciennes, 1918, no. 35; Lille, 1933, no. 28; Paris, 1937, no. 241; Brussels, 1947–48, no. 7; Ghent, 1950, no. 1; Berlin, 1964, no. 2; Paris, 1967-2, no. 396; London, 1972, no. 30; Lille, 1988–89, no. 14; Avignon, 1989.

LITERATURE

Dinaux, 1847, p. 200; Gonse, 1874, p. 118; Gonse, 1877, p. 91; Houdoy, 1877, p. 81; Lille, 1889, p. 12; Lenglart, 1893, no. 67; Harrisse, 1898, pp. 14, 134, nos. 544, 1184; Gonse, 1900, pp. 158–59, ill.; Marmottan, 1913, pp. 48–53, ill. opp. p. 50; Valenciennes, 1918, no. 35, ill. p. 178; Beaucamp, 1928, pp. 32–33; de Poncheville, 1931, pp. 56–60, 208–13, ill. p. 60; Ghent, 1950, no. 1, pl. 11; Hallam, 1981, p. 620, fig. 7; Oursel, 1984, pp. 55–56, ill.; Laveissière, in Lille, 1988–89, p. 14; Avignon, 1989, p. 54, ill.

LOUIS-LÉOPOLD BOILLY

French

La Bassée 1761–1845 Paris

31 *Portrait of a Man*

About 1800

Oil on canvas, 22 x 18 1/8 in. (56 x 46 cm.)

Pendant to the *Portrait of a Young Woman* (cat. no. 32)

Inv. no. 1949

Boilly is particularly well known for his small-scale, bust-length portraits—generally 22 x 17 cm.—but he is equally

celebrated for his consummate skill and a certain innovative approach toward painting full-length portraits. This is apparent in the present work and its pendant, which, by their similarity in format, pose, setting, and handling, very likely represent a married couple.[1] Here, the artist shows a man in a rural setting engaged in a task: He holds a billhook in one hand and a branch in the other, and is about to put the finishing touches on a wooden bridge he is building on his property. Pausing in his physical activity, he presents an image of the "gentleman farmer"—a reflection of the Anglomania that swept through France in the early part of the nineteenth century.

From the beginning of his career, Boilly, like the English painters Gainsborough and Reynolds, favored portraits in outdoor settings, depicting his sitters against landscape backgrounds that reflected their moods. Thus, the *Poet in Love* (about 1790; Whereabouts unknown) shows a man seated on a bench in an arbor, alongside a climbing rosebush and with a variety of recognizable plants at his feet. This keen sensitivity to nature[2] is even more pronounced in a group of portraits executed under the Directoire and the Consulat: among them, that of Antoine-Thomas-Laurent Goupil (Paris, Galerie Dru, 1930), the Brezin brothers (formerly collection of the painter Gérard and the Seligmann collection), and of Christophe-Philippe Oberkampf, his two sons, and his eldest daughter in front of the Jouy factory (formerly Collection Henri Mallet, 1898).

The elegantly dressed man in the Lille portrait is somewhat casually posed before a panoramic landscape. In the classical treatment of the subject and the clear and precise delineation of the compositional elements—especially those denoting the man's occupation and his social standing—the portrait reflects the aesthetics of David,[3] while the smooth and meticulous technique recalls the porcelain-like effect of the brushwork in Dutch paintings of the seventeenth century, which Boilly began to collect early on.[4] Nevertheless, the emphasis here is on a particular, sentimental sort of mood, heightened by the importance afforded the background landscape, which is suffused by a soft, golden, changeable light (this is even more true of the pendant *Portrait of a Young Woman*, cat. no. 32).

Indeed, in the first decade of the nineteenth century Boilly, along with such contemporaries as Prud'hon, Gérard, and Gros, formulated a pre-Romantic type of portrait, portraying refined but melancholic figures like the man in the present painting and the young woman in the following one.

AS-DW

1 The identities of the couple remain unknown. Harrisse, 1898, makes no mention of either this portrait or its pendant.

2 As an art collector Boilly especially favored landscape paintings, and his enthusiasm for them never waned. Landscapes comprised the majority of paintings from his collection that he sold in 1829 (see de La Monneraye, 1929).

3 Boilly was a great admirer of David, his contemporary, and even paid him special homage in the remarkable *Painting of the "Consecration" Exhibited in the Grand Salon of the Louvre* of 1810 (60 x 81 cm.; New York, Private collection).

4 See the *Catalogue du précieux cabinet de tableaux des écoles hollandaise, flamande et française de M. Boilly, peintre* . . . , Paris, April 13 and 14, 1829.

PROVENANCE
Acquired along with its pendant, the *Portrait of a Young Woman*, from Galerie Cailleux, Paris, 1980.

EXHIBITIONS
Lille, 1988–89, no. 35; Yokohama–Hokkaido–Osaka–Yamaguchi, 1991–92, no. 3.

LITERATURE
Oursel, in Oursel and Scottez, 1980, pp. 309–10, fig. 1; Oursel, 1984, p. 57; Scottez-De Wambrechies, 1988, p. 129; Scottez-De Wambrechies, in Lille, 1988–89, no. 35, ill. p. 107; Scottez-De Wambrechies, in Brejon and Scottez, 1991, no. 3, ill. p. 20.

LOUIS-LÉOPOLD BOILLY

French

La Bassée 1761–1845 Paris

32 *Portrait of a Young Woman*

About 1800

Oil on canvas, 22 x 18 1/8 in. (56 x 46 cm.)

Pendant to the *Portrait of a Man* (cat. no. 31)

Inv. no. 1950

An elegant young woman stands in a grotto near a cascading river. She has removed her cloak, her hat, and one of her gloves and appears to be consciously posing, yet she leans against the rock with a casual air, and glances into the distance with a dreamy and nostalgic gaze. Her identity remains unknown. What seems likely to have been a compositional study for the painting was sold at auction in Paris.[1] (The drawing, entitled *Woman before a Fireplace*, is listed in Harrisse's catalogue raisonné of the artist's work.)[2] The costume, pose, and expression of the young woman are analogous to those in the painting; only the setting is different. In the drawing she is shown in a bourgeois interior, resting against the mantel of a fireplace in which a fire is burning. Instead of a hat, in her right hand she holds an open book, which she reads by candlelight, but her reading has been interrupted by a reverie, and she stares off into space. The cloak is also included, but it has been cast onto an armchair in the background. The squaring of the drawing for transfer and the liveliness of the line and of the figure's expression suggest that the painter, satisfied with his arrangement, opted to change the background to a natural setting only at the last minute: The river, the trees, and especially the grotto create a romantic ambiance more in keeping with the young woman's pensive mood. This marks Boilly's first step toward the development of a pre-Romantic sensibility, and it finds parallels primarily in the work of his contemporary Baron Gros. The latter's *Portrait of Christine Boyer* (1801; Paris, Musée du Louvre) is very similar in conception to the present picture, and there, too, the sitter's meditative expression and her graceful pose are set off by the landscape.

Other works from the same period as this portrait display Boilly's fidelity to the new aesthetic, although without renouncing the example of David's style: the clear narratives and ordered compositions, the life-like details, and the meticulous handling of the paint, which was influenced by seventeenth-century Dutch painting. Notable among these contemporary works by Boilly are *Mme Oberkampf and Her Two Daughters in the Park at Jouy* (1803; Private collection; the pendant to the male portrait mentioned in the preceding entry), the *Portrait of Mme Tallien and Her Daughter* (formerly Mühlbacher collection), and *The Wait* (sale of the Charpentier collection, Paris, December 2, 1958, no. 116, ill.).

As is the case with all of the portraits mentioned above, the present one is a masterful work in every respect, from its romantic conception to the clear and fluid composition, the sober yet sensitive handling of the paint, and the delicacy of the brushwork, which lends an impressive palpability to the natural setting, the fabrics of the costume, and the ribbons of the hat. Boilly's supreme command of color, already evident in his first commissions—which predate the Revolution[3]—is further revealed in this portrait: The grayish-green and ocher color scheme is discreetly but harmoniously offset by the blue of the ribbon and the orange of the gloves. A golden but nonetheless vibrant light skillfully modulates the space.

AS-DW

1 Laurin, Guilloux, and Buffetaux, June 12, 1972, no. 16, ill. (45 x 36 cm.; black chalk and gray wash, heightened with white, on gray paper, squared for transfer).

2 See Harrisse, 1898, p. 169, no. 968.

3 For example, the works commissioned by Calvet de Lapalun from 1789 to 1792, four of which are in the museum in Saint-Omer: *The Visit, The Impromptu Concert, Ce qui allume l'amour l'éteint,* and *The Jealous Lover* (see Lille, 1988–89, nos. 2–5).

PROVENANCE

Acquired along with its pendant, the *Portrait of a Man,* from Galerie Cailleux, Paris, 1980.

EXHIBITIONS

Lille, 1988–89, no. 36; Yokohama–Hokkaido–Osaka–Yamaguchi, 1991–92, no. 4.

LITERATURE

Oursel, in Oursel and Scottez, 1980, pp. 309–10, fig. 2; Oursel, 1984, pp. 54, 188, no. 36, ill.; Scottez-De Wambrechies, 1988, p. 129, ill. p. 131; Scottez-De Wambrechies, in Lille, 1988–89, no. 36, ill. p. 109; Scottez-De Wambrechies, in Brejon and Scottez, 1991, no. 4, ill. p. 21.

LOUIS-LÉOPOLD BOILLY

French

La Bassée 1761–1845 Paris

---

33   *Trompe-l'oeil Still Life with Coins, on a Pedestal Table*

About 1808–14

Oil on vellum set into mahogany, painting, 18 7/8 x 23 5/8 in. (48 x 60 cm.); pedestal table, height, 29 7/8 in. (76 cm.)

Signed (at the upper right, on the label): *M. Boilly, rue Meslée 12 à Paris*

Inv. no. 1896

Set into the top of an Empire-style pedestal table, or *guéridon,* this trompe-l'oeil still life by Boilly includes scattered piles of coins, a magnifying glass, a pocketknife, a quill, two nails, some playing cards, a piece of broken glass, drops of glue, and a mailing label from a newspaper showing Boilly's address in 1806 (until 1829): 12, rue Meslée, Paris. A clipping from *The Connoisseur* dated November 1902, found in a drawer in the table, notes that the table was once in Napoleon's study at the Château de Saint-Cloud. This may explain why the coin with Napoleon's profile is set slightly apart from the others in the painting. Boilly's work was much appreciated by the emperor, and we know that the artist collaborated with Baron Gérard on a commission from the Manufacture de Sèvres for a tabletop decorated with portraits of the imperial family.[1]

From the beginning of his career Boilly manifested a strong interest in trompe l'oeil, which he explored in monochromatic gray or brown grisaille paintings that resemble engravings,[2] in imitations of marble bas-reliefs,[3] and in polychrome trompe-l'oeil still lifes composed of various objects, one of the first examples of which dates to his early years in Arras (1780–85).[4] Boilly admirably experimented with all of the pictorial and symbolic possibilities of trompe l'oeil—a very old art form that became especially popular in the seventeenth and eighteenth centuries in France and in the Northern and Southern Netherlands. Harrisse catalogued as many as twenty-two works of this type in Boilly's oeuvre.[5] The artist's sense of humor and inventiveness are particularly evident in such a work as the *Trompe l'oeil Representing an Old, Torn Painting Seen from Behind.*[6] In a more satirical vein, Boilly gave vent to his anger at the abuse of power by art critics in a work that was exhibited to much acclaim at the Salon of the Year IX (1800; no. 38): Among other objects seen through a broken window are two half-open brochures entitled *Arlequin au Museum* and *Jocrisse au Museum* and the caption *Artistes, voilà vos censeurs (Artists, here are your censors).*[7]

Two other versions of the Lille trompe-l'oeil tabletop exist: one, painted on a round slab of white marble, depicts coins, signed letters, a quill, and a portrait in miniature of a man;[8] the other, entitled *Coins,* is painted on cardboard and mounted on the top of a small table.[9]

The Lille trompe-l'oeil tabletop is a veritable masterpiece of virtuosity in which the painter evidently took pleasure in tackling an assortment of visual effects with consummate skill by introducing a variety of illusionistic elements: Not only did he depict the traditional piece of broken glass and the magnifying glass, but he even imitated drops of glue on paper, indicated shadows, and included a miniature painting of a spectator pressing his nose in amazement against the glass. In its deformity, the latter's face resembles a caricature—a genre that Boilly practiced with equal facility, and which reached its apogee in the series known as the *Grimaces* (1823–28). A second miniature, set slightly back from the first, reveals Boilly's talents as a portraitist by providing a signature in the form of a self-portrait. The varied yet spare composition, the subtle humor of certain details, the perfection of the illusionistic treatment, and the mixture of genres attest to Boilly's expertise as a painter as well as to the humanistic aspects of his work.

AS-DW

1 See Harrisse, 1898, p. 29.

2 See, for example, *Ah! It Will Do* (Saint-Omer, Musée Sandelin), the *Young Woman Seated on a Window Ledge* (London, National Gallery), and *Our Little Soldiers* (Musée de Douai, La Chartreuse).

3 Compare *The Triumph of Amphitrite* and *The Triumph of Galatea,* copies after bas-reliefs by Clodion (see Lille, 1988–89, p. 140).

4 Formerly in the collection of Lenglart, Lille, and of the actor Sacha Guitry; acquired by the Sterling and Francine Clark Art Institute, Williamstown, 1981.

5 See Harrisse, 1898, p. 68.

6 87 x 32 cm.; sale of the comte de Pourtalès collection, 1865.

7 See Harrisse, 1898, pp. 21, 78, no. 24.

8 Diameter, 47 cm.; sale of the Linet collection, Paris, Palais Galliéra, March 23, 1963, no. 4, ill.; Private collection, Switzerland.

9 22 x 27 cm.; see Harrisse, 1898, p. 138, no. 589.

PROVENANCE

Table from Napoleon's study at the Château de Saint-Cloud; sold, London, November 1902;* acquired on the Paris art market, 1974.

* See *The Connoisseur*, November 1902, IV, no. 15, item no. R 632, ill.

EXHIBITION

Lille, 1988–89, no. 42.

LITERATURE

Oursel, 1976, p. 388, ill. p. 389; Milman, 1982, p. 89, ill.; Oursel, 1984, p. 57, ill. 83, p. 224; Scottez-De Wambrechies, 1988, p. 132, ills. pp. 132–33; Laveissière, in Lille, 1988–89, p. 15; Scottez-De Wambrechies, in Lille, 1988–89, no. 42, ill. p. 121; Siegfried, 1992 (forthcoming).

FRANCISCO DE GOYA Y LUCIENTES

Spanish

Fuendetodos 1746–1828 Bordeaux

34 *Time* (*Le temps*; *Les vieilles*)

About 1808–12

Oil on canvas, 71 1/4 x 49 1/4 in. (181 x 125 cm.)

Inscribed (at the bottom right): X 23

Inv. no. 50

From 1808 to 1814 Spain was in a state of political flux. On March 18, 1808, Charles IV abdicated in favor of his son Ferdinand VII. Barely a month later Ferdinand VII relinquished the crown to Napoleon, who, in turn, placed his brother Joseph Bonaparte on the throne. The outbreak of the War of Independence (the Peninsular War) at the end of May 1808 changed the lives of the Spanish people. With the support of British troops under Wellington the Spanish staged a massive revolt against Napoleon's invasion that lasted some six years (1808–14). All these events helped to fuel Goya's imagination. Indeed, some of Goya's most memorable works date from this period: the *Disasters of War* of 1810–14,[1] *The Second of May 1808* of 1814 (Madrid, Museo del Prado),[2] *The Third of May 1808* of 1814 (Madrid, Museo del Prado),[3] the *Duke of Wellington on Horseback* of 1812 (London, Wellington Museum),[4] as well as a series of large genre paintings that include *Time* and *The Letter* (see cat. no. 35).

Time has a double significance. It is both a *vanitas* and a biting critique of the libertine Queen Maria Luisa.[5] The composition of *Time* and its moralizing message are similar to those of an engraving, *Vanity with Death* (fig. 1), by Hendrick Hondius after Jacob de Gheyn the Younger (1565–1629).[6] Even if Goya did not own this engraving, he would certainly have seen it or a similar one in the large print collection of his friend Sebastián Martínez. De Gheyn's depiction of a beautiful, young, buxom and bejeweled woman in the presence of an old hag was a common means of moralizing on the transitory nature of life. Goya, however, immediately confronts the viewer with the hag's ravaged old age and only alludes to youth by showing the hag comparing her mirrored image with a miniature that may well represent her in her younger days. A mirror, with *Que tal?* ("How goes it?") inscribed on the back, is being held by a syphilitic maidservant for the hag to look into.[7] Father Time, clutching a broom

FIGURE 1. Hendrick Hondius, after Jacob de Gheyn the Younger. *Vanity with Death*. Engraving. The Metropolitan Museum of Art, New York. The Elisha Whittelsey Collection. The Elisha Whittelsey Fund, 1949

(traditionally he is pictured holding a scythe or an hourglass), appears to shed light onto the mirror, which enlightens the old hag to the fact that, despite her expensive garb, she is no longer the fresh, young, innocent woman of the miniature. One of Father Time's roles is to unveil Truth.[8] The diamond-studded arrow that ornaments the old hag's orange-blond hair is similar to the one worn by Queen Maria Luisa in Goya's *The Family of Charles IV* of 1800–1801 (Madrid, Museo del Prado);[9] an arrow purportedly was given to Queen Maria Luisa by her lover Manuel de Godoy in 1800. Certainly, this painting of the royal family was so famous that it would have been impossible not to associate the hag in *Time* with the queen herself. Maria Luisa and, indeed, the entire Spanish royal family had lost favor with the Spanish people; at the time that Goya painted this picture the throne of Spain, abandoned by the royal family, was occupied by Napoleon's brother Joseph.

Time, the *Maja and Celestina on a Balcony* (D. Bartolomé March Servera),[10] and the *Majas on a Balcony* (Private collection)[11] were painted from about 1808 to 1812. All three works appear in the inventory of October 1812, confirming that by this date they had been completed.[12] X rays of *Time* and of the *Maja and Celestina on a Balcony* reveal that Goya painted over compositions by a different artist.[13] During the war years (1808–14) supplies were difficult to come by and it is understandable that Goya would have used whatever canvases he could obtain, even if they already had been painted.

AN

1 See Gassier and Wilson, 1971, nos. 993–1148.

2 See Gassier and Wilson, 1971, no. 982.

3 See Gassier and Wilson, 1971, no. 984.

4 See Gassier and Wilson, 1971, no. 896.

5 See López-Rey, 1964, pp. 59–61.

6 This engraving was brought to my attention by Walter Liedtke.

7 Several works by Goya include a mirror and a mirror image. There exists a series of six drawings (see Gassier and Wilson, 1971, nos. 648–653) depicting mirror images; of these the closest to *Time* is the drawing *Hasta la muerte* (Madrid, Museo del Prado; see Gassier and Wilson, 1971, no. 562).

8 Father Time is also depicted in the *Allegory on the Adoption of the Constitution of 1812* of 1812–14 (Stockholm, Nationalmuseum; see Gassier and Wilson, 1971, no. 695; Pérez-Sánchez and Sayre, in Madrid–Boston–New York, 1988–89, no. 74).

9 See Gassier and Wilson, 1971, no. 783.

10 See Gassier and Wilson, 1971, no. 958.

11 See Gassier and Wilson, 1971, no. 959.

12 After the death of Goya's wife, Josefa Bayeau, in 1812, an inventory was drawn up of property to be given to their son Xavier. Subsequently, an initial *X* (for Xavier), followed by a number, was painted in white in one of the lower corners of the paintings (see de Salas,

1964, pp. 99–110; Gassier and Wilson, 1971, pp. 246–47, appendix I, p. 381). An *X23* is clearly visible at the bottom right corner of *Time*. However, both the *Maja and Celestina on a Balcony* and the *Majas on a Balcony* have lost their marks. The mark *X24* formerly on the *Maja and Celestina on a Balcony* is visible in a black-and-white photograph from the Moreno Archives (see Gassier and Wilson, 1971, p. 256, no. 958) and the *X24* formerly on the *Majas on a Balcony* is visible in a photograph in the archives of the Galerie Durand-Ruel, Paris (see Gassier and Wilson, 1971, p. 256, no. 959).

13 I have not seen an X ray of the *Majas on a Balcony* (Private collection). See Arturo Gilardoni, Riccardo Ascani Orsini, and Silvia Taccani, *X-rays in Art.* Como, 1977, pp. 164–67.

PROVENANCE

The artist's son Xavier Goya, Madrid, by 1812 until 1825; purchased by Baron Isidore-Justin-Séverin Taylor (1789–1879), art adviser to King Louis-Philippe;* King Louis-Philippe, by 1838; Posthumous sale, London, Messrs. Christie & Manson, *Catalogue of the Pictures Forming the Celebrated Spanish Gallery of His Majesty the Late King Louis-Philippe*, May 6–7, 13–14, 20–21, 1853, no. 169; purchased by Durlacher for 4 pounds 15 shillings; Warneck, by 1873; purchased by M. Sauvage for FFr 2,000, Mme Gentil for FFr 500, and M. Reynart for FFr 500; Gift of M. Sauvage, Mme Gentil, and M. Reynart, 1874.

* See catalogue number 35.

EXHIBITIONS

Valenciennes, 1918, no. 140; Paris, 1938, no. 21; Ghent, 1950, no. 37; Paris, 1963-2, no. 123; Berlin, 1964, no. 17; The Hague–Paris, 1970, no. 43.

LITERATURE

Gassier and Wilson, 1971, pp. 243, 245–46, 256 n. 961, p. 266, no. 961, ill.; Baticle and Marinas, 1981, pp. 271–72, *annexe* no. 24; Oursel, 1984, p. 49, colorpl.; Heckes, 1991, pp. 93–100, fig. 2.

FRANCISCO DE GOYA Y LUCIENTES

Spanish

Fuendetodos 1746–1828 Bordeaux

---

35 *The Letter* (*Les jeunes*; *Femme lisant une lettre*)
About 1814–19
Oil on canvas, 71 1/4 x 49 1/4 in. (181 x 125 cm.)
Inv. no. 9

Goya derived this genre scene of a lady and her maidservant, set against a backdrop of laundresses, from two of his earlier works, *The Parasol* of 1777 and *The Laundresses* of 1780 (both Madrid, Museo del Prado; see figs. 1, 2). However, in the present painting, completed about thirty-five years after the *Laundresses*, the underlying message of moral laxity has become more biting. Whereas the lapdog, synonymous with lust

FIGURE 1. Francisco de Goya y Lucientes. *The Parasol*. Oil on canvas. Museo del Prado, Madrid

FIGURE 2. Francisco de Goya y Lucientes. *The Laundresses*. Oil on canvas. Museo del Prado, Madrid

or animal passion,[1] slumbered on his mistress's lap in *The Parasol*, in the Lille painting he is shown jumping up at his mistress. Goya further accentuates the licentious undertones of the work by delineating the woman's bodice using thick white paint, which contrasts dramatically with her thinly painted black dress, thus calling attention to her breasts. Ignoring the viewer, the young woman—her face in full sunlight despite the parasol—looks down at the letter in her right hand. It is the maidservant, fiddling with the parasol, whose face is in the shade. In the background, thinly painted in monochromatic tones, are the haggard laundresses hard at work, with the fruits of their labor hanging up to dry on barely visible branches. Goya has come a long way from his early cartoon for a tapestry in which he depicted laundresses, young and dewy eyed, seated in a lush, green Arcadian setting.[2] Here, they add yet another undercurrent of promiscuity to the picture. In eighteenth-century painting, laundresses were often depicted as sexually accessible and even promiscuous, and in 1790 a royal decree had been issued prohibiting the laundresses who worked along the banks of the Manzanares River in Madrid from "hailing passers by, making obscene gestures, and gathering around peaceful middle class citizens."[3] It is not accidental that the laundress at the far right of the composition arrests our attention and draws us into the picture.

Unlike *Time* (cat. no. 34), *The Letter* does not appear in the inventory drawn up after the death of Josefa Goya in 1812; most likely it was painted at least two years later.[4] In *The Letter* Goya placed the figures farther from the picture plane, as he had done in *The Forge* of about 1812–19 (New York, Frick Collection; also not included in the 1812 inventory); conversely in the *Maja and Celestina on a Balcony*, the *Majas on a Balcony*, and *Time*—all of which were painted from about 1808 to 1812—the figures appear close to the picture plane. In addition, both *The Forge* and *The Letter* display a similar monochromatic palette, which foreshadows Goya's black paintings of 1819–20.

The identity of the woman reading the letter remains undetermined, although it has been proposed that she may be either the young Queen Maria Luisa[5] or Leocadia Weiss, with whom Goya was amorously involved from about 1812 until his death. The second suggestion seems the more plausible.[6] Indeed, a comparison of the young woman in *The Letter* and the sitter in the later work of 1820–23 *La Leocadia* (Madrid, Museo del Prado) reveals a striking similarity.

Over the years, *Time* and *The Letter* have been considered either as pendants or as part of a series of genre pictures.[7] However, they were painted within an interval of about four years, making it unlikely that they were conceived as pendants. Instead, the two pictures in Lille are probably part of a series of large figure paintings that Goya worked on over a period of about eleven years (1808–19).[8] Four of these paintings, including *Time* and *The Letter*, are devoted to women, and each conveys a social message that links them together. Although both *The Letter* and *Time* were owned by King Louis-Philippe, he chose not to exhibit *Time*; perhaps he found it too macabre.

AN

1 See Posner, 1973, pp. 77–83.

2 Goya also depicted laundresses in another oil painting and in three drawings: a cartoon for a tapestry *Laundresses* (fig. 2), the *Three Washerwomen: Album B. 45* (New York, The Metropolitan Museum of Art; see Gassier and Wilson, 1971, no. 411), the *Useful Work: Album E. 37* (Private collection; see Gassier and Wilson, 1971, no. 1406), and the *Washerwomen* (Madrid, Biblioteca Nacional; see Gassier and Wilson, 1971, no. 1847).

3 See Tomlinson, 1889, p. 101.

4 See catalogue number 34, note 12.

5 See Heckes, 1991, pp. 97–100.

6 See Gassier and Wilson, 1971, pp. 242–43.

7 For a comprehensive summary of writings on the question of whether these pictures are pendants or part of a series see Heckes, 1991, pp. 93–94.

8 These include the *Maja and Celestina on a Balcony* of about 1808–12 (166 x 108 cm.; D. Bartolomé March Servera; see Gassier and Wilson, 1971, no. 958), the *Majas on a Balcony* of about 1808–12 (166 x 107 cm.; Private collection; see Gassier and Wilson, 1971, no. 959), *Time* of about 1808–12 (181 x 125 cm.; see cat. no. 34), *The Letter* of about 1814–19 (the present work), and *The Forge* of about 1812–19 (181.6 x 125 cm.; New York, Frick Collection; see Gassier and Wilson, 1971, no. 965).

PROVENANCE

The artist's son Xavier Goya, Madrid, until 1825; purchased by Baron Isidore-Justin-Séverin Taylor (1789–1879), art adviser to King Louis-Philippe;* King Louis-Philippe, by 1838; Galerie Espagnol, Paris, 1838, no. 104; Posthumous sale, London, Messrs. Christie & Manson, *Catalogue of the Pictures Forming the Celebrated Spanish Gallery of His Majesty the Late King Louis-Philippe*, May 6–7, 13–14, 20–21, 1853, no. 353; purchased by Durlacher for 21 pounds; Warneck, by 1873; purchased by the Musée des Beaux-Arts for FFr 7,000, 1874.

* In 1825 Baron Taylor purchased eight paintings from Xavier Goya for 15,500 *réaux*; see the receipt in the Archives Nationales, Paris, O (4) 1725.

EXHIBITIONS

Valenciennes, 1918, no. 139; Paris, 1938, no. 20; Ghent, 1950, no. 36; Paris, 1963-2, no. 126; Berlin, 1964, no. 18; The Hague–Paris, 1970, no. 42.

LITERATURE

Gassier and Wilson, 1971, pp. 242–43, colorpl. p. 243, pp. 245, 256 n. 962, p. 266, no. 962, ill.; Baticle and Marinas, 1981, p. 85, no. 104, ill.; Oursel, 1984, pp. 190–91, no. 37, colorpl.; Heckes, 1991, pp. 93–100, fig. 1.

JEAN-LOUIS-ANDRÉ-THÉODORE GERICAULT

French

Rouen 1791–1824 Paris

---

36 *The Race of the Barberi Horses*

1817

Oil on paper, mounted on canvas, 17 3/4 x 23 5/8 in. (45.1 x 60 cm.)

Inv. no. 475

Horses played an important role in the life and oeuvre of Théodore Gericault. His first Salon painting, depicting a victorious officer on horseback, was *The Charging Chasseur* (*L'officier de chasseurs à cheval de la garde chargeant*; Paris, Musée du Louvre, Inv. no. 4885), which won him a gold medal at the Salon of 1812. Two years later *The Charging Chasseur* was exhibited once again, along with two new paintings that also conspicuously include horses, *The Wounded Cuirassier* (*Le cuirassier blessé*; Paris, Musée du Louvre, Inv. no. 4886) and the *Artillery Exercise on the Grenelle Plain* (now lost). In July 1814, Gericault joined the cavalry of the king's musketeers, remaining with them until October 1815, when he then focused on winning the 1816 Prix de Rome—a prestigious competition for students at the École des Beaux-Arts in Paris. Although Gericault did not win the prize, the twenty-five-year-old artist was able to travel to Italy in early September 1816 with the help of an annuity provided by his mother. He arrived in Rome in November, having already spent a month in Florence studying the works of the Old Masters.

The most thrilling event of the Roman Carnival—a week of festivities that ended on the last Sunday before Lent—was the race of the Barberi horses.[1] The horses ran the length of the Corso, one thousand six hundred and fifty yards, from the Piazza del Popolo to the Piazza Venezia. This memorable event caught the attention of both artists and writers alike: Goethe, Mme de Staël, Alexandre Dumas, Fragonard, Horace and Carle Vernet, just to name a few. Perhaps the most telling account is that given by Goethe, who described the races from their inception, "the moment when the excitement of the thousands of spectators reaches its peak," to the often dramatic conclusion, when either the horses are "skillfully caught and tied up in an enclosure" or "the grooms in the Piazza Venezia fail to catch their horses," and, "again crowded with people, accidents . . . occur."[2] Gericault, too, was captivated by the races, which he wit-

36

nessed during the week of February 6, 1817. Indeed, until his departure for Paris in September, Gericault devoted most of his time to making drawings and paintings of the *Moza*, the start of the race, and of the *Ripresa*, the end of the race, for an ambitious project that never came to fruition. Numerous drawings by Gericault of the races are known, but of the more than twenty oil studies that he devoted to this subject only five remain; one of these is the Lille painting and another the Baltimore picture mentioned below.[3]

The Race of the Barberi Horses, as Lorenz Eitner convincingly argues, appears to depict the *Moza*, and not the *Ripresa* as previously had been thought.[4] Although no starting rope is

FIGURE 1. Jean-Louis-André-Théodore Gericault. *Riderless Racers at Rome*. 1817. Oil on paper, mounted on canvas. Walters Art Gallery, Baltimore

visible, barely detectable at the far right of the composition is a red-draped stand with spectators, and at the far left are part of the wooden stand as well as the three windows of a palazzo. All of these elements are more summarily depicted in the *Riderless Racers at Rome* of 1817 (Baltimore, Walters Art Gallery, Inv. no. 37.189; see fig. 1), which, of the four paintings, is the closest to the Lille work. Whether the *Race of the Barberi Horses* is the *Ripresa* or the *Moza* is moot; what is important is that in the Lille painting Gericault has condensed the event and used it to portray the conflict between man and beast. The stands and the palazzo are secondary; the focus rather is on the grooms in their colorful Phrygian caps, and their struggle to hold down the rearing Barberi horses. The raking light, which falls from left to right, highlighting the head and the flank of the rearing white horse in the center and the face of the groom to the far right, only

intensifies the sense of drama. Scarcely discernible in the left foreground is a secondary scene: a blue-caped peasant fleeing from a runaway horse, with a fallen figure just behind him—a vignette that recalls Raphael's *Expulsion of Heliodorus from the Temple* in the Stanza d'Eliodoro of the Palazzo Vaticano.

Eitner called the *Race of the Barberi Horses* "a milestone in [Gericault's] work and in French art of the period."[5] The mass of struggling bodies bathed in dramatic lighting foreshadows Gericault's most important painting, *The Raft of the Medusa* of 1819 (Paris, Musée du Louvre, Inv. no. RF 4884), begun soon after his return to Paris from Rome.

AN

1 The race of the Barberi horses was a tradition that began in 1567 and lasted until 1884. For a good history of the race see Bazin, 1990, IV, pp. 35–66.

2 See Goethe, 1982, pp. 462–64.

3 See Clément, 1879-2, p. 100. The other related works by Gericault are the *Start of the Barberi Race* (Paris, Musée du Louvre, Inv. no. RF 2042), the *Start of the Barberi Race* (Malibu, The J. Paul Getty Museum, Inv. no. 85.PA.406), and the *Four Youths Holding a Running Horse* (Rouen, Musée des Beaux-Arts, Inv. no. 866.3.1). All three are oil on paper mounted on canvas; they are of the same dimensions (45 x 60 cm.) except for the work in the Getty museum (20 x 29 cm.), and date from 1817. Gericault also did numerous drawings, two of which relate to the Lille painting: the Study for *The Barberi Horses* (Stockholm, Nationalmuseum, Inv. no. 37.1981; 14.2 x 27.3 cm.) and the *Men Struggling with Horses* (Truro, England, Royal Institution of Cornwall County Museum and Art Gallery; 16.8 x 27 cm.); both are pen and pencil on tracing paper and date, as well, from 1817.

4 See Eitner, 1983, p. 123.

5 See Eitner, 1983, p. 124.

PROVENANCE

Possibly included under no. 81, as *Huit tableaux esquisses dont six représentent des courses de Rome: 250 F*, in the posthumous inventory of the artist's collection; probably included in the posthumous sale of the contents of Gericault's studio, Paris, Hôtel Bullion, November 2–3, 1824, no. 13, as *Dix-huit esquisses: courses, portraits, chevaux et cavaliers;** Mme Maracci, until 1901; Gift of Mme Maracci, 1901.

* See Eitner, 1959, p. 119.

EXHIBITIONS

Valenciennes, 1918, no. 131; Recklinghausen, 1959, no. 107; Berlin, 1964, no. 16; Los Angeles–Detroit–Philadelphia, 1971–72, no. 40; Calais–Arras–Douai–Lille, 1975–76, no. 30; Rome, 1979–80, no. 15; San Francisco, 1989, no. 17; Paris, 1991–92-1, no. 116.

LITERATURE

Murphy, 1972, n.p., fig. 2; Grunchec, 1978, p. 104, no. 107, pl. XX; Eitner, 1983, pp. 123–24, 302 pl. 21, 337 n. 82; Oursel, 1984, pp. 192–93, no. 38, colorpl.; Bazin, 1990, IV, pp. 73, 212, no. 1383, ill., colorpl. (detail); Laveissière, in Laveissière and Michel, 1991, pp. 98, 105 colorpl. 175, p. 360, no. 117.

EUGÈNE DELACROIX

French

Charenton–Saint-Maurice 1798–1863 Paris

---

37 *Medea About to Murder Her Children*

Oil on canvas, 102 3/8 x 65 in. (260 x 165.1 cm.)

Signed and dated (at the lower left): EUG.DELACROIX/ 1838.

Inv. no. 542

Like Gericault, Delacroix was a pupil of the neoclassical painter Pierre-Narcisse Guérin (1774–1833), but he was also influenced by earlier artists such as Rubens and the Venetians Titian and Veronese. His first major painting was the *Barque of Dante* (Paris, Musée du Louvre), which was shown at the Salon of 1822. Five years later, at the Salon of 1827–28, he exhibited the colossal *Death of Sardanapalus*, which at the time was severely criticized for its incoherent composition and for falling outside the standards of decorum exemplified by the work of Delacroix's principal rival, Jean-Auguste-Dominique Ingres.

In 1832 Delacroix accompanied the French ambassador, the comte de Mornay, on a diplomatic mission to Morocco. Delacroix's North African experience was fundamental to his subsequent development as an artist, and he continued to paint Moroccan subjects for the rest of his life. Among his masterpieces in this genre are the *Women of Algiers in Their Apartment* of 1834 (Paris, Musée du Louvre) and *Arabs Skirmishing in the Mountains*, which was executed in 1863 (Washington, D.C., National Gallery of Art).

Delacroix undertook the decoration of the Salon du Roi in the Palais-Bourbon in Paris in 1833, and during most of the following decade he was engaged in the execution of murals for the Deputies' Library in the same building. He painted the dome of the Peers' Library in the Palais du Luxembourg, Paris, from 1841 to 1845, and in 1849 he was entrusted with the decoration of the Chapel of the Holy Angels in the church of Saint-Sulpice. The last project occupied Delacroix until 1861, two years before his death. The artist was also a talented printmaker as well as an innovative and highly accomplished draftsman.

Delacroix had considered executing a picture of Medea as early as 1820, when he noted in a sketchbook, "Médée tue ses 2 enfants."[1] In 1824 Delacroix wrote in his journal, "Médée m'occupe,"[2] but he probably did not begin work on the present painting until 1836.[3] The picture is signed and dated 1838, and it was shown at the Salon that year. Greatly admired by contemporary critics, the painting was purchased by the State for the museum in Lille on July 31, 1838, for the sum of 4,000 francs.[4]

According to legend, Medea was the wife of Jason, whom she had helped to obtain the Golden Fleece and by whom she had had two sons. When Jason abandoned her for Glauce, the daughter of the king of Corinth, the vengeful Medea murdered the two children. The tragedy is the subject of plays by Euripides, Seneca, Longepierre, Glover, and Legouvé. Lee Johnson notes that the most likely source for Delacroix's interpretation of the story is a play by Corneille in which one scene takes place in a grotto, although the actual location of the murder is not specified.[5]

In composition, *Medea About to Murder Her Children* reveals Delacroix's keen interest in Italian Renaissance painting. Even though he never went to Italy, he was familiar with the collections of the Louvre and executed numerous drawings after works by Old Masters. The critic Étienne-Jean Delécluze was the first to point out similarities with Correggio's *Jupiter and Antiope* (Paris, Musée du Louvre),[6] and the compact, pyramidal composition of Delacroix's painting recalls both Raphael's Florentine Madonnas and Andrea del Sarto's *Charity* (Paris, Musée du Louvre).

Some twenty years after he completed the picture now in Lille Delacroix returned to the subject of Medea, further developing ideas that he had begun to explore in his studies for the earlier painting. A variant, signed and dated 1859, was formerly in the Nationalgalerie, Berlin, but was destroyed during World War II.[7] Two reduced replicas of the picture in Lille, both signed and dated 1861 but possibly begun somewhat earlier, are in the Louvre and in a private collection in Paris.[8]   WMG

1 Paris, Musée du Louvre, Département des Arts Graphiques, Inv. no. RF 9153, folio 8 (recto). The date July 13, 1820, appears on folio 16 (verso). See Sérullaz, 1984, no. 1745, ill.; Johnson, 1981–89, III, p. 80, under no. 261.

2 *Journal*, March 4, 1824.

3 See Johnson, 1981–89, III, p. 73, under no. 259.

4 See Sérullaz, 1963-1, pp. 184–85, under no. 245.

5 See Johnson, 1981–89, III, p. 80, under no. 261.

6 *Journal des Débats*, March 8, 1838. See Johnson, 1981–89, III, p. 80, under no. 261.

7 See Johnson, 1981–89, III, no. 333, IV, pl. 152.

8 See Johnson, 1981–89, III, nos. 343, 344, IV, plates 153, 154, respectively.

PROVENANCE

Acquired by the State for the Musée des Beaux-Arts, 1838.

37: detail

EXHIBITIONS

Paris, Salon of 1838, no. 456; Paris, 1855, no. 2913; Paris, 1885, no. 130; Valenciennes, 1918, no. 95; Basel, 1921, no. 68; Paris, 1930, no. 90; Paris, 1937, no. 318; Zurich, 1939, no. 327; Paris, 1963-1, no. 249; Berlin, 1964, no. 11; Edinburgh–London, 1964, no. 40.

LITERATURE

Johnson, 1981–89, III, no. 261, IV, pl. 79 (with complete bibliography); Oursel, 1984, no. 39, ill.

EUGÈNE DELACROIX

French

Charenton–Saint-Maurice 1798–1863 Paris

38   *Medea About to Murder Her Children*

Oil on canvas, 18 1/8 x 15 in. (46 x 38 cm.)

Inv. no. 933

According to Lee Johnson, this freely painted oil sketch may have been executed as early as 1836, when Delacroix wrote to his friend Frédéric Villot (1809–1875), "J'ai commencé la *Médée* qui se débrouille; nous verrons."[1] The sketch corresponds rather closely to the finished painting, although in the latter Delacroix abandoned the blue cape that here swirls up behind the head of Medea.

                                                                WMG

1 *Correspondance*, I, p. 416. See Johnson, 1981–89, III, p. 73, under no. 259.

PROVENANCE

Posthumous sale of the contents of Delacroix's studio, Paris, Hôtel Drouot, February 22–27, 1864, no. 139.

EXHIBITIONS

Valenciennes, 1918, no. 96; Recklinghausen, 1959, no. 70; Recklinghausen–Utrecht, 1962, no. 31; Bern, 1963–64, no. 43; Paris, 1963-1, no. 250; Bremen, 1964, no. 37; Montauban, 1967, no. 221; Moscow–Leningrad, 1968–69, no. 29; Paris, 1973; Sydney–Melbourne, 1980–81, no. 25.

LITERATURE

Johnson, 1981–89, III, no. 259, IV, pl. 78 (with complete bibliography).

EUGÈNE DELACROIX

French

Charenton–Saint-Maurice 1798–1863 Paris

39   Preparatory drawings for *Medea About to Murder Her Children*

A.   *Two Sketches of Medea About to Murder Her Children*; *Head of a Boy*; *Study of Saint Sebastian*

Pen and brown ink, and brown wash, 8 1/8 x 13 in. (20.7 x 33 cm.)

Inscribed in pen and brown ink (at the upper margin): *l'air*; (to the right of center): *ombres plus claires/ dans les . . . jaunes.*

Inv. Pluchart 1281

At the posthumous sale of the contents of Delacroix's studio in 1864 the city of Lille acquired for the Musée des Beaux-Arts some twenty-seven studies for *Medea About to Murder Her Children*.[1] Most of these drawings are directly related to the painting in Lille (see cat. no. 37), although, according to Alfred Robaut and later to Lee Johnson, at least one of them may have been executed later, in connection with the lost variant painted in 1859.[2] Two further preparatory drawings for the picture in Lille are in the Musée du Louvre, Paris,[3] and another is in the Musée Bonnat in Bayonne.[4]

This sheet is one of several preparatory drawings in which Medea is represented facing right.[5] Johnson suggests that these may be the earliest of Delacroix's studies for the painting, since two of them are on the same sheets of paper as sketches for the figure of Saint Sebastian in the *Saint Sebastian Tended by the Holy Women*, which was executed in 1836 and is now in the church of Saint-Michel in Nantua.[6]

                                                                WMG

1 Paris, Hôtel Drouot, February 22–27, 1864, no. 335: "Médée furieuse (1838). Dessins et croquis. 27 feuilles."

2 Pluchart 1274. See Robaut, 1885, no. 669, ill., p. 490; Johnson, 1981–89, III, p. 80, under no. 261.

3 Inv. nos. RF 9356, RF 22966 (verso). See Sérullaz, 1984, I, nos. 259, ill., 260 (verso), ill.

4 Inv. no. 209 (N.I. 557). See Sérullaz, in Ducourau and Sérullaz, 1979, no. 53, ill. Johnson remarks that the drawing in Bayonne "has more in common with the design of the painting dated 1859, while seeming to have been drawn in conjunction with the picture of 1838" (Johnson, 1981–89, III, pp. 80–81, under no. 261).

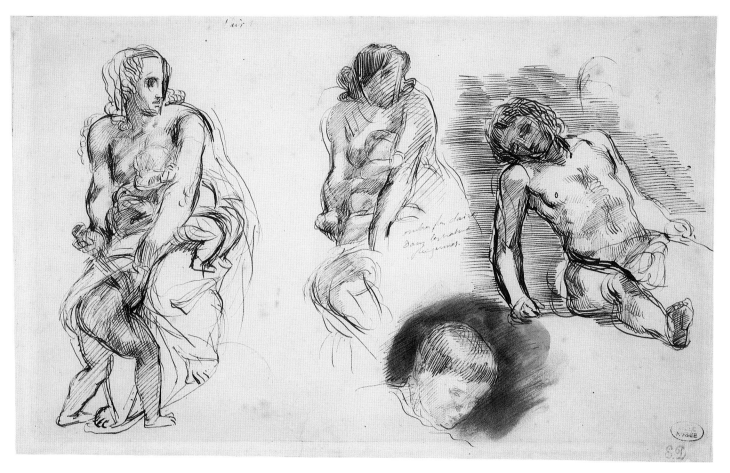

39 A

5 Medea also faces right on a sheet of studies for the *Medea* and the
Saint Sebastian (Pluchart 1279; Sérullaz, 1963-1, no. 247, ill.; Oursel,
1974-2, no. 26, pl. 78) and in a red-chalk sketch on tracing paper,
which was acquired by the Musée des Beaux-Arts, Lille, from Alfred
Robaut in 1878 (Pluchart 1296; Sérullaz, 1963-1, no. 248, ill.).

6 See Johnson, 1981–89, IV, no. 422, pl. 230.

PROVENANCE

Eugène Delacroix (Lugt Suppl. 838 a); Posthumous sale of the contents
of Delacroix's studio, Paris, Hôtel Drouot, February 22–27, 1864, part
of no. 335.

LITERATURE

Pluchart, 1889, no. 1281.

B. *Medea About to Murder Her Children*

Graphite, 8 13/16 x 6 1/2 in. (22.4 x 16.5 cm.)

There are scattered stains.

Inscribed in graphite (along the bottom edge): *Connu . . . à . . .*

Inv. Pluchart 1266

This study is very close in composition to the oil sketch (cat.
no. 38), although here Medea holds a dagger in each hand
and is pursued by a group of figures who appear at the
entrance to the grotto. Johnson remarks that the omission of
these figures from the finished work "enhances the drama by
leaving the object of Medea's fearsome attention to the
imagination."[1]

WMG

1 See Johnson, 1981–89, III, p. 80, under no. 261.

PROVENANCE

Eugène Delacroix (Lugt Suppl. 838 a); Posthumous sale of the contents
of Delacroix's studio, Paris, Hôtel Drouot, February 22–27, 1864, part
of no. 335.

EXHIBITIONS

Recklinghausen, 1959, no. 71; Paris, 1963-1, no. 257; London–
Cambridge–Birmingham–Glasgow, 1974–75, no. 27.

LITERATURE

Robaut, 1885, part of no. 670; Pluchart, 1889, no. 1266; Sérullaz,
1963-1, no. 253, ill.; Oursel, 1974-2, no. 27, pl. 81; Johnson, 1981–89,
III, p. 80, under no. 261.

39 B

C. *The Right Arm and Torso of Medea*; *Study for the Head of
Medea*

Graphite on pink paper, 8 5/8 x 10 13/16 in. (22 x 27.5 cm.)

Inv. Pluchart 1293

The pose of the nude figure in this drawing is virtually
identical to that of Medea in the oil sketch (cat. no. 38). In the
painting Medea is seen frontally, so that her right arm con-
ceals the contour of her left side.

WMG

PROVENANCE

Eugène Delacroix (Lugt Suppl. 838 a); Posthumous sale of the contents
of Delacroix's studio, Paris, Hôtel Drouot, February 22–27, 1864;
Alfred Robaut.

EXHIBITION

Paris, 1963-1, no. 258.

LITERATURE

Pluchart, 1889, no. 1293; Sérullaz, 1963-1, no. 254, ill.; Johnson, 1981–
89, III, p. 80, under no. 261.

39 C

39 D

39 E

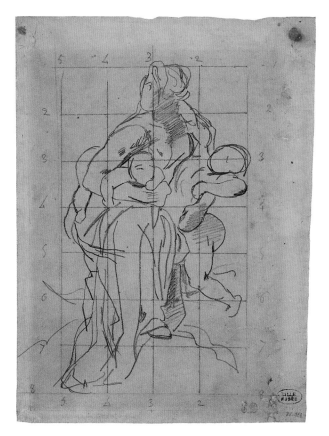

39 F

D. *The Left and Right Arm of Medea*

Graphite on beige paper, 6 7/8 x 8 5/8 in. (17.5 x 22 cm.)

Inv. Pluchart 1292

In this drawing Medea's left forearm is more sharply fore-shortened than in the painting of the same subject (cat. no. 37), whereas her right arm corresponds closely to that in the finished work.

WMG

PROVENANCE

Eugène Delacroix (Lugt Suppl. 838 a); Posthumous sale of the contents of Delacroix's studio, Paris, Hôtel Drouot, February 22–27, 1864, part of no. 335.

LITERATURE

Robaut, 1885, part of no. 670; Pluchart, 1889, no. 1292; Johnson, 1981–89, III, p. 80, under no. 261.

E. *Three Sketches of Medea About to Murder Her Children*

Pen and brown ink, 8 1/4 x 12 13/16 in. (21 x 32.5 cm.)

Inv. Pluchart 1276

In these vigorous studies Medea steps forward with her right foot and holds a dagger in her right hand, while the older of the two children reaches up with his right arm. The figures are posed similarly to those in the lost version of *Medea About to Murder Her Children*, which was formerly in the Nationalgalerie, Berlin, but was apparently destroyed during World War II. The picture was signed and dated 1859, but was evidently begun in or before 1855.[1]

WMG

1 Johnson, 1981–89, III, p. 150, under no. 333.

PROVENANCE

Eugène Delacroix (Lugt Suppl. 838 a); Posthumous sale of the contents of Delacroix's studio, Paris, Hôtel Drouot, February 22–27, 1864, part of no. 335.

EXHIBITIONS

Paris, 1963-1, no. 253; London–Cambridge–Birmingham–Glasgow, 1974–75, no. 28.

LITERATURE

Robaut, 1885, part of no. 670; Pluchart, 1889, no. 1276; Sérullaz, 1963-1, no. 249, ill.; Oursel, 1974-2, no. 28, pl. 79; Johnson, 1981–89, III, p. 80, under no. 261.

F. *Medea About to Murder Her Children*

Graphite on tracing paper, squared in red chalk, 8 5/8 x 6 1/8 in. (22 x 15.5 cm.)

The drawing is lined.

Inv. Pluchart 1268

This study has much in common with the picture in Lille (cat. no. 37) but, like catalogue number 39E, it was probably made in connection with the lost 1859 version of the painting. In both the present drawing and the painting of 1859 Medea steps forward with her right foot and holds the dagger in her right hand. The poses of the two children in this drawing are also similar to those in the painting. Nevertheless, in the 1859 painting Medea wore a crown and her head was turned so that more of her face was visible.

WMG

PROVENANCE

Eugène Delacroix (Lugt Suppl. 838 a); Posthumous sale of the contents of Delacroix's studio, Paris, Hôtel Drouot, February 22–27, 1864, part of no. 335.

LITERATURE

Robaut, 1885, part of no. 670; Pluchart, 1889, no. 1268; Johnson, 1981–89, III, p. 80, under no. 261.

GUSTAVE COURBET

French

Ornans 1819–1877 La Tour de Peilz

40 *After Dinner at Ornans (Un après-dîner à Ornans)*

1848–49

Oil on canvas, 76 3/4 x 101 1/8 in. (195 x 257 cm.)

Inv. no. 522

Gustave Courbet arrived in Paris late in the fall of 1839, at the age of twenty, and almost immediately he began to submit works every year to the Paris Salon. However, his paintings were not accepted for exhibition until 1844, and his reputation was only firmly established with his contributions to the Salon of 1849.[1] As reported by Champfleury, the champion of Realism who soon became one of Courbet's closest friends, "Courbet forces open the doors of the Salon [of 1849] with nine [seven] paintings. Yesterday nobody

40

knew his name: today his name is on everyone's lips" ("Courbet force les portes du Salon [de 1849] avec neuf [sept] tableaux. Personne hier ne savait son nom: aujourd'hui il est dans toutes les bouches."[2]

Of the eleven works Courbet sent to the Salon, only seven—not nine—were accepted, and of these four were landscapes, two were genre scenes, and one was a portrait.[3] The genre scene *Un après-dîner à Ornans* had the greatest impact on the critics: "Courbet dared paint a life-size genre piece" ("Courbet a osé peindre un tableau de genre de grandeur naturelle") Champfleury noted,[4] but he was not the only one to appreciate the significance of this painting. The jury, which in 1849 was selected, exceptionally, by the exhibiting artists and not by the Académie, and which counted among its members Delacroix and Ingres, decided to award Courbet a gold medal[5] (gold medal recipients did not have to go through the selection committee until 1857, when the regulations for the Salon were altered). At the close of the exhibition, the painting was acquired by the State and given to the Musée des Beaux-Arts in Lille. "Had I been asked to choose a destination for the picture," Courbet wrote, "I would certainly have thought of one less distinguished and less honorable" ("J'aurais eu à choisir un emplacement que certainement je le lui aurais choisi moins beau et moins honorable").[6]

As of 1849, artists participating in the Salons were expected to supply *notices* (or entries) for their works. Courbet provided the following to accompany *Un après-dîner à Ornans*: "It was the month of November, we were at our friend Cuenot's house. Marlet had come in from hunting, and we had asked Promayet to play the violin for my father" ("C'était au mois de novembre, nous étions chez notre ami Cuenot, Marlet revenait de la chasse, et nous avions engagé Promayet à jouer du violon devant mon père").[7] Courbet explains in his *notice* that the month is November, but of this there is no doubt: Dead leaves lie next to the coal bucket at the bottom right, the figures are clad in heavy clothing, and the entire picture is steeped in dark autumnal colors, enlivened with afternoon highlights. Four characters are gathered around a table, its white tablecloth freshly stained with red wine and topped with wine bottles, heavy glasses, and bread. On closer examination, however, it becomes apparent that the focus of the painting is in reality the figure of Courbet's childhood friend the violinist Alphonse Promayet (1822–1872). Promayet has the fixed attention of both Urbain Cuenot,[8] the host, who sits pensively in the background, and of Marlet,[9] who is seated at the center of the picture, lighting

his pipe with a piece of kindling wood from the fire. Even Courbet's father, Éléonor Régis Courbet (1798–1882), who, at this point, has been lulled to sleep by the music, faces the musician. The inanimate objects, such as the flagstones and the chairs, have been used by Courbet to further direct the viewer's glance toward Promayet.

After Dinner at Ornans, painted during the winter of 1848, was Courbet's first attempt at a large-scale canvas and his first major Realist work. As Linda Nochlin has pointed out, Courbet's use of almost life-size figures in an everyday setting elevates the rural genre scene to the level of a history painting, in much the same way as Louis Le Nain had done with his *Repas de paysans* of 1642 (Paris, Musée du Louvre, Inv. no. M.I. 1088).[10] It was perhaps the achievement of *After Dinner at Ornans* that prompted Courbet to continue in this vein, and to paint two of his most well-known works, *A Burial at Ornans*, begun late in the summer of 1849, and *The Artist's Studio* of 1855 (both in Paris, Musée d'Orsay, Inv. nos. RF 325, RF 2257).

AN

1 Courbet submitted works to the Salons of 1841, 1842, and 1843, but none of the entries was accepted (see Paris–London, 1977–78, p. 24 [p. 24]).

2 See Champfleury, 1973, p. 154.

3 Courbet exhibited the following works at the Salon of 1849: *Le peintre* (no. 450), *M. N. T. [Marc Trapadoux] examinant un livre d'estampes* (no. 451), *La vendange à Ornans, sous la Roche-du-Mont* (no. 452), *La vallée de la Loue, prise de la Roche-du-Mont; le village qu'on aperçoit des bords de la Loue est Montgesoye* (no. 453), *Vue du château de Saint-Denis, le soir, prise du village de Scey-en-Varais (Doubs)* (no. 454), *Un après-dîner à Ornans* (no. 455), *Les communaux de Chassagne; soleil couchant* (no. 456); see Paris, *Salon de 1849* (reprinted, New York and London, 1977).

4 See Champfleury, 1973, p. 154.

5 For a compilation of statements devoted to Courbet's works exhibited at the Salon of 1849 see Fernier, 1949.

6 See Riat, 1906, p. 68.

7 Archives du Musée du Louvre, Paris; reprinted in Paris–London, 1977–78, p. 94 (p. 206).

8 The figure was thought to be Courbet until Marie-Thérèse de Forges correctly pointed out that this was, indeed, Cuenot, the host. See de Forges, 1973, p. 35.

9 It is not clear whether this figure is meant to be Adolphe or Tony Marlet: Both brothers were friends of Courbet.

10 See Nochlin, 1976, p. 62.

PROVENANCE

Bought by the State for FFr 1,500 at the Salon of 1849 and given to the Musée des Beaux-Arts, 1849.

EXHIBITIONS

Paris, 1849, no. 455; Valenciennes, 1918, no. 75; Basel, 1921, no. 25; Paris, 1973, no. 41; Paris–London, 1977–78, no. 18.

LITERATURE

Riat, 1906, pp. 64–68; Léger, 1929, p. 43; Meltzoff, 1942, p. 264, fig. 5; Fernier, 1949, pp. 1–7, ill.; Macdonald, 1969, pp. 68–69 n. 17; Fermigier, 1971, pp. 24–28, ill. (details); Nochlin, 1971, p. 194; de Forges, 1972, p. 452, fig. 2, pp. 453–54 n. 8; Champfleury, 1973, pp. 154–55; de Forges, 1973, pp. 34–36, no. 41, ill.; Nochlin, 1976, pp. 59–65, fig. 52; Fernier, 1977, I, pp. 56–57, ill.; Toussaint, in Toussaint and de Forges, 1977, pp. 27, 94–96, no. 18, ill.; Toussaint, in Toussaint and de Forges, 1978, pp. 27, 206–8, no. 134, ill.; Fried, 1990, pp. 85–110.

JEAN-BAPTISTE-CAMILLE COROT(?)

French

Paris 1796–1875 Ville d'Avray

---

41   *Castel Sant'Angelo*

Oil on paper mounted on canvas, 10 5/8 x 15 3/4 in. (27 x 40 cm.)

Signed (at the bottom right): COROT

Inv. no. 544

Ever since the fifteenth century Italy has held an attraction for artists from the North, and the establishment of national art academies in Rome further served to focus activity in the south. By the 1820s, sketching out of doors had become part of academic practice, and the sites of Rome and its environs became favored motifs in the works of young artists.[1]

The Castel Sant'Angelo was among the most popular sites in Rome. Paintings of it survive from the sixteenth century, and by the beginning of the nineteenth century it had become both an icon of Rome and a venerable formula of classical design.[2] The castle was originally conceived as the mausoleum of the emperor Hadrian (A.D. 76–138). Construction of the enormous circular building was begun by Hadrian about A.D. 130 and was completed one year after his death, in A.D. 139. In the Early Middle Ages the tomb was surrounded by ramparts and became the citadel of Rome. According to legend, while praying for the cessation of the plague of 590, Saint Gregory the Great saw an angel sheathing his sword on top of the fortress. The saint's vision presaged the end of the plague, and since then the castle has borne the name of the holy angel.

Jean-Baptiste-Camille Corot, one of the most important of the landscape artists working in Italy during the first half of the nineteenth century, was also seduced by the castle, and he painted the monument from two different vantage points. The first was situated across the Tiber, and he positioned himself so that he was looking toward Saint Peter's basilica and the castle; the paintings that resulted are the *View of Saint Peter's and the Castel Sant'Angelo* of about 1826–28 (San Francisco, The Fine Arts Museums),[3] the *View of Saint Peter's and the Castel Sant'Angelo* also of 1826–28 (Paris, Private collection),[4] and the *View of Saint Peter's and the Castel Sant'Angelo* of about 1835–40 (Whereabouts unknown).[5] Corot's second viewpoint was from upstream, and excluded Saint Peter's, as seen in the *Castel Sant'Angelo* of about 1826–28 (Paris, Musée du Louvre, Inv. no. RF 1622).[6] Indeed, the *Castel Sant'Angelo* in Lille incorporates the same view as the Paris painting.

Over the years the painting in Lille has been attributed to both Corot and Caruelle d'Aligny (1798–1871), in neither case convincingly. Alfred Robaut, who began the catalogue raisonné of Corot's oeuvre during the artist's lifetime, was the first to voice suspicion about the present work. As Robaut noted, "Camille Benoit, marchand de tableaux et photographe à Lille, avait offert au Musée cette toile achetée par lui à la Vente d'Aligny et sur son affirmation erronée on a posé sur le cadre une cartouche de Corot, tandis que c'est d'*Aligny*. Exécution propre, régulière et parfois dure" ("Camille Benoit, art dealer and photographer in Lille, gave the museum this painting, purchased by him at the d'Aligny sale and under his [Benoit] misguided assertion a plaque [with the name] COROT was placed on the frame—whereas the work is by d'*Aligny*. Precise, regular and sometimes harsh in treatment") and "au Musée de Lille, École d'Aligny (ne pas confondre avec Corot) c'est lisse et *régulier* sans caprice avec sécheresses trop nombreuses pour Corot" ("in the Musée de Lille, School of d'Aligny [not to be confused with Corot], it [the painting] is smooth and *methodical* without caprice, too dry for Corot").[7] Germain Bazin's important monograph on Corot, published in 1942, reiterated Robaut's comments.[8] Although Hélène Toussaint reascribed the painting to Corot in 1976,[9] it was included in an exhibition of the works of Caruelle d'Aligny in 1979, and subsequently in the catalogue raisonné of his oeuvre in 1988.[10]

Corot worked in the company of many French artists in Rome, any one of whom could have painted the Lille picture: Prosper Barbot; Jacques-Raymond Brascassat, Jules-Louis-Philippe Coignet, André Giroux, François Bouchot, Julien-Léopold Boilly, François-Antoine-Léon Fleury, Guillaume Bodinier, François-Édouard Bertin, and Caruelle d'Aligny. Thus, further research needs to be done in order to identify definitively the author of this sensitive work in Lille.   AN

1 In his recent book, Peter Galassi sheds new light on the uncharted territory of plein-air painting during the first half of the nineteenth century. See Galassi, 1991.

2 Wolfgang Kroenig devoted an entire article to the history of the depictions of the Castel Sant'Angelo, from the fresco of 1580 by Mattheus Bril (1550–1583) to a work by Oswald Achenbach of 1883. See Wolfgang Kroenig, "Storia di una Veduta di Roma," *Bollettino d'Arte*, no. 57, 1972, pp. 165–98.

3 See Robaut, 1905, II, no. 70. There is also a preparatory drawing for this work in the Museum Boymans-van Beuningen, Rotterdam; see Galassi, 1991, ill. p. 156.

4 See Robaut, 1905, II, no. 70 bis.

5 See Robaut, 1905, II, no. 71.

6 See Robaut, 1905, II, no. 73.

7 See Robaut, 1927, Dc.282.n fol. 81; reprinted in Bazin, 1973, pp. 104–5 n. 7 a.

8 See Bazin, 1942, pp. 69 ff., ills.

9 See Toussaint, in Rome, 1975–76, no. 38.

10 See Aubrun, 1979, no. 1; Aubrun, 1988, no. 8.

PROVENANCE

Théodore Caruelle d'Aligny, until 1871; Posthumous sale of the collection of Caruelle d'Aligny, Paris, Hôtel Drouot, March 8 and 9, 1878, no. 65; purchased by Camille Benoit, Lille; Gift of Camille Benoit, 1882.

EXHIBITIONS

Valenciennes, 1918, no. 70; Ghent, 1950, no. 4; Berlin, 1964, no. 9; Rome, 1975–76, no. 38; Bremen, 1977–78, no. 11; Orléans–Dunkirk–Rennes, 1979, no. 1; Yokohama–Hokkaido–Osaka–Yamaguchi, 1991–92, no. 14.

LITERATURE

Robaut, 1927, Dc.282. n fol. 81; Bazin, 1942, p. 69, ill. p. 71; Bazin, 1973, pp. 88 ff., 104–5 n. 7 a, p. 109 n. 32; Toussaint, in Rome, 1975–76, no. 38, ill., and colorplate cover; Aubrun, 1979, n.p., no. 1, ill.; Oursel, 1984, pp. 196–97, no. 40, colorpl.; Aubrun, 1988, pp. 63–65, no. 8, ill.; Scottez-De Wambrechies, in Brejon and Scottez, 1991, colorpl. p. 31, p. 157, no. 14.

VINCENT VAN GOGH

Dutch

Zundert 1853–1890 Auvers-sur-Oise

42 *Study of Cows, after Jacob Jordaens* (after an etching by Paul-Ferdinand Gachet)

June 1890

Oil on canvas, 21 5/8 x 25 5/8 in. (55 x 65 cm.)

Inv. no. 1765

Throughout his decade-long career, Vincent van Gogh made copies after the works of other artists. In 1880 he took up copying to learn the rudiments of figure drawing; just prior to his suicide in 1890, in Auvers-sur-Oise, he again turned to the drawing exercises in Charles Bargue's *Cours de dessin*, in order to restore to his work the discipline he felt it had lost. As one scholar has succinctly noted, van Gogh ended his career just as he had begun it: by copying Bargue.[1]

Of the four copies van Gogh executed in Auvers-sur-Oise (from May 20 to July 29, 1890), three are drawings after the first *exercices de fusain* in Bargue. The fourth is the present oil, based on Paul-Ferdinand Gachet's 1873 etching after Jacob Jordaens's *Study of Cows* (see cat. nos. 43, 5). It is van Gogh's last painted copy and the only work in this genre from the Auvers period. Distinct from the copies after Bargue, this painting can be better understood in relation to the some thirty copies in oil after other artists that van Gogh had undertaken in Saint-Rémy, just prior to his arrival in Auvers. At the end of his life, van Gogh came to appreciate not only the didactic value of copying but also its creative potential.

Over the course of his year-long confinement in the asylum at Saint-Rémy (May 1889–May 1890), van Gogh gave various reasons for copying. Some were practical. He copied as an antidote to the long, dreary hours spent indoors and the restrictions institutional life placed on him, and so as to "not lose sight of the figure, even though I have no models at the moment."[2] (All but one of his Saint-Rémy copies, *The Plow*, were based on compositions with figures.) He found consolation and pleasure in the activity of copying,[3] as well as in the end result: He did not especially like to see his own works adorning his bedroom, and thus he copied pictures by other artists to use as decoration.[4]

Van Gogh considered his copies as "translations" or "improvisations," likening them to a musician's interpretation of Beethoven. He would let "the black and white by Delacroix or Millet or something made after their work pose . . . as a subject. And then . . . improvise color," keeping in mind their pictures, and "the vague consonance of colors which are at least right in feeling."[5] These translations of black-and-white images (prints, reproductions, photographs) "into the language of color" were for van Gogh more than mere exercises. He saw copying as potentially "more useful" than his own painting, since it was a means by which he could propagate the work of great masters such as Millet.[6] These goals, van Gogh felt, lent ample justification to the practice of copying.

As to taking on the role of copyist or interpreter himself, van Gogh confessed: "Nowadays there are so many

people who do not feel they are made for publicity, but who support and strengthen what others do. Those who translate books, for instance. The engravers, the lithographers.''[7] He asked why painters must "*be nothing but composers . . . it isn't like that in music*," where the performer's "*interpretation* of a composer is something."[8]

Although van Gogh had "scruples of conscience," fearing criticism about his copying, "lest it should be plagiarizing,"[9] his earliest critics were quick to defend his efforts against ridicule of this kind. With particular sensitivity to van Gogh's artistic aims, Johan de Meester (writing in 1890 and 1891 in the Dutch papers *Algemeen Handelsblad* and *Nederland*, respectively) and Octave Mirbeau (in 1891 in *L'Écho de Paris*) pioneered the first discussions of van Gogh's "copies." As Mirbeau plainly stated, these were "not strictly speaking copies, these exuberant and imposing restitutions. They are, rather, interpretations through which the painter manages to re-create the works of others, to make them his own while preserving their original spirit and special character."[10] De Meester reiterated, "Such preservation was his goal. . . . Often armed with nothing more than a small engraving, [van Gogh] copied the composition of the master, respecting the integrity of Millet's subject and sentiment while at the same time endeavoring . . . to fully preserve his own character."[11]

These observations are borne out when one compares van Gogh's *Study of Cows* to the Gachet etching on which it was based. The painting remains fairly faithful to the overall composition and character of the print. Van Gogh respected the general poses and placement of the cows, as well as the light-and-dark gradations of tone, from the shaded portions of the cows' bodies to the relation between sky and ground. However, in adopting the rectangular composition of the print to the nearly square format of his canvas, van Gogh extended the sky at the top and the bodies of the animals at the bottom. In terms of the foreground animals, the result was not entirely successful; the two cows are closer together, and he seems not to have understood, or been able to translate effectively, the pose of the cow at the right.[12] Van Gogh added a certain naïveté of detail to his version in the sweet, almost child-like faces of the cows; the reeds and the crow at the right; and the flower buds at the left. He also articulated the ground as a grassy field, which rises both at the left and right of the composition. Yet, it is by means of his animated brushwork and high-keyed palette of acid yellows, vibrant greens, and ochers that van Gogh ultimately transforms the image into a work unmistakably his own.

Van Gogh did not mention the *Study of Cows* in his correspondence. Gachet's son, the only source for the genesis of this painting, notes that van Gogh had responded enthusiastically to the print, especially to its history and its sentimental value for Dr. Gachet (see cat. no. 43); he had asked for a proof, and returned the next day with his oil painting.[13]

There is no doubt that the subject would have appealed to van Gogh. Often, motifs in his Auvers paintings recall those in his Dutch works. Likewise, in the subjects he chose to copy in 1889–90 we see a complete reversion to the taste he had maintained before leaving the Netherlands for France. Van Gogh had known and admired the work of Jacob Jordaens,[14] and he was also entirely familiar with the rich Northern tradition of cattle pictures, from seventeenth-century examples to those by his Hague School contemporaries. During his years in The Hague (January 1882–December 1883), van Gogh had studied with his cousin Anton Mauve and had had contact with a number of artists who had practiced this genre of painting, among them the cattle painter *par excellence* Willem Maris. Their works provided the example for van Gogh's early efforts along these lines (two studies of a cow lying down and another, *Cows in the Meadow*, have been assigned to his Hague period).[15] To van Gogh's year in Nuenen (December 1884–November 1885) dates a handful of paintings and thumbnail sketches of carts and plows pulled by oxen.[16] After his Dutch period, cows are not found again in van Gogh's oeuvre until 1890, when they reappear in two oils—his copy after Millet, *Noon: Rest* (Paris, Musée d'Orsay), and the present painting—in a panoramic view of the Auvers countryside in watercolor (London, Tate Gallery), and in two Auvers sketches showing figures and cows in a field (Amsterdam, Rijksmuseum Vincent van Gogh).[17] These drawings are distinctive, not for their summary treatment of the animals (one, from a sketchbook, depicts three cows in profile; the other shows three cows in alternate views—profile, three-quarter, and from the rear), but for their attendant color notes. These notes, written clearly beneath the cows in the sketchbook drawing—and which read, from left to right, *brun rouge, noir, brun rouge*—suggest that van Gogh may, indeed, have contemplated in Auvers a painting with cows in a field. Was the study after Gachet an exercise toward this end? Or is it simply a reflection of van Gogh's renewed interest in, and nostalgia for, his Northern heritage?

Van Gogh's letters and portraits offer penetrating characterizations of his doctor and companion in Auvers. However, he wrote sparingly about Gachet as an artist.

Although van Gogh knew it would give the doctor "great pleasure," he seems never to have "replicated the *Pietà* by Delacroix" for him.[18] Nor—because of the artist's suicide in July 1890—did van Gogh's hopes for their collaboration on a series of prints after his paintings ever come to fruition.[19] Yet, in this painting van Gogh succeeded not only in acknowledging Gachet as an artist and in presenting him with a copy, but in realizing a collaborative effort between painter and etcher that was rooted in a Northern tradition they both shared.

SAS

1 See Chetham, 1976, pp. 46–47.

2 Quotations from van Gogh's correspondence are followed by standard numerical designations for the letters as reprinted in *The Complete Letters of Vincent van Gogh*, 3 vols., Boston, 1958. Letters written to his brother, Theo, have been abbreviated as LT, and those to his sister Wil as W. This quote is from LT 607.

3 See LT 607.

4 See W 14.

5 See LT 607.

6 See LT 611, 623.

7 See LT 623.

8 See LT 607. That van Gogh would devise for himself and then opt for a supportive or secondary role is symptomatic of other attitudes held at that time regarding the making, exhibiting, and selling of his art. Not coincidentally, such attitudes made their appearance just when van Gogh learned that his "work was having some success" (LT 629 a). In this context, see the Introduction in Stein, 1986, pp. 24–26.

9 See LT 625.

10 See Octave Mirbeau, "Vincent van Gogh," in *L'Écho de Paris*, March 31, 1891; reprinted in Stein, 1986, p. 269.

11 See Johan de Meester, "Vincent van Gogh," in *Nederland*, March 1891; reprinted in Stein, 1986, p. 264.

12 These awkward passages stem from weaknesses in the print (see cat. no. 43). It should be noted that van Gogh, like Jordaens, cropped the pair of cows in the foreground so that more of the cows' torsos are seen, and he added a patch of grass between the two animals. The format of van Gogh's canvas is also closer to that of the original painting. These similarities, which may suggest knowledge of the original, are curious. Van Gogh did not know the Jordaens oil study firsthand, and, according to Gachet's son, the work "did not exist in reproduction" at the time. Are these references explainable, mere coincidence, or do they challenge the painting's attribution, wholly or in part? (De la Faille left it out of his manuscript for the 1970 edition of his catalogue raisonné of van Gogh's works, but it was accepted as authentic by the editors of that volume; see de la Faille, 1970, no. F 822.)

It is perhaps likely that in trying to resolve the poses of the cows at the bottom of the composition van Gogh consulted with Gachet about the original painting; he may have adopted these features from Gachet's preparatory drawing or earlier watercolor (unfortunately neither work is known, and there is no evidence that van Gogh had seen them); or he may have simply arrived at his solution to the foreground independently. It is always possible that the painting was completed or reworked by Gachet after van Gogh's death, but this proposal cannot be seriously entertained without the benefit of sufficient technical examination of the canvas.

13 See Gachet, 1954-2, n.p.

14 See LT 438, 439, 443.

15 These works are presently known only through poor-quality photographs. They are reproduced in de la Faille, 1970, nos. 1 b, 1 c, 15. (Hereafter in the notes, works will be cited by their de la Faille [F] numbers.) A rather ambitious watercolor of a meadow, with a sprinkling of cows and peasants in the middle ground (F 916), also dates to this period.

16 See, for example, F 38, 39, 172, 1142, 1144. Van Gogh, earlier and later, had explored the subjects of plowing or carting loads, but in these works horses or donkeys carry the burden instead of cows.

Animals do not figure very prominently in van Gogh's oeuvre. However, perhaps as a result of Gachet's menagerie, his last drawings, including some twenty-two pages of an Auvers sketchbook, do show a keener interest in animal studies—mostly of horses, but also of dogs, chickens, cows, and donkeys. (See van der Wolk, 1987, sketchbook [SB] 7, nos. 10, 12, 22, 31, 69, 70, 99, 107, 125, 138, 141, 144–147, 149–154, 156; and de la Faille, nos. F 1622, 1730, 1609, 1610, 1631, 1731, 1654 *v*, 1652, 1615, respectively.) In addition to the present painting, van Gogh treated the subject of animals in his copies after other artists' works: Note the donkey in the foreground of his copy after Millet's *Morning: Going Out to Work* (F 684), the oxen in his version of Millet's *Noon: Rest* (F 686), and the horse in his rendition of Delacroix's *Good Samaritan* (F 633).

17 Only one of the drawings, *Sketch of Cows and Children*, is reproduced in de la Faille (as F 1632). The other, a page from a sketchbook, is illustrated in van der Wolk, 1987, in SB 7 as no. 69.

18 See LT 638. Hulsker, 1980, p. 485 n. 12, convincingly argued that neither of the two van Gogh copies after Delacroix's *Pietà* (F 630, 757) could have been made for Gachet; Hulsker was the first to assign both versions to Saint-Rémy.

19 The two men collaborated once on the etching—a portrait of Gachet—that van Gogh made under the doctor's tutelage in Auvers.

PROVENANCE

Paul-Ferdinand Gachet, Auvers, 1890, until his death in 1909; by descent to his son, Paul Gachet, Auvers, 1909, until 1950; Gift of Paul Gachet, 1950.

EXHIBITIONS

Lille, 1951, no. 293; Paris, 1954–55, no. 49; Recklinghausen, 1959, no. III; Paris, 1960, no. 63; Pau, 1980, no. 84; Dordrecht–Leeuwarden, 1988–89, no. 65.

LITERATURE

De la Faille, 1928, I, p. 232, no. 822; de la Faille, 1939, p. 557; Gachet, 1954-2; Châtelet, 1970-1, pp. 204–5, no. 95; de la Faille, 1970, pp. 308–9, no. 822; Hulsker, 1980, p. 476, no. 2095.

PAUL-FERDINAND GACHET
(PSEUD. PAUL VAN RYSSEL)

French

Lille 1828–1909 Auvers-sur-Oise

---

43 *Study of Cows, after Jacob Jordaens*

November 1873

Etching, 3 7/8 x 5 3/8 in. (10 x 13.7 cm.)

Signed (at the lower left): *P. van.Ryssel Scult*; inscribed
(at the lower right): *Jordáens pinx*

Inv. no. W. 4046

Dr. Paul-Ferdinand Gachet maintained a medical practice in
Paris and, from 1872, a country home in Auvers-sur-Oise,
just northwest of the city. There, he became friend and
patron to a number of Impressionist and Post-Impressionist
painters who had worked in the area, including Pissarro,
Guillaumin, Renoir, Sisley, Cézanne, and Vincent van
Gogh. He had known Corot and Courbet, Daumier and
Daubigny, Champfleury and Victor Hugo, and enjoyed
friendships with the leading printmakers of his day. An art
collector, man of letters, and freethinker, Gachet was also a
painter and etcher; he used the pseudonym van Ryssel, which
in Flemish means "of Lille," the city where he was born.

Unlike his contribution to the graphic arts, Gachet's
efforts as a painter were limited and largely derivative. By
the early 1870s, he had abandoned the somber realism of
paintings in the manner of his friend Armand Gautier for
landscapes modeled after the works of Pissarro and
Guillaumin, whose high-keyed palettes and atmospheric effects he emulated. Gachet's etchings date from 1872 and were
initiated in Paris under the influence of Richard Lesclide,
founder of *Paris à l'eau-forte* (in 1873), and by Guillaumin and
Pissarro in Auvers.[1]

Although Gachet's talents as a printmaker were applied
mostly to copying the works of his Impressionist friends, he
was among the original contributors to Lesclide's period-
ical—perhaps the most important forum for the technical
innovations in etching that took place in Paris in the
mid-1870s. Gachet, who as early as 1874 was using fine
aquatint in conjunction with stop-out varnish, shared with
his fellow *cuisiniers* Henri-Charles Guérard and Félix-Hilaire
Buhot a predominant interest in experimenting with novel
"recipes" for creating different surface effects. A number of
new processes in biting and inking plates were introduced at
the time, including both regular and liquid aquatint, stop out,

sulfur tint, lift ground, and open biting.[2] Since the revival of
etching in the 1860s—under the pen of Baudelaire and the
etching needles of such artists as Millet, Daubigny, Félix
Bracquemond, and Charles Meryon—concerns had
changed. For the new generation of etchers, emphasis had
shifted away from whether subtleties of tone could be sustained in multiple printings to a preoccupation with the
richness of the individual impression, the "*belle épreuve*."
Gachet's wide circle of friends embraced both generations,
from Bresdin and Meryon (both before and after his mental
illness) to Guillaumin and Buhot (to whom Gachet dedicated
the set of prints now conserved in the Bibliothèque Nationale,
Paris).

The present etching was made in November 1873 after
a painting Gachet had long admired in the museum in his
native town of Lille—Jacob Jordaens's *Study of Cows* (cat. no.
5). A "strange composition," and "veritably unknown" at
the time, the Jordaens painting was a work about which
Gachet "always spoke with emotion."[3] According to the
recollections of his son, some twenty-three years earlier—
about 1850—Gachet had made a watercolor after the same
painting. The etching was preceded by a drawing made at the
Lille museum, and was printed upon Gachet's return to
Auvers. (The preliminary sketch and earlier watercolor are
lost.) Gachet printed at least three states of the present etching. It was presumably the version here that served as the
basis for van Gogh's 1890 oil painting of the subject (see cat.
no. 42).

In the etching Gachet has respected the integrity of the
original in terms of the poses and grouping of the five cows in
a landscape while also preserving some of the vitality of
Jordaens's composition. Yet, he has rather inexpertly translated the spirit of the whole. The strength and character of
Jordaens's animals have been mitigated in the print by the
way Gachet cropped and framed the cows (extending the
area of sky around the trio at the top, but cutting off the pair
at the bottom above their legs); by their vapid expressions; by
the modeling, which conveys little feeling for anatomy or
variation in color; and by the reduction of the landscape—
with its sense of time, elevation, and dryness—to a dark,
undefined ground. Judged on its own merits and in relation
to other etchings by Gachet, this is an early and otherwise
unexceptional print—save for its historical and artistic role
as intermediary between the painting by Jordaens and that
by van Gogh.   SAS

1 Guillaumin seems to have instructed Gachet in his first plate. See
   Jean Adhémar and Jacques Lethère, *Bibliothèque Nationale, Cabinet des*

Estampes, Inventaire du fonds français après 1880, VIII, Paris, 1954, pp. 294, 295, no. 6 (first and third states). In the summer and fall of 1873, the year the present etching was made, Gachet had worked in the company of Cézanne; he also published his first print in *Paris à l'eau-forte*.

2 In addition to the monograph by Gachet's son (see Gachet, 1954-1), valuable contributions to the subject of Gachet's work in the context of printmaking in Paris in the mid-1870s have been made, more recently, by Douglas Druick and Peter Zegers in their introduction to Sue Welsh Reed and Barbara Stern Shapiro, *Edgar Degas: The Painter as Printmaker*. Boston, Museum of Fine Arts, 1987; see especially pp. xxxi–xxxii, lii.

3 See Gachet, 1954-2, n.p.

PROVENANCE
Gift of Paul Gachet *fils*, 1950.

LITERATURE
Gachet, 1954-1, no. 6, p. 45; Gachet, 1954-2.

DONATELLO (DONATO DI NICCOLÒ DI BETTO BARDI)

Italian

Florence, about 1386–1466 Florence

44 *The Feast of Herod*

Marble, 19 5/8 x 28 1/8 in. (50 x 71.5 cm.)

Inv. no. 1912

Among Donatello's many original contributions, none lays greater claim to attention than his sculpture in exceptionally low relief, "*rilievo schiacciato*" (or "squashed relief")—a term used by Vasari to convey the impression in these works of layers of space and incident packed into just a few centimeters of depth. Only a handful of Donatello's exercises in this genre survive. In addition to the present example, there is the *Ascension and Giving of the Keys to Saint Peter* (London, Victoria and Albert Museum), which, like the relief in Lille, also almost certainly formed part of the Medici collections. The Lille *Feast of Herod* is generally identified as the "panel of marble with many figures in low relief and other things in perspective, that is, of Saint John, by Donatello," which was valued at thirty florins in the inventory of the possessions of Lorenzo de' Medici, just after the latter's death in 1492.

Donatello had business relations with the paterfamilias Cosimo de' Medici and with the Medici bank from 1425. A likely first owner may have been one of Cosimo's sons—

either Piero "the Gouty" (Lorenzo's father) or Giovanni—both connoisseurs documented as interesting themselves in small works by Donatello. By the time of Lorenzo's death, Palazzo Medici in Florence contained among its decorations four sculptures described as by Donatello. The Lille relief was probably meant from the start to be an object for private contemplation, not part of a greater whole. In any case, in Palazzo Medici it was shown in an antechamber in Lorenzo's apartments that served as an especial treasury, containing small paintings by Giotto, Fra Angelico, and Fra Filippo Lippi, as well as two Donatello Madonnas.

When the relief left the Medici collections and how it came into the possession of Jean-Baptiste-Joseph Wicar are unknown; the 1834 Wicar inventory describes it merely as "a little bas-relief of Saint John." According to Perkins (1864), John Charles Robinson appears to have been the first to ascribe it to Donatello—an attribution that has satisfied the majority of scholars, who mostly agree upon dating it about 1435, near the time of the stucco roundels with scenes from the life of Saint John the Evangelist in the Old Sacristy of San Lorenzo in Florence. Doubters including Pope-Hennessy (1986) allege a lack of coordination between narrative and settings, and the relief has sometimes even been assigned to an artist of a later generation. Trudzinski (1986), author of the most detailed account, sustains the attribution to Donatello and convincingly shows how the master arrived at a synchronization of characters and structures through an avid, wide-ranging consultation of classical and medieval sources—especially of illuminated codices of the ninth to twelfth centuries that locate sacred subjects in emphatic architectural settings.

The Gospels of Matthew and Mark agree that after Salome danced for her stepfather, Herod, on his birthday, she was granted the favor of John the Baptist's head, which, placed on a charger, she then presented to her mother, Herodias. Donatello employs thirty figures to narrate these events, moving from right to left. Salome dances in a palace courtyard before an arcade that is cut off by a staircase on the right, serving as a device to group nearby figures. At left the tetrarch, his wife, and guests sit at a table in a loggia while the Baptist's head, barely delineated, is proffered by a kneeling servant. Only one of the guests, his hand covering his eyes, and the woman seated on the foreground bench seem to react.

Donatello had already depicted this subject in the famous bronze relief for the Siena Baptistery font about ten years earlier. It is a model of illusionistic perspective, with

layers of figures in well-ordered spatial recession, even if it is relatively claustrophobic. The Lille relief displays the most radically searching pursuit of perspectival accuracy by any artist before Leonardo da Vinci. Its construction results from Donatello's immediate grappling with the principles of perspective promulgated by his friend Leon Battista Alberti in his treatise *Della pittura*, completed in 1435. As Morolli (1989) shrewdly observes, the relief could serve as a kind of marble frontispiece to the treatise. Briefly stated, Alberti's system establishes perspective by making orthogonals meet at a vanishing point, using a grid and a module to control proportions and degrees of recession. Donatello's orthogonals converge to the left of center, above the head of the seated woman. Everything is subservient to this organization. The railings at the right seem magnetized leftward. The marks of scoring that control the orthogonals sometimes crisscross the figures and the architecture. Precisely comparable scorings in the Old Sacristy stucco roundels are visible since their recent cleaning. Donatello surely knew that the perspectival emphasis would be enhanced by the creamy white stone's directional graining, veins of pale gray moving upper right to lower left, parallel to the tops of the railings, and further activating the extraordinarily rich and complex surface. Other technical features to be noted are the simple self-molding—much like that in the *Madonna of the Clouds* in the Museum of Fine Arts, Boston—and the brusquely hacked back of the marble, curved and thinning to the sides.

Donatello's wholehearted application of logic means that figures get cut off at the level of their heads by the architecture, as in real life and as in the Old Sacristy roundels, and sometimes they become unusually compressed. Salome has to be observed attentively before it is discovered that she is dancing in front of two musicians, for just the skulls and instruments and the hand of one alone are visible. Farther left, there is not quite space enough to give full value to the delicate fictive hangings behind the table, representing angels enframing a seated woman (repeated). A deliberate solecism is the massive baby dozing on the stairs at right, to this writer the only disappointing feature in the relief as far as Donatello's authorship is concerned. The boy is in the same plane as the soldier-observers to the left of him and should therefore be considerably smaller. The only rationale for his size is to accentuate the spatial recession.

Contemporaries may have sensed a magical semblance of order, but the ambiguities that resulted from all this painstaking research were to be the delight of Mannerist artists in ensuing decades. The motif of the stairs would occupy the

youthful Michelangelo's attention when he was planning his marble relief *The Madonna of the Stairs* (Florence, Casa Buonarroti). Kauffmann (1935) pointed out that Rosso Fiorentino appropriated the setting wholesale in a fresco painted at Fontainebleau.

It appears never to have been recognized that Donatello approached the subject in terms of continuous narrative, thereby causing further complication. This conventional form of pictorial license, beloved of the Florentines from the Middle Ages but not, one would think, especially to Donatello's taste, permitted an artist to repeat characters in a scene in order to get across more than one event in a tale. It is a question of illogic serving logic. Donatello only used continuous narrative once before, in the Siena *Feast of Herod*, where we glimpse the Baptist's head on the salver carried ceremoniously in the background before it reappears to confront a startled Herod. In the Lille relief, it is Salome who is repeated, for the figure generally referred to as "the woman on the bench" can really be no one but she. It was the Italian custom to show the separate stages of this story in a single enframement. Thus, Giotto at Arezzo and Masolino at Castiglione Olona show Salome's dance and her presentation taking place beneath separate structures but within the same setting. Fra Filippo Lippi in Prato Cathedral painted three Salomes in one space, and in the presentation scene she has visibly rearranged her toilette. The "woman on the bench" has the refined peplum and hairnet of the dancing princess but her dress now has sleeves. Like Fra Filippo's concomitant figure, this Salome has had time to compose herself somewhat; the Gospels provide her with an exit and an entrance to allow the adjustment. A telling point in favor of this identification is that nobody is looking any longer at the dancing Salome. She flutters at some distance farther back than the soldier-onlookers, who gaze past her toward the table. Another feature is that the lines of perspective draw attention to the seated woman. It perhaps seems strange to find the same character repeated so closely in a single composition, but in an authoritative Trecento setting of the narrative, over the entrance portal of the Baptistery in Pisa, Salome is shown back to back with herself. There, as with the present relief, it would be fitting to spell out the subject as The Dance of Salome and the Feast of Herod.

Donatello's two Salomes are the figures in this relief most obviously studied from ancient models. The dancing Salome derives from the maenads of Roman marble urns and silver reliefs, while the seated Salome's twisted pose is that of Venus in the "Bed of Polycleitus," a much-admired relief then in the collection of Donatello's rival, Lorenzo Ghiberti. The motif suited Donatello's interpretation of the Salome story, for the sharp, contradictory nature of her movement underscores the villainy of her deed and suggests her own horrified reaction to it. Continuous narration may have been a surprisingly conventional usage for Donatello to adopt, but his reasons for doing so were entirely in character. Like the choice of pose, it offered motivational advantages that he seized upon as a sculptor famously involved with the psychology of his subjects.

JDD

LITERATURE

Perkins, 1864, I, n. p. 146; Müntz, 1888, p. 64; Janson, 1957, II, pp. 129–31; Bennett and Wilkins, 1984, pp. 140–42; Herzner, in Detroit–Fort Worth, 1985–86, pp. 118–19; Pope-Hennessy, 1986, pp. 68–69; Trudzinski, 1986, pp. 96–143; Morolli, 1989, p. 48.

PIERRE-JEAN DAVID D'ANGERS

French

Angers 1788–1856 Paris

---

45 Four Models for the *Gutenberg Monument*: *The Benefits of Printing in Europe*; *Asia*; *Africa*; *and America*

Terracotta: each, 15 x 22 7/8 in. (38.1 x 58.1 cm.)

Europe signed and dated (cut off by lower right edge of frame): DAV[ID] / 184[0]

Asia signed (effaced by chipped lower right corner): DAVI[D]

Inv. nos. 71–74

David d'Angers, his success consolidated with his work on the pediment of the Panthéon in Paris (1834–37), soon undertook another project celebrating genius, in the form of his monument to the father of European printing, Johannes Gutenberg. The city of Mainz already had Bertel Thorvaldsen's monument to its native son, but Strasbourg laid claim to Gutenberg through his residence there in the 1430s and 1440s. It was probably in 1836, when Strasbourg organized a "secular fête" in Gutenberg's memory, that David was approached for a monument, which he would tailor to his libertarian, arch-republican tastes. At his own expense, David made the models for the statue and the four reliefs on its base, depicting the benefits extended to the continents (the traditional four) through the printed word. A public subscription would pay for the casting in bronze. The statue was erected in 1840, but the bronze reliefs, commissioned in 1839, were not installed until 1844. They basically follow the Lille models, although local controversy occasioned one modification.

There are complex borrowings from traditional iconography throughout the monument, which were appropriate to the printer of the Bible as well as to David's wish to emphasize the humanitarian consequences of the invention. The statue holds a page inscribed with words from Genesis 1:3, "and there was light." The reliefs for the base have sacramental overtones in the altar-like placement of the printing press in all four. Each scene extends hope to the young, employing children among the beneficiaries. In *The Benefits of Printing in Europe*, the relief for the front side of the monument, nine voracious readers are grouped much like musical angels at the foot of a Renaissance Madonna.

Preliminary drawings for the reliefs are in the Musée des Beaux-Arts in Angers. That for *Europe* has stick figures, each given a name, and the final bronze relief also bears inscriptions allowing us to identify some outstanding characters in the terracotta, whose features are not all fully evolved. To the left of center, Dürer with his flowing hair is already fully recognizable, but Voltaire beside him is less so. A romantically draped, pensive Descartes has pride of place in front of the printing press, and just to the right stands Luther in a fur-trimmed robe. The choice of subjects rekindled ancient sectarian hatreds in Strasbourg. Ultramontane forces objected strenuously to the inclusion of Luther. David responded in conciliatory fashion with an intermediate design, placing the French orator and theologian Bossuet prominently at the extreme left, as if to moderate Lutheran influence. This stage of the design is known from the cast-lead relief on the base of a second example of the statue in the courtyard of the Imprimerie Nationale in Paris. The gesture failing to win over extremists, it was decided to eliminate both Luther and Bossuet from the relief in Strasbourg. David agreed to substitute Erasmus for Bossuet and Montesquieu for Luther in his final design—but under protest at the citizens' show of "intolerance, which I thought had been extinguished forever."

Asia presents a variety of Orientals, mostly potentates, receiving the written word. At the center, two Europeans and three Brahmins exchange books for manuscripts. In the model, the inscription on the press is indecipherable. At the

Europe

Asia

Africa

America

far right, beneath a Buddhistic divinity, two Hindu matrons stand reverentially by as their offspring pore over their texts, their heads ranged in delightful cadence. Their teacher, bending over to guide their study, is Théodore-Marie Pavie, a prodigious polyglot from David's home city of Angers.

In *Africa,* only MOT ("word") is legible on the base of the printing press. This, the most *mouvementé* of the models, reveals most as to David's egalitarian beliefs. A long-contemplated project of his had been to create a colossal monument to the abolition of slavery. At the left in the relief, little Africans are tutored by young Europeans. To the left of center, William Wilberforce, champion of the emancipation movement, plants a hand on the press while receiving the thankful embrace of a youth clutching a book. Above, more Africans rapturously claim their printed copies. At the right, David explicitly equates education with liberty as three other pioneers of the movement, Thomas Clarkson, the marquis de Condorcet, and the Abbé Grégoire, release slaves from bondage. Overhead, slave women bounce their babies in the fresh air of freedom. In the final relief, the Africans no longer wear loincloths. Their nudity, while permissible enough in accordance with neoclassical compositional convention, underscores their newly freed status.

For *America,* David concentrated on the United States. To the left of center, Washington and Lafayette fraternize. Franklin, alongside the press, brandishes a tablet inscribed DROïTS / DE L'HOMME / ET DU / CYTOYEN ("Rights of Man and of the Citizen"). Farther along, past John Adams, Simón Bolívar accepts the grateful homage of native South Americans. The groups at the extreme left and right were greatly clarified in the final relief, as were many details in all four. Yet the Lille sketches established the bronze reliefs' salient formal characteristic: their harsh figural style, obtained through a vigorous deployment of the modeler's stick, the *ébauchoir.* This corduroy effect was deliberately carried over to the bronzes for maximum textural excitement.

JDD

PROVENANCE

The artist; given to M. Martin, Strasbourg; given to Hélène Leferme, daughter of David d'Angers; Bequest of Mme Leferme to the Louvre, 1900; assigned to the Musée des Beaux-Arts, 1903.

LITERATURE

Jouin, 1878, II, pp. 491, 492; Huchard, 1885, pp. 54–56; Le Normand-Romain, 1990, pp. 43–50; Driskel, 1991, pp. 359–80; de Caso, 1992, p. 242 n. 2.

Drawings

Drawings in the Musée des Beaux-Arts, Lille

WILLIAM M. GRISWOLD

The collection of French and, in particular, Italian Old Master drawings preserved in the Musée des Beaux-Arts in Lille is among the richest in Europe. Many sheets now in Lille once belonged to the history painter and portraitist Jean-Baptiste-Joseph Wicar (see cat. no. 29), who bequeathed a magnificent group of drawings to the local Société des Sciences in 1834, thus forming the nucleus of the present collection. A native of Lille and a devoted pupil of Jacques-Louis David, Wicar spent most of his adult life in Italy. In 1797 he was named a member of the committee entrusted by Napoleon with the selection of works of art to be appropriated from Italian collections for export to Paris. Wicar seems to have begun his own collection of Old Master drawings at about this time.

Between 1795 and his death in 1834, Wicar assembled not one but three successive collections of drawings. It was probably in 1796 that Wicar gave the drawings he had acquired up to that time to a certain Giuseppe Giustini of Florence for temporary safekeeping. A short time later Giustini evidently turned over Wicar's collection to an unscrupulous father and son by the name of Pamparoni, who subsequently sold the contents of the three strongboxes containing the drawings to the Florentine painter Antonio Fedi. In 1799 Fedi offered a selection of these sheets to the English dealer William Young Ottley (1771–1836), who eventually sold them to the portrait painter, connoisseur, and insatiable collector Sir Thomas Lawrence (1769–1830). Wicar did not learn of the theft of his collection until July 1800, by which time he was unable to initiate the return of the drawings from England.

In 1801 Wicar settled permanently in Rome, where he enjoyed a successful career as a painter and again began to collect drawings. Nevertheless, in 1823 he was obliged to sell his second collection to another English dealer, Samuel Woodburn (1786–1853), in order to finance the construction of a town house in Rome. Wicar's collection was subsequently resold by Woodburn to Thomas Dimsdale, after whose death it, too, was acquired by Lawrence. More

FIGURE 1. Jacques-Louis David. *The Oath of the Horatii*. Pen and black ink, and gray wash, heightened with white, over graphite

than a decade after Lawrence's death in 1830 part of his superb collection of drawings was purchased by public subscription for the Ashmolean Museum in Oxford.[1] Other drawings that belonged first to Wicar and later to Lawrence were eventually acquired by the British Museum and the Musée du Louvre.[2]

Shortly after disposing of his second collection Wicar undertook the formation of a third, and in 1824 he was able to buy back from Antonio Fedi many of the drawings that had been stolen from him some twenty-five years earlier. When Wicar died in Rome on February 27, 1834, he owned an outstanding group of drawings by Raphael (see cat. nos. 51–59), as well as works by Filippino Lippi (see cat. no. 47), Fra Bartolommeo (see cat. nos. 48– 50), Andrea del Sarto, and Pontormo (see cat. nos. 60–61). Wicar's collection was particularly rich in drawings by seventeenth- and eighteenth-century Florentine painters, such as Jacopo Chimenti da Empoli (see cat. no. 68), Carlo Dolci (see cat. no. 75), and Giovanni Domenico Ferretti (1692–1768), and he possessed a number of fine works by French artists—notably, a superb study by David for *The Oath of the Horatii* (fig. 1).[3] After Wicar's death, ownership of his munificent bequest to the Société des Sciences was transferred to the city of Lille, and the collection was exhibited in the Hôtel de Ville until its removal to the Palais des Beaux-Arts (Musée des Beaux-Arts) at the end of 1891.

Over the years the collection has been much enlarged by purchases, gifts, and bequests. The great majority of French drawings in Lille was acquired in the second half of the nineteenth century, and today the Musée des Beaux-Arts boasts fine examples of the work of Nicolas Poussin (1594–1665; see fig. 2),

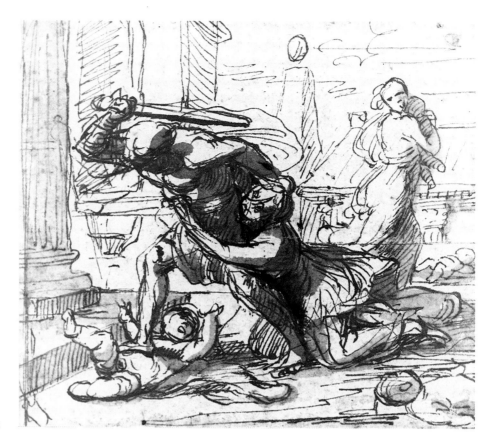

FIGURE 2. Nicolas Poussin. *The Massacre of the Innocents*. Pen and brown ink, and brown wash

Claude Gillot (1673–1722), Antoine Watteau (1684–1721), Nicolas Lancret (1690–1745), Hubert Robert (see cat. no. 80), Jean-Baptiste Greuze, and Théodore Gericault (see cat. no. 83), among many others. A number of these sheets were presented to the museum by local collectors, while drawings by Jean-Auguste-Dominique Ingres (see cat. no. 82), Pierre Puvis de Chavannes (see cat. no. 85), and Ignace-Henri-Jean-Théodore Fantin-Latour (1836–1904) were given by the artists who made them. One of the most spectacular additions to the museum's rapidly growing collection was the purchase of some thirty studies for the *Medea About to Murder Her Children*, at the posthumous sale of the contents of Delacroix's studio in 1864 (see cat. no. 39 A–F).

Although most of the drawings in Lille are by French and Italian artists, all the major schools are represented. The museum owns a number of fine sheets by German draftsmen, including a portrait by Albrecht Dürer (1471–1528) of Lucas van Leyden (see fig. 3)[4] and an early drawing of Saint John the Baptist by Lucas Cranach the Elder (1472–1553),[5] as well as works by the Flemish artist Anthony van Dyck (1599–1641) and by the Dutch painters Jan van Goyen (1595–1656) and Cornelis Saftleven (1607–1681). Recent acquisitions include a composition study by Joachim Wtewael for *The Raising of Lazarus* (cat. no. 86) and a vigorous red- and black-chalk sketch of two cows by Jacob Jordaens (see cat. no. 88). Growth of the collection continues unabated,

FIGURE 3. Albrecht Dürer. *Portrait of Lucas van Leyden.* Metalpoint

and in 1989 the museum purchased a splendid drawing of the Transfiguration by one of Raphael's most gifted and idiosyncratic followers, Polidoro da Caravaggio (1490/1500–1543 ?).

Despite its high quality and remarkable depth, the drawings collection in Lille was long familiar only to specialists. An unillustrated catalogue by Charles Benvignat of 1,436 drawings—of which some 1,300 originally belonged to Wicar—was published in 1856, and Henry Pluchart's indispensable *Musée Wicar, Notice des dessins, cartons, pastels, miniatures et grisailles exposés . . .* appeared in 1889. At that time the collection of drawings numbered 2,838 examples.

In recent decades the museum's holdings have become known to a much wider public, in large part because of exhibitions in Lille and elsewhere in Europe. Sixty-one drawings by Raphael and his immediate circle were exhibited at the Musée des Beaux-Arts in 1961, and more than one hundred Italian drawings from the fifteenth through the eighteenth century were shown in Amsterdam, Brussels, and Lille in 1967–68. Another exhibition of Italian drawings from the Musée des Beaux-Arts took place at the Galleria degli Uffizi in Florence, in 1970, whereas the first in a series of shows devoted to works by French draftsmen was organized in 1974 at the Heim Gallery in London. The last exhibition was followed in 1983 by a show of neoclassical drawings in Lille and, most recently, by an exhibition of nineteenth-century French paintings and watercolors, which opened in Yokohama, Japan, in 1991. From 1989 to 1992 an important group of Italian drawings, many of them previously unpublished, was shown in Lille and, with some significant modifications, at the Wallraf-Richartz Museum in Cologne, while an exhibition of drawings by Florentine artists of the seventeenth and the eighteenth century was held in Florence in 1991. The present selection of forty-nine drawings from the Musée des Beaux-Arts provides the American public with its first glimpse of this extraordinary collection.

1 The following sheets in the Ashmolean Museum, Oxford, belonged first to Wicar and then to Lawrence: see Parker, 1956, nos. 27 (Perugino), 42 (style of Jacopo della Quercia), 44 (Luca Signorelli ?), 45 (Lo Spagna), 245 (Giulio Romano), 292, 295, 307–309, 311–313, 315–319, 328–330, 332–337, 341, 343–345 (Michelangelo), 352–354, 360, 368, 369 (copies after Michelangelo), 372, 375 (followers of Michelangelo), 377, 378* (Antonio Mini ?), 411 (Raffaele da Montelupo), 452, 453 (?) (Passarotti), 462, 466 (Baldassare Peruzzi), 503, 515, 519, 526, 534, 541, 544, 550–552, 564, 566, 567, 572, 576, 580, 581, 582 (?), 590, 592 (Raphael), 625 (artist unknown), 639, 645, 649, 658, 659, 665 f (after Raphael), 692 (Andrea del Sarto), 727 (Giovanni da Udine), 761 (Taddeo Zuccaro).

2 Among them are twenty-two drawings by Michelangelo now in the British Museum (see Wilde, 1953, nos. 6, 10, 13, 15–17, 32, 42, 52–54, 58, 61, 63, 71, 72, 76–78, 81, 82, 102).

3 Pluchart 1194. See Sérullaz, in Lille, 1983, no. 15, ill.; Sérullaz, in Paris–Versailles, 1989–90, no. 71, ill.

4 Pluchart 918. See Strauss, 1974, pp. 2046–48, no. 1521/26, ill.

5 Pluchart 914. See Rosenberg, 1960, p. 15, no. 4, ill.

BARTOLOMEO MONTAGNA

Italian

Orzinuovi (Brescia), about 1450–1523 Vicenza

---

46   *The Virgin and Child*

Black chalk and gray wash, heightened with white, on gray-green paper, 13 x 8 1/2 in. (33.1 x 21.6 cm.)

Inscribed in pen and brown ink (beneath the right foot of the Virgin): I.B.

Inv. Pluchart 58

A pupil of the Venetian painter Giovanni Bellini (about 1430–1479), Bartolomeo Montagna was active primarily in Vicenza. His altarpieces and devotional pictures betray the influence of his master as well as that of Antonello da Messina (about 1430–1479), who was in Venice from 1475 to 1476. In Verona, Montagna executed scenes from the life of Saint Blaise in the church of Santi Nazzaro e Celso, and in 1512 he painted the *Recognition of the Body of Saint Anthony* in the Scuola del Santo, Padua. From later that year until his death in 1523 Montagna was in Vicenza, where his work had considerable impact upon the stylistic development of the next generation of local artists.

This meticulous drawing is a preparatory study for the *Virgin and Child with Saints Sebastian and Jerome* (fig. 1) in the Gallerie dell'Accademia, Venice, originally painted for the church of San Sebastiano, Verona.[1] The circumstances of the commission are unknown; however, according to two early guidebooks, the picture once bore the date 1507.[2] The drawing is close to the finished work, although in the painting there are slight differences in the arrangement of the drapery, and the Virgin's gaze is directed downward.

Lionello Puppi cites two further studies for the painting: a vigorous pen sketch for the figure of Saint Sebastian (Modena, Galleria e Museo Estense)[3] and a brush drawing of Saint Jerome (Paris, Musée du Louvre, Département des Arts Graphiques).[4]

WMG

1 See Puppi, 1962, pp. 64, 128–29, fig. 149.

2 See Dal Pozzo, 1718, p. 262; Maffei, 1732, p. 184; cited in Puppi, 1962, p. 128. The date is no longer legible.

3 Inv. no. 793. See Puppi, 1962, p. 148, fig. 152.

4 Inv. no. 5604. See Puppi, 1962, p. 151, fig. 151.

PROVENANCE

Jean-Baptiste-Joseph Wicar (Lugt 2568).

EXHIBITIONS

Paris, 1956-1, no. 149; Amsterdam–Brussels–Lille, 1967–68, no. 66; Florence, 1970, no. 63; Lille, 1984, no. 119; Marseilles, 1987, no. 55; Lille, 1989–90, no. 1; Cologne, 1990–91, no. 3.

LITERATURE

Benvignat, 1856, no. 34; Gonse, 1877, p. 387 (Montagna ?); Pluchart, 1889, no. 58 (attributed to Giovanni Bellini); Morelli, 1891–92, p. 153; Borenius, 1909, p. 104 (by or after Montagna); Parker, 1927, p. 33, no. 58, ill.; Venturi, 1927, p. 154; Laclotte, 1956, no. 149, pl. LX; Puppi, 1962, pp. 64, 145, fig. 150; Châtelet, 1967, no. 66, pl. 4; Châtelet, 1970-2, no. 63, fig. 50; Oursel, 1984, pp. 85–86, fig. 62; Brejon de Lavergnée, 1989-2, no. 1, ill.; Brejon de Lavergnée, in Cologne, 1990–91, no. 3, ill.

FIGURE 1. Bartolomeo Montagna. *The Virgin and Child with Saints Sebastian and Jerome.* Oil (?) on wood. Gallerie dell'Accademia, Venice

FILIPPINO LIPPI

Italian

Prato, about 1457–1504 Florence

---

47   *A Sibyl and Two Angels with Books*

Pen and brown ink, 3 3/16 x 5 5/8 in. (8.1 x 14.4 cm.)

Inscribed in pen and brown ink (on the verso): *Albert Badi . . . : Fra Filippi*

Inv. Pluchart 633

The son of Fra Filippo Lippi (about 1406–1469), Filippino studied first with his father and then with Botticelli (1445–1510). In the early 1480s in Florence he completed the cycle of frescoes begun sixty years earlier by Masaccio (1401–1428) in the Brancacci Chapel at Santa Maria del Carmine, and in 1487 he undertook the decoration of the Strozzi Chapel in Santa Maria Novella. The latter project was interrupted in 1488 when Filippino was invited to Rome to fresco the walls and ceiling of the Carafa Chapel in Santa Maria sopra Minerva. Four years later he returned to Florence and resumed work in the Strozzi Chapel, which he finished in 1502.

Philip Pouncey identified this lively pen sketch as a study for one of the sibyls in the vault of the Carafa Chapel.[1] The decoration of the chapel was commissioned from Filippino by Cardinal Oliviero Carafa, and work began shortly after the artist's arrival in Rome in September 1488. He completed the frescoes in 1492.

The Cumaean, Tiburtine, Delphic, and Hellespontine sibyls occupy the four compartments of the vault. The frescoes on the altar wall represent the Annunciation and the Assumption of the Virgin; those on the wall to the right of the entrance depict the Triumph of Saint Thomas Aquinas and the miracle of his chastity. The *Combat of Virtues and Vices* executed by Filippino on the left-hand wall of the chapel has been destroyed.

Pouncey associated the present drawing with the figure of the Cumaean sibyl. The resemblance between drawing and fresco is not persuasive, however, and Gail Geiger, in her monograph on Filippino's work in the Carafa Chapel, plausibly suggests that the sheet in Lille is instead a study for the Hellespontine sibyl.[2] Although the Hellespontine sibyl was repainted in the seventeenth century, and its original appearance is unknown, the repainted figure is posed similarly to the one in the present study, her body turned slightly to the left and her right arm raised. She is, moreover, accompanied by two angels, whereas the Cumaean sibyl is flanked by four.

The British Museum possesses a somewhat damaged metalpoint drawing that corresponds very closely to the Cumaean sibyl.[3]

WMG

1 See Pouncey, 1964, p. 286.

2 See Geiger, 1986, pp. 65–66: the *Cumaean Sibyl*, pl. 18, the *Hellespontine Sibyl*, pl. 21. According to Geiger (p. 71 n. 28), the repainted figure may be the work of Niccolò Berrettoni (1637–1682).

3 Inv. no. 1946-7-13-215. See Popham and Pouncey, 1950, I, no. 132, II, pl. CXXVII.

PROVENANCE

Jean-Baptiste-Joseph Wicar (Lugt 2568).

EXHIBITIONS

Amsterdam–Brussels–Lille, 1967–68, no. 54; Florence, 1970, no. 53; Lille, 1989–90, no. 7; Cologne, 1990–91, no. 10.

LITERATURE

Benvignat, 1856, no. 1153; Gonse, 1877, p. 396 (probably Filippino Lippi); Pluchart, 1889, no. 633 (anonymous Italian); Berenson, 1961, II, no. 1343 A; Viatte, 1963, no. 54; Pouncey, 1964, p. 286, pl. 30 b; Châtelet, 1967, no. 54; Châtelet, 1970-2, no. 53, fig. 44; Shoemaker, 1977, p. 222, no. 54, fig. 54; Geiger, 1986, pp. 65–66, pl. 26, p. 71 n. 28; Brejon de Lavergnée, 1989-2, no. 7, ill.; Brejon de Lavergnée, in Cologne, 1990–91, no. 10, ill.

FRA BARTOLOMMEO
(BACCIO DELLA PORTA)

Italian

Florence 1472–1517 Florence

---

48 *Standing Draped Man, Seen from Behind*

Black chalk, heightened with white, on beige paper,
11 1/16 x 5 13/16 in. (28.1 x 14.8 cm.)

Inscribed in pen and brown ink (at the upper right): 24

Inv. Pluchart 34

A pupil of the workman-like Florentine painter Cosimo Rosselli (1439–1507), the young Fra Bartolommeo was profoundly influenced by the art of Piero di Cosimo (1461/62–1521), Domenico Ghirlandaio (1449–1494), and Leonardo da Vinci (1452–1519). The present sheet, executed early in Fra Bartolommeo's career, is typical of his masterful figure and drapery studies in black chalk on prepared paper. The drawing was long thought to be a study for the figure of Saint Joseph in the *Presentation in the Temple* (Florence, Galleria degli Uffizi)—one of two small paintings executed by Fra Bartolommeo in about 1497 as shutters for a lost tabernacle that once housed a marble relief by Donatello.[1]

However, in 1971 Christian von Holst suggested a more plausible connection between this sheet and Fra Bartolommeo's monumental fresco of *The Last Judgment* (fig. 1).[2] The largest and most ambitious project the young artist had ever undertaken, this fresco originally occupied part of a wall in the Chiostro delle Ossa of the Arcispedale di Santa Maria Nuova, Florence, but it was detached in the nineteenth century and is now in the Museo di San Marco.

The *Last Judgment* was commissioned by Gerozzo Dini on January 8, 1499, and was to be completed by the following July. Nevertheless, work was apparently still in progress when Fra Bartolommeo began his novitiate at the monastery of San Domenico in Prato in July 1500. At that point, the artist's friend and sometime partner Mariotto Albertinelli took over and, using drawings and cartoons by Fra Bartolommeo, executed the figures of the Saved and the Damned in the lower half of the composition. The fresco was finished by March 11, 1501.

In all, more than sixty preparatory drawings for the *Last Judgment* survive. Almost all of them are chalk studies of single figures, and many are preserved in the Museum Boymans-van Beuningen, Rotterdam.[3] The sheet in Lille is a study for the man at the far right among the Damned in the

FIGURE 1. Fra Bartolommeo (Baccio della Porta). *The Last Judgment.* Fresco. Museo di San Marco, Florence

fresco. Another drawing for the same figure, somewhat closer to the finished work, is in the Gabinetto Disegni e Stampe of the Uffizi.[4]

WMG

1 See von der Gabelentz, 1922, I, pp. 135–37, figs. 1, 2; Fischer, 1990, pp. 36–37, figs. 1, 2.

2 See von der Gabelentz, 1922, I, pp. 137–40, fig. 3; Fischer, 1990, pp. 43–45, fig. 9.

3 See Fischer, 1990, nos. 4–18, ill., figs. 11, 13, 15, 17, 18, 21–23, 25, 27–30.

4 Inv. no. 518 E. See von Holst, 1974, p. 283, fig. 11.

PROVENANCE

Jean-Baptiste-Joseph Wicar (Lugt 2568).

EXHIBITIONS

Paris, 1965–66, no. 31; Amsterdam–Brussels–Lille, 1967–68, no. 15; Florence, 1970, no. 16; Lille, 1989–90, no. 12; Cologne, 1990–91, no. 19.

LITERATURE

Benvignat, 1856, no. 249; Gonse, 1877, p. 401; Pluchart, 1889, no. 34; Morelli, 1891–92, col. 377; Berenson, 1903, II, no. 393; Knapp, 1903, pp. 40, 252, 318, pl. 14; von der Gabelentz, 1922, II, p. 114, no. 256; Venturi, IX, I (1925), p. 232, fig. 152; Berenson, 1938, II, no. 393; Fossi, in Florence, 1954, p. 9, under no. 8; Berenson, 1961, II, no. 393; Viatte, 1963, no. 39; Châtelet, 1967, no. 15; Châtelet, 1970-2, no. 16, fig. 10; von Holst, 1974, p. 283, fig. 10; Ames-Lewis, 1981, p. 56, fig. 27; Oursel, 1984, p. 86; Brejon de Lavergnée, 1989-2, no. 12, ill.; Brejon de Lavergnée, in Cologne, 1990–91, no. 19, ill.

FRA BARTOLOMMEO
(BACCIO DELLA PORTA)

Italian

Florence 1472–1517 Florence

---

49   *Two Male Religious Embracing*; *Study of Drapery*;
      Two Studies of a Reclining Man

Black chalk, heightened with white, on beige paper,
8 7/16 x 10 7/8 in. (21.4 x 27.6 cm.)

Inv. Pluchart 36

Verso: *Reclining Man*

Black chalk, heightened with white, on beige paper

Inv. Pluchart 39

Between July 1500, when Fra Bartolommeo entered the monastery of San Domenico in Prato, and late 1504, when he undertook the execution of the *Vision of Saint Bernard* (Florence, Galleria degli Uffizi), he gave up painting to pursue a religious life. Afterward, he took up painting again, and in April 1508 he was in Venice, where his work was influenced by the rich palette of Giovanni Bellini. Later the same year, he and his former associate Mariotto Albertinelli formed a new and highly successful partnership.

Three of the studies on the recto of the Lille sheet are connected with the *Mystic Marriage of Saint Catherine*, now in the Musée du Louvre, Paris, but originally in the church of San Marco, Florence (fig. 1).[1] The altarpiece, which is dated 1511, represents the spiritual marriage of Saint Catherine of Siena to the Christ Child in the presence of the Virgin and eight other saints: Peter, Vincent, Stephen, Francis of Assisi, Dominic, Paul, Lawrence (?), and Catherine of Alexandria. In March 1512 the picture was purchased by the Florentine government and given to the departing French ambassador, Jacques Hurault; eventually it was replaced by another painting of the same subject, also by Fra Bartolommeo (Florence, Galleria dell'Accademia).[2] The drawing of two embracing figures at the left on the present sheet is a study for Saints Francis and Dominic, who appear in the background just to the right of the Virgin in the painting. Their embrace alludes to a passage in *The Golden Legend* of Jacobus de Voragine: One night Saint Dominic had a vision in which he and Saint Francis were appointed by Christ as warriors against the vices of pride, concupiscence, and avarice. When Saint Dominic saw Saint Francis in church the next day, "he ran to him and greeted him with pious kisses and embraces."[3] Fra Bartolommeo treated this subject on several occasions; the

FIGURE 1. Fra Bartolommeo (Baccio della Porta). *The Mystic Marriage of Saint Catherine*. Oil on wood. Musée du Louvre, Paris

poses of Saints Francis and Dominic in the *Mystic Marriage of Saint Catherine* are similar to those of the figures in a frescoed lunette in the Ospizio della Maddalena, in Le Caldine, near Florence.[4]

Chris Fischer has identified a number of preparatory drawings for the Louvre painting.[5] The three compositional studies in Florence,[6] Lille,[7] and London,[8] respectively, indicate that the two mendicant saints were at first much more prominent, kneeling in the foreground in front of the throne of the Virgin. In subsequent drawings, however, the two figures are relegated to the background, possibly at the insistence of the Dominican friars for whom the picture was painted. Another drawing of the same two saints, similar to the study in Lille, is in the Museum Boymans-van Beuningen, Rotterdam.[9]

Near the right margin of the present sheet are two small sketches of a half-reclining male figure. The same figure is repeated on a larger scale on the reverse of the drawing and on the reverse of a study in Rotterdam for the *Carondelet Madonna*, which was commissioned from Fra Bartolommeo in 1511 and finished in 1512.[10] According to Fischer, these drawings may be studies for the figure of Saint Joseph in a lost or unexecuted *Holy Family* of about 1511–12.[11]

WMG

49: verso

1 See von der Gabelentz, 1922, I, pp. 155–57, fig. 10; Fischer, 1982, pp. 167–70, fig. 1; Fischer, 1990, pp. 189–90, fig. 105.

2 See von der Gabelentz, 1922, I, pp. 157–58, fig. 11.

3 *The Golden Legend of Jacobus de Voragine.* Granger Ryan and Helmut Ripperger, trans. New York, 1969, p. 417.

4 See von der Gabelentz, 1922, I, p. 170; Fahy, 1974, pp. 15, 17, fig. 10; Fischer, 1990, p. 212, fig. 121.

5 See Fischer, 1982, pp. 170–80, figs. 2–18.

6 Gabinetto Disegni e Stampe degli Uffizi, Inv. no. 408 F. See Fischer, 1982, p. 170, fig. 2; Fischer, 1990, p. 190, fig. 106.

7 Musée des Beaux-Arts, Pluchart 43. See Fischer, 1982, p. 171, fig. 3; Fischer, 1986, no. 49, fig. 64; Fischer, 1990, p. 191, fig. 107.

8 Victoria and Albert Museum, Dyce 150. See Fischer, 1990, p. 191, fig. 108.

9 Vol. M 122. See Fischer, 1990, no. 55, ill.

10 Vol. M 54. See Fischer, 1990, no. 66, ill.

11 See Fischer, 1990, p. 249, under no. 66.

PROVENANCE

Jean-Baptiste-Joseph Wicar (Lugt 2568).

EXHIBITIONS

Amsterdam–Brussels–Lille, 1967–68, no. 13; Florence, 1970, no. 13; Paris, 1982, no. 10; Lille, 1989–90, no. 13; Cologne, 1990–91, no. 20.

LITERATURE

Benvignat, 1856, nos. 251 (recto), 254 (verso); Merson, 1862, II, p. 166; Gonse, 1877, pp. 401–2; Gruyer, 1886, p. 41, ill. (detail of recto); Pluchart, 1889, nos. 36 (recto), 39 (verso); Berenson, 1903, II, no. 394; Knapp, 1903, pp. 318, 319, 265, 266, respectively; von der Gabelentz, 1922, I, p. 156, II, pp. 114–15, no. 258; Venturi, IX, I (1925), p. 290 n. 1, fig. 203 (recto); Berenson, 1938, II, no. 394; Bacou, 1957, p. 62; Berenson, 1961, II, no. 394, III, fig. 395 (recto); Viatte, 1963, no. 43; Châtelet, 1967, no. 13, pl. 16 (recto); Châtelet, 1970-2, no. 13, fig. 8 (recto); Fahy, 1974, p. 15; Béguin, 1982, no. 10; Fischer, 1982, p. 173, fig. 9 (recto), n. 52; Oursel, 1984, p. 86; Fischer, 1986, p. 99, under no. 49; Brejon de Lavergnée, 1989-2, no. 13, ill. (recto and verso); Fischer, 1990, p. 211, under no. 55, p. 213, fig. 122 (recto), p. 249, under no. 66, p. 251, fig. 158 (verso); Brejon de Lavergnée, in Cologne, 1990–91, no. 20, ill.

FRA BARTOLOMMEO
(BACCIO DELLA PORTA)

Italian

Florence 1472–1517 Florence

---

50   *Sheet of Studies: Two Heads; Three Hands; The Head of Christ*

Red chalk, 8 1/4 x 10 1/4 in. (21 x 26 cm.)

Inv. Pluchart 37

Verso: *Standing Male Religious with Right Arm Raised*

Red chalk

Inv. Pluchart 38

The heads and hands at the left on the recto of the sheet are related to a damaged painting of Saint Vincent Ferrer (fig. 1), formerly over the door to the sacristy in the church of San Marco and now in the Museo di San Marco, Florence.[1] Above the figure, who points upward, there was originally a small roundel representing Christ as judge; it is now in the Casa Vasari in Arezzo. On the verso of the sheet is another study for the figure of the Dominican saint, shown from the knees up, as he is in the painting. Two further drawings of Vincent Ferrer, both in the Museum Boymans-van Beuningen, Rotterdam, appear on the same sheets as figure studies for Fra Bartolommeo's *Mystic Marriage of Saint Catherine* (Paris, Musée du Louvre).[2] This circumstance indicates that the undated *Saint Vincent Ferrer* might have been executed at about the same time as the *Mystic Marriage*, which is signed and dated 1511.[3]

The head of Christ carrying the cross is a study for a devotional picture (Florence, Museo di San Marco) that

50: verso (detail)

FIGURE I. Fra Bartolommeo (Baccio della Porta). *Saint Vincent Ferrer* (detail). Oil on wood. Museo di San Marco, Florence

is inscribed ORAT QUO PICTORE, followed by a date that has been read as 1511 (by Knapp) and as 1514 (by most other scholars).[4] In light of the fact that the drawing is on the same sheet as the series of studies for the *Saint Vincent Ferrer*, the earlier date assigned to the painting by Knapp is most likely to be correct.

WMG

1 See Gabelentz, 1922, II, pp. 165–66; Fischer, 1990, p. 199, under no. 51, p. 201, fig. 113.

2 Vol. M 128 and Vol. N 48. See Fischer, 1990, nos. 53, ill., 51, ill., respectively. For a discussion of the Louvre picture see also catalogue number 49.

3 As suggested by Chris Fischer (1990, p. 199, under no. 51).

4 See Knapp, 1903, pp. 255–56 (the picture said to be dated 1511, "nicht 1514, wie offenbar nach einer Retouche zu lesen ist"); Gabelentz, 1922, pp. 169–70 (the picture said to be dated 1514).

PROVENANCE

Jean-Baptiste-Joseph Wicar (Lugt 2568).

EXHIBITIONS

Amsterdam–Brussels–Lille, 1967–68, no. 14; Florence, 1970, no. 15; Lille, 1989–90, no. 15; Cologne, 1990–91, no. 22.

LITERATURE

Benvignat, 1856, nos. 252 (recto), 253 (verso); Gonse, 1877, p. 402; Pluchart, 1889, nos. 37 (recto), 38 (verso); Morelli, 1891–92, col. 377; Berenson, 1903, II, no. 2724 (as Giovanni Antonio Sogliani); Knapp, 1903, pp. 257, 319, fig. 98 (verso); Gabelentz, 1922, I, pp. 165, 170, II, p. 115, no. 259; Berenson, 1938, II, no. 2724 (as Giovanni Antonio Sogliani); Bacou, 1957, p. 62; Berenson, 1961, II, no. 2724 (as Giovanni Antonio Sogliani); Viatte, 1963, no. 45; Châtelet, 1967, no. 14; Châtelet, 1970-2, no. 15, fig. 9 (recto); Brejon de Lavergnée, 1989-2, no. 15, ill. (recto and verso); Fischer, 1990, p. 199, under no. 51, p. 201, figs. 114 (verso), 115 (recto); Brejon de Lavergnée, in Cologne, 1990–91, no. 22, ill. (recto and verso).

RAPHAEL (RAFFAELLO SANTI)

Italian

Urbino 1483–1520 Rome

---

51   *The Coronation of Saint Nicholas of Tolentino*

Black chalk, over stylus underdrawing, squared in black chalk, 16 1/8 x 10 3/8 in. (40.9 x 26.3 cm.)

There are scattered stains.

Inv. Pluchart 474

Verso: *Head of a Man, Two Studies of Drapery, Four Studies of Birds, Façade of a Palace*

Black chalk (the head of a man and the studies of drapery) and pen and brown ink (the studies of birds and the façade of a palace)

Inv. Pluchart 475

This drawing is a study for Raphael's earliest documented painting, *The Coronation of Saint Nicholas of Tolentino*, which was commissioned on December 10, 1500, by Andrea di Tommaso Baronci for his chapel in the church of Sant' Agostino in Città di Castello; the painting was finished by September 13, 1501.[1] The altarpiece, executed by Raphael in collaboration with the little-known painter Evangelista di Pian di Meleto (1458–1549), remained in Sant'Agostino until the end of the eighteenth century. On September 30, 1789, the altarpiece was badly damaged in an earthquake. The ruined picture was sold to Pope Pius VI, and a short time later it was replaced with a partial copy by Ermenegildo Costantini (1731–1791).[2]

Four fragments of the original altarpiece survive: two of angels—in the Pinacoteca Tosio Martinengo, Brescia,[3] and the Musée du Louvre[4]—and a fragment with the Virgin and one with God the Father, both in the Museo di Capodimonte, Naples.[5] Yet another fragment, a half-length figure of Saint Augustine, may once have belonged to Jean-Baptiste-Joseph Wicar, but its present whereabouts is unknown.[6] On the basis of the surviving fragments in Brescia, Paris, and Naples; the copy still in Città di Castello; and preparatory drawings in Lille and in Oxford, it has been possible to reconstruct the original appearance of the altarpiece.

Flanked by four angels and wearing the black habit of the Augustinian order, Saint Nicholas of Tolentino was shown standing, with a crucifix in his right hand and an open book in his left. Satan lay prostrate beneath his feet, while half-length figures of God the Father, the Virgin, and Saint Augustine appeared overhead, holding crowns. With the exception of Saint Augustine, who wears a bishop's miter and

cope, the figures in the drawing are represented in contemporary dress, and were evidently studied from life. In the present drawing, the architectural setting and the figure of Saint Nicholas are indicated with just a few strokes of chalk, and only one of the four angels in the painting is included.

A drawing in the Ashmolean Museum, Oxford, contains, on the recto, studies in black chalk for the left and right hands of Saint Nicholas, for the right forearm of Saint Augustine, and for the head of the angel on the far left in the altarpiece;[7] on the verso are a sketch of the same angel and a full-length study from life for the figure of Saint Augustine.

The principal drawing on the verso of the present sheet is a study for the head of Saint Nicholas. As with most of the figures shown on the recto, this sensitive sketch was drawn from a live model, probably a studio assistant, or *garzone*. On the same sheet are two studies for the drapery of the angel on the left in the finished work. The architectural drawing in the lower right-hand corner may have been inspired by the ducal palace in Raphael's native city of Urbino.

WMG

1 See Dussler, 1971, pp. 1–2, pl. 6 (reconstruction); Béguin, in Paris, 1983–84, pp. 69–72, under no. 1, p. 71, fig. 2 (reconstruction).

2 Illustrated by Béguin, in Paris, 1983–84, p. 71, fig. 1.

3 See Dussler, 1971, pp. 2–3, pl. 4; Béguin, in Paris, 1983–84, p. 21, ill., no. 2, ill.

4 See Béguin, in Paris, 1983–84, p. 20, ill., no. 1, ill.

5 See Dussler, 1971, pp. 1–2, pl. 5 (*God the Father*); Béguin, in Paris, 1983–84, p. 21, ill., no. 3, ill. (*God the Father*), no. 3 a, ill. (*Head of the Virgin*).

6 See Béguin, in Paris, 1983–84, p. 71, under no. 1.

7 See Parker, 1956, no. 504 (recto and verso), pl. CXVI (recto); Joannides, 1983, p. 138, no. 17, ill. (recto and verso); Oberhuber, 1983, no. 14, ill. (recto), no. 16, ill. (verso); Viatte, in Paris, 1983–84, p. 166, under no. 2, figs. 23, 22 (recto and verso, respectively).

PROVENANCE

Jean-Baptiste-Joseph Wicar (Lugt 2568).

EXHIBITIONS

Brussels, 1954–55, no. 121; Lille, 1961, no. 5; Berlin, 1964, no. 70; Paris, 1965–66, no. 233; Amsterdam–Brussels–Lille, 1967–68, no. 79; Lille, 1968, no. 79; Florence, 1970, no. 76; Lille, 1983-2, no. 1; Paris, 1983–84, nos. 1 (recto), 2 (verso); Lille, 1984, no. 126; Lille, 1989–90, no. 18; Cologne, 1990–91, no. 25.

LITERATURE

Oberhuber, 1983, p. 556, nos. 12, ill. (recto), 13, ill. (verso); Viatte, in Paris, 1983–84, pp. 163–67, nos. 1, ill. (recto), 2, ill. (verso), with complete bibliography; Shearman, in Rome, 1984, p. 112, no. 2-1-1, ill. (verso); Ames-Lewis, 1986, p. 19, pl. VI, pp. 20, 26–29, fig. 21 (recto), pp. 33–34; Gregori, 1987, fig. 326 b (recto); Brejon de Lavergnée, 1989-2, no. 18, ill. (recto and verso); Brejon de Lavergnée, in Cologne, 1990–91, no. 25, ill. (recto and verso).

51: recto

51: verso

RAPHAEL (RAFFAELLO SANTI)

Italian

Urbino 1483–1520 Rome

52 *Seated Youth Holding a Book*

Metalpoint on white prepared paper, 9 7/8 x 7 1/8 in.
(25 x 18 cm.)

Inv. Pluchart 442

Verso: *Two Archers*

Pen and brown ink, over stylus underdrawing

Inv. Pluchart 443

This charming sketch of a youth holding an open book was long thought to be a study for Raphael's *Solly Madonna* of about 1500–1501 (Berlin, Staatliche Museen Preussischer Kulturbesitz).[1] In that painting, however, the composition is reversed: The Virgin holds a book in her right hand, and she cradles the foot of the Christ Child in her left. Sir John Pope-Hennessy was the first to recognize that the Lille drawing is more closely related to another, slightly later painting of the Virgin and Child (fig. 1), which was acquired by the Norton Simon Museum of Art, Pasadena, in 1972.[2]

Three other studies for the Norton Simon painting, all of which have at one time or another been associated with the *Solly Madonna*, are in English public collections. The first in the sequence, a pen-and-ink study for the whole composition, is in the Ashmolean Museum, Oxford;[3] on the verso of the Oxford drawing is another study of the Christ Child, his pose virtually identical to that of the corresponding figure on the recto.[4] A sheet of landscape studies, also in the Ashmolean Museum, is directly related to the background of the painting in Pasadena.[5] Finally, a metalpoint drawing of the head of the Virgin, probably executed after the present *garzone* study for the entire figure, is in the British Museum, London.[6]

Both the drawing in Lille and the *Head of the Virgin* in the British Museum belong to a group of seven sheets that Oskar Fischel believed were part of a single, now widely dispersed sketchbook.[7] This suggestion today seems unlikely, but all seven drawings associated with the so-called "Large Umbrian Silverpoint Sketchbook" are identical in style and technique. Four of them, including catalogue number 53, are studies for Raphael's Oddi Altarpiece of about 1503. It therefore seems reasonable to assume that the four drawings associable with the *Virgin and Child* in the Norton Simon Museum of Art were executed during the same period, a supposition borne out by the style of the painting.

FIGURE 1. Raphael. *The Virgin and Child with a Book*. Oil on wood. Norton Simon Art Foundation, Pasadena

On the verso of the present sheet is a sketch of two archers, which presents problems of attribution analogous to those posed by the drawing on the verso of catalogue number 53. In both cases the stylus underdrawing seems to be by Raphael, but the contours of the figures have been clumsily reinforced in pen and ink, presumably by a later hand. The figure on the left in the present example is copied from Luca Signorelli's *Martyrdom of Saint Sebastian* (Città di Castello, Pinacoteca Comunale), a painting with which Raphael would no doubt have been familiar. Since the figure on the right does not appear in Signorelli's altarpiece, it has been suggested that Raphael was copying a lost preparatory drawing for the *Martyrdom of Saint Sebastian* rather than the finished work.[8]

WMG

1 Inv. no. 141. See Dussler, 1971, p. 4, pl. 8.

2 Illustrated in Dussler, 1971, fig. 18; Pope-Hennessy, 1970, fig. 158, pp. 178–81.

3 See Parker, 1956, no. 508 a (recto); Gere and Turner, 1983, no. 16, ill.; Joannides, 1983, p. 141, no. 32 *r*, ill.

4 See Parker, 1956, no. 508 a (verso); Joannides, 1983, p. 141, no. 32 *v*, ill.

5 See Parker, 1956, no. 508 b (recto and verso); Gere and Turner, 1983, no. 17, ill. (recto); Joannides, 1983, p. 141, nos. 33 *r*, ill., 33 *v*, ill.

6 Inv. no. 1895-9-15-611. See Gere and Turner, 1983, no. 18, ill.; Joannides, 1983, p. 142, no. 35 *r*, ill.

7 See Fischel, 1913–45, I, nos. 16, 18–19, 21–22, 41, 50–51, ill. Fischel, followed by Parker (1956, nos. 511 a, 511 b), believed nos. 21–22 were cut from the same sheet.

8 See Fischel, 1913–45, text vol., under no. 50; Viatte, in Paris, 1983–84, p. 197, under no. 31.

PROVENANCE

Antonio Fedi; Jean-Baptiste-Joseph Wicar (Lugt 2568).

EXHIBITIONS

Lille, 1961, nos. 17 (recto), 18 (verso); Paris, 1965–66, no. 236; Amsterdam–Brussels–Lille, 1967–68, no. 81; Florence, 1970, no. 78; Lille, 1983-2, no. 8; Paris, 1983–84, nos. 30 (recto), 31 (verso); Lille, 1989–90, no. 22; Cologne, 1990–91, no. 27.

LITERATURE

Gere and Turner, 1983, p. 37, under no. 18; Oberhuber, 1983, no. 68, ill. (recto); Viatte, in Paris, 1983–84, pp. 195–97, nos. 30, ill. (recto), 31, ill. (verso), with complete bibliography; Ames-Lewis, 1986, p. 15, pl. IV (recto), pp. 16–17, 24, 59; Brejon de Lavergnée, 1989-2, no. 22, ill. (recto and verso); Brejon de Lavergnée, in Cologne, 1990–91, no. 27, ill. (recto).

RAPHAEL (RAFFAELLO SANTI)

Italian

Urbino 1483–1520 Rome

---

53 *Head and Hands of a Youth*

Metalpoint on gray prepared paper, 10 1/2 x 7 3/4 in. (26.6 x 19.6 cm.)

Inv. Pluchart 440

Verso: *Two Seated Youths*

Traces of black chalk, and pen and brown ink, over stylus underdrawing

Inv. Pluchart 441

This sheet is one of a number of preparatory drawings for Raphael's *Coronation of the Virgin* (fig. 1),[1] now in the Pinacoteca at the Vatican. The painting was commissioned by Alessandra di Simone degli Oddi for her chapel in the church of San Francesco al Prato in Perugia. *The Coronation of the*

FIGURE 1. Raphael. *The Coronation of the Virgin*. About 1503. Oil on wood, transferred to canvas. Pinacoteca Vaticana, Vatican City

Virgin is usually dated to about 1503, the year in which the exiled Oddi family returned to Perugia following the flight of their rivals, the Baglioni. Recently, however, it has been suggested that the main part of the altarpiece was executed a little earlier, in 1502, and the predella from 1503 to 1504.[2]

The picture represents the Virgin seated before Christ on a bank of clouds, flanked by music-making angels. Below them, the apostles are gathered around the tomb of the Virgin, which is empty but for the roses and lilies that grew there after her Assumption into heaven. The facial types and the graceful demeanor of the figures, as well as the clear division of the composition into two distinct registers, reflect the influence of Raphael's slightly older Umbrian contemporaries, Perugino and Pinturicchio.

53: verso

sively retouched in pen and brown ink. Although it is now virtually impossible to detect Raphael's hand in this sketch, it nevertheless seems to be an original study for the Oddi Altarpiece and not just a copy.

WMG

1 Inv. no. 334. See Dussler, 1971, p. 10, plates 26–28 (the predella), 29; Pierluigi De Vecchi, in Rome, 1984–85, no. 1, ill. Fischel (1913–45, I, nos. 15–27, ill.) identified ten studies for *The Coronation of the Virgin*; A. E. Popham recognized another in the Royal Library, Windsor (Popham and Wilde, 1949, no. 788, pl. 46). See also Joannides, 1983, nos. 38–50, ill.

2 The hypothesis was put forward by Fabrizio Mancinelli and Pierluigi De Vecchi at the symposium "Raphael before Rome" in Washington, D.C., 1983. Cited by De Vecchi, in Rome, 1984–85, pp. 15–16, under no. 1.

3 See Fischel, 1913–45, I, nos. 18–19, ill. (Oxford, Ashmolean Museum, Inv. nos. 511 a, 511 b), no. 22, ill. (London, British Museum, Inv. no. Pp. 1–67).

PROVENANCE
Jean-Baptiste-Joseph Wicar (Lugt 2568).

EXHIBITIONS
Lille, 1961, nos. 9 (recto), 10 (verso); Paris, 1965–66, no. 234; Lille, 1983-2, no. 2; Paris, 1983–84, nos. 21 (recto), 22 (verso); Lille, 1989–90, no. 19.

LITERATURE
Ferino-Pagden and Oberhuber, in Oberhuber, 1983, p. 560, no. 47, ill. (recto), p. 559, no. 38, ill. (verso); Viatte, in Paris, 1983–84, pp. 184–87, nos. 21, ill. (recto), 22, ill. (verso), with complete bibliography; Ames-Lewis, 1986, p. 32, fig. 31 (verso), pp. 33, 154 n. 21; Brejon de Lavergnée, 1989-2, no. 19, ill. (recto and verso).

The head and hands on the recto of the present drawing correspond to those of Saint Thomas, who stands behind the open sarcophagus in the lower register of the painting. The saint gazes upward at the figure of the Virgin and holds in his hands her girdle, which she lowered to him at the Assumption. In the painting, only the position of the fingers of Saint Thomas's right hand differs slightly from the preparatory drawing, which in every other respect anticipates the finished work.

There are three other metalpoint studies for the Oddi Altarpiece.[3] Metalpoint was a technique popular in Florence and in Umbria during the second half of the fifteenth century and was frequently employed by the young Raphael. Unlike most of his contemporaries, however, he used metalpoint with a freedom that is usually associated with black chalk.

On the verso of the present sheet is a *garzone* study for the figures of the Virgin and God the Father in *The Coronation of the Virgin*, drawn with the stylus and then lightly strengthened in black chalk. Later, however, the drawing was exten-

RAPHAEL (RAFFAELLO SANTI)

Italian

Urbino 1483–1520 Rome

54 *Head of a Youth Wearing a Cap*

Black chalk, heightened with white, on gray-brown paper, 8 3/8 x 7 5/16 in. (21.2 x 18.6 cm.)

Inv. Pluchart 461

There is an obvious similarity between the present drawing and the head of the angel playing the tambourine at the far left in Raphael's Oddi Altarpiece of about 1503, now in the Pinacoteca Vaticana (see fig 1 in cat. no. 53). In a *garzone* study for the angel (Oxford, Ashmolean Museum), the youth-

ful model wears a cap identical to the one worn by the figure in the Lille drawing.[1]

Raphael possessed prodigious talent as a portraitist, as his paintings amply demonstrate. This sensitive study of the head of a young man is clearly a portrait as well, and Anna Forlani Tempesti's suggestion that it might not be directly related to the Oddi Altarpiece seems entirely plausible.[2]

The Lille drawing probably dates from about 1503, and, not surprisingly, the physiognomy of the sitter (perhaps the studio assistant who posed for the Oxford drawing) reflects Umbrian prototypes. Nevertheless, Forlani Tempesti has pointed out that Raphael may also have been influenced by the innumerable metalpoint studies of heads executed by the Florentine artist Lorenzo di Credi (about 1460–1537).[3]

WMG

1 See Fischel, 1913–45, I, no. 18, ill.; Parker, 1956, no. 511 a; Gere and Turner, 1983, no. 20, ill.

2 Cited by Viatte, in Paris, 1983–84, p. 194, under no. 29.

3 See, for example, Dalli Regoli, 1966, nos. 42, 44, 45, 52, 55, 56, 57, 60, 84, 87, 114, 117, figs. 87, 89, 98, 94, 96, 100, 99, 105, 118, 120, 119, 125, respectively.

PROVENANCE

Jean-Baptiste-Joseph Wicar; Antonio Fedi; Jean-Baptiste-Joseph Wicar (Lugt 2568).

EXHIBITIONS

Lille, 1961, no. 15; Berlin, 1964, no. 71; Paris, 1965–66, no. 236; Amsterdam–Brussels–Lille, 1967–68, no. 80; Florence, 1970, no. 77; Lille, 1983-2, no. 9; Paris, 1983–84, no. 29; Lille, 1989–90, no. 21; Cologne, 1990–91, no. 26.

LITERATURE

Oberhuber, 1983, no. 75, ill.; Viatte, in Paris, 1983–84, p. 194, no. 29, ill., with complete bibliography; Brejon de Lavergnée, 1989-2, no. 21, ill.; Brejon de Lavergnée, in Cologne, 1990–91, no. 26, ill.

RAPHAEL (RAFFAELLO SANTI)

Italian

Urbino 1483–1520 Rome

55 *The Holy Family in a Landscape, with Saints John the Baptist, Anne, and Joachim*

Pen and brown ink, over stylus underdrawing and traces of black chalk, squared in red chalk (bottom half), 13 7/8 x 9 1/4 in. (35.3 x 23.4 cm.)

The top of the sheet is arched.

Inv. Pluchart 458

Verso: autograph letter from Raphael to Domenico di Paride Alfani

Pen and brown ink

Inv. Pluchart 459

FIGURE 1. Domenico di Paride Alfani, after a design by Raphael. *The Holy Family, with Saints and Angels.* Tempera on wood. Galleria Nazionale dell'Umbria, Perugia

The Virgin is seated in a panoramic landscape with the Christ Child standing before her. Saint Joseph, at the right, offers Christ a pomegranate, emblematic of the Resurrection, while the infant Saint John the Baptist, at the left, directs the attention of the viewer toward Christ. Saints Anne and Joachim, the parents of the Virgin, stand behind the main figures, and overhead cherubs play a tambourine, pipes, and a triangle.

Between 1504 and 1508 Raphael spent most of his time in Florence, where he was influenced by the work of Fra Bartolommeo, Leonardo da Vinci, and Michelangelo. Toward the end of this period he supplied the present sheet to the Umbrian painter Domenico di Paride Alfani (about 1480–after 1553), who utilized the design for an altarpiece, formerly in the church of San Simone dei Carmini, Perugia (now Perugia, Galleria Nazionale dell'Umbria; see fig. 1).[1] Alfani later reused the pose of the Christ Child in another altarpiece (dated 1504), *The Virgin and Child Enthroned with Four Saints and Angels* (Perugia, Galleria Nazionale dell'Umbria),[2] although there the figure is reversed.

On the verso of the Lille drawing is a letter in which Raphael asks Alfani to remind Atalanta Baglioni of Perugia that she still owes him money.[3] This request is usually associated with Raphael's *Entombment*, now in the Galleria Borghese, Rome.[4] One of the last and most sophisticated works of Raphael's Florentine period, *The Entombment* was commissioned by Baglioni for her chapel in the church of San Francesco al Prato in Perugia. Since *The Entombment* bears the date 1507, it is likely that Raphael drew the *modello* for Alfani's *Holy Family* at about the same time.

In composition, *The Holy Family* is more complex than Raphael's earlier representations of the Virgin and Child, and, in this respect, bears some resemblance to *The Entombment*. In handling, however, the drawing is rather dry, and there are no significant pentimenti. The style of the sheet may be explained partly by its function, for it must always have been intended as a *modello* for the use of another artist. The precise pen work is similar to that of a study by Raphael, now at Windsor Castle, also datable to about 1507.[5]

WMG

1 See Santi, 1985, no. 173, ill. (Pompeo di Anselmo and Domenico Alfani).

2 See Santi, 1985, no. 163, ill.

3 *Recordo avoi menecho che me mandiate le istranboti de riciardo di quella tenpesta che ebbe andando [in] uno viagio e/ che recordiate a Cesarino che me manda quella predicha e recomandatemi a lui ancora ve ricoro che voi solecitate/ madona le atala[n]te che me manda li denari e vedete davere horo e dite a cesarino che ancora lui recorda e soleciti/ a se io poso altro p[er]voi avisatime.*

4 See Dussler, 1971, pp. 23–24, pl. 67.

5 Inv. no. 12738. See Popham and Wilde, 1949, no. 790, pl. 47; Gere and Turner, 1983, no. 58, ill.

PROVENANCE

Blanchard (?); Jean-Baptiste-Joseph Wicar; Antonio Fedi; marchese della Penna, Perugia; Jean-Baptiste-Joseph Wicar (Lugt 2568).

EXHIBITIONS

Lille, 1961, no. 32; Berlin, 1964, no. 73; Paris, 1965–66, no. 237; Lille, 1983-2, no. 14; Paris, 1983–84, nos. 54 (recto), 55 (verso); Lille, 1989–90, no. 26.

LITERATURE

Oberhuber, 1983, no. 212, ill. (recto); Viatte, in Paris, 1983–84, pp. 223–25, nos. 54, ill. (recto), 55, ill. (verso), with complete bibliography; Brejon de Lavergnée, 1989-2, no. 26, ill. (recto).

RAPHAEL (RAFFAELLO SANTI)

Italian

Urbino 1483–1520 Rome

---

56 *Seated Draped Figure*

Point of the brush, and brown wash, heightened with white, over metalpoint underdrawing, squared in metalpoint; around the figure is a circle drawn with a compass and stylus, and below is a line in pen and brown ink, 16 x 10 3/8 in. (40.6 x 26.4 cm.)

Inv. Pluchart 471

Verso: *Sketch of Two Male Nudes*

Pen and brown ink

Inv. Pluchart 472

In 1508, Pope Julius II della Rovere invited Raphael to Rome, where he immediately undertook the lion's share of the decoration of Julius's private apartments on the second floor of the Palazzo Vaticano. Raphael finished his frescoes in the Stanza della Segnatura in 1511, and he had begun work in the adjacent Stanza d'Eliodoro when Julius II died in 1513. Under Julius's successor, Pope Leo X de'Medici, Raphael completed the frescoes in the Stanza d'Eliodoro and, with considerable studio assistance, he executed those in the Stanza dell'Incendio from 1514 to 1517.

During Julius's lifetime, the Stanza della Segnatura was the pope's private library. Accordingly, the decorative scheme illustrates the four main branches of learning, each of which is represented on the ceiling by a female allegorical

FIGURE 1. Raphael. *Disputa*. Fresco. Stanza della Segnatura, Palazzo Vaticano, Vatican City

figure. On the walls below the figures of Theology, Poetry, and Philosophy, respectively, Raphael painted the now-famous *Disputa* (fig. 1), the *Parnassus* (fig. 1 in cat. no. 57), and the *School of Athens*; beneath the personification of Jurisprudence is a less-unified composition that encompasses two narrative scenes (*Tribonian Hands the Pandects to the Emperor Justinian* and *Pope Gregory IX Hands the Decretals to Saint Raymond*), and which surrounds the embrasure of a large window, on top of which are seated the cardinal virtues of Fortitude, Prudence, and Temperance.

The first large fresco painted by Raphael in the Stanza della Segnatura was the *Disputa* of about 1509–10,[1] in which God the Father appears above the figure of Christ, whose hands are raised to display his wounds. Christ is accompanied by the Virgin and Saint John the Baptist, and flanked by six saints and six patriarchs seated on a semicircular cloud bank, no doubt inspired by Fra Bartolommeo's fresco of *The Last Judgment* (fig. 1 in cat. no. 48), now in the Museo di San Marco, Florence. In the center of the composition is the dove of the Holy Spirit, which descends toward a monstrance on an altar in the lower register. The rest of the bottom part of the fresco is occupied by groups of theologians in animated discussion about the Eucharist.

The present drawing, executed with the point of the brush in brown wash, heightened with white, is a study for the figure of Christ. Here, Raphael's main interest was the arrangement of the drapery; the rest of the figure is barely indicated. The pose of Christ in the finished work differs very little from that of the figure in the drawing, which presumably was executed at a fairly advanced stage in the design of the fresco.

Catherine Monbeig-Goguel has pointed out that the broad use of wash and white heightening to indicate the distribution of light on the folds of drapery might have been inspired by Leonardo da Vinci, whose drapery studies on linen Raphael could have seen sometime between 1504 and 1508, when he was in Florence.[2] Another possible source is the work of Fra Bartolommeo, whose influence Francis Ames-Lewis has detected in other drapery studies for the *Disputa*.[3]

On the verso of the present drawing is a quick pen sketch of two figures; they represent Abraham and Saint Paul, who are shown seated at the far right in the fresco.

WMG

1 See Dussler, 1971, pp. 71–73, pl. 123.
2 See Paris, 1983–84, p. 240, under no. 68.

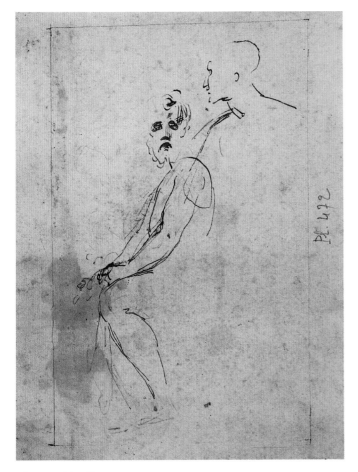

56: verso (detail)

3 See Ames-Lewis, 1986, pp. 96–98. According to Vasari, contact between Raphael and Fra Bartolommeo was mutually beneficial; Raphael taught Fra Bartolommeo perspective, but at the same time he emulated the older artist's use of color (Vasari-Milanesi, 1906, IV, pp. 183–84).

PROVENANCE

Jean-Baptiste-Joseph Wicar; Antonio Fedi; Jean-Baptiste-Joseph Wicar (Lugt 2568).

EXHIBITIONS

Lille, 1961, no. 14; Lille, 1983-2, no. 31; Paris, 1983–84, nos. 68 (recto), 69 (verso); Lille, 1989–90, no. 27; Cologne, 1990–91, no. 30.

LITERATURE

Oberhuber, 1983, nos. 308, ill. (verso), 314, ill. (recto); Monbeig-Goguel, in Paris, 1983–84, pp. 240–41, nos. 68, ill. (recto), 69, ill. (verso), with earlier bibliography; Ames-Lewis, 1986, p. 86, pl. XV, pp. 95–96; Monbeig-Goguel, 1987, I, p. 385, II, fig. 178 (recto); Brejon de Lavergnée, 1989-2, no. 27, ill. (recto and verso); Brejon de Lavergnée, in Cologne, 1990–91, no. 30, ill. (recto and verso).

RAPHAEL (RAFFAELLO SANTI)

Italian

Urbino 1483–1520 Rome

---

57 *Seated Male Nude Playing the* Lira da Braccio

Pen and brown ink, over traces of stylus underdrawing, 13 3/4 x 9 3/8 in. (34.9 x 23.8 cm.)

Inv. Pluchart 452

Verso: *Two Studies of Drapery on a Standing Male Figure*

Pen and brown ink, over traces of stylus underdrawing

Inv. Pluchart 453

This drawing of a nude youth playing the *lira da braccio* is a study for the figure of Apollo in Raphael's *Parnassus* in the Stanza della Segnatura (fig. 1; see also cat. no. 56). The fresco was begun about 1510, immediately after Raphael finished the *Disputa*, and bears the date 1511. Apollo is shown seated before a copse of laurel trees on Mount Parnassus accompanied by his companions, the Muses. The central group is flanked by various poets, including Sappho, Homer, Petrarch, Virgil, and Dante. The frescoed wall is interrupted by a large window, affording a view of the slope of the Vatican Hill, which, in Roman times, was held to be sacred to Apollo.

Except for the fact that in the fresco Apollo is represented partly draped and looking upward, the drawing corresponds quite closely to the finished work. A print by Marcantonio Raimondi (about 1480–before 1534) records an earlier project by Raphael for the *Parnassus*,[1] and indicates that Apollo originally was to hold a lyre, for which a *lira da braccio* was substituted in the fresco. The *lira da braccio* in the drawing is described with great precision: It is a five-stringed instrument, the fifth string to be plucked with the thumb. In the fresco, the *lira da braccio* has nine strings, symbolic of the nine Muses.

On the verso of the drawing is a study for the drapery of the blind poet, Homer, who stands to the left of Apollo in the *Parnassus*. The Musée des Beaux-Arts, Lille, also owns another study for the drapery of Homer on the verso of which is a preparatory drawing for the feet of the poets Horace and Ovid.[2]

A copy of the drawing on the recto of the present sheet is preserved in the Musée Bonnat, Bayonne.[3]

WMG

1 *The Illustrated Bartsch*, XXVI (1978), no. 247 (200), ill.

FIGURE 1. Raphael. *Parnassus*. 1511. Fresco. Stanza della Segnatura, Palazzo Vaticano, Vatican City

2 Inv. Pluchart 445 (recto), 446 (verso); Monbeig-Goguel, in Paris, 1983–84, nos. 80, ill. (recto), 81, ill. (verso).

3 Inv. no. 1385. See Bean, 1960, no. 139, ill.

PROVENANCE

Jean-Baptiste-Joseph Wicar; Antonio Fedi; Jean-Baptiste-Joseph Wicar (Lugt 2568).

EXHIBITIONS

Brussels, 1954–55, no. 127; Lille, 1961, no. 44; Berlin, 1964, no. 74; Paris, 1965–66, no. 242; Lille, 1983-2, no. 34; Paris, 1983–84, nos. 78 (recto), 79 (verso); Lille, 1989–90, no. 28.

LITERATURE

Oberhuber, 1983, nos. 365, ill. (recto), 368, ill. (verso); Monbeig-Goguel, in Paris, 1983–84, nos. 78, ill. (recto), 79, ill. (verso), with complete bibliography; Cordellier, 1985, p. 98, notes 33, 37; Ames-Lewis, 1986, pp. 46, 90, fig. 106 (verso), p. 91, fig. 108 (recto), pp. 92, 96; Brejon de Lavergnée, 1989-2, no. 28, ill.

57: verso

RAPHAEL (RAFFAELLO SANTI)

Italian

Urbino 1483–1520 Rome

---

58 *The Virgin and Child with the Infant Saint John the Baptist; Other Studies of the Virgin and Child; The Plan and Elevation of a Building*

Red chalk, partly gone over with pen and brown ink, 16 5/8 x 10 3/4 in. (42.2 x 27.3 cm.)

The group of the Virgin and Child with the infant Saint John the Baptist is drawn in red chalk and partly gone over in pen and brown ink; the studies of the Virgin and Child at the upper left and the lower right are in pen and brown ink; and the plan and the elevation of a building at the upper right are in red chalk.

Inv. Pluchart 456

Verso: *Seated Youth*

Red chalk

Inv. Pluchart 457

This magnificent sheet comprises a series of studies for Raphael's celebrated *Alba Madonna* (fig. 1), now in the National Gallery of Art, Washington, D.C.[1] The painting was probably executed in 1511 for the Florentine humanist Paolo Giovio (1483–1552), and was acquired by the Alba family of Spain in 1688. In style, the *Alba Madonna* demonstrates the importance Raphael continued to attach to works that he had seen in Florence between 1504 and 1508. The shape of the painting—a tondo—is typically Florentine, and the composition owes much to Leonardo da Vinci's *Virgin and Child with Saint Anne* (Paris, Musée du Louvre) and Michelangelo's *Taddei Tondo* (London, Royal Academy of Arts). The *Alba Madonna* is nevertheless more monumental than any of Raphael's earlier, comparatively intimate Virgin and Child compositions, and the complexity of the poses of the three figures parallels his work in the Stanza della Segnatura.

The principal study on the recto of the sheet corresponds quite closely to the painting. In the finished work the figures are somewhat smaller in relation to the circular frame, allowing for a more extensive landscape background, and the lamb—which, here, Saint John the Baptist presents to the Christ Child—has been abandoned.[2] Moreover, in the painting Christ's right arm is raised—a possibility Raphael had begun to explore in the course of making the present drawing.

At the lower right is a pen sketch of an infant in a complicated pose reminiscent of that of the Christ Child in the *Bridgewater Madonna*, which was executed prior to Raphael's departure from Florence and is now on loan from the duke of Sutherland to the National Gallery of Scotland, Edinburgh.[3] The sheet also contains two small pen sketches of the seated Virgin in profile, holding the Christ Child in her arms. Once again, Raphael has taken pains to establish the relationship between the figures and the framing lines that delimit the composition. These sketches anticipate two later paintings by Raphael, the *Madonna della Sedia* (Florence, Palazzo Pitti)[4] and the *Madonna della Tenda* (Munich, Alte Pinakothek),[5] both of which, however, date from about 1513–14.

The elevation and floor plan of a building in the upper right corner have been variously interpreted: Faul Joannides has suggested that these are studies for the building under construction in the background of the *Disputa*,[6] John Shearman believes they are more likely to be studies for an ephemeral structure,[7] whereas Stefano Ray hypothesizes that they could be related to a now-destroyed loggia overlooking the Tiber, which was erected about 1511 for one of Raphael's principal patrons, Agostino Chigi.[8]

FIGURE 1. Raphael. *The Alba Madonna.* About 1511. Oil on wood, transferred to canvas. National Gallery of Art, Washington, D.C. Andrew W. Mellon Collection

58: verso

The splendid drawing on the verso, sketched from a male model, is a study for the figure of the Virgin in the *Alba Madonna*. Like the principal study on the recto, it is executed in red chalk, the medium that Raphael evidently preferred during the last decade of his life.

WMG

1 Inv. no. 24. See Pope-Hennessy, 1970, pp. 205–6, fig. 192; Dussler, 1971, pp. 35–36, pl. 72; Shapley, 1979, I, pp. 386–89, II, pl. 277; Brown, 1983-2, pp. 168–77, pl. 15, fig. 108.

2 Another study for the figure of the infant Saint John, closer to the finished work than is the present sheet, is in the Museum Boymans-van Beuningen, Rotterdam (Inv. no. I.110; Joannides, 1983, p. 203, no. 279, ill.; Oberhuber, 1983, no. 387, ill.).

3 See Pope-Hennessy, 1970, pp. 189–90, fig. 174; Dussler, 1971, p. 23, pl. 60.

4 Inv. no. 151. See Pope-Hennessy, 1970, pp. 216–17, frontispiece ill.; Dussler, 1971, p. 36, pl. 84.

5 Inv. no. H.G. 797. See Pope-Hennessy, 1970, pp. 215–16, fig. 200; Dussler, 1971, p. 39, pl. 87.

6 See Joannides, 1983, p. 202, under no. 278 *r*.

7 See Shearman, in Rome, 1984, p. 116, under no. 2.1.7.

8 See Ray, in Rome, 1984, p. 119.

PROVENANCE

Jean-Baptiste-Joseph Wicar; Antonio Fedi; Jean-Baptiste-Joseph Wicar (Lugt 2568).

EXHIBITIONS

Brussels, 1954–55, no. 124; Lille, 1961, no. 33; Berlin, 1964, no. 75; Paris, 1965–66, no. 240; Amsterdam–Brussels–Lille, 1967–68, no. 87; Florence, 1970, no. 84; Lille, 1983-2, no. 278; Paris, 1983–84, nos. 103 (recto), 104 (verso); Lille, 1989–90, no. 30; Cologne, 1990–91, no. 33.

LITERATURE

Oberhuber, 1983, nos. 384, ill. (recto), 385, ill. (verso); Monbeig-Goguel, in Paris, 1983–84, p. 39, ill., nos. 103, ill. (recto), 104, ill. (verso), with complete bibliography; Incerpi, in Florence, 1984, p. 154, fig. 61 (recto), p. 157, under no. 13; Ray, in Rome, 1984, p. 119, ill. (detail of recto); Shearman, in Rome, 1984, pp. 116–17, no. 2.1.7, ill. (recto); Ames-Lewis, 1986, pp. 11, 24, figs. 19 (recto), 20 (verso); Brejon de Lavergnée, 1989-2, no. 30, ill. (recto and verso); Brejon de Lavergnée, in Cologne, 1990–91, no. 33, ill. (recto and verso).

RAPHAEL (RAFFAELLO SANTI)

Italian

Urbino 1483–1520 Rome

59 *Standing Youth*

Pen and brown ink, over stylus underdrawing, 15 3/4 x 10 3/16 in. (40 x 25.9 cm.)

Inv. Pluchart 439

In Rome, Raphael decorated two chapels for the powerful banker Agostino Chigi—one in the church of Santa Maria del Popolo[1] and the other in Santa Maria della Pace.[2] Neither project was completed according to Raphael's designs. For the Chigi Chapel in Santa Maria della Pace, Raphael planned an altarpiece, the *Resurrection*, which was never painted, although several preparatory drawings survive.[3] The altarpiece was to be flanked by two bronze roundels, *The Incredulity of Saint Thomas* and *Christ in Limbo* (fig. 1), and the surface of the surrounding wall was to be decorated with frescoes of prophets and sibyls. The frescoes were painted and the two roundels cast, but the latter were never installed in the chapel. Executed probably by the sculptor Lorenzetto (Lorenzo di Ludovico di Guglielmo Lotti; 1490–1541), and based on drawings by Raphael, the roundels are now at the Abbey of Chiaravalle.[4]

The present sheet, drawn with a stylus and partly reinforced in pen and ink, is a study from life for the figure of Christ in the *Christ in Limbo*, the roundel that was to be placed to the right of the *Resurrection*. The pose of the figure in the drawing and in the sculpture is similar, but in the latter Christ is bearded and enveloped in fluttering drapery. A composition study by Raphael for the same roundel is in the Galleria degli Uffizi, Florence.[5]

The chronology of Raphael's work in Santa Maria della Pace is problematic. Michael Hirst, who reconstructed the original scheme of the decoration, argued that the frescoes might have been painted in 1513–14.[6] The style of the drawing in Lille, however, suggests a somewhat earlier date, perhaps 1511–12. Such a date would be compatible with Vasari's account, according to which the decoration of the chapel was executed at approximately the same time as Raphael's *Galatea*—about 1511–12—in Agostino Chigi's villa (the Farnesina) on the other side of the Tiber.[7]

WMG

1 See Shearman, 1961, pp. 129–60; Dussler, 1971, pp. 95–96, plates 155–156.

59

2 See Hirst, 1961, pp. 161–85; Dussler, 1971, pp. 93–95, plates 153–154.

3 See Joannides, 1983, pp. 208–10, nos. 304–311, ill.

4 See Hirst, 1961, pp. 175–78, plates 31 c (*Christ in Limbo*), 32 c (*The Incredulity of Saint Thomas*).

5 Gabinetto Disegni e Stampe, Inv. no. 1475 E. See Hirst, 1961, pp. 175–76, pl. 31 b; Joannides, 1983, p. 212, no. 315 *r*, ill. (see also p. 211, nos. 312, ill., 313, ill., both of which are studies for the *Incredulity of Saint Thomas*).

6 See Hirst, 1961, p. 165.

7 Vasari–Milanesi, 1906, IV, p. 340: ". . . Agostino Chisi [*sic*], sanese, . . . fece non molto dopo allogazione d'una cappella; e ciò per avergli poco innanzi Raffaello dipinto in una loggia del suo palazzo, oggi detto i Chisj [*sic*] in Trastevere, con dolcissima maniera, una Galatea. . . ."

PROVENANCE

Jean-Baptiste-Joseph Wicar (Lugt 2568).

EXHIBITIONS

Amsterdam–Brussels–Lille, 1967–68, no. 91; Florence, 1970, no. 88; Lille, 1983-2, no. 37; Paris, 1983–84, no. 105; Lille, 1989–90, no. 31; Cologne, 1990–91, no. 34.

LITERATURE

Oberhuber, 1983, no. 402, ill.; Monbeig-Goguel, in Paris, 1983–84, no. 105, ill., with complete bibliography; Ferino-Pagden, in Florence, 1984, p. 313, under no. 18, fig. 52; Monbeig-Goguel, 1987, I, p. 384, II, figs. 176, 177; Brejon de Lavergnée, 1989-2, no. 31, ill.; Brejon de Lavergnée, in Cologne, 1990–91, no. 34, ill.

FIGURE 1. Lorenzetto (Lorenzo di Ludovico di Guglielmo Lotti), after a design by Raphael. *Christ in Limbo*. Bronze relief. Abbey of Chiaravalle

PONTORMO (JACOPO CARRUCCI)

Italian

Pontorme 1494–1556 Florence

---

60 *Three Studies of a Male Nude*

Red chalk, 15 5/8 x 10 7/16 in. (39.8 x 26.5 cm.)

Inv. Pluchart 162

Verso: *Seated Draped Figure Turned to the Right*; *Study of Drapery*

Black chalk

Inv. Pluchart 163

This remarkable sheet was attributed to Bartolommeo Ammanati (1511–1592) by Louis Gonse but correctly identified as the work of Pontormo in Pluchart's 1889 catalogue of drawings in Lille. Janet Cox-Rearick was the first to notice that the drawing is a study for the *Pharaoh with His Butler and Baker* (fig. 1)—one of four panels executed by Pontormo as part of the decoration of the bedchamber of Pierfrancesco Borgherini; all four panels are now in the National Gallery, London.[1]

The decoration of the room, commissioned about 1515 to celebrate the marriage of Borgherini to Maria Acciaioli, comprised a series of paintings of scenes from the life of Joseph, which were set into the walls of the room, the bed, and the fronts of cassoni.[2] Other paintings from this ensemble—by Andrea del Sarto (1486–1530), Francesco Granacci (1469–1543), and Francesco Ubertini, called Bacchiacca (1494–1557)—are in the Galleria degli Uffizi and the Palazzo Pitti, Florence; the National Gallery, London; and the Galleria Borghese, Rome.[3]

The story of Pharaoh's chief butler and chief baker is told in Genesis 40: 1–23. The two servants had been imprisoned for having offended their master. Joseph, who had already been jailed on the spurious charge of attempting to violate Potiphar's wife, offered to interpret their dreams. Three days after Joseph had explained to them the meaning of their dreams, his prophecies came true, and the butler was restored to his post and the baker hanged from a tree. In the upper part of Pontormo's painting, which is dated by Cox-Rearick to 1517, the butler leaves the prison by a flight of stairs, escorted by guards, while below, he gives Pharaoh his cup, and the baker is led away to be hanged.

The present drawing contains three studies for the prison guard at the top of the stairs in the painting. None of

FIGURE 1. Pontormo (Jacopo Carrucci). *Pharaoh with His Butler and Baker*. Oil on wood. National Gallery, London

the figures on the sheet corresponds exactly in pose to the draped figure in the finished work, but the one on the far left is closely related to a drawing in the Uffizi, which Cox-Rearick calls "the final nude study for the figure."[4] Although the lower part of the figure in the drawing in Florence is similar to that of the figure at the left in the present sheet, in the former study the head and torso are more or less in profile, as in the painting, instead of turned away.

The Lille drawing is a superb example of Pontormo's virtuoso handling of red chalk, his preferred medium. In technique the sheet owes much to drawings by Pontormo's teacher, Andrea del Sarto, whereas the energetic nude figures reflect the influence of Michelangelo's lost cartoon for *The Battle of Cascina*.

On the verso of the sheet is a black-chalk study of a heavily draped figure holding a book. Cox-Rearick identified this study as an early preparatory drawing for the figure of Saint John the Evangelist in Pontormo's *Virgin and Child with Saints Joseph, John the Evangelist, Francis, James, and John the Baptist*, dated 1518, in the church of San Michele Visdomini, Florence.[5] In the painting, however, Saint John is posed very

differently: The position of the legs and the arrangement of the folds of the drapery in the drawing were utilized for the figure of Saint Joseph holding the Christ Child.

Old copies of the recto of the Lille drawing are in the Gabinetto Disegni e Stampe of the Uffizi and in a Japanese private collection.[6] Also in Lille is a black-chalk sketch of the figure kneeling at the foot of the staircase in the painting.[7]

WMG

1 The following panels were executed by Pontormo: *Joseph Sold to Potiphar, Pharaoh with His Butler and Baker, Joseph's Brothers Beg for Help*, and *Jacob with Joseph in Egypt*. See Forster, 1966, pp. 130–32, nos. 8, 9, 7, 10, respectively, and figs. 12, 8, 9, 15, respectively; Berti, 1973, nos. 41, 42, 40, 43, ill., respectively; Braham, 1979, pp. 754–65, figs. 15, 16, 8, 6, respectively.

2 For a hypothetical reconstruction of the decoration of the bedchamber of Pierfrancesco Borgherini, see Braham, 1979, pp. 754–65, fig. 2.

60: verso

3 Andrea del Sarto: *Scenes from the Early Life of Joseph; Pharaoh Consults Joseph about His Dreams* (both Florence, Palazzo Pitti); see Braham, 1979, figs. 3, 5. Bacchiacca: *Joseph Receives His Brothers on Their Second Visit to Egypt, Joseph Pardons His Brothers* (both London, National Gallery), *Joseph Orders the Imprisonment of His Brothers, Simeon Taken to Prison, The Search for the Silver Cup, The Finding of the Cup* (all Rome, Galleria Borghese); see Braham, 1979, figs. 9–14. Granacci: *Joseph Taken to Prison, Joseph Introduces His Father to Pharaoh* (both Florence, Uffizi); see Braham, 1979, figs. 4, 7.

4 Gabinetto Disegni e Stampe, Inv. no. 6690 F recto. See Cox-Rearick, 1981, I, no. 26, II, fig. 35.

5 See Forster, 1966, p. 133, no. 13, fig. 14; Berti, 1973, pl. XVII, no. 53, ill.

6 Gabinetto Disegni e Stampe, Inv. no. 442 F. See Clapp, 1916, fig. 44 (as Pontormo). For the drawing in a Japanese private collection, see Yamanaka, 1981, no. 7, ill.

7 Pluchart 2175. See Cordellier, 1986, no. 84, ill.; Westfehling, in Cologne, 1990–91, no. 43, ill.

PROVENANCE

Jean-Baptiste-Joseph Wicar (Lugt 2568).

EXHIBITIONS

Berlin, 1964, no. 69; Paris, 1965–66, no. 222; Amsterdam–Brussels–Lille, 1967–68, no. 76; Florence, 1970, no. 73; Paris, 1986–87, no. 83; Lille, 1989–90, no. 36; Cologne, 1990–91, no. 42.

LITERATURE

Benvignat, 1856, nos. 1429 (recto), 1430 (verso); Gonse, 1877, p. 555; Delacre, 1931, p. 139; Berenson, 1938, II, no. 2252 b; Bacou, 1957, pp. 27, ill. (recto), 62; Grassi, 1958, p. 243, pl. 208 (recto); Berenson, 1961, II, no. 2252 b; Viatte, 1963, no. 89; Cox-Rearick, 1964, I, p. 28 (recto), nos. 25 (recto), 45 (verso), II, figs. 34 (recto), 51 (verso); Berti, 1965, p. 8, no. V, pl. V (recto); Châtelet, 1967, no. 76, pl. 28 (recto); Châtelet, 1970-2, no. 73, figs. 59 (recto), 60 (verso); Berti, 1973, no. 42[1], ill. (recto); Cox-Rearick, 1981, I, p. 28 (recto), nos. 25 (recto), 45 (verso), II, figs. 34 (recto), 51 (verso); Yamanaka, 1981, p. 122, fig. 5, p. 170; Oursel, 1984, p. 86, pl. V; Cordellier, 1986, no. 83, ill. (recto); Brejon de Lavergnée, 1989-2, no. 36, ill. (recto and verso); Brejon de Lavergnée, in Cologne, 1990–91, no. 42, ill. (recto and verso).

PONTORMO (JACOPO CARRUCCI)

Italian

Pontorme 1494–1556 Florence

---

61   *Saint Michael*

    Black chalk, 15 1/8 x 6 3/16 in. (38.4 x 15.7 cm.)

    Inv. Pluchart 568

    Verso: *Two Studies of a Seated Male Nude*

    Red chalk

    Inv. Pluchart 569

61

Formerly classified as the work of Timoteo Viti (1469–1523), this lively drawing was attributed to Pontormo by A. E. Popham.[1] The sheet is a study for the figure of Saint Michael in a painting of Saints John the Evangelist and Michael the Archangel that originally framed a niche in the chapel dedicated to the Virgin in the church of San Michele in the artist's hometown of Pontorme.[2] The picture, datable to about 1519, is now in the Museo della Collegiata in nearby Empoli.

In both the painting and the preparatory drawing in Lille, Saint Michael holds a balance in his left hand. With his right foot he subdues the devil, here represented by an impish putto rather than by the usual dragon. The dense chiaroscuro of the drawing is replaced in the painting by light colors, crisp contours, and a pristine surface that anticipate later works by the artist.

A study for the figure of Saint John the Evangelist, in every respect similar to the present sheet, is in the Gabinetto Disegni e Stampe of the Uffizi.[3] To the right of the figure of the Evangelist in the Uffizi drawing are two studies for the right hand of Saint Michael. Also in the Uffizi is a meticulous study in red chalk for the legs of the archangel.[4]

Janet Cox-Rearick associates the red-chalk studies of a seated youth on the verso of the present drawing with the putto at the feet of Saint Michael. However, Barbara Brejon de Lavergnée points out that the figure in the drawing is much older than the one in the painting, and their poses are not all that similar. She suggests that the drawing might instead be connected with Pontormo's frescoes in the Medici villa at Poggio a Caiano, another project undertaken by the artist in 1519.[5]

WMG

1 See Pouncey, 1964, p. 290.

2 See Forster, 1966, pp. 135–36, no. 18, figs. 22 (*Saint John the Evangelist*), 24 (*Saint Michael*); Berti, 1973, plates XXI A (*Saint John the Evangelist*), XXI B–XXII (*Saint Michael*), nos. 61 (*Saint John the Evangelist*), 62 (*Saint Michael*), ill.

3 Gabinetto Disegni e Stampe, Inv. no. 6571 F recto. See Forlani Tempesti, 1970, no. 6, ill.; Cox-Rearick, 1981, I, no. 98, II, fig. 101.

4 Gabinetto Disegni e Stampe, Inv. no. 6506 F recto. See Forlani Tempesti, 1970, no. 7, ill.; Cox-Rearick, 1981, I, no. 101, II, fig. 100.

5 See Forster, 1966, pl. III, p. 136, no. 19, fig. 29; Berti, 1973, plates XXIX–XXXI, no. 67, ill.

PROVENANCE

Jean-Baptiste-Joseph Wicar (Lugt 2568).

EXHIBITIONS

Amsterdam–Brussels–Lille, 1967–68, no. 77; Florence, 1970, no. 74; Lille, 1989–90, no. 37; Cologne, 1990–91, no. 44.

LITERATURE

Benvignat, 1856, nos. 1427 (recto), 1428 (verso); Pluchart, 1889, nos. 568, 569 (as Timoteo Viti); Bacou, 1957, p. 62; Viatte, 1963, no. 88; Cox-Rearick, 1964, I, p. 34 (recto), nos. 99 (verso), 100 (recto), II, figs. 102 (recto), 103 (verso); Pouncey, 1964, p. 290, pl. 39; Forster, 1966, p. 136, under no. 18; Châtelet, 1967, no. 77; Châtelet, 1970-2, no. 74, figs. 61 (recto), 63 (verso); Forlani Tempesti, 1970, under no. 7; Berti, 1973, no. 62[1], ill.; Oursel, 1984, p. 86; Brejon de Lavergnée, 1989-2, no. 37, ill. (recto and verso); Brejon de Lavergnée, in Cologne, 1990–91, no. 44, ill. (recto and verso).

61: verso

GIULIO ROMANO (GIULIO PIPPI)

Italian

Rome 1499–1546 Mantua

---

62 *Christ with Arms Extended, in a Glory of Angels*

Pen and brown ink, over traces of black chalk,
13 3/8 x 9 1/4 in. (34 x 23.5 cm.)

Inv. Pluchart 462

Verso: *Study of Drapery*

Black chalk

Raphael's heir and the most distinguished of his many pupils, Giulio Romano participated in the decoration of the Stanza d'Eliodoro and the Stanza dell'Incendio in the Palazzo Vaticano and played a major part in the execution of the frescoes in the Loggia di Psiche at the Villa Farnesina in Rome. After Raphael's death in 1520, Giulio and his colleague Gianfrancesco Penni (1488 ?–1528 ?) were charged with the decoration of the largest of the Vatican Stanze, the Sala di Costantino. In 1524 Giulio accompanied Baldassare Castiglione to Mantua, where he entered the service of Federigo II Gonzaga (1500–1540), and a short time later Giulio undertook the design, construction, and frescoed decoration of the Palazzo del Tè; the project, his masterpiece, was finished about 1535. Giulio remained in Mantua, closely allied to the Gonzaga family, until his death in 1546.

The present study for a Resurrection or an Ascension was attributed to Raphael in Pluchart's catalogue of 1889 but recognized by Michael Hirst and later by Konrad Oberhuber as the work of Giulio Romano. The sheet is related to a drawing of the same subject in the Musée Bonnat, Bayonne, which Hirst has identified as a study by Raphael for a painting intended for the altar of the Chigi Chapel in Santa Maria della Pace, Rome, but never executed.[1] As Sylvia Ferino-Pagden has pointed out, the drawing by Giulio is more iconic than the sketch by Raphael; the relatively static figure of Christ is seen frontally, and the angels flanking him are arranged symmetrically in a circle.[2]

Fischel identified the coat of arms shown in the lower half of the drawing as that of the prince of Wales. The drawing may therefore date from about 1521—the year in which Pope Leo X awarded Henry VIII the title of "Defender of the Faith." Another study for a Resurrection, also by Giulio Romano and perhaps executed at about the same time, is in the Musée du Louvre, Paris.[3]   WMG

62: verso

1 Inv. no. 683. See Bean, 1960, no. 132, ill.; Hirst, 1961, pp. 171–73, pl. 30 a; Joannides, 1983, p. 208, no. 304, ill.

2 See Ferino-Pagden, in Mantua, 1989, p. 253.

3 Inv. no. 3468.

EXHIBITIONS

Lille, 1961, no. 61 (as Circle of Raphael); Mantua, 1989; Cologne, 1990–91, no. 47.

LITERATURE

Benvignat, 1856, no. 687; Ruland, 1876, p. 46, no. 3; Pluchart, 1889, no. 462 (as Raphael); Fischel, 1898, no. 395 (as Circle of Raphael); Fischel, 1913–45, VIII, under no. 387 (as Penni ?); Hirst, 1961, p. 173 n. 71 (as Giulio Romano ?); Oberhuber, 1972, pp. 34–35, fig. 27; Paris, 1983–84, p. 322; Brejon de Lavergnée, 1989-2, p. 86; Ferino-Pagden, in Mantua, 1989, p. 253, ill.; Westfehling, in Cologne, 1990–91, no. 47, ill.

ATTRIBUTED TO GIULIO ROMANO
(GIULIO PIPPI)

Italian

Rome 1499–1546 Mantua

---

63 *Seated Nude Youth*

Red chalk, over stylus underdrawing, 16 x 10 3/8 in.
(40.5 x 26.3 cm.)

The drawing is lined.

Inv. Pluchart 481

This is a study for the figure of Emperor Lothair I (r. 840–
55), painted in bronze monochrome, in the Stanza dell'Incendio in the Palazzo Vaticano (see fig. 1).[1] The decoration of
the room, consisting of scenes from the lives of Popes Leo III
and Leo IV, was designed and executed by Raphael and his
assistants for Pope Leo X from 1514 to 1517. Lothair I appears on the dado beneath the fresco representing the victory
of Leo IV over the Saracens at Ostia, the port of Rome. The
subject provided a historical precedent for the political aims
of Leo X, who wished to organize a crusade against the
Turks. Since Lothair I was one of the most powerful allies of
Leo IV, he is appropriately included among the secular
princes frescoed on the lower part of the wall. The pose of the
figure in the drawing corresponds closely to that of the
emperor in the fresco, except that in the latter he is represented bearded and in armor, and holds the staff of a banner
with the arms of Leo X in his right hand.

Most of the frescoes in the Stanza dell'Incendio were
executed by Raphael's assistants, and the role of the master in
designing these works is still problematic. A number of
garzone studies for figures in *The Battle of Ostia* may be attributed to Raphael, although Giulio Romano appears to have
been entrusted with both the cartoon and the execution of
the fresco. This sheet is generally ascribed to Giulio, who,
according to Vasari, was largely responsible for the monochrome figures on the dado.[2] Fischel was the first to suggest
that the Lille drawing is the work of Giulio—an opinion with
which the present writer concurs. Yet, because this drawing
is very close in style to figure studies by Raphael, its authorship remains uncertain, and the possibility that it might,
indeed, be by him cannot be entirely excluded.[3]

An old copy of this drawing is preserved in the Kupferstichkabinett, Staatliche Museen Preussischer Kulturbesitz, Berlin.[4]

WMG

FIGURE 1. Giulio Romano (Giulio Pippi). *Emperor Lothair I* (detail).
Fresco. Stanza dell'Incendio, Palazzo Vaticano, Vatican City

1 For the decoration of the Stanza dell'Incendio see Dussler, 1971, pp.
82–86, plates 139–142. For the contribution of Giulio Romano see
Hartt, 1958, I, pp. 13–15, 21–24, II, figs. 10–22.

2 See Vasari-Milanesi, 1906, V, p. 524: "Aiutò anco a Raffaello
colorire molte cose nella camera di Torre Borgia, dov'è l'incendio
di Borgo, e particolarmente l'imbasamento fatto di colore di
bronzo; la contessa Matilda, il re Pipino, Carlo Magno, Gottifredi
Buglioni re di Ierusalem, con altri benefattori della Chiesa, che sono
tutte bonissime figure."

3 See Monbeig-Goguel, in Paris, 1983–84, pp. 270–71, under no. 91.

4 Inv. no. KdZ 21555. Cited by Monbeig-Goguel, in Paris, 1983–84,
p. 271, under no. 91.

PROVENANCE

Antonio Fedi; Jean-Baptiste-Joseph Wicar (Lugt 2568).

EXHIBITIONS

Lille, 1961, no. 59; Amsterdam–Brussels–Lille, 1967–68, no. 36; Florence, 1970, no. 39; Lille, 1983-2, no. 36; Paris, 1983–84, no. 91 (as
Circle of Raphael).

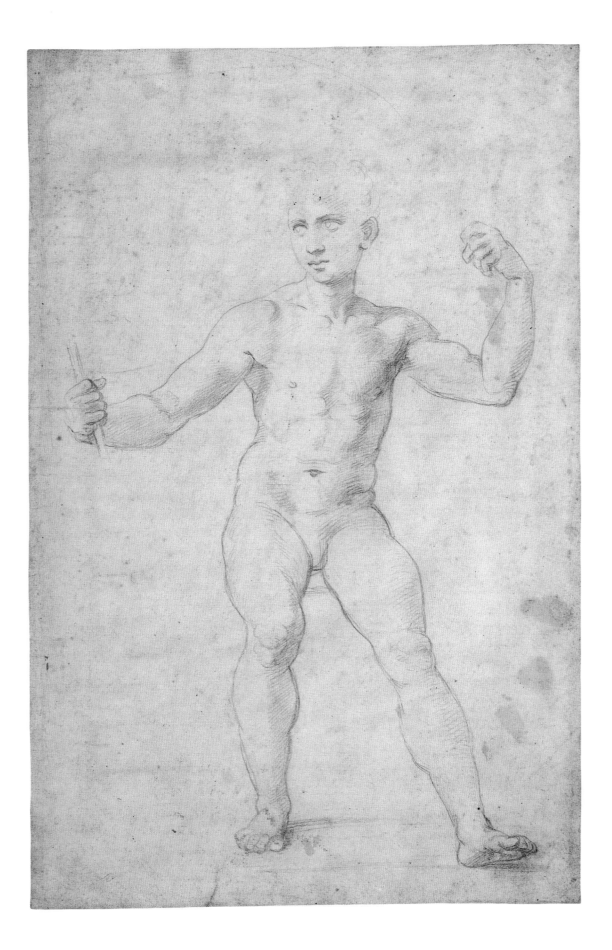

LITERATURE

Benvignat, 1856, no. 734; Pluchart, 1889, no. 481 (as Raphael); Morelli, 1891–92, col. 441, no. 99 (as not by Raphael); Fischel, 1898, p. xxx, no. 204 (as Giulio Romano); Gonse, 1904, p. 222; Hartt, 1958, I, pp. 24, 287, no. 10, II, fig. 22 (as Giulio Romano); Châtelet, 1967, no. 36, pl. 29; Châtelet, 1970-2, no. 39, fig. 32; Dussler, 1971, p. 86 (as Giulio Romano); Oberhuber, 1972, p. 121, no. 437, pl. 40 (as Giulio Romano); Joannides, 1983, p. 229, no. 379, ill. (as Giulio Romano); Monbeig-Goguel, in Paris, 1983–84, no. 91, ill. (as Circle of Raphael), with complete bibliography.

LELIO ORSI

Italian

Novellara 1511–1587 Novellara

---

64 *Design for a Frieze with Adam and Eve*

Pen and brown ink, and brown wash, heightened with white, over traces of black chalk, on light brown paper, squared in black chalk, 4 3/8 x 15 5/8 in. (11.1 x 39.8 cm.)

The drawing is lined.

Inv. Pluchart 342

64

Lelio Orsi was a native of the small town of Novellara, near Reggio Emilia. Little is known about his training as an artist, but it is clear that he was much influenced by the work of Pellegrino Tibaldi and especially by that of Correggio, whose light effects and fervent expression Orsi emulated throughout his career. From 1554 to 1555 Orsi was in Rome, where he was inspired by the art of Michelangelo, and his later paintings and drawings betray a profound debt to both North and Central Italian sources.

At one time ascribed to Giovanni da Udine, the present sheet was attributed to Orsi by Giovanni Battista Toschi, who associated it with two studies of comparable format in the Galleria degli Uffizi.[1] In 1563 Orsi was commissioned to design the façades of a number of houses in Novellara, and although none of his façade paintings survive, the composition of the Lille drawing suggests that it is a study for a lost decoration of this type. Within an acanthus scroll enlivened by a ram, a horse, and a goat, Adam and Eve accept the forbidden fruit of the tree of knowledge, which is proffered to them by a serpent with the head of a woman. Another drawing in Lille—almost identical in size and technique—represents a similar frieze inhabited by the figures of Apollo and Diana (see fig. 1).[2] The juxtaposition of Old Testament and mythological subjects in these two drawings reflects a tendency in sixteenth-century thought to emphasize the continuity of Christianity and pagan culture.[3]

According to Nora Clerici Bagozzi, both studies in Lille may date from about 1552–54, just prior to Orsi's sojourn in Rome.[4]

WMG

1 Gabinetto Disegni e Stampe, Inv. nos. 1620 E, 1640 E. See Clerici Bagozzi, in Reggio Emilia, 1987–88, nos. 28, 7, respectively, ill.

2 Pluchart 341. See Clerici Bagozzi, in Reggio Emilia, 1987–88, no. 62, ill.; Brejon de Lavergnée, 1989-2, no. 42, ill.

3 For a discussion of this current in Renaissance art and thought see Davidson, 1985, pp. 39 ff.

4 See Clerici Bagozzi, in Reggio Emilia, 1987–88, p. 91, under no. 62.

PROVENANCE

Paul Delaroche (?); Martial Pelletier (?); Louis-Léopold Boilly.

EXHIBITIONS

Reggio Emilia, 1987–88, no. 61; Lille, 1989–90, no. 41.

LITERATURE

Pluchart, 1889, no. 342 (as Giovanni da Udine); Toschi, 1900, pp. 17–18; Venturi, IX, 6 (1933), p. 633; Salvini and Chiodi, 1950, pp. XIV, 88, no. 2; Salvini, 1951, p. 82; Gregori, 1953, p. 55; Villani, 1953–54, pp. 71, XII, no. 43; Hoffman, 1975, pp. 106, 195, no. 47 B, fig. 76; Verzelloni, 1977–78, pp. 147–67, 211, 212, no. 7; Romani, 1982, pp. 48, 49, 59 n. 70, fig. 21; Romani, 1984, p. 35 n. 43; Clerici Bagozzi, in Reggio Emilia, 1987–88, no. 61, ill.; Brejon de Lavergnée, 1989-2, no. 41, ill.

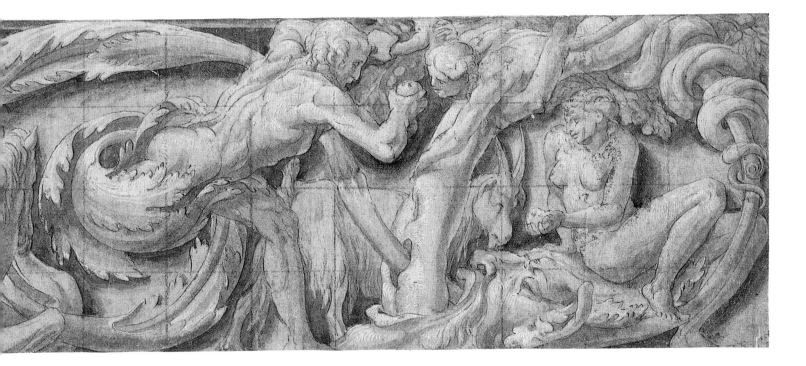

FIGURE 1. Lelio Orsi. *Design for a Frieze with Apollo and Diana*. Drawing. Musée des Beaux-Arts, Lille

GIORGIO VASARI

Italian

Arezzo 1511–1574 Florence

---

65   *The Death of Saint Sigismund*

Pen and brown ink and brown wash, over black chalk,
11 1/4 x 7 15/16 in. (28.6 x 20.2 cm.)

The drawing is pasted onto a mount decorated by
Vasari with framing motifs in pen and brown ink,
16 5/8 x 11 5/8 in. (42.1 x 29.6 cm.).

Inscribed in pen and brown ink (beneath the two figures
flanking the central scene): ABCD/EF; GHIK/Z [?] O

Inv. Pluchart 549

A painter, architect, art historian, and collector, Giorgio
Vasari began his career as a pupil of the French glass painter
Guillaume Marcillat (1475–1529/37). In 1524 he moved
from his hometown of Arezzo to Florence, where he assisted
Andrea del Sarto and received further instruction from Baccio Bandinelli (1493–1560) and Rosso Fiorentino (1495–
1540). In 1532 he visited Rome. There he studied works by
Michelangelo, Raphael, and Raphael's followers Perino del
Vaga (1501–1547) and Polidoro da Caravaggio (1490/1500–
1543 ?). Vasari undertook the decoration of his own house,
the Casa Vasari in Arezzo, in 1542, and four years later he
began work in the Gran Salone of the Palazzo della Can-
celleria in Rome. Between 1555 and 1572 he and a team of
talented assistants decorated several rooms in the Palazzo
della Signoria in Florence. Toward the end of his life he
painted part of *The Last Judgment* in the cupola of the Duomo
in Florence, a project that was completed after Vasari's death
by Federico Zuccaro (1540/41–1609). Vasari is known today
primarily for his biographies of artists, *Le vite de' più eccelenti
pittori, scultori ed architettori*, first published in 1550 and revised
and expanded in 1568.

The Lille sheet is a study for the *Death of Saint Sigismund*,
an altarpiece formerly in the Martelli Chapel of the church
of San Lorenzo in Florence.[1] The picture, commissioned
from Vasari by Pandolfo di Piero Martelli on October 14,
1549, was finished during the summer of the following year; it
was destroyed during the eighteenth century, and the present
drawing is the only surviving record of its appearance.

Saint Sigismund was the son of Gundobad, King of
Burgundy. After his succession to the throne, Sigismund was
captured by the sons and heirs of Clovis I, King of France,
and, with the rest of his family, was put to death by being

thrown into a well. The drawing shows Sigismund's wife and
two sons about to be murdered, while three soldiers attack
the prostrate figure of the saint in the foreground. The setting
in the drawing mimics the architecture of the church of San
Lorenzo, with the altar wall surrounding the painting shown
decorated with feigned statues of allegorical figures.

The sheet once formed part of the artist's personal
collection. Vasari was the first systematic collector of drawings, and his *Libro de' disegni* was intended to illustrate the
entire history of Italian art. The drawings Vasari owned
were mounted in large albums, each page of which he decorated with an elaborate pen-and-wash border. The decoration of surviving pages from the *Libro de' disegni* is often
architectural in character, but in this case the surround
imitates a sixteenth-century picture frame. The museum in
Lille possesses another drawing by Vasari, similarly mounted
on a page from the *Libro de' disegni*.[2]

WMG

1 See Barocchi, 1964-3, p. 132, under no. 38.

2 Pluchart 547. See Brejon de Lavergnée, 1989, no. 43, ill.; Brejon de
   Lavergnée, in Cologne, 1990–91, no. 51, ill. The drawing is a study
   for the *Abraham Entertaining the Three Angels*, formerly in the refectory
   of the monastery of San Michele in Bosco, Bologna. A third drawing
   by Vasari from the *Libro de' disegni* is currently on the art market in
   London; see Kliemann, in Arezzo, 1981, no. 37 f (then in a private
   collection in Calenzano).

PROVENANCE

Giorgio Vasari (Lugt 2480, 2858); Jean-Baptiste-Joseph Wicar (Lugt
2568).

EXHIBITIONS

Amsterdam–Brussels–Lille, 1967–68, no. 111; Florence, 1970, no. 112.

LITERATURE

Gonse, 1877, p. 555; Pluchart, 1889, no. 549; Morelli, 1891–92, col. 343;
Kurz, 1937–38, p. 43; Bacou, 1957, p. 28, ill.; Barocchi, 1964-2, p. 296;
Barocchi, 1964-3, pp. 35, 103–4, 131, under no. 37ª, p. 132, no. 38, ill.;
Châtelet, 1967, no. 111, pl. 31; Châtelet, 1970-2, no. 112, fig. 94; Ragghianti Collobi, 1974, I, p. 165, II, fig. 502; Brejon de Lavergnée, 1989-2,
p. 93, under no. 43; Brejon de Lavergnée, in Cologne, 1990–91, p. 152,
under no. 51.

GIOVANNI BATTISTA NALDINI

Italian

Florence 1537–1591 Florence

---

66   *Four Figures*: *Study for a Pietà*

Black chalk, 7 7/8 x 11 1/16 in. (20 x 28.1 cm.)

There are scattered stains. The drawing is lined.

Inv. Pluchart 659

Philip Pouncey was the first to recognize this drawing as a characteristic work by the Florentine Mannerist painter Giovanni Battista Naldini. Naldini was a pupil of Jacopo Carrucci, called Pontormo, and later was an assistant to Giorgio Vasari, with whom he participated in the decoration of the Palazzo Vecchio in Florence. About 1570, Naldini supplied two small paintings for the Studiolo of Francesco I de' Medici in the Palazzo Vecchio, and during the following two decades he produced a number of altarpieces for the Florentine churches of Santa Maria Novella and Santa Croce. His numerous drawings reflect not only the influence of Pontormo, his master, but also that of Pontormo's teacher, Andrea del Sarto (1486–1530).

This drawing of four youths posed in contemporary dress is evidently a study for a Pietà, or Lamentation—the theme of several paintings and a great many drawings by Naldini.[1] In composition, the sheet corresponds most closely to a fresco of the Pietà that Naldini executed for the tomb of Michelangelo in the church of Santa Croce: There, the figure on the right is Saint John the Evangelist; the one in the center, holding the hand of Christ, is the Virgin; and the one on the left is Saint Mary Magdalene.

Less than a month after the death of Michelangelo on February 18, 1564, plans were made to erect a splendid sepulcher in his native city.[2] The project was a collaborative effort, financed by the artist's nephew, Leonardo Buonarroti; planned by Vincenzo Borghini; designed by Vasari; and executed by a team of young sculptors that included Battista Lorenzi (1527/28–1594), Valerio Cioli (1529–1599), and Giovanni Bandini (1540–1599). The monument as it stands today consists of three allegorical figures (Painting, Sculpture, and Architecture) seated on a sarcophagus surmounted by a marble bust of Michelangelo. Naldini's fresco, for which he received payment in 1578, is in the marble frame above the bust of the deceased.

WMG

1 See Viatte, 1967, pp. 384–86, plates 23–26.

2 For a discussion of the project see Pope-Hennessy, 1985, pp. 366–69.

PROVENANCE

Jean-Baptiste-Joseph Wicar (Lugt 2568).

LITERATURE

Pluchart, 1889, no. 659 (as anonymous Italian); Viatte, 1963, no. 71; Viatte, 1967, pp. 384, 386 n. 12, pl. 26.

GIOVANNI BATTISTA NALDINI

Italian

Florence 1537–1591 Florence

---

67   *The Pentecost*

Black chalk, and brown wash, 9 1/8 x 7 1/4 in. (23.2 x 18.4 cm.)

The drawing is lined.

Inv. Pluchart 336

The subject of this sketch would be unclear were it not very similar to several other drawings by Naldini, all of which represent the Pentecost (see below). The kneeling figure with arms crossed, in the upper center of the composition, is the Virgin, while the agitated figures who surround her represent Christ's disciples. The present sheet probably has been trimmed at the top, for the dove of the Holy Spirit that is visible above the head of the Virgin in the other drawings does not appear here.

The drawing in Lille closely resembles a pen-and-ink study in the Galleria degli Uffizi, Florence.[1] In two additional drawings—one formerly in a private collection in Paris,[2] and the other (squared for transfer) in the Musée du Louvre[3]—the composition is reversed. Two other drawings of the Pentecost—one in the Uffizi,[4] and one formerly in the Rudolf collection[5]—seem to be by the same hand, but they are less close in composition to the study in Lille.

All of these drawings have in the past been ascribed to Naldini, but Paola Barocchi has recently proposed that the two sheets in the Uffizi and the sketch in Lille are instead the work of Naldini's pupil Francesco Morandini (about 1544–1597), better known as Il Poppi, after the name of his hometown.[6] However, despite differences in quality between the various drawings in the group, most scholars are inclined to

67

accept the attribution of all six sheets to Naldini rather than to his less-gifted pupil.[7] In this context, it is noteworthy that the drawing in Lille has been ascribed to Naldini since at least the nineteenth century, if not earlier.

None of these drawings corresponds to a known painting. Several in the group—of which the Lille drawing may be the first in the sequence—have been associated with an altarpiece of the Pentecost in the church of the Badia, Florence; it is the only painting of this subject listed by Adolfo Venturi as the work of Naldini.[8] However, the picture in Florence is now thought to be by another sixteenth-century artist, Mirabello Cavalori (about 1510/20 – about 1572), and in any case the resemblance is generic. The painting in connection with which this group of drawings was made is now presumably lost, or perhaps was never executed.

WMG

1 Gabinetto Disegni e Stampe, Inv. no. 7449 F. See Barocchi, 1964-1, p. 141, fig. 26, p. 142 (as Francesco Morandini, called Il Poppi). See also Monbeig-Goguel, 1972, p. 86, under no. 87; Petrioli Tofani, 1982, p. 84.

2 Sale, London, Sotheby's, June 28, 1979, no. 48, ill.; see Petrioli Tofani, 1982, p. 81, fig. 41, p. 84. This drawing was recently on the art market in London.

3 Département des Arts Graphiques, Inv. no. 1355. See Monbeig-Goguel, 1972, no. 87, ill.

4 Gabinetto Disegni e Stampe, Inv. no. 750 F. See Petrioli Tofani, 1982, p. 81, fig. 40, p. 84.

5 Sale, London, Sotheby's, July 4, 1977, no. 100, ill.

6 See Barocchi, 1964-1, p. 142.

7 For a discussion of Francesco Morandini, called Il Poppi, as a draftsman see Giovannetti, 1991.

8 See Venturi, IX, 5 (1932), p. 267 (as Naldini); Sestan, Adriani, and Guidotti, 1982, pp. 124, 142 notes 279, 280, ill.

PROVENANCE
Jean-Baptiste-Joseph Wicar (Lugt 2568).

LITERATURE
Benvignat, 1856, no. 630; Pluchart, 1889, no. 336; Viatte, 1963, no. 70; Barocchi, 1964-1, p. 141, fig. 27, p. 142 (as Francesco Morandini, called Il Poppi); Monbeig-Goguel, 1972, p. 86, under no. 87; Petrioli Tofani, 1982, pp. 84, 88 n. 40.

JACOPO CHIMENTI DA EMPOLI

Italian

Florence 1551–1640 Florence

68 *Old Woman Holding a Staff, and Five Studies of Her Left Hand*

Black chalk, heightened with white, on gray-green paper, 14 7/8 x 10 5/16 in. (37.7 x 26.2 cm.)

Inv. no. 1265

Jacopo Chimenti da Empoli was a pupil of Maso da San Friano (about 1532–1571), but like many of his contemporaries he was also influenced by earlier Florentine artists such as Fra Bartolommeo, Andrea del Sarto, and Pontormo. His austere, decorous style is associated with the Counter-Reformation. The Galleria degli Uffizi in Florence possesses more than four hundred drawings by the artist, and the Musée des Beaux-Arts, Lille, with twenty-two sheets, owns the second largest group.

The present drawing was attributed to Empoli by Christel Thiem, who recognized it as a study from life for the figure of the prophetess Anna in *The Presentation in the Temple* (fig. 1), formerly in the Museo della Collegiata, Empoli, but destroyed during World War II.[1] The altarpiece, which was signed and dated 1604, was commissioned by Tommaso Zeffi for his chapel in the church of Santo Stefano, Empoli. In the painting, the left hand of the prophetess was obscured by the figure of the Virgin, who was shown kneeling in front of her. An autograph replica with some minor variations, signed and dated 1606, is in a private collection in Florence.[2]

The story of the Presentation in the Temple is told in the Gospel according to Saint Luke (2: 22–38). Simeon, a devout man and—as recounted in the protevangelium—the successor of Zacharias as high priest of the Temple, had miraculously been given to understand that he would not die before he had seen the Messiah. Upon taking the infant Jesus into his arms, Simeon "blessed God, and said, Lord, now lettest thou thy servant depart in peace, . . . For mine eyes have seen thy salvation, Which thou hast prepared before the face of all people; A light to lighten the Gentiles, and the glory of thy people, Israel." The aged prophetess Anna witnessed the event, "and coming in that instant, gave thanks likewise unto the Lord, and spoke of him to all those who looked for redemption in Jerusalem."

Three further studies for *The Presentation in the Temple* survive. The first in the sequence is a pen-and-wash drawing

68

of the whole composition, in the Ashmolean Museum, Oxford.[3] Another composition study, more precise in execution and very close to the painting, is in the Uffizi.[4] Chalk drawings such as the study in Lille must have been made in connection with all the major figures in the picture. Of these figure studies, only the present sheet and a sensitive black-chalk drawing of the head and shoulders of the Virgin, now in the Uffizi, have thus far been identified.[5]

WMG

1 See Thiem, 1977, p. 273, under no. 16, fig. 233; Marabottini, 1988, no. 47, ill.

2 See Marabottini, 1988, no. 48, ill.

3 See Parker, 1956, no. 213; Marabottini, 1988, no. 47 a, ill.

4 Gabinetto Disegni e Stampe, Inv. no. 950 F. See Marabottini, 1988, no. 47 b, ill.

5 Gabinetto Disegni e Stampe, Inv. no. 840 F. See Marabottini, 1988, no. 47 c, ill.

PROVENANCE

Jean-Baptiste-Joseph Wicar (Lugt 2568).

LITERATURE

Thiem, 1977, no. 16, ill.; Marabottini, 1988, no. 47 d, ill.

FIGURE 1. Jacopo Chimenti da Empoli. *The Presentation in the Temple* (destroyed during World War II). Oil on wood. Formerly Museo della Collegiata, Empoli

244

IL CIGOLI (LUDOVICO CARDI)

Italian

Castelvecchio di Cigoli 1559–1613 Rome

---

69   *The Virgin Mary, Seated*

Black and red chalk, heightened with white, on blue paper, 15 5/8 x 9 7/8 in. (39.8 x 25.1 cm.)

The drawing is lined.

Inscribed in graphite (at the bottom left): *Pl: 207 / 185 Carlo Dolci.*

Inv. Pluchart 207

Ludovico Cardi, better known as Il Cigoli, began his training as a pupil of Alessandro Allori. He later studied with the architect Bernardo Buontalenti and in the workshop of Santi di Tito. The sober naturalism of paintings by Santi di Tito had considerable impact upon the development of Cigoli's style. Always a brilliant colorist, Cigoli was particularly influenced by the work of Federico Barocci and by sixteenth-century Venetian painting. From 1604 until his death in 1613, Cigoli was active principally in Rome. There he painted major altarpieces for Saint Peter's and for San Paolo fuori le Mura, and he frescoed the dome of the Cappella Paolina in Santa Maria Maggiore.

Catherine Monbeig-Goguel was the first to recognize this drawing as a fine and characteristic work by Cigoli.[1] According to Miles Chappell,[2] the sheet is a study for the figure of the Virgin in a painting of the Lamentation, which is now in the Palazzo Vescovile in Colle di Val d'Elsa in southern Tuscany (fig. 1).[3] The composition of the Colle di Val d'Elsa picture is similar to that of another *Lamentation* by Cigoli (Vienna, Kunsthistorisches Museum), which was executed for the Florentine merchant Antonio de' Bardi about 1599, and taken to Vienna in 1792 as part of an exchange of works of art between Ferdinand III de' Medici, Archduke of Tuscany, and his brother Francis II, Emperor of Austria.[4]

The painting in Colle di Val d'Elsa differs from the Vienna *Lamentation* in that it contains fewer figures and is square rather than vertical in format. Moreover, in the Colle di Val d'Elsa picture Saint John the Evangelist replaces the turbaned man (possibly Joseph of Arimathaea) who supports the head and shoulders of Christ in the painting in Vienna, and Mary Magdalene stands at the right, behind the figure of the Virgin. Chappell has pointed out that an eighteenth-century inscription—visible only in an old photograph of the reverse of the Colle di Val d'Elsa painting—suggests that the

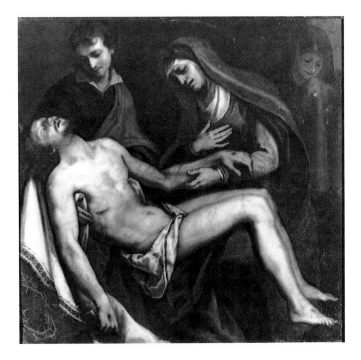

FIGURE 1. Il Cigoli (Ludovico Cardi). *The Lamentation*. Oil on canvas. Palazzo Vescovile, Colle di Val d'Elsa

picture was executed in 1605;[5] the technique and handling of the present study are consistent with this fairly late date.

A composition study in pen and blue wash (Paris, Musée du Louvre) is indisputably connected with the *Lamentation* in Colle di Val d'Elsa.[6] The Musée du Louvre also owns a preparatory drawing for the Vienna *Lamentation*,[7] and Christel Thiem has identified a sheet in the Kupferstichkabinett, Berlin, as a study for the body of the dead Christ in the same picture.[8]   WMG

1 According to Barbara Brejon de Lavergnée (verbal communication).

2 Letter of October 29, 1991.

3 See Faranda, 1986, pp. 144–45, no. 44, ill.

4 See Faranda, 1986, pp. 143–44, pl. XXVI, no. 42, ill.

5 Cited by Viatte, in Viatte and Monbeig-Goguel, 1981, p. 39, under no. 19; and in Viatte, 1988, p. 97, under no. 156.

6 Département des Arts Graphiques, Inv. no. 881. See Viatte, in Viatte and Monbeig-Goguel, 1981, no. 19, ill.; Viatte, 1988, no. 156, ill.

7 Département des Arts Graphiques, Inv. no. 880. See Faranda, 1986, pp. 143–44, no. 42 a, ill.; Viatte, 1988, no. 145, ill.

8 Inv. no. KdZ 18539. See Thiem, 1977, no. 39, ill.

PROVENANCE

Jean-Baptiste-Joseph Wicar (Lugt 2568).

LITERATURE

Pluchart, 1889, no. 207 (as Carlo Dolci).

ANDREA BOSCOLI

Italian

Florence, about 1560–1607 Florence

---

70 *Elijah Visited by an Angel*

Pen and brown ink, and watercolor, 6 3/16 x 19 5/8 in. (15.7 x 50 cm.)

The drawing is lined.

Inv. Pluchart 665

The subject of this unusual drawing is taken from I Kings 19: 4–8: Having fled the wrath of Jezebel, the aged prophet Elijah falls asleep beneath a broom tree. There, an angel appears to him bearing bread and water, and commands him to arise and eat. The sustenance brought to him by the angel gives Elijah the strength to continue his journey to Horeb, "the mount of God."

In Lille, the drawing was formerly classified as anonymous, but it was recognized as the work of Andrea Boscoli by A. E. Popham and Philip Pouncey.[1] A pupil of Santi di Tito (1536?–1603), Boscoli was profoundly influenced by German and Netherlandish prints. Not surprisingly, the precise, linear style of this highly finished drawing recalls that of engravings.

Since watercolors are exceedingly rare in Boscoli's oeuvre the function of the drawing is unclear. It does not correspond to any of the artist's known paintings. Nevertheless, Anna Forlani Tempesti has pointed out that its subject and oblong format suggest that the sheet might have been drawn in connection with a lost or unexecuted decoration for a refectory.[2]

WMG

1 According to Thiem, 1977, p. 298, under no. 47.

2 See Florence, 1986–87, p. 107, under no. 2.50.

PROVENANCE

Jean-Baptiste-Joseph Wicar (Lugt 2568).

EXHIBITIONS

Florence, 1986–87, no. 2.50; Lille, 1989–90, no. 63.

LITERATURE

Benvignat, 1856, no. 1237; Pluchart, 1889, no. 665 (as anonymous Italian); Thiem, 1977, no. 47, ill.; Forlani Tempesti, in Florence, 1986–87, no. 2.50, ill.; Brejon de Lavergnée, 1989-2, no. 63, ill.

248

GUIDO RENI

Italian

Bologna 1575–1642 Bologna

71 *Half-length Figure of an Old Man*

Red chalk, heightened with white, on beige paper, 16 3/8 x 8 5/8 in. (41.7 x 21.9 cm.)

The sheet is irregular in shape; the margins have been made up to form a rectangle. The drawing is lined.

Inv. Pluchart 395

Like his younger contemporaries Francesco Albani (1578–1660) and Domenico Zampieri (1581–1641)—better known as Domenichino—Guido Reni began his career in Bologna as a pupil of the Flemish expatriate Denys Calvaert (about 1540–1619). In 1595 he joined the Accademia degli Incamminati, directed by the Carracci family. Reni's earliest major work, *The Coronation of the Virgin* (Bologna, Pinacoteca Nazionale), reflects the combined influence of Calvaert's Late Mannerism and the naturalistic style favored by the Carracci. From 1601 to 1614 Reni was in Rome, where he received numerous prestigious commissions, among them the decoration of the ceiling of the Casino of the Palazzo Pallavicini-Rospigliosi (1614). Between 1614, when he returned to Bologna, and his death there in 1642, Reni was the city's leading painter. His late works, such as *The Flagellation* (Bologna, Pinacoteca Nazionale), are thinly painted in a limited palette of pale, silvery hues.

The present sheet was utilized, in reverse, for the figure holding a book on the far right in *The Fathers of the Church Contemplating the Immaculate Conception* (fig. 1), now in the Hermitage, Saint Petersburg.[1] The painting, which was formerly in the collection of the marchese de Angelis in Rome, and of Robert Walpole at Houghton Hall, Norfolk, represents six Fathers of the Church—Jerome, Ambrose, Augustine of Hippo, Gregory the Great, John Chrysostom, and Basil the Great—with the Virgin Immaculate seated on clouds overhead. Her arms crossed, she gazes up toward the word *Yahweh*, inscribed in Hebrew letters at the top of the canvas. The Saint Petersburg picture is dated by Otto Kurz to about 1635, and by Stephen Pepper to 1624–25.

The figure in the study in Lille reappears, in reverse, in a pen-and-wash drawing of the entire composition, in the Kupferstichkabinett, Berlin.[2] The latter sheet, which differs considerably from the painting, was published by von Boehn as an autograph study for the painting. It has, however, been

FIGURE 1. Guido Reni. *The Fathers of the Church Contemplating the Immaculate Conception.* Oil on canvas. Hermitage, Saint Petersburg

rejected by Pepper, and may be a copy after a lost sketch by Reni for the Saint Petersburg picture.

W M G

1 See von Boehn, 1910, p. 41, fig. 37, p. 102; Kurz, 1937, p. 219; Pepper, 1984, p. 250, no. 98, pl. 124; Pepper, 1988, p. 255, no. 87, pl. 80.

2 Inv. no. 5002. See von Boehn, 1910, p. 43, fig. 38, p. 102; Kurz, 1937, p. 219; Pepper, 1984, p. 250, under no. 98; Pepper, 1988, p. 255, under no. 87.

PROVENANCE

Jean-Baptiste-Joseph Wicar (Lugt 2568).

EXHIBITIONS

Amsterdam–Brussels–Lille, 1967–68, no. 95; Florence, 1970, no. 92, fig. 81; Lille, 1989–90, no. 67.

LITERATURE

Benvignat, 1856, no. 346; Pluchart, 1889, no. 395; von Boehn, 1910, p. 40, fig. 36; Châtelet, 1967, no. 95, pl. 40; Roli, 1969, pp. 20–21, pl. 26; Viatte, 1969, p. 53; Châtelet, 1970-2, no. 92, fig. 81; Brejon de Lavergnée, 1989-2, no. 67, ill.

250

OTTAVIO LEONI

Italian

Rome, about 1578–1630 Rome

---

72   *Portrait of a Man Wearing a Ruff*

Black chalk, heightened with white, on buff paper,
8 9/16 x 6 1/8 in. (21.8 x 15.5 cm.)

The drawing is lined.

An illegible inscription in pen and brown ink at the lower margin has been partly cut off.

Inv. Pluchart 285

During the first three decades of the seventeenth century, Ottavio Leoni was among the most accomplished and prolific portraitists working in Rome. The son of an artist, he was a member of the Accademia di San Luca in 1604 and served as Principe of the academy in 1614. Although he is believed to have executed numerous painted portraits, very few of these have come to light, and Leoni is best known today for his many surviving drawings in black (or red and black) chalk, heightened with white, on blue or buff paper. Leoni's drawn portraits are relatively small in scale, and they are distinguished by their naturalism.[1]

The Musée des Beaux-Arts, Lille, possesses an outstanding group of drawings by Ottavio Leoni.[2] Two other portrait drawings in Lille have recently been attributed to Ottavio's son, Ippolito, who emulated his father's style.[3]

The present work is perhaps the finest portrait by Ottavio Leoni in the collection. The sitter has not been identified, and the date of the drawing is uncertain. Most of Leoni's portrait drawings are inscribed with the month and year in which they were executed, as well as a number. These numbers are sequential, with the series beginning in 1615 and ending in 1629, shortly before the artist's death. The Lille sheet has unfortunately been trimmed at the lower margin, leaving only traces of Leoni's inscription. Nevertheless, Carmen Roxanne Robbin has kindly pointed out that after about 1620 Leoni generally used red and black chalk together. She therefore dates this drawing, executed in black chalk only, to before 1619.

WMG

1 See Spike, 1984, pp. 12–16.

2 Pluchart, 1889, nos. 279, 280, 283–285.

3 Pluchart, 1889, nos. 281, 282. See Amsterdam–Brussels–Lille, 1967–68, nos. 51, 52, pl. 5 (attributed to Ottavio Leoni); Spike, 1984, pp. 16, 19 (attributed to Ippolito Leoni).

PROVENANCE

Jean-Baptiste-Joseph Wicar (Lugt 2568).

LITERATURE

Benvignat, 1856, no. 1233; Pluchart, 1889, no. 285; Robbin, 1990, no. 322, ill. 268.

252

PIETRO DA CORTONA
(PIETRO BERRETTINI)

Italian

Cortona 1596–1669 Rome

73 *Anne of Austria Attended by Four Allegorical Figures*

Black chalk on beige paper, 13 1/4 x 8 1/4 in.
(33.6 x 21 cm.)

The drawing is lined.

Inscribed in graphite (at the lower right): *P da Cortona*

Inv. Pluchart 63

A native of the Tuscan hill town of Cortona, south of Arezzo, Pietro Berrettini, better known as Pietro da Cortona, was a pupil of the Florentine painter Andrea Commodi (1560–1638). In 1612 he accompanied Commodi to Rome, where, in 1614, he entered the studio of another Florentine painter, Baccio Ciarpi (1578–about 1644). During these years Pietro da Cortona studied ancient Roman sculpture, as well as paintings by Raphael, Titian (about 1488/90–1576), and Veronese (about 1528–1588), and works by Annibale Carracci (1560–1609) and Bernini (1598–1680). For Marchese Marcello Sacchetti he executed frescoes in the Villa Sacchetti at Castel Fusano (1626–29). From 1633 to 1639 he decorated the vault of the Gran Salone in the Palazzo Barberini, Rome, with a vast fresco, *The Glorification of the Reign of Pope Urban VIII Barberini*, which marks the peak of the development of Pietro da Cortona's exuberant High Baroque style. From 1640 to 1647 he was in Florence, where he decorated a number of rooms in the Palazzo Pitti. Stylistically, the frescoes that he painted in Florence anticipate the classical restraint of works such as *Saint Ivo, Advocate of the Poor* (Rome, Sant'Ivo), which the artist left unfinished when he died in 1669.

The present drawing was engraved in reverse by Karl Audran (1594–1674) for the frontispiece of Le Moyne's *La galerie des femmes fortes*. The book was published in Paris in 1647 by A. de Sommaville, and other editions were issued by J. Elsevier in Leiden in 1660 and by C. Angot in Paris the same year.[1] The subject of the engraving is described by Roger-Armand Weigert: A putto places a crown on Anne of Austria, who is attended by two allegorical figures, while two other women carve her name in the pedestal on which she stands.

WMG

1 See Weigert, 1939, pp. 208–9, no. 304 (1647 edition); Châtelet, 1967, p. 32, under no. 73.

PROVENANCE

Gift of Lucien Rouzé-Huet (Lugt 1742).

EXHIBITIONS

Amsterdam–Brussels–Lille, 1967–68, no. 73; Florence, 1970, no. 70; Lille, 1989–90, no. 77.

LITERATURE

Pluchart, 1889, no. 63; Briganti, 1962, p. 305; Châtelet, 1967, no. 73, pl. 45; Châtelet, 1970-2, no. 70, fig. 56; Briganti, 1982, p. 291; Brejon de Lavergnée, 1989-2, no. 77, ill.

PIER FRANCESCO MOLA

Italian

Coldrerio 1612–1666 Rome

---

74   *The Abduction of Europa*

Pen and brown ink and brown wash, over red chalk, 10 5/8 x 8 3/16 in. (27.1 x 20.8 cm.)

Inscribed in pen and brown ink (at the top left): 20; (at the bottom left): *Mola*; (at the bottom right): 28

Inv. no. 3187

Pier Francesco was the son of Giovanni Battista Mola (1585–1665), an architect and the author of a celebrated guidebook to Rome. As a young man, Pier Francesco was a pupil first of Prospero Orsi (about 1558–1663) and then of Giuseppe Cesari, Il Cavaliere d'Arpino (1568–1640). Between 1633 and 1647 Mola traveled extensively in northern Italy, where he was exposed to Venetian painting, as well as to the art of Guercino (1591–1666). Mola was also profoundly influenced by the work of his somewhat older contemporary Nicolas Poussin. During the last twenty years of his life he was active principally in Rome, where he executed frescoes in the churches of Il Gesù and San Marco, as well as in the Palazzo del Quirinale (*Joseph Making Himself Known to His Brethren* of 1657) and the Palazzo Costaguti. Like Salvator Rosa (1615–1673) and Pietro Testa (1612–1650), Mola was keenly interested in the expressive potential of landscape, which plays a major part in many of his paintings.

This hitherto unpublished sheet is a fine and characteristic example of Mola's highly pictorial drawing style. According to Greek mythology, Europa was the daughter of Agenor, King of Tyre. Jupiter fell in love with her and, in the guise of a white bull, carried her off to Crete. In the present drawing the unsuspecting Europa is helped onto the bull by her attendants, who adorn the animal with garlands of flowers.

Early sources attribute two paintings of this subject to Mola.[1] However, just one, now in the Bayerische Staatsgemäldesammlungen, Schloss Schleissheim, survives today.[2] The picture at Schleissheim is an early work, greatly influenced by Francesco Albani's *Rape of Europa* in the Galleria degli Uffizi in Florence;[3] unlike the present drawing it is horizontal in format and depicts the helpless Europa being carried out to sea while her companions look on in dismay.

The style of the Lille drawing suggests that it may date from the 1650s.

WMG

1 See Laureati, in Lugano–Rome, 1989–90, p. 148, under no. I.3.
2 Inv. no. 924. See Lugano–Rome, 1989–90, no. I.3, ill.
3 Inv. no. 1366. See Lugano–Rome, 1989–90, no. IV.4, ill.

CARLO DOLCI

Italian

Florence 1616–1686 Florence

---

75   *Saint John the Evangelist on Patmos*

Black and red chalk, heightened with white, on gray prepared paper, 8 7/8 x 12 11/16 in. (22.6 x 32.2 cm.)

Inv. Pluchart 204

A pupil of Jacopo Vignali (1592–1664), Carlo Dolci was famous among his aristocratic clientele for his portraits and pietistic devotional images. Dolci's paintings are meticulous in execution, influenced on the one hand by the Tenebrism of Caravaggio (1571–1610) and on the other by the pristine surfaces of pictures by earlier Florentine artists such as Bronzino (1503–1572), Alessandro Allori (1535–1607), and Cigoli. The intensity of religious feeling that distinguishes most of his work was condemned by later critics as excessively sentimental.

One of a number of drawings by Dolci in the Musée des Beaux-Arts, Lille, the present sheet is a study from the model for the *Vision of Saint John the Evangelist on Patmos* (fig. 1) in the Galleria Palatina, Palazzo Pitti, Florence.[1] The figure in the drawing corresponds almost exactly to that of Saint John in the painting, except that in the latter he is bearded and clearly meant to be much older. The subject of the painting is taken from the Book of Revelation (the Apocalypse). Exiled

by the Roman emperor Domitian to the island of Patmos, John was believed to have had a series of visions foretelling the Second Coming of Christ. Dolci's painting represents the apparition to Saint John of "a woman clothed with the sun, with the moon under her feet, and upon her head a crown of twelve stars" (Revelation 12: 1–6). Saint John also saw before him "a great red dragon, having seven heads and ten horns, and seven crowns upon his heads." The eagle standing behind the recumbent figure of the saint in the painting is John's usual attribute, emblematic of his divine inspiration.

The painting now in the Palazzo Pitti appears in a late-seventeenth-century inventory of the property of Vittoria della Rovere, one of Dolci's principal patrons.[2] In 1986 Charles McCorquodale suggested that it might be the *modello* for a painting recorded by Filippo Baldinucci as having been executed for Pier Francesco Rinuccini.[3] That painting, which was signed and dated 1657, seems to have remained in the Rinuccini family until 1852, when it was sold to an English collector; its present whereabouts is unknown.[4]

WMG

1 See Cantelli, 1983, p. 69, plates 315, 316. The connection between the drawing and the painting was established by Marco Chiarini.

2 According to Marco Chiarini. Cited by Brejon de Lavergnée, 1989-2, p. 149, under no. 86.

3 See McCorquodale, in Florence, 1986–87, *Biografie*, p. 82. See Baldinucci, 1845–47, V, p. 351: "Dipinse la bella figura quanto il naturale del san Giovanni Evangelista, in atto di vedere la misteriosa visione della donna vestita di sole, che conculca il dragone: e questo quadro ebbe per trecento scudi il marchese Pier Francesco Rinuccini."

4 See McCorquodale, 1977, pp. 55, 59 notes 7, 8.

PROVENANCE

Jean-Baptiste-Joseph Wicar (Lugt 2568).

EXHIBITION

Lille, 1989–90, no. 86.

LITERATURE

Benvignat, 1856, no. 180; Pluchart, 1889, no. 204; Brejon de Lavergnée, 1989-2, no. 86, ill.

FIGURE 1. Carlo Dolci. *The Vision of Saint John the Evangelist on Patmos*. Oil on canvas. Galleria Palatina, Palazzo Pitti, Florence

FRANCESCO GUARDI

Italian

Venice 1712–1793 Venice

---

76   *The Villa del Timpano Arcuato*

Pen and brown ink and brown wash, over traces of black chalk, 12 x 18 3/8 in. (30.5 x 46.7 cm.)

Inscribed in graphite (at the bottom left): *Fr^{co} Guardi*

Inv. Pluchart 273

Arguably the greatest *vedutista*, or view painter, of the eighteenth century, Francesco Guardi was one of a family of artists that included his father, Domenico, his two brothers, Gian Antonio and Nicolò, and his son, Giacomo. Francesco began work as a figure painter in the atelier of his older brother, Gian Antonio. His earliest Venetian views, much influenced by the work of Canaletto, date from the 1750s, but it was not until after 1760 that Francesco emerged as an independent and innovative artistic personality. He is best known today for his atmospheric renderings of Venice and the terra firma, his paintings and drawings of events such as the disastrous fire at San Marcuola in 1789, and his imaginary views, or *capricci*.

Winslow Ames was the first to point out that this superb drawing is related to a painting by Francesco Guardi in a private collection in London.[1] A different view of the same villa (now destroyed) appears in the background of another painting by Guardi that represents the garden façade of the neighboring Villa Loredan, on the outskirts of Paese, near Treviso.[2] Two other paintings from the same series, also owned privately, depict the façade of the Villa Loredan[3] and the gardens of the Palazzo Contarini dal Zaffo in Venice, respectively.[4] In the late eighteenth century the Villa Loredan was inhabited by John Strange, British Resident in Venice from 1773 to 1790. Strange was one of Guardi's principal patrons, and it seems likely that he commissioned the four paintings.

A number of preparatory drawings for this series survive. Studies for the entrance gate and for the façade of the Villa Loredan are in the collections of the Metropolitan Museum[5] and the Rhode Island School of Design in Providence.[6] A view from the front windows and one from the back windows of the villa—neither of which corresponds to a known painting—are in the Fodor Collection, Amsterdam,[7] and the Ashmolean Museum, Oxford.[8] A splendid drawing of the gardens of the Palazzo Contarini dal Zaffo is also in the Ashmolean Museum.[9] James Byam Shaw has suggested that the artist executed these drawings in 1778, while en route to his family home in the Val di Sole.

On the verso of the drawing in Providence is a slight pen sketch of the façade of the "Villa del Timpano Arcuato," so called on account of its unusual curved pediment.[10] The more elaborate drawing in Lille corresponds almost exactly to the painting in London, except that in the latter there are more figures, a carriage in the foreground, and a horse-drawn chaise in the distance.

WMG

1 See Ames, 1963, pp. 37–39, fig. 1; Morassi, 1973, I, no. 683, II, figs. 639, 641.
2 See Morassi, 1973, I, no. 682, II, figs. 640, 642.
3 See Morassi, 1973, I, no. 681, II, figs. 636–638.
4 See Morassi, 1973, I, no. 680, II, fig. 635.
5 Rogers Fund, 1937, 37.165.69. See Morassi, 1975, no. 422, fig. 424; Bean and Griswold, 1990, no. 93, ill.
6 Inv. no. 57.250. See Morassi, 1975, no. 421, fig. 421; Giles, in Providence, 1983, no. 21, ill.
7 Inv. no. A-18423. See Morassi, 1975, no. 425, fig. 427; Koevoets, 1976, no. 23, ill.
8 See Parker, 1956, no. 1016; Morassi, 1975, no. 424, fig. 426.
9 See Parker, 1956, no. 1014, pl. CCXVIII; Morassi, 1975, no. 419, fig. 422.
10 See Ames, 1963, p. 39, fig. 2 (detail); Giles, in Providence, 1983, p. 74, under no. 21.

PROVENANCE

E. Desperet (Lugt 721); Marmontel; Beurnonville; sale of the Beurnonville collection, Paris, 1885.

EXHIBITIONS

Berlin, 1964, no. 63; Amsterdam–Brussels–Lille, 1967–68, no. 39; Florence, 1970, no. 43; Paris, 1971, no. 103.

LITERATURE

Bacou, 1957, p. 62; Ames, 1963, pp. 37–39, pl. 21; Bean, 1964, under no. 46; Châtelet, 1967, no. 39, pl. 54; Châtelet, 1970-2, no. 43, fig. 37; Bean and Stampfle, 1971, p. 87, under no. 207; Morassi, 1973, I, p. 437, under no. 683; Morassi, 1975, no. 426, fig. 428.

SIMON VOUET

French

Paris 1590–1649 Paris

---

77   *Study of a Seated Male Figure Facing Right*

Black chalk, heightened with white, on brown paper,
11 3/4 x 8 7/8 in. (29.8 x 22.7 cm.)

Inv. Pluchart 1706

The figure in this drawing, who appears to be seated on clouds and is holding a banderole, recalls the angels in two *modelli*[1] by Vouet (London, Private collection). The *modelli* are related to the second altarpiece commissioned from the artist for Saint Peter's in Rome, an *Adoration of the Cross*, which was destroyed in the eighteenth century but is known through several sketches. The pose and the low viewpoint adopted for this figure and for an angel in the upper part of the *Ecstasy of Saint Francis of Paola*—one of Vouet's Roman compositions, known from an engraving by Claude Mellan (1598–1688)[2]—are quite similar. Here, the type of elegant youth, with stylized profile and curly hair, is realistically rendered in the artist's Italianate, Caravaggesque style, which suggests that the Lille drawing could date to his Roman period, about 1625–26. Drawings by Vouet from his years in Rome, however, are quite rare, and there is little general agreement on those studies that have been attributed to him.[3] The attributions of the drawings executed in wash are the most convincing. For example, the artist used this technique in the Princeton *Saint Peter Healing the Sick with His Shadow*, which J.-P. Cuzin relates to Vouet's first commission for an altarpiece for Saint Peter's,[4] and in the partial study for the *Allegory of the House of Savoy* (Reims, Musée Saint-Rémi), which was engraved by Mellan in Rome.[5]

Despite the scarcity of extant works from this first part of Vouet's career, the few wash drawings by him that have come down to us all belong to the early period.[6] The graphic work that he produced in Paris is composed entirely of detail studies drawn in black chalk and heightened with white.

Nevertheless, Vouet's observation of nature, his drawings from the model, and even the facial types of the figures in these vigorous studies would be unthinkable without an Italian precedent, and it seems likely that Vouet already drew in this manner while he was in Rome. The Lille drawing may be considered a typical example of Vouet's Italian style. Recently Pierre Rosenberg compared a fine study by Vouet executed in black chalk to the figure of a young man in the *Martyrdom of Saint Catherine*, a painting from the artist's Roman period known through an engraving by Mellan and from several painted copies.[7]

It was precisely through the use of black chalk that Vouet—ever attentive to the rendering of form—revealed his talents and contributed significantly to the renewal of an artistic idiom in Paris. The atelier that he established when he returned to the French capital in 1627 placed a premium on creativity, teaching, and the practice of drawing, and this met with great success.

BBL

1 See Schleier, 1972, pp. 91–92, figs. 43, 44.

2 See Préaud, 1988, no. 78, ill.; Ficacci, 1989, p. 188, no. 26, ill.

3 See Paris, 1990–91, p. 358 n. 1, for a summation of this issue.

4 See Cuzin, 1987, pp. 359–70.

5 See Paris, 1990–91, no. 66, ill.

6 This is also true in the case of two preparatory wash drawings made for documented paintings executed soon after the artist's return from Italy: a *Last Supper* (drawing; Berlin, Staatliche Museen Preussischer Kulturbesitz, Kupferstichkabinett) for the Lorette painting (see Rosenberg, 1972) and an *Assumption* (drawing; Paris, Musée du Louvre, Département des Arts Graphiques) for the altarpiece in the church of Saint-Nicolas-des-Champs in Paris (see Paris, 1990–91, no. 69, ill.).

7 See Rosenberg, 1990-1, pp. 310–14.

PROVENANCE
Bequest of Dubrunfaut to the Musée des Beaux-Arts, 1883.

EXHIBITIONS
London–Cambridge–Birmingham–Glasgow, 1974–75, no. 93, pl. 2; Paris, 1990–91, no. 67, ill.

LITERATURE
Pluchart, 1889, no. 1706; Brejon de Lavergnée, 1987, no. VI, ill.

CHARLES LE BRUN

French

Paris 1619–1690 Paris

---

78 *Project for the Frontispiece of the Thesis of Charles d'Orléans*

Red chalk and brown wash on four sheets of paper joined together, 41 x 27 1/2 in. (104 x 70 cm.)

Inv. Pluchart 1505

This large, ambitious drawing, rediscovered and identified at the time of the exhibition "Au temps du roi soleil, les peintres de Louis XIV" in Lille in 1968,[1] is a preparatory study for the frontispiece of the thesis defended by Charles d'Orléans, Comte de Saint-Pol, on August 1, 1664. There is an engraving after the drawing by Gilles Rousselet (1610–1686), in reverse and with slight variations (see fig. 1).[2]

The allegories, clearly indicated only on the engraving, were described about 1700 by Claude Nivelon: "[The thesis] that followed in 1664 was ingeniously devised to show what His Majesty had achieved, through foresight and courage, for the good of his kingdom. . . . The Prince appears armed and seated on a rearing horse that tramples Blind Fury [wearing a blindfold] and Rebellion [wielding a dagger], both of them armed and reeling before him; Ignorance [with donkey's ears] and Fear [with a hare] are represented on the other side as a partially draped male figure who appears to be trying to stand up and flee. These four subjects represent what happened to enemies both inside and outside the kingdom . . ." ("Celle [la thèse] qui suit en 1664 est ingénieusement inventée pour représenter ce que Sa Majesté a exécuté par sa prévoyance et sa valeur pour le bien de son royaume. . . . Le Prince y paroit armé et monté sur un cheval qui abat en se cabrant ou renverse l'aveugle fureur [avec son bandeau] et la rébellion [avec son poignard] toutes deux armées et trébuchantes devant lui, et l'ignorance [avec ses oreilles d'âne] et la crainte [avec son lièvre] sont représentées de l'autre côté sous la figure d'un homme en partie couvert d'une draperie, paroissant se vouloir relever et fuir. Ces quatre sujets représentent ce qui s'est passé tant de la part des ennemis du dehors que du dedans le royaume . . .").[3]

The drawing shows Louis being crowned by Glory (Divine Providence in the engraving), seen resting against a globe ornamented with fleurs-de-lis and held by Love of Country, while Renown proclaims her grandeur. Winged putti hold shields with inscriptions designating the scenes to be depicted in the engraving, including *Ste Empoule* (the

FIGURE 1. Gilles Rousselet, after Charles Le Brun. *Louis XIV on Horseback.* Engraving. Cabinet des Estampes, Bibliothèque Nationale, Paris

baptism of King Clovis), *la pucelle* (Joan of Arc), *les armes de France, bataille de Rocroy,* and *mariage du Roy.* According to Nivelon's somewhat confused interpretation, the shields, which are connected by a chain, are meant to symbolize the continuity of the virtues of the monarchy through the centuries.

The Lille drawing, which may be dated to the same year as the thesis (1664), is a fairly early work by Le Brun. The artist already enjoyed great success, having been made director of the Manufacture Royale des Gobelins in 1663; shortly afterward, he was officially named *Premier peintre du roi* as well as "director and keeper of His Majesty's paintings and drawings collection." During his career, Le Brun designed several such frontispieces for treatises by important personages. He carefully worked out these compositions in detail studies, compositional drawings, and monochromatic oil sketches.[4]

Lydia Beauvais has found no drawings related to the Lille composition among those by Le Brun preserved in the Musée du Louvre in Paris.[5] The pictorial effect of the present drawing is enhanced by the liberal use of wash in combination with red chalk, the strong contrasts of light and shadow, and the large format of the sheet. These qualities make it clear that despite his new, official duties, Le Brun still maintained an interest in designing frontispieces for theses and books.

The grand theme of the king on horseback triumphing over adversity appears numerous times in the artist's oeuvre, as, for example, in the frontispiece to Jacques-Nicolas Colbert's theological thesis (defended at the Sorbonne December 30, 1677),[6] and in the project for an equestrian monument intended for the colonnade of the Louvre,[7] which was entrusted to Girardon but never realized. In the sketch for a medallion in bas-relief to be executed by the sculptor Antoine Coysevox for a mantelpiece in the Salon de la Guerre at Versailles,[8] Le Brun once again depicted the king on horseback, this time in antique-style dress, trampling his enemies under his horse's hooves.

BBL

1 See Thuillier, in Lille, 1968, p. 67, no. 110.

2 See Véronique Meyer, "Gilles Rousselet et la gravure d'interprétation en France au XVIIe siècle," Ph.D. diss., Paris IV, Sorbonne, 1984, no. 280; the author points out that Charles d'Orléans (1649–1672) was the son of the duc de Longueville. The engraving is not included in Daniel Wildenstein, "Les oeuvres de Charles Le Brun d'après les graveurs de son temps," Gazette des Beaux-Arts, LXVI (July–August 1965), pp. 1–58.

3 See Nivelon, ms. fr. 12987, about 1700, p. 284. We wish to thank Mme Beauvais for providing us with Nivelon's text as well as bibliographical assistance.

4 For the monochromatic oil sketches see Sylvain Laveissière's entry on the composition of The Triumph of Religion engraved by Gerard Edelinck (1640–1707), in Nouvelles acquisitions du Département des peintures (1987–1990), Paris, Musée du Louvre, 1991, pp. 81–83.

5 In a letter of 1992 to this author.

6 See Thuillier, 1963, p. LXV.

7 See Beauvais and Méjanès, in Paris, 1985–86, pp. 68–70.

8 See Guy Kuraszewski, "La cheminée du Salon de la Guerre au château de Versailles," Bulletin de la Société de l'Histoire de l'Art français (meeting of October 5, 1974), 1975, pp. 63–69.

PROVENANCE

Gift of Jules and Auguste Lenglart, 1877.

EXHIBITIONS

Lille, 1968, no. 110; London–Cambridge–Birmingham–Glasgow, 1974–75, no. 64.

LITERATURE

Pluchart, 1889, no. 1505; Thuillier, in Lille, 1968, p. 67, no. 110, ill.; Oursel, 1974-2, no. 64, pl. V.

JOSEPH-FRANÇOIS PARROCEL

French

Avignon 1704–1781 Paris

79   *The Adoration of the Magi*

Black chalk, heightened with white, 15 7/8 x 12 5/8 in. (40.5 x 32 cm.)

Inscribed in pencil (at the right center): *J. Parrocel inven. et Pinxit 1751*

Inv. no. 2589

FIGURE 1. Joseph-François Parrocel. *The Adoration of the Magi*. Oil on canvas. Cathedral of Amiens

265

This is a preparatory drawing for the large altarpiece of *The Adoration of the Magi*, which the artist executed for the Chapel of Saints Peter and Paul in the Cathedral of Amiens (see fig. 1). The painting, which differs in several details from the Lille drawing, bears the coat of arms of the canon Cornet de Coupel, who commissioned the decoration of the chapel in 1749.[1] The altar itself was constructed by Dron, a carpenter from Amiens, and the chapel was consecrated by Mgr. de La Motte on June 21, 1751, which corroborates the date on the drawing. M. Foucart, in Amiens, has pointed out the similarity in style between the painting in Amiens Cathedral and the series of four canvases painted by the artist for the sacristy of the Abbey of Valloires and dated 1753: *The Adoration of the Shepherds*, *The Flight into Egypt*, *Christ among the Doctors*, and *Christ in the Garden of Gethsemane*.[2]

Joseph-François belonged to the celebrated Parrocel family from Montbrison. An ancestor, Barthélémy, had established himself in Brignoles, and during the seventeenth and eighteenth centuries the family produced many painters who were active in the Var or in Avignon. However, Joseph-François, a student of his father, Pierre, was not from the same branch of the family as Joseph (painter to Louis XIV) and his son Charles; they were the most famous members of this dynasty of artists and pursued their careers in Paris. Joseph-François traveled to Rome in 1736, and in 1753 he was accepted into the Académie Royale de Peinture et de Sculpture in Paris.

Parrocel's black-chalk studies combine a sensitivity to the classical tradition with the refined handling that is characteristic of eighteenth-century drawings. Rapid strokes define the figures and their facial features without disturbing the coherence of the whole. The monumentality of the Lille sheet, its balanced composition, and the skillful distribution of light and shadow recall the finest drawings of the seventeenth century.

BBL

1 See Oursel, 1974-2, no. 76.

2 We wish to thank M. Foucart for supplying a photograph of the painting.

PROVENANCE
Purchased from M. Hennaert, Ypres, 1898.

EXHIBITION
London–Cambridge–Birmingham–Glasgow, 1974–75, no. 76.

HUBERT ROBERT

French

Paris 1733–1808 Paris

80 *Colonnade in Ruins*

Pen and black ink, and watercolor, 31 1/2 x 30 3/8 in. (80 x 77 cm.)

Signed and dated in pen and black ink on the pedestal of the statue (at the lower right): H. ROBERT D 1780 ·

Inv. Pluchart 1194

This sheet is a splendid example of Hubert Robert's watercolors of Roman ruins peopled by small-scale figures in contemporary dress. From 1754 to 1765 the artist was a *pensionnaire* at the Académie de France in Rome, where he was taught perspective by the view painter Giovanni Paolo Panini (1691/92–1765). Robert was, moreover, an exact contemporary, friend, and fellow student of Jean-Honoré Fragonard (1732–1806), whose red-chalk drawings are sometimes nearly indistinguishable from his own. Upon his return to Paris, Robert continued to produce paintings and drawings based upon the sites he had visited and sketched while he was in Rome.

This unusually large drawing is signed and dated 1780. Comparable watercolors of ruined colonnades seen in perspective are in the Metropolitan Museum[1] and in a private collection in Paris.[2] A red-chalk drawing, datable to 1779 and similar in detail to the sheet in Lille, was formerly in a New York private collection;[3] in that drawing the architecture and staffage correspond (in reverse) to those in the present work, but that sheet is decidedly horizontal instead of nearly square in format. An unsigned replica of the Lille drawing was acquired directly from the artist by the architect H. Trou in 1796. In 1933 the replica and its pendant, *Interior of a Ruined Palace*, both slightly smaller than the Lille sheet, were in the collection of Mme Paul Fournier.[4]

Views such as this one clearly derive from the ruins of Roman public buildings—for example, the Baths of Caracalla and the Baths of Diocletian. These works, however, are caprices, intended to evoke the picturesque quality of Roman ruins in general rather than a particular site. In this respect, Robert's work was directly inspired by the *capricci* of his teacher, Panini.

WMG

1 Bequest of Alexandrine Sinsheimer, 1958, 59.23.68. See Bean, 1986, no. 267, ill.

2 See Carlson, 1978, no. 49, ill.

3 See *French Master Drawings, Renaissance to Modern: A Loan Exhibition* (exhib. cat.). New York, Charles E. Slatkin Galleries, 1959, no. 57, ill.

4 See Sterling, 1933, no. 69, pl. 70 (replica of the present drawing), no. 70 (pendant to no. 69).

PROVENANCE

Purchased from M. Lecomte, Paris, about 1887.

EXHIBITIONS

London–Cambridge–Birmingham–Glasgow, 1974–75, no. 89; Lille, 1983-1, no. 144.

LITERATURE

Pluchart, 1889, no. 1470; Oursel, 1974-2, no. 89, pl. 25; Carlson, 1978, p. 124, under no. 49; Scottez, in Lille, 1983-1, no. 144, ill.

LOUIS-LÉOPOLD BOILLY

French

La Bassée 1761–1845 Paris

---

81 *Portrait of a Little Girl* (Boilly's Daughter?)

Graphite on two sheets of white vellum pasted together, 8 1/2 x 6 5/8 in. (21.6 x 16.9 cm.)

Inv. Pluchart 1113

A little girl wearing an Empire-style dress is shown in a garden. She is leaning on a large, flat stone on which there is some sheet music entitled CHANT, to which she points with her right hand. Her identity unfortunately is not known; however, her oval face, full cheeks, prominent eyes, and small mouth are not unlike the features of Boilly's own children, whom he often depicted during the first half of his career. The girl in the Lille study may be compared with one of the three figures identified as the artist's children in a drawing owned by a Mme B. of Lille in 1911;[1] with one of the faces of the figures in the central group in Boilly's painting *The Arrival of the Coach in the Cour des Messageries in Paris* (exhibited at the Salon of 1804; Paris, Musée du Louvre), which represents the artist's family in the company of Lethière;[2] and with the child in a *Portrait of One of the Artist's Sons*.[3] Not only are the facial features of the sitters in the two previously mentioned works similar to those of the little girl in the Lille drawing, but these works are also close in spirit to the Lille sheet: The likenesses of the children are rendered with the same tender and unconstrained feeling as are Boilly's portraits of his family, while his commissioned portraits are more objec-

tively drawn and painted. It is therefore likely that the present work is a portrait of one of the artist's daughters, either from his first marriage in 1787, to Marie-Madeleine Desligne of Arras (died 1795), or from his second marriage, to Adelaïde-Françoise Leduc of Paris, in 1795. With his first wife he is said to have had one daughter and five sons, and with his second wife two daughters (who died in infancy) and three sons, the eldest of whom, Julien-Léopold, born in 1796, also became a painter. Marmottan mentions a painting in the Lütz collection entitled *Portrait of the Artist's Daughter*.[4] Yet the question remains: Which of Boilly's daughters is portrayed here?

The Lille drawing, long forgotten in the storerooms of the Musée des Beaux-Arts until the exhibition at the Heim Gallery in London in 1974, reveals one of the many facets of Boilly's talent: his ability as a draftsman, which was greatly appreciated by connoisseurs and critics alike. Very painstaking and methodical in his work, Boilly is said to have produced between four and five hundred drawings, including compositional as well as detail studies, sketches from life, and preparatory drawings for lithographs, in addition to commissioned and family portraits. As Harrisse, one of his finest biographers, wrote: "The sureness of Boilly's hand, and his perfect understanding of costume, attitude, and type are even more visible in his drawings and sketches done in pencil, pen and ink, and wash [than in his other work]. In this domain, we would say he is the equal of the best draftsmen of his day."[5] Indeed, the grace of the child's informal pose and the impish charm of her face are accentuated by the delicate pencil strokes and shading and by the fluid yet straightforward handling. This powerful and personal image of a little girl in a romantic, natural setting is typical of the art of the first decade of the nineteenth century, and serves to enhance our appreciation of Boilly's work.

AS-DW

1 The figure to the far right, who appears a little younger than the sitter in the Lille drawing (black chalk). See Victor Champier, *L'art dans les Flandres françaises aux 17e et 18e siècles . . . Exposition rétrospective de Roubaix*, Lille, 1911, pl. XXXVI.

2 See Harrisse, 1898, p. 78.

3 Black chalk, 33 x 26 cm.; sold, Paris, Paulme, May 13, 1929, no. 7, ill.

4 See Marmottan, 1913, p. 231.

5 See Harrisse, 1898, p. 55.

PROVENANCE

Gift of Lucien Rouzé,* Lille, January 8, 1872.

* Rouzé, a collector from Lille, gave several drawings to the Musée des Beaux-Arts, including *The Music Lesson*, another sheet by Boilly.

EXHIBITIONS

London–Cambridge–Birmingham–Glasgow, 1974–75, no. 5; Lille, 1988–89, no. 43.

LITERATURE

Pluchart, 1889, no. 1113; Harrisse, 1898, p. 171, no. 994; Oursel, 1974-2, no. 5, pl. 66; Scottez-De Wambrechies, in Lille, 1988–89, no. 43, ill. p. 143.

JEAN-AUGUSTE-DOMINIQUE INGRES

French

Montauban 1780–1867 Paris

82 Drapery study for an angel in *The Vow of Louis XIII*

Black chalk, stumped and heightened with white, on blue-gray paper, 14 x 14 in. (35.6 x 35.6 cm.)

Inscribed (at the center) in black chalk: *grand / clair*.

Inv. Pluchart 1483

A pupil of the neoclassical painter Jacques-Louis David, Jean-Auguste-Dominique Ingres was awarded the Prix de Rome in 1801. Five years later he traveled to Rome, where he was to remain until 1820. During this period Ingres painted *La grande baigneuse* (1808) and *La grande odalisque* (1814), both now in the Musée du Louvre, Paris, and executed numerous portrait drawings of French tourists. Between 1820 and 1824 Ingres was in Florence. He spent most of the next decade in Paris, only to return to Rome in 1835 as director of the Académie de France. By 1841 he was again in Paris, where in 1862 he painted one of his last major works, *Le bain turque* (Musée du Louvre). He died less than five years later, at the age of eighty-six.

The present drawing is a study for the *Vow of Louis XIII* (fig. 1) in the Cathedral of Notre-Dame in Ingres's hometown of Montauban, near Toulouse, in southern France.[1] The commission was awarded to Ingres by the Minister of the Interior in 1820. The painting was executed entirely in Florence and was not completed until 1824, when it was shown in the Salon. It was finally installed in the choir of the cathedral of Montauban in 1826.

The painting records Louis XIII's dedication of his kingdom to the Virgin of the Assumption in 1636. Two angels are shown pulling aside curtains to reveal the Virgin and Child seated on clouds. Below, the king kneels before an altar,

FIGURE 1. Jean-Auguste-Dominique Ingres. *The Vow of Louis XIII.* 1824. Oil on canvas. Cathedral of Notre-Dame, Montauban

offering his crown and scepter up to heaven. Ingres's sources for the painting include the *Sistine Madonna* (Dresden, Gemäldegalerie) and the *Madonna di Foligno* (Rome, Pinacoteca Vaticana) by Raphael, as well as the *Vow of Louis XIII* (Caen, Musée des Beaux-Arts) by Philippe de Champaigne (1602–1674), which was executed in 1638.

The present sheet is a drapery study for the angel pulling back the curtain at the right in the painting. The pose of the figure is the same as that in another drawing by Ingres, which includes both angels.[2] The latter study, drawn from the nude model, is one of a number of preparatory sketches for the *Vow of Louis XIII* in the Musée Ingres in Montauban.[3] In the painting, the angel's left knee, which is bent in the Lille sketch, has been straightened so that both legs are extended,

271

and the drapery falls to the figure's right ankle instead of revealing the whole thigh. Daniel Ternois cites two further drapery studies for the angels in the *Vow of Louis XIII* in the museum in Bern.[4]

WMG

1 See Ternois, in Paris, 1967–68, no. 131, ill.

2 Inv. no. 867.2577. See Ternois, in Paris, 1967–68, no. 135, ill.; Ekelhart-Reinwetter, 1991, no. III.7, ill.

3 See Ternois, in Paris, 1967–68, nos. 132–135, ill.; Ekelhart-Reinwetter, 1991, nos. III.1–III.8, ill.

4 See Ternois, in Paris, 1967–68, p. 194, under no. 136.

PROVENANCE

Gift of the artist, 1866.

EXHIBITIONS

Washington–Cleveland–Saint Louis–Cambridge–New York, 1952–53, no. 113; Rome–Milan, 1959–60, no. 122; Montauban, 1967, no. 90; Paris, 1967–68, no. 136; London–Cambridge–Birmingham–Glasgow, 1974–75, no. 56; Lille, 1983-1, no. 110.

LITERATURE

Gonse, 1877, p. 94; Pluchart, 1889, no. 1483; Mabilleau, 1894, p. 381, ill.; *Choix de dessins*, 1926, pl. 42; Alazard, 1950, pl. LV; Millier, 1955, pl. 19; Ternois, in Paris, 1967–68, no. 136, ill.; Oursel, 1974-2, no. 56, pl. 67; Scottez, in Lille, 1983-1, no. 110, ill.

JEAN-LOUIS-ANDRÉ-THÉODORE GERICAULT

French

Rouen 1791–1824 Paris

---

83 *The Murderers of Fualdès Carrying His Body to the Aveyron*

Graphite, black chalk, and brown wash, heightened with white, on beige paper, 8 3/8 x 11 5/16 in. (21.3 x 28.7 cm.)

Inscribed in pen and dark brown ink (at the upper right): *N° 169-catalogue / de M. Clément.*

Inv. Pluchart 1395

In the autumn of 1817, Gericault returned to Paris after a disappointing sojourn in Rome. A short time later, he executed a series of at least seven drawings based on the brutal murder of the magistrate Antoine-Bernardin Fualdès, which had taken place at Rodez earlier that year. Gericault's drawings depict a number of different episodes from the story,

including the conspiracy to assassinate Fualdès, Fualdès dragged into the brothel in which the murder took place, the murder of Fualdès, the body of Fualdès carried to the Aveyron, the body of Fualdès thrown into the river, and the assassins' escape. Gericault evidently intended to work up one of these drawings into a large painting for the Salon of 1819. Eventually, however, he abandoned the project, having found an even more dramatic and politically explosive subject in the tragic shipwreck of the *Medusa* off the coast of West Africa.

This is one of two studies for *The Body of Fualdès Carried to the Aveyron*. The second drawing, similar in composition but less highly finished than the sheet in Lille, was formerly in the collection of the duke of Treviso; its present whereabouts is unknown.[1] Other drawings from the set, all more schematic than the present sheet, are in the collection of Louis-Antoine Prat in Paris;[2] the Musée des Beaux-Arts, Rouen;[3] and elsewhere.[4] Although the drawings may have been inspired by a series of lithographs published in 1818 by Sébastien Coeuré (born 1778),[5] Gericault's heroic interpretation of the scene from the story owes much to his experience in Italy. The muscular nudes reflect his exposure to works by Michelangelo, while the composition of the drawing in Lille is clearly indebted to that of Raphael's *Entombment* in the Galleria Borghese, Rome.

WMG

1 See Berger, 1955, p. 81, no. 56, ill.

2 *The Murder of Fualdès*; see Berger, 1955, p. 81, no. 55, ill.; Rosenberg, 1990-1, p. 29, ill., no. 76, ill.

3 *The Escape of the Assassins of Fualdès*, Inv. no. 1389. See Berger, 1955, p. 81, no. 59, ill.; Rosenberg, 1990-1, p. 186, fig. 2.

4 For the whole series, see Berger, 1955, pp. 80–81, nos. 54–59, ill.

5 See Eitner, 1983, pp. 156–57, fig. 144 (*Fualdès Dragged into the House of Bancal*), p. 342 n. 63.

PROVENANCE

Gift of M. Lehoux, 1883.

EXHIBITIONS

London–Cambridge–Birmingham–Glasgow, 1974–75, no. 42; Paris, 1991–92-1, no. 166.

LITERATURE

Clément, 1879-1, p. 364, no. 165; Pluchart, 1889, no. 1395; Rosenthal, 1905, p. 168; Trévise, 1924, p. 301; Courthion and Cailler, 1947, p. 186; Huyghe, 1948, p. 173, pl. 23; Berger, 1955, pp. 28–29, 55, 81, no. 57, ill.; Aimé-Azam, 1956, pp. 162, 342; Del Guercio, 1963, p. 148, fig. 163; Eitner, 1972, fig. T; Oursel, 1974-2, no. 42, pl. 77; Eitner, 1983, pp. 156, 159, fig. 147, p. 342 n. 62; Rosenberg, 1990-1, p. 186, fig. 1; Michel, in Paris, 1991–92-1, no. 166, ill. 211.

EUGÈNE DELACROIX

French

Charenton–Saint-Maurice 1798–1863 Paris

---

84   *The Abduction of Rebecca*

Pen and brown ink, squared in white chalk,
10 3/16 x 7 15/16 in. (25.9 x 20.2 cm.)

Inv. Pluchart 1261

This vigorous drawing is a study for *The Abduction of Rebecca* (fig. 1), now in the Metropolitan Museum.[1] The painting illustrates an episode from chapter 32 of Sir Walter Scott's *Ivanhoe*. Locksley (Robin Hood) and King Richard have sacked Sir Reginald Front-de-Boeuf's castle, Torquilstone, rescuing Ivanhoe. Rebecca, however, is abducted from the castle on the orders of the Templar Sir Brian de Bois-Guilbert, who appears at the far right in Delacroix's composition. In the foreground, Rebecca is shown being carried off on horseback by two of the Templar's Saracen slaves.

The painting is signed and dated 1846 and was exhibited in the Salon that year. There, it was criticized by some for its sloppy draftsmanship but praised by others, including Baudelaire, for the expressive intensity of Delacroix's palette. In 1888, the picture was acquired by David C. Lyall of Brooklyn, New York, and some fifteen years later it was purchased by the Metropolitan Museum, thus becoming one of the first works by Delacroix to enter an American public collection.

The drawing corresponds quite closely to the painting, although the castle is farther to the right and somewhat lower in the study than in the finished work. The still life in the foreground of the painting is also missing from the present sheet. Two other studies for the painting, both executed in graphite, are in the Musée du Louvre, Paris: One is a drawing for the entire composition, similar to the sheet in Lille but freer in execution;[2] the other is a fragmentary sketch for the three figures in the foreground.[3]

In 1858, Delacroix executed a second painting of this subject (Paris, Musée du Louvre).[4] The later version differs from the one in New York in that the castle looms larger in the composition, and Bois-Guilbert himself is shown carrying Rebecca.   WMG

1 See Baetjer, 1980, I, p. 46, III, p. 555, ill.; Johnson, 1981–89, III, no. 284, IV, pl. 102.

FIGURE 1. Eugène Delacroix. *The Abduction of Rebecca*. 1846. Oil on canvas. The Metropolitan Museum of Art, New York. Wolfe Fund, 1903, Catherine Lorillard Wolfe Collection

2 Département des Arts Graphiques, Inv. no. RF 3704. See Sérullaz, 1984, I, no. 367, ill.

3 Département des Arts Graphiques, Inv. no. RF 3705. See Sérullaz, 1984, I, no. 368, ill.

4 See Johnson, 1981–89, III, no. 326, IV, pl. 103. A preparatory drawing for this version of the painting is in the Département des Arts Graphiques of the Louvre (Inv. no. RF 9529); Sérullaz, 1984, I, no. 472, ill.

PROVENANCE

Eugène Delacroix (Lugt Suppl. 838 a); Posthumous sale of the contents of Delacroix's studio, Paris, Hôtel Drouot, February 22–27, 1864, no. 354; Gift of the baron de Laage, sometime between 1864 and 1889.

EXHIBITIONS

Paris, 1963-1, no. 358; Bern, 1963–64, no. 193; Kyoto–Tokyo, 1969, no. D 22; London–Cambridge–Birmingham–Glasgow, 1974–75, no. 30.

LITERATURE

Gonse, 1877, p. 92; Robaut, 1885, no. 973; Pluchart, 1889, no. 1261; Meier-Graefe, 1922, p. 172, ill.; Roger-Marx, 1933, pl. 46; Sérullaz, 1963-1, under no. 355; Sérullaz, 1963-2, p. 34, ill.; Oursel, 1974-2, no. 30, pl. 83; Johnson, 1981–89, III, p. 112, under no. 284; Sérullaz, 1984, I, under no. 367.

PIERRE PUVIS DE CHAVANNES

French

Lyons 1824–1898 Paris

---

85 *Le sommeil*

Conté crayon and oil paint on cream-colored paper,
14 1/2 x 22 7/8 in. (36.9 x 58 cm.)

Signed in Conté crayon (at the bottom left):
Puvis Ch . . . .

Inv. no. 1358 *bis*

Pierre Puvis de Chavannes is best known for his large-scale works, and during the second half of the nineteenth century he was the leading muralist in France. The present drawing appears to be the definitive study for *Le sommeil*, a painting on canvas that is now in the Musée des Beaux-Arts, Lille.[1] The picture is signed and dated 1867 and was shown in the Salon that year.

The subject was inspired by a passage from Virgil's *Aeneid* (II: 268–269): "Tempus erat, quo prima quies mortalibus aegris / incipit" ("It was the hour when for weary mortals their first rest begins"). The artist's intention was not to illustrate Virgil's text, since the lines quoted in the *livret* of the Salon refer to the slumber of the Trojan people after they brought the wooden horse of the Greeks inside the walls of their city. For Puvis, however, the passage evokes the untroubled sleep of weary men and women of all ages, here seen in a mysterious moonlit landscape.

Numerous preparatory drawings for the painting survive, including four other studies in Lille.[2] The Musée des Beaux-Arts also possesses an oil sketch on canvas, which differs substantially from the finished work.[3] A pen-and-wash study for the entire composition, in the Metropolitan Museum (see fig. 1),[4] is inscribed in Latin with the relevant passage from the *Aeneid*; the Museum's drawing corresponds very closely to the painting and to the present oil sketch on paper, which may have been among the last studies executed for *Le sommeil*. The Metropolitan Museum also owns a reduced replica of the painting.[5]

WMG

1 Inv. no. 625. See Foucart, in Paris–Ottawa, 1976–77, no. 63, ill.

2 One is illustrated by Foucart, in Paris–Ottawa, 1976–77, no. 66. For other preparatory drawings for *Le sommeil*, see Foucart, in Paris–Ottawa, 1976–77, p. 88, under no. 63, nos. 67–69, ill.

3 Inv. no. 1722. See Foucart, in Paris–Ottawa, 1976–77, no. 65, ill.; Scottez-De Wambrechies, in Brejon and Scottez, 1991, no. 41, colorpl.

4 Rogers Fund, 1909, 10.45.19. See Foucart, in Paris–Ottawa, 1976–77, p. 88, under no. 63.

5 Bequest of Theodore M. Davis, 1915, Theodore M. Davis Collection, 30.95.253. See Baetjer, 1980, I, p. 145, III, p. 586, ill.; Foucart, in Paris–Ottawa, 1976–77, p. 88, under no. 63.

EXHIBITION
Yokohama–Hokkaido–Osaka–Yamaguchi, 1991–92, no. 76.

LITERATURE
Scottez-De Wambrechies, in Brejon and Scottez, 1991, no. 76, ill.

FIGURE 1. Pierre Puvis de Chavannes. *Le sommeil*. Drawing. The Metropolitan Museum of Art, New York. Rogers Fund, 1909

JOACHIM WTEWAEL

Dutch

Utrecht 1566–1638 Utrecht

---

86   *The Raising of Lazarus*

Pen and brown ink, with wash, 12 x 16 5/8 in.
(30.5 x 42.2 cm.)

Inv. no. W 3307-969-3

This highly accomplished drawing is in some sense a "preparatory study" for Wtewael's painting in Lille (see cat. no. 11).[1] However, it differs from several of the drawings by Wtewael that have been called preparatory studies in that the execution reveals not the slightest hesitation in composition or in the rendering of details, there is less shading with wash than usual, and the artist employed a system of hatching with parallel lines in discrete areas that creates an almost diagrammatic effect, specifically in Christ's cloak and in the open grave.[2] These qualities suggest that the drawing was made at the end of a preparatory process and is in fact a finished statement, or *modello*, for presentation to a patron. Upon approval, the drawing could have been squared for transfer to the much larger canvas support. In this case, Wtewael made substantial revisions and additions to the composition, the most important of which were noted in the discussion of catalogue number 11.

The date of the drawing would probably be very close to that of the painting, which is considered here to be about 1600. The drawing's somewhat more mannered style need not be explained by chronological distance; with respect to line the stylistic distinction is partly dependent upon the differences in medium. The influence of Abraham Bloemaert, through Jan Muller's engraving (see fig. 1 in cat. no. 11), is also a factor—in particular, with regard to the "inversion," as it is often termed, in the scale of primary and secondary figures. It may be significant, however, that the gesticulating figure to the left in Bloemaert's painting, whom the artist equipped with a spade, is closer to the corresponding figure in Wtewael's painting than to the one in the drawing.[3] Additional sources and less-finished preparatory drawings must have contributed also to the creation of this sophisticated work.

WL

1 The drawing is so described in Lowenthal, 1986, p. 88.

2 Compare Lowenthal, 1986, plates 6, 12, 13, 29, 34, all of which are called preparatory studies on pp. 83, 87, 87, 99, 102, respectively. Two drawings differ substantially from the finished work (see figs. 11–13). The extensively washed drawings in Stockholm and in Florence for paintings in Stuttgart and in The Hague (see Lowenthal, 1986, figs. 26–29) would appear to be preparatory studies in the usual sense. A drawing in Oslo, squared for transfer, was presumably for the version of the *Judgment of Paris* in Stuttgart (see Lowenthal, 1986, figs. 33, 34). In these drawings Wtewael rather thoroughly works out the shading that will model figures and distinguish spaces in the final paintings. A proper study of Wtewael's drawings and their function remains to be written.

3 Spear, 1965, pp. 69–70 n. 13, fig. 3, considers this figure to have been derived from an engraving after Federico Zuccaro's *Raising of Lazarus* in the Grimani Chapel of San Francesco della Vigna, Venice (as noted by Lowenthal, 1986, p. 88).

PROVENANCE
Purchased from Paul Prouté, Paris, 1969.

LITERATURE
Lowenthal, 1986, pp. 83, under no. A-4, 87, under no. A-9, 88, under no. A-10 (the Lille painting), pl. 15.

JACOB JORDAENS

Flemish

Antwerp 1593–1678 Antwerp

---

87   *The Descent from the Cross*

Pen and brown ink, and brown wash, with underdrawing
in black chalk, 7 5/8 x 4 7/8 in. (19.5 x 12.3 cm.)

Inv. no. 963-31

This quick pen sketch after Rubens's altarpiece in Lille (see
cat. no. 1) was made by Jordaens about 1617. The drawing's
purpose is clearly not to record the composition but to absorb
its ideas, which Jordaens varies slightly yet deliberately.
Christ's left arm has evidently fallen to his side and the figure
to the upper right has straightened somewhat, as if his still-
extended hand has just released its burden. The other figure
at the top of the cross extends his right—not his left—arm, a
gesture that recalls the figure in the same place in Rubens's
Antwerp *Descent* (fig. 1 in cat. no. 1), where, however, he is the
younger not the older man. Again Jordaens seems to suggest
that Christ's body has fallen free. Indeed, Christ's back is
bent at a greater angle than in Rubens's painting; the Virgin's right hand now extends under Christ's arm, as if lend-
ing support, and Mary Magdalene has sunk lower to the
ground. That Jordaens wished to concentrate on these different reactions may be indicated also by the elimination of
Mary Cleophas. The figure of Saint John appears to be
naked to the waist, more upright, and more heroic, as if at the
crucial moment he became a match for the massive, shirtless
Roman just below Christ in Rubens's *Raising of the Cross*
(Antwerp Cathedral). These significant departures from
Rubens's composition in such a comparatively slight sketch
reveal that Jordaens's rapid pen strokes responded to an even
quicker mind.

WL

PROVENANCE
Pierre Dubaut, Paris; Ludwig Burchard (1886–1960), London; Matthiesen Gallery, London, 1963; acquired from the Matthiesen Gallery
by the Musée des Beaux-Arts, 1963.

EXHIBITIONS
Berlin, 1964, no. 67; Antwerp–Rotterdam, 1966–67, no. 9.

LITERATURE
D'Hulst, 1956, pp. 74, 305, 321, no. 11, fig. 36; Białostocki, 1964, pp.
516–17, fig. 11; Held, 1967, p. 96; d'Hulst, 1974, I, no. A 40, fig. 45;
d'Hulst, 1982, p. 78, fig. 46.

JACOB JORDAENS

Flemish

Antwerp 1593–1678 Antwerp

---

88   *Two Cows*

Red chalk, heightened with black and white chalk,
9 x 15 1/4 in. (22.9 x 38.6 cm.)

Inscribed (at the top): *Witge [plekt]* ? [white spotted] ?

Inv. no. W-3957

The cows in this drawing recently acquired by the Musée des
Beaux-Arts resemble two of the animals Jordaens depicted in
the *Study of Cows* (cat. no. 5), the oil sketch also in Lille. This
similarity, and that shared by other related works, suggests
that the present drawing was probably made about the same
time as the oil sketch, which some scholars place in the 1620s
but which may also date from about 1630–35.

Jordaens did represent cows in related poses during the
early 1620s, as in a compositional sketch for an Adoration of
the Shepherds (on the art market in 1980–81),[1] and in a pen-
and-ink drawing, *Homage to Ceres*, in the Courtauld Institute
Galleries, London.[2] In the former drawing the cow is similar
to the one at the left in the present sketch—but in reverse—
and the head is held even lower, in apparent deference to the
Christ Child in Mary's lap. In the Courtauld Institute drawing the pose is the same as in the Lille study but the head is
lifted and turned so that the cow faces the viewer. This was
not the first time that Jordaens depicted an animal from such
a low and diagonal view from the rear: See, for example, the
goat in *The Mocking of Ceres*, a pen-and-ink sketch dating from
about 1618–20 in the Musée des Beaux-Arts, Orléans.[3]

A cow very like the one at the left in the Lille study, but
with a less rounded back, higher shoulder blades, horns, and
a more mature head, is found in Jordaens's *Mercury and Argus*,
a canvas of the early 1620s in the Musée des Beaux-Arts,
Lyons.[4] However, support for dating the Lille drawing to
about a decade later comes from evidence of renewed interest
in this particular problem of foreshortening, as seen in the
cows studied from the same angle in two drawings of the
Adoration of the Shepherds, one in the Graphische Sammlung Albertina, Vienna, and the other in the National Gallery of Scotland, Edinburgh.[5] The most persuasive indication of an early 1630s date is provided by the surprisingly
similar description of a pig in a drawing, *Two Pigs* (fig. 1), in
the Amsterdams Historisch Museum, Amsterdam,[6] which

may explain the oddly porcine appearance of the young cow at the left in the present sketch. The Amsterdam drawing is in the same medium, also with white heightening, and like the Lille drawing it bears a color notation in red chalk. A ground plane was added in watercolor below the pig at the left, but not for the other, which is drawn in profile looking to the right and with incomplete legs. The latter animal was reversed when the two pigs were placed in the background of a painting dating from the early 1630s, the *Odysseus Threatening Circe* (formerly New York, Collection Mrs. Ruth K. Palitz).[7] The most comparable use of either cow in the Lille drawing—predictably, the one at the left—occurs in the *Ulysses Taking Leave of Circe*, a painting of about 1640 in the Museo de Arte, Ponce, Puerto Rico,[8] but it would be rash to insist upon the connection given the fecundity of farmyard life in Jordaens's "Odysseus" paintings and tapestry designs alone,[9] not to mention the rest of his oeuvre.[10]   WL

1 See d'Hulst, 1974, I, no. A 66, fig. 75; sold, Amsterdam, Sotheby's, November 17, 1980, no. 70; London, Baskett & Day, 1981.

2 See d'Hulst, 1974, I, no. A 67, fig. 76.

3 See d'Hulst, 1974, I, no. A 49, fig. 56.

4 See d'Hulst, 1982, p. 108, fig. 74.

5 See d'Hulst, 1974, I, nos. A 94, A 95, figs. 104, 105.

6 See d'Hulst, 1974, I, no. A 107, fig. 119; d'Hulst, 1982, p. 145, fig. 106.

7 See d'Hulst, 1982, p. 144, fig. 105.

8 See Jaffé, 1968, no. 58, fig. 58; cited by d'Hulst, 1982, p. 144.

9 See d'Hulst, 1982, pp. 142–48, 296–97.

10 For example, see d'Hulst, 1974, II, nos. A 321, A 373, figs. 338, 392, and copies after Jordaens's drawings, such as nos. C 23, C 54, C 61, C 75, C 78, figs. 500, 537, 553, 556.

PROVENANCE

Skippe Collection; P. & D. Colnaghi & Co., New York, 1988; purchased from Colnaghi, 1988.

FIGURE 1. Jacob Jordaens. *Two Pigs*. Black and red chalk, with traces of white body color and watercolor. Amsterdams Historisch Museum, Amsterdam

Appendix: What Does the Future Hold for Museums?

MARC FUMAROLI

In 1891, the concept of the Museum was commonplace whether in the Vienna of the Hapsburgs or in Republican Lille, in Paris or in New York. All that was necessary was for it to be implemented and then lavishly elaborated upon. Yet today, doubts are setting in. Questions are being asked, especially in the large cities, as to the purpose of these enormous "apparatuses" for exhibiting works of art, which are being invaded by more and more massive crowds of tourists for whom such "intellectual recreation" can only be hasty and superficial at best. Has the education of our citizens through exposure to works of art—such as was envisioned by the leaders of the French Revolution—been replaced by merely pandering to the jaded curiosity and banal pastimes of the masses? An ever-widening gap exists between the technicality of increasingly specialized curators behind the scenes and the monotonous uproar of the hordes of tourists and their guides in the galleries. One of the fortunate aspects of provincial museums today, such as the one in Lille, is that they are spared the worst overflow of crowds that plagues museums in the major capitals. Yet the same question arises for all museums: What is their function now, two centuries after their birth? Under what conditions can they hope to persist without reneging on their promise? To deny it would mean to jeopardize their original purpose, with which they were charged by their founders, the heirs of the Enlightenment: to develop an eye, an intellect, and a taste for the arts, first in the artist, and then in the public. To educate, to teach, is perhaps not incompatible with tourist "culture" and activities aimed at the masses, but the difficulties, and even the contradictions, have become apparent. Museums today are faced with a new challenge, and if it is not adequately met, then the very soundness of the Museum as an institution will be called into question.

As early as 1925, long before this challenge was recognized, Paul Valéry, in an essay entitled "The Problem of Museums," which has remained largely unknown, launched a radical critique of the museums of his day, such as they were then, the tranquil and undisputed heirs of the Revolution, improved upon in the nineteenth century. Paul Valéry was not a historian—he even had an aversion to history—but his description of the Museum, filtered through the eyes of a poet, puts down certain of its features, which can also be explained by history. Valéry began rather abruptly, "I do not like museums very much. There are many admirable ones, but none that is delightful. These notions of classification, conservation, and public usefulness—which are obvious and appropriate—have very little to do with delight."

This "delight" is far from the conceptual aesthetics of Winckelmann, Baumgarten, or Hegel. Valéry is restating an idea first voiced by David, as the art critic Étienne-Jean Delécluze relates: "Viewing masterpieces in the Museum might produce scholars or Winckelmanns, but an artist? Never!"

For the poet, such "delight" is incompatible with assembling objects or works of art, however beautiful they may be, in an official place, subject to administrative and disciplinary regulations, even if justified by an educational ideal. What does Valéry mean by "delight"? For him, it is the quintessential experience of beauty, intimate and unforeseeable, inspiring, like love or happiness. There is something incommensurable between order in art and the political, administrative, ideological, and technical order of the Museum. With a single word, Valéry questions the civic concept of the Fine Arts as formulated first under the Enlightenment and then during the Revolution, and which the modern State has inherited. He echoes the indignant criticism that Quatremère de Quincy expressed on the occasion of the pillaging of Italy—a living museum in spite of itself—for the benefit of a monstrous Museum filled with scattered fragments, a veritable morgue of the arts:

> Soon, I no longer know what I have come to do in this waxen desert, which resembles a temple and a salon, a graveyard and a school. Have I come to educate myself, to seek instruction, to fulfill a duty, or to do what is expected of me? Or is it not just some rather peculiar kind of exercise, a promenade strangely impeded by beautiful things, hindered at every turn by masterpieces, left and right, among which one must navigate like a drunkard between bars. . . . How tiresome, I say to myself, and how barbaric! All of this is inhuman. None of this is pure. What a paradox, this assemblage of wonders, independent but at odds, and which are even like mortal enemies when they are not alike. . . . Something quite insane results from the proximity of these lifeless phantoms. They are jealous of one another and they vie for the gaze that acknowledges their existence. From every corner they call upon my undivided attention. They trigger the live spot within that draws the body toward what attracts it. . . . The ear could never stand to hear ten orchestras at once. The mind can neither follow nor conduct several distinct operations at the same time, and there is no such thing as simultaneous reasoning. Yet, the eye, because of the mobility of its field of vision and its instantaneous perception, is obliged to take in a portrait and a seascape, a kitchen scene and a triumph, figures in the most varied conditions and dimensions; not only that, but it must

absorb in the same glance [color] harmonies and manners of painting that are completely unrelated. Just as the sense of sight is offended by this abuse of space that we call a collection, so is the intelligence no less overworked by a confined group of important works. The more beautiful they are, the more exceptional they are as products of human ambition, and the more they have to be kept distinct. They are rare objects whose creators would have liked very much for them to remain unique.

Had Paul Valéry read Quatremère de Quincy? His reservations about the Museum, as a poet, reiterate, after one hundred and thirty years, the opposition between artistic sensitivity and the incarceration of art in the Museum, upon which the polemics of Quatremère's *Lettres* had been based in 1796. Yet, in 1925, eighteenth-century Italy was no longer the only homeland of Beauty for Valéry: "I do not believe that ancient Egypt, China, or Greece, which were wise and refined civilizations, ever made use of this system of juxtaposing works that devour one another. They did not arrange incompatible objects of pleasure together with registration numbers, and according to abstract principles." The poet concludes with an observation that Quatremère would surely have approved of: "I suddenly perceived a vague clarity. A response arose within me, detached itself little by little from my impressions, and demanded to be expressed. Painting and Sculpture, the demon of Explanation tells me, are abandoned children. Their mother is dead, their mother, Architecture. As long as she was alive, she gave them their place, their function, their limits. They were refused the freedom to wander. They had their space, their particular light, their subjects, their alliances. . . . As long as she was alive, they knew what they wanted. . . . Farewell, this thought says to me, I shall go no further."

To go further would have meant to recognize openly that architecture, the supreme art of the great religious civilizations and, for them, the metaphor of the sacred and cosmic order underlying the passage of time and the world of appearances, had not survived the triumph of modern Reason. The "Great Chain of Being" that the temples and palaces had symbolized—giving meaning to the paintings, sculpture, and art objects that adorned them—had been broken. The French Revolution, in turning this metaphysical rupture into a political act, had not been content to overthrow the theological structure of monarchy by divine right: It had interrupted the spontaneous generation of forms that was in accord with this structure and with its harmonic counterpart—the sacred order of the world. Hegel, summing up the consequences of the French Revolution, spoke of the "end of the artistic period." Indeed, henceforth Beauty no longer was required to link the visible order with the divine and invisible; it was no longer indispensable everywhere that men work, pray, and converse. Beauty retreated, withdrawing into the rarefied works that preserve her memory. These works must now be isolated, grouped together, exhibited, and preserved in the name of learning and enjoyment. In the modern world, the function of the Museum is to guarantee the commemoration of Beauty a sort of stage, very formal yet marginal at the same time. The nineteenth century witnessed the slow death of the traditional academies and craftsmen—the two surviving roots of the arts under the Ancien Régime. It saw the gradual shrinking of the space given over to art and craftsmanship, as this narrow and circumscribed space—the Museum—became the object of a more pompous official cult. The nineteenth century also saw the emergence for the first time of the "*artiste maudit*." These painters—from Manet to Cézanne, van Gogh to Picasso—owed everything to the Museum; their greatest dream was to be admitted into it. Marcel Duchamp, a master of black humor, called attention to the exile of art in the Museum with his "practical jokes" that he called "Ready-mades." The tragic sense of destiny that the modern world reserves for art is as strong in Duchamp as in Valéry, although it manifests itself in the work of the poet and in that of the humorist through very different means of expression. Exhibiting a urinal, with an inventory number and a label, in a museum was Duchamp's way of satirizing both the Museum as an art "reservation" (in the sense of an Indian reservation) and the utilitarian and practical nature of our modern society, indifferent to the arts, but all the more eager to conceal this indifference by officially assigning them a place. By the 1930s, the uneasiness of artists vis-à-vis the Museum—their last refuge—was even stronger than it had been when the Museum was born, in 1796.

Ever since then, these qualms seem to have been swallowed up in the triumphant proliferation and increasing success of museums worldwide. The late twentieth century might well be called "the Age of Museums," in the words of Germain Bazin. Museums have become more numerous, much more complete, and are visited far more often than in the nineteenth century. The restoration, preservation, and scientific study of works of art have benefited from advances in technology. The displays of permanent collections or of temporary exhibitions today call upon the resources of lighting technicians and the talents of set designers for theater, opera, and films. Behind the scenes or "on stage," the great modern Museum has become a veritable factory where multi-faceted shows are produced, which, with the aid of massive advertising campaigns, draw an uninterrupted flow of tourists and sightseers. Cafeterias, bookshops, and boutiques, as well as lectures and concerts, have made visiting a museum even more comfortable and appealing: The Museum is a "must" on many an itinerary in our consumer and leisure society.

Paul Valéry could still avail himself of the extreme luxury of criticizing the Museum of the nineteenth century, adopting the terms and the arguments of Quatremère de Quincy, who had been familiar with the arts during the Ancien Régime. Yet, the nineteenth-century Museum, wherever it has survived—still untouched by modern renovations or blatant commercialism—has become, in turn, a threatened work of art, our last palace, our last temple, a harmonious entity that remains very moving for us today. It still presents art objects and architecture according to a unified vision, such as the Beaux-Arts tradition was able to achieve at the beginning of this century, and its stability is in marked contrast to the flood of contemporary art in our modern museums. The last museums of the nineteenth century, precisely because they are out of fashion and frequented in lesser numbers, today stand as familiar and poetic dwellings in which works of art are at home, and where they can be contemplated in relative privacy, without hordes of onlookers. In these museums, for the most part in the provinces, we can rediscover some of the delight offered by the most perfect of them all: the Dulwich Picture Gallery in London. This English collection, a gem of its kind, was created during the French Revolution and the Empire. Neoclassical in style, it was designed by the great architect Sir John Soane, and has become a model for post-Modernism today. There are no crowds at the Dulwich gallery, but only silence, and illumination is provided by windows in the roof, which flood the paintings with natural light. Yet, there is also something vaguely funereal, echoing a pre-Romantic sensibility and at the same time rekindling an idealism and a passion for Beauty. It was refined and delicate sensations such as these that Quatremère de Quincy—after Poussin and Claude, as well as David—sought in the streets and squares of Rome, but which, since the Revolution, one finds in the shelter of the galleries of our art museums. It was this kind of emotion that Proust's Bergotte experienced upon seeing the famous "little section of yellow wall" in Vermeer's *View of Delft* on exhibition at the Jeu de Paume. In the provinces of Europe, but also in the United States—for example, at the Isabella Stewart Gardner Museum or the Kimbell Art Museum—such "chapel-like" museums have remained faithful to or revived nineteenth-century museology, and have thus acquired an incomparable appeal. They are our temples, for peaceful contemplation and meditation. They invite us on a spiritual journey to another world, the world of beautiful and mysterious forms. This is the effect that Dominique de Menil had in mind when she built her austere museum in Houston.

It is in this sense, and because of its relative archaism, that the nineteenth-century Museum—which nourished the great artist-rebels of the time—has become a model and a recourse against the excesses of modern society. These days, such museums can only be found far from the large urban metropolises. Yet, even then, there is the temptation to follow the pattern of the big-city museum, to go the way of the "grand spectacle" or of the commercial gallery, whose only aim seems to be to attract the largest crowds. This purpose subverts and denies the one that the inventors of the Museum, the descendants of the Enlightenment, envisioned for it: the awakening of artistic genius through contact with works of genius, and the development of artistic taste through the careful comparison of masterpieces. How can these democratic and civic tasks still be fulfilled today if they must be subordinated to such ephemeral needs as the wholesale satisfaction of indeterminate touristic obligations or the mechanical and sheep-like curiosity of museum goers? How can any artistic vocations be cultivated or the eye trained amidst a hubbub reminiscent of the subway or the public square, which, more often than not, assaults the visitor who comes in good faith to the galleries of our major museums? It should be recognized, however, that from the very beginning there was an element of abstraction in the idea of the Museum, an impersonal side, like a bureaucratic and scientific reserve, which could produce a chilling, intimidating, and ultimately sterilizing effect. Another temptation for the modern museum, apart from mass consumption, is excessive pedantry. The philosophers of the Enlightenment formulated the educational mission of the Museum on the notion of "genius" and on the selection of "masterpieces" that would make genius contagious or, at the least, simply evident. The erudition of the modern art historian is directed toward turning the museum into a scientific reflection of his or her competence and professional advancement. A commercial gallery on the one hand, the Museum is thus threatened with becoming a clinic or a place for scholarly dissection on the other. In such a setting, neither taste, nor pleasure, nor talent can find any outlet. Valéry already feared for these "delights." Despite the influx of noisy and bustling crowds, they have not succeeded in bringing life to the museum. Such large numbers of people are even more abstract and alien to art than the bureaucratic and scientific silence derided by the poet. How, then, to remedy this peril? While remaining faithful to its original mission, how can the Museum be saved from its success and restored to a vital role in the world of tomorrow?

First it must resist the temptation to be a unique model. We are no longer living in the Napoleonic era. The monumental, encyclopedic, and universal Museum, visited by all of humanity, may have its justification in a large metropolis, but it cannot be repeated everywhere, even on a lesser scale. The time has come for a diversity of museums—in size, atmosphere, and contents. Those cities fortunate enough to have a small or a medium-sized museum with a history, or "pedigree," should modernize it, to be sure, but without violating its own traditions and proportions, and retaining its individual spirit. An old, or relatively old, museum should be conceived of as a work of art to be preserved with equal care and moderation, restoring its basic form when necessary, for it responded to a tangible need for unity, of which artists are the best interpreters. Accordingly, even the most majestic museums have lessons to learn from their more modest counterparts: The more they are able to present attractive collections and in moderate proportions, the more they will succeed in diversifying their public and in avoiding the danger of overflowing with vast quantities of art and visitors. The chapels must be cared for even more than the naves. What is most distressing is to see a lonely crowd traipsing through a space intended for a friendly encounter, a private confrontation, or a lovers' rendezvous. After having succumbed to the temptation to adapt to a society governed by the conspicuous consumption of the leisure classes, the Museum must now strive to recover its initial purpose: to promote Beauty. It will come about that much more easily if the museum is small or medium sized. The future belongs to the provincial museum.

However, reviewing its ties to the "École" does not mean that the museum must become a school. Nothing is more disturbing to the serenity of works of art (which are unique and living entities, not inanimate objects), or to the love for them that one hopes to instill in the public, than the pedagogical double-talk that, in addition to the commotion of the crowds today, all too often makes visits to a museum mechanical and claustrophobic experiences. Everything that contributes to these massive and inattentive processions of visitors works against the institution's basic purpose. Perhaps it would be useful, at this point, to recall that the word *museum*, so cold and abstract in its Latin form, had other connotations in the original Greek, *Mouseion*: It signified the temple of the Muses, daughters of Memory, lovers of silence, contemplation, and poetic enthusiasm. It is the task of both the architect and the museum curator to give the works of art entrusted to their care and safekeeping the same treatment required by a living person, each one of whom is unique. The daylight and the space around the objects—whether majestic or intimate—must be adjusted according to what suits them and is conducive to their own well-being while also satisfying the visitor's imagination and appetite for beauty. As much as a science, this task is also an act of love and a sign of taste, and indirectly may well be a more effective educational tool than all the lectures and spectacular and costly presentations at a museum's disposal.

On the other hand, school, insofar as it precedes the Museum in our experience, can and should see to it that a museum visit is as rich an experience as possible. Education is out of place in the galleries and in front of works of art. A trip to a museum, to the greatest degree possible, should once more become an event, a unique and intense encounter. It can, of course, be prepared for long in advance in school, through the study of art history, and even through the disciplines of drawing, engraving, and painting. For this preliminary education to succeed, there must be a collaboration and an exchange of information among museum curators and teachers, university professors, and instructors in specialized institutions. The preparation for a museum visit is best addressed in study rooms and seminars—namely, in a variety of scholarly surroundings. Such coordination of activity on a grand scale would make the museum experience (and even work in a museum, such as the copying of Old Masters, which is now back in fashion) a high point in a long cycle of learning and reflection. It is under these conditions that the face-to-face encounter with both the actual reality and the mystery of beautiful objects can truly become a revelation.

Museums, of course, cannot be closed to tourism, but, as was the practice of the Commission des arts, under the Convention, certain hours may be set aside solely for artists, students, or art lovers who have provided sufficient proof of their studiousness, passion, and perseverance. The massive increase in the number of visitors to museums is no substitute for policy. Having been created for the purpose of instruction, the Museum must uphold this educational principle as the criterion against which it measures its choices, and it must apply its best efforts to this task, even if it winds up reaching only a minority of its public. Among the Museum's concerns, art must take precedence over the reception and dispersal of crowds. There is a great future ahead for the Museum—this grand institution of the Age of Enlightenment, put into practice during the French Revolution—but only on the condition that it does not betray the ideals of its founders. Museums must be able to withstand unscathed the flood of mass culture, or else they will become just another hobby, like any other pastime. May the Museum resist, and face the opposition with equal measures of knowledge, serenity, and taste.

List of Exhibitions

Catalogues listed in the Bibliography by author are cross-referenced below.

Amsterdam, 1926
"Exposition rétrospective d'art français," Musée de l'État.

Amsterdam, 1971
"Hollandse schilderijen uit Franse musea," Rijksmuseum.

Amsterdam–Brussels–Lille, 1967–68
"Dessins italiens du Musée de Lille," Amsterdam, Rijksmuseum; Brussels, Bibliothèque Royale de Belgique; and Lille, Palais des Beaux-Arts (*see* Châtelet, 1967).

Antwerp–Rotterdam, 1966–67
"Tekeningen von Jacob Jordaens," Antwerp, Rubenshuis; and Rotterdam, Museum Boymans-van Beuningen.

Augsburg–Cleveland, 1975–76
"Johann Liss," Augsburg, Rathaus; and Cleveland, Cleveland Museum of Art.

Avignon, 1989
"La mort de Bara," Musée Calvet.

Basel, 1921
"Exposition de peinture française," Kunsthalle.

Berlin, 1964
"Meisterwerke aus dem Museum in Lille," Schloss Charlottenburg.

Berlin, 1966
"Deutsche Maler und Zeichner des 17. Jahrhunderts," Schloss Charlottenburg.

Bern, 1963–64
"Eugène Delacroix," Kunstmuseum.

Bremen, 1964
"Eugène Delacroix," Kunsthalle.

Bremen, 1977–78
"Zurück zur Natur," Kunsthalle.

Brussels, 1910
"Exposition d'art ancien: l'art belge au XVIIᵉ siècle," Musée de Cinquantenaire.

Brussels, 1947–48
"De David à Cézanne," Palais des Beaux-Arts.

Brussels, 1954–55
"L'Europe humaniste," Palais des Beaux-Arts.

Brussels, 1963
"Le siècle de Bruegel," Musées Royaux des Beaux-Arts.

Brussels, 1965
"Le siècle de Rubens," Musées Royaux des Beaux-Arts.

Cologne, 1990–91
"Raffael und die Zeichenkunst der italienischen Renaissance: Meisterzeichnungen aus dem Musée des Beaux-Arts in Lille und aus eigenem Bestand," Wallraf-Richartz-Museum, Graphische Sammlung.

Dordrecht–Leeuwarden, 1988–89
"Meesterlijk vee: nederlandse veeschilders 1600–1900," Dordrecht, Dordrechts Museum; and Leeuwarden, Fries Museum.

Edinburgh–London, 1964
"Delacroix: An Exhibition of Paintings, Drawings and Lithographs Sponsored by the Edinburgh Festival Society and Arranged by the Arts Council of Great Britain in Association with the Royal Scottish Academy," Edinburgh, Royal Scottish Academy; and London, Royal Academy of Arts.

Florence, 1954
"Mostra di disegni dei primi manieristi italiani," Gabinetto Disegni e Stampe degli Uffizi.

Florence, 1970
"Disegni di Raffaello e di altri italiani del Museo di Lille," Gabinetto Disegni e Stampe degli Uffizi (*see* Châtelet, 1970-2).

Florence, 1986–87
"Il Seicento fiorentino: arte a Firenze da Ferdinando I a Cosimo III," Palazzo Strozzi.

Ghent, 1950
"Quarante chefs-d'oeuvre du Musée de Lille," Museum voor Schone Kunsten.

Ghent, 1954
"Roelandt Savery," Musée des Beaux-Arts.

Grenoble–Rennes–Bordeaux, 1988–89
"Laurent de La Hyre, 1606–1656: l'homme et l'oeuvre," Grenoble, Musée de Grenoble; Rennes, Musée des Beaux-Arts et d'Archéologie; and Bordeaux, Musée des Beaux-Arts (*see* Rosenberg and Thuillier, 1988).

The Hague–Paris, 1970
"Goya," The Hague, Mauritshuis; and Paris, Orangerie des Tuileries.

Helsinki–Brussels, 1952–53
"P. P. Rubens: esquisses, dessins, gravures," Helsinki, Ateneumin Taidemuseo; and Brussels, Musées Royaux des Beaux-Arts.

Kortrijk, 1976
"Roeland Savery," Stedelijk Museum voor Schone Kunsten.

Kyoto–Tokyo, 1969
"Eugène Delacroix," Kyoto, Municipal Museum; and Tokyo, National Museum.

Lille, 1889
"Exposition historique du Centenaire de 1789," Mairie de Lille.

Lille, 1933
"Cent tableaux du Musée de Lille," Musée des Beaux-Arts.

Lille, 1951
"Lille accroissements," Musée des Beaux-Arts.

Lille, 1961
"Collection J. B. Wicar du Musée de Lille: dessins de Raphael," Musée des Beaux-Arts.

Lille, 1968
"Au temps du roi soleil: les peintres de Louis XIV (1660–1715)," Palais des Beaux-Arts.

Lille, 1970
"Cent chefs-d'oeuvre du Musée de Lille," Musée des Beaux-Arts.

Lille, 1974
"La Collection d'Alexandre Leleux," Musée des Beaux-Arts.

Lille, 1981
"Donation d'Antoine Brasseur," Musée des Beaux-Arts.

Lille, 1983-1
"Autour de David: dessins néo-classiques du Musée des Beaux-Arts de Lille," Musée des Beaux-Arts.

Lille, 1983-2
"Dessins de Raphaël du Musée des Beaux-Arts de Lille," Musée des Beaux-Arts.

Lille, 1984
"Le Chevalier Wicar: peintre, dessinateur et collectionneur lillois," Musée des Beaux-Arts.

Lille, 1988–89
"Boilly, 1761–1845: un grand peintre français de la Révolution à la Restauration," Musée des Beaux-Arts.

Lille, 1989–90
"Renaissance et baroque: dessins italiens du Musée de Lille," Musée des Beaux-Arts (see Brejon de Lavergnée, 1989-2).

Lille–Arras–Dunkirk, 1972–73
"Peinture hollandaise," Lille, Musée des Beaux-Arts; Arras, Musée d'Arras; and Dunkirk, Musée des Beaux-Arts.

Lille–Calais–Arras, 1977
"La peinture flamande au temps de Rubens," Lille, Musée des Beaux-Arts; Calais, Musée des Beaux-Arts; and Arras, Musée d'Arras.

Lille–Calais–Arras–Douai, 1975–76
"Peinture française, 1770–1830," Lille, Musée des Beaux-Arts; Calais, Musée des Beaux-Arts; Arras, Musée d'Arras; and Douai, Musée de Douai, La Chartreuse.

Lille–Dunkirk–Valenciennes, 1980
"La peinture française des 17e et 18e siècles," Lille, Musée des Beaux-Arts; Dunkirk, Musée des Beaux-Arts; and Valenciennes, Musée des Beaux-Arts.

London, 1972
"The Age of Neo-Classicism," Royal Academy of Arts and Victoria and Albert Museum.

London–Cambridge–Birmingham–Glasgow, 1974–75
"From Poussin to Puvis de Chavannes: A Loan Exhibition of French Drawings from the Collections of the Musée des Beaux-Arts at Lille," London, Heim Gallery; Cambridge, Fitzwilliam Museum; Birmingham, City Museum and Art Gallery; and Glasgow, Glasgow Art Gallery and Museum (see Oursel, 1974-2).

Los Angeles–Detroit–Philadelphia, 1971–72
"Gericault," Los Angeles, Los Angeles County Museum of Art; Detroit, Detroit Institute of Arts; and Philadelphia, Philadelphia Museum of Art.

Mantua, 1989
"Giulio Romano," Palazzo del Tè and Palazzo Ducale.

Marseilles, 1987
"Sublime indigo," Centre de la Vieille Charité.

Meaux, 1988–89
"De Nicolò dell'Abate à Nicolas Poussin: aux sources du classicisme, 1550–1650," Musée Bossuet.

Montauban, 1967
"Ingres et son temps: exposition organisée pour le centenaire de la mort d'Ingres," Musée Ingres.

Montreal, 1980
"Largillierre and the Eighteenth-Century Portrait," Montreal Museum of Fine Arts (see Rosenfeld, 1980).

Moscow–Saint Petersburg, 1987
"Chefs-d'oeuvre du Musée des Beaux-Arts de Lille," Moscow, Pushkin Museum; and Saint Petersburg, Hermitage.

Orléans–Dunkirk–Rennes, 1979
"Théodore Caruelle d'Aligny (1798–1871) et ses compagnons," Orléans, Musée des Beaux-Arts; Dunkirk, Musée des Beaux-Arts; and Rennes, Musée des Beaux-Arts (see Aubrun, 1979).

Paris, 1855
"Exposition universelle: notice historique et analytique des peintures . . . exposées dans les galeries des portraits historiques au Palais du Trocadéro," Palais du Trocadéro.

Paris, 1860
"Tableaux et dessins de l'école française, principalement du XVIIIe siècle, tirés de collections d'amateurs," Galerie Martinet, 26, boulevard des Italiens.

Paris, 1885
"Exposition Eugène Delacroix au profit de la souscription destinée à élever à Paris un monument à sa mémoire," École Nationale des Beaux-Arts.

Paris, 1907
"Exposition Chardin et Fragonard," Galerie Georges Petit.

Paris, 1913
"David et ses élèves," Palais des Beaux-Arts

Paris, 1929
"Exposition des oeuvres de J. B. S. Chardin," Galerie Pigalle.

Paris, 1930
"Eugène Delacroix: centenaire du romantisme," Musée du Louvre.

Paris, 1937
"Chefs-d'oeuvre de l'art français," Exposition Universelle, Palais National des Arts.

Paris, 1938
"Peintures de Goya des collections de France," Musée de l'Orangerie.

Paris, 1954–55
"Van Gogh et les peintres d'Auvers-sur-Oise," Orangerie des Tuileries.

Paris, 1956-1
"De Giotto à Bellini: les primitifs italiens dans les musées de France," Orangerie des Tuileries (see Laclotte, 1956).

Paris, 1956-2
"De Watteau à Prud'hon," Gazette des Beaux-Arts.

Paris, 1960
"Vincent van Gogh, 1853–1890," Musée Jacquemart-André.

Paris, 1963-1
"Eugène Delacroix (1798–1863): exposition du centenaire," Musée du Louvre (see Sérullaz, 1963-1).

Paris, 1963-2
"Trésors de la peinture espagnole: églises et musées de France," Musée des Arts Décoratifs, Palais du Louvre.

Paris, 1965
"Le décor de la vie privée en Hollande au XVIIe siècle," Institut Néerlandais.

Paris, 1965–66
"Le XVIᵉ siècle européen: peintures et dessins dans les collections publiques françaises," Musée du Petit Palais.

Paris, 1967-1
"La vie en Hollande au XVIIᵉ siècle," Musée des Arts Décoratifs.

Paris, 1967-2
"Les grandes heures de l'Amitié Franco-Suédoise," Hôtel de Rohan.

Paris, 1967–68
"Ingres," Musée du Petit Palais.

Paris, 1970–71
"Le siècle de Rembrandt: tableaux hollandais des collections publiques françaises," Musée du Petit Palais.

Paris, 1971
"Venise au dix-huitième siècle: peintures, dessins et gravures des collections françaises," Orangerie des Tuileries.

Paris, 1973
"Autoportraits de Courbet," Musée du Louvre.

Paris, 1977–78
"Le siècle de Rubens dans les collections publiques françaises," Grand Palais.

Paris, 1982
"Le XVIᵉ siècle florentin au Louvre," Musée du Louvre (see Béguin, 1982).

Paris, 1983–84
"Hommage à Raphaël: Raphaël dans les collections françaises," Grand Palais.

Paris, 1986–87
"Hommage à Andrea del Sarto," Musée du Louvre.

Paris, 1990–91
"Vouet," Grand Palais.

Paris, 1991–92
"Géricault," Grand Palais.

Paris–Cleveland–Boston, 1979
"Chardin, 1699–1779," Paris, Grand Palais; Cleveland, Cleveland Museum of Art; and Boston, Museum of Fine Arts (see Rosenberg, 1979).

Paris–Detroit–New York, 1974–75
"French Painting, 1774–1830: The Age of Revolution," Paris, Grand Palais; Detroit, Detroit Institute of Arts; and New York, The Metropolitan Museum of Art.

Paris–London, 1977–78
"Gustave Courbet (1819–1877)," Paris, Grand Palais; and London, Royal Academy of Arts.

Paris–Milan, 1988–89
"Seicento: le siècle de Caravage dans les collections françaises," Paris, Grand Palais; and Milan, Palazzo Reale.

Paris-Ottawa, 1976–77
"Puvis de Chavannes," Paris, Grand Palais; and Ottawa, National Gallery of Canada.

Paris–Philadelphia–Fort Worth, 1991–92
"Loves of the Gods: Mythological Painting from Watteau to David," Paris, Grand Palais; Philadelphia, Philadelphia Museum of Art; and Fort Worth, Kimbell Art Museum (see Bailey, 1991).

Paris–Versailles, 1989–90
"Jacques-Louis David, 1748–1825," Paris, Musée du Louvre; and Versailles, Musée National du Château.

Pau, 1980
"Vive la vache," Musée des Beaux-Arts.

Philadelphia–Berlin–London, 1984
"Masters of Seventeenth-Century Dutch Genre Painting," Philadelphia, Philadelphia Museum of Art; Berlin, Staatliche Museen Preussischer Kulturbesitz, Gemäldegalerie; and London, Royal Academy of Arts.

Recklinghausen, 1959
"Die Handschrift des Künstlers," Städtische Kunsthalle.

Recklinghausen, 1962
"Idee und Vollendung," Städtische Kunsthalle.

Recklinghausen–Utrecht, 1962
"Miracula Christi," Recklinghausen, Städtische Kunsthalle; and Utrecht, Aartsbisschoppelijk.

Reggio Emilia, 1987–88
"Lelio Orsi, 1511–1587: dipinti e disegni," Teatro Valli.

Rome, 1975–76
"Corot (1796–1875): dipinti e disegni di collezioni francesi," Accademia di Francia in Roma (Villa Medici).

Rome, 1979–80
"Géricault," Accademia di Francia in Roma (Villa Medici).

Rome, 1981–82
"David e Roma," Accademia di Francia in Roma (Villa Medici).

Rome–Milan, 1959–60
"Il disegno francese da Fouquet a Toulouse-Lautrec," Milan, Palazzo Reale; Rome, Palazzo Venezia.

Rotterdam, 1991
"Perspectives: Saenredam and the Architectural Painters of the Seventeenth Century," Museum Boymans-van Beuningen.

San Francisco, 1989
"Gericault, 1791–1824," The Fine Arts Museums of San Francisco, California Palace of the Legion of Honor.

Strasbourg, 1987
"L'amour de l'art: le goût de deux amateurs pour le baroque italien," Musée des Beaux-Arts.

Sydney–Melbourne, 1980–81
"The Revolutionary Decades," Sydney, Art Gallery of New South Wales; and Melbourne, National Gallery of Victoria.

Valenciennes, 1918
"Geborgene Kunstwerke aus dem besetzten Nordfrankreich," Musée de Peinture et de Sculpture.

Washington–Cleveland–Saint Louis–Cambridge–New York, 1952–53
"French Drawings: Masterpieces from Five Centuries," Washington, D.C., National Gallery of Art; Cleveland, Cleveland Museum of Art; Saint Louis, City Art Museum; Cambridge, Fogg Art Museum; and New York, The Metropolitan Museum of Art.

Yokohama–Hokkaido–Osaka–Yamaguchi, 1991–92
"La peinture française au XIXième siècle: le Musée des Beaux-Arts de Lille," Yokohama, Sogo Museum of Art; Hokkaido, Hokkaido Obihiro Museum; Osaka, Museum of Art Kintetsu; and Yamaguchi, Yamaguchi Prefectural Museum of Art (see Brejon and Scottez, 1991).

Zurich, 1939
"Eugène Delacroix," Kunsthaus.

Selected Bibliography

Ackley, 1980
Ackley, Clifford S. *Printmaking in the Age of Rembrandt*. Exhibition catalogue. Boston, Museum of Fine Arts; and Saint Louis, Saint Louis Art Museum, 1980–81. Boston, 1980.

Aimé-Azam, 1956
Aimé-Azam, Denise. *Mazeppa. Géricault et son temps*. Paris, 1956.

Alazard, 1950
Alazard, Jean. *Ingres et l'Ingrisme*. Paris, 1950.

Alden and Beresford, 1989
Alden, Mary, and Richard Beresford. "Two Altar-pieces by Philippe de Champaigne: Their History and Technique." *The Burlington Magazine* 131 (June 1989), pp. 395–406.

Alexander, 1976–77
Alexander, David. *The Dutch Mezzotint and England in the Late Seventeenth Century*. Exhibition catalogue. York, York City Art Gallery; and London, Geffrye Museum, 1976–77. York, England, 1976.

Ames, 1963
Ames, Winslow. "The 'Villa del Timpano Arcuato' by Francesco Guardi." *Master Drawings* 1, no. 3 (1963), pp. 37–39.

Ames-Lewis, 1981
Ames-Lewis, Francis. *Drawing in Early Renaissance Italy*. New Haven and London, 1981.

Ames-Lewis, 1986
Ames-Lewis, Francis. *The Draftsman Raphael*. New Haven and London, 1986.

Amman and Sachs, 1568
Amman, Jost, and Hans Sachs. *The Book of Trades (Ständebuch)*. Frankfurt am Main, 1568. Reprint, with introduction by Benjamin A. Rifkin. New York, 1973.

Amsterdam, 1971
Hollandse schilderijen uit Franse musea. Exhibition catalogue. Amsterdam, Rijksmuseum, 1971. Amsterdam, 1971.

Amsterdam, 1976
Tot lering en vermaak. Exhibition catalogue, with introduction by E. de Jongh and entries by Jan Baptist Bedaux, Peter Hecht, E. de Jongh, Jeroen Stumpel, and Rik Vos. Amsterdam, Rijksmuseum, 1976. Amsterdam, 1976.

Amsterdam, 1982
The Ceramic Load of the "Witte Leeuw" (1613). Exhibition catalogue, edited by C. L. van der Pijl-Ketel. Amsterdam, Rijksmuseum, 1982. Amsterdam, 1982.

Amsterdam, 1984
Masters of Middelburg. Exhibition catalogue, by Noortje Bakker, Ingvar Bergström, Guido Jansen, Simon H. Levie, and Sam Segal. Amsterdam, K. and V. Waterman Gallery, 1984. Amsterdam, 1984.

Amsterdam–Groningen, 1983
The Impact of a Genius: Rembrandt, His Pupils and Followers in the Seventeenth

Century. Exhibition catalogue, by Albert Blankert, Ben Broos, Ernst van de Wetering, Guido Jansen, and Willem van de Watering. Amsterdam, K. and V. Waterman Gallery; and Groningen, Groninger Museum, 1983. Amsterdam, 1983.

Antwerp, 1977
P. P. Rubens: schilderijen, olieverfschetsen, tekeningen. Exhibition catalogue, by R.-A. d'Hulst et al. Antwerp, Koninklijk Museum voor Schone Kunsten, 1977. Antwerp, 1977.

Antwerp–Münster, 1990
Jan Boeckhorst 1604–1668: medewerker van Rubens. Exhibition catalogue, by Hans Vlieghe et al. Antwerp, Rubenshuis; and Münster, Westfälisches Landesmuseum für Kunst, 1990. Freren, Germany, 1990.

Arezzo, 1981
Giorgio Vasari. Exhibition catalogue, by Laura Corti, Margaret Daly Davis, Charles Davis, Julien Kliemann, and Anna Maria Maetzke. Arezzo, Casa Vasari, 1981. Arezzo, 1981.

Aubrun, 1979
Aubrun, Marie-Madeleine. *Théodore Caruelle d'Aligny (1798–1871) et ses compagnons*. Exhibition catalogue. Orléans, Musée des Beaux-Arts; Dunkirk, Musée des Beaux-Arts; and Rennes, Musée des Beaux-Arts, 1979. Nantes, 1979.

Aubrun, 1988
Aubrun, Marie-Madeleine. *Théodore Caruelle d'Aligny (1798–1871): catalogue raisonné de l'oeuvre peint, dessiné, gravé*. Paris, 1988.

Augsburg–Cleveland, 1975–76
Johann Liss. Exhibition catalogue, by Rüdiger Klessman, Ann Tzeutscher-Lurie, Louise S. Richards, and Bruno Bushart. Augsburg, Rathaus; and Cleveland, Cleveland Museum of Art, 1975–76. Augsburg, 1975.

Avignon, 1989
La mort de Bara. Exhibition catalogue, by Marie-Pierre Foissy-Aufrère, Jean-Clément Martin, Régis Michel, Édouard Pommier, and Michèle Vorelle. Avignon, Musée Calvet, 1989. Avignon, 1989.

Bacou, 1957
Bacou, Roseline. "Ils existent. Le saviez-vous?" *L'Oeil* 28 (April 1957), pp. 22–29, 62.

Bader, 1976
Bader, Alfred. *The Bible through Dutch Eyes*. Exhibition catalogue. Milwaukee, Milwaukee Art Center, 1976. Milwaukee, 1976.

Baetjer, 1980
Baetjer, Katharine. *European Paintings in The Metropolitan Museum of Art by artists born in or before 1865: A Summary Catalogue*. 3 vols. New York, 1980.

Bailey, 1991
Bailey, Colin, with the assistance of Carrie A. Hamilton. *Loves of the Gods: Mythological Painting from Watteau to David*. Exhibition catalogue. Paris, Grand Palais; Philadelphia, Philadelphia Museum of Art; and

Fort Worth, Kimbell Art Museum, 1991–92. Fort Worth and New York, 1991.

Baldinucci, 1845–47
Baldinucci, Filippo. *Notizie dei professori del disegno da Cimabue in qua.* 5 vols. Florence, 1845–47. Reprint (7 vols.). Florence, 1974–76.

Barocchi, 1964-1
Barocchi, Paola. "Appunti su Francesco Morandini da Poppi." *Mitteilungen des Kunsthistorischen Institutes in Florenz* 11, nos. 2–3 (1964), pp. 117–48.

Barocchi, 1964-2
Barocchi, Paola. *Complementi al Vasari pittore.* Florence, 1964.

Barocchi, 1964-3
Barocchi, Paola. *Vasari pittore.* Milan, 1964.

Barrelet, 1959
Barrelet, James. "Chardin du point de vue de la verrerie." *Gazette des Beaux-Arts* (May–June 1959), pp. 305–14.

Baticle and Marinas, 1981
Baticle, Jeannine, and Cristina Marinas. *La galerie espagnole de Louis-Philippe au Louvre, 1838–1848.* Paris, 1981.

Bauch, 1960
Bauch, Kurt. *Die frühe Rembrandt und seine Zeit.* Berlin, 1960.

Baudouin, 1977
Baudouin, Frans. *P. P. Rubens.* Antwerp, 1977.

Baudouin, 1980
Baudouin, Frans. "À propos de l'iconographie d'un tableau de Rubens à Lille: l'influence de Sainte Thérèse d'Avila." In *Festschrift für Eduard Trier zum 60. Geburtstag*, pp. 165–75. Berlin, 1980.

Baudouin, 1981
Baudouin, Frans. "Quelques remarques concernant *La Sainte Marie-Madeleine en extase* de Rubens au Musée des Beaux-Arts à Lille." In *Ars Auro Prior: Studia Ioanni Białostocki Sexagenario Dicata*, pp. 483–87. Warsaw, 1981.

Bauman and Liedtke, 1992
Bauman, Guy C., and Walter A. Liedtke, eds. *Flemish Paintings in America.* Antwerp, 1992.

Bazin, 1942
Bazin, Germain. *Corot.* Paris, 1942.

Bazin, 1967
Bazin, Germain. *The Museum Age.* New York, 1967.

Bazin, 1973
Bazin, Germain. *Corot.* Paris, 1973.

Bazin, 1990
Bazin, Germain. *Le Voyage en Italie.* Vol. 4 of *Théodore Géricault: étude critique, documents et catalogue raisonné.* Paris, 1990.

Bean, 1960
Bean, Jacob. *Inventaire général des dessins des musées de province. 4: Bayonne, Musée Bonnat. Les dessins italiens de la collection Bonnat.* Paris, 1960.

Bean, 1964
Bean, Jacob. *100 European Drawings in The Metropolitan Museum of Art.* New York, 1964.

Bean, 1986
Bean, Jacob, with the assistance of Lawrence Turčić. *Fifteenth–Eighteenth Century French Drawings in The Metropolitan Museum of Art.* New York, 1986.

Bean and Griswold, 1990
Bean, Jacob, and William Griswold. *Eighteenth Century Italian Drawings in The Metropolitan Museum of Art.* New York, 1990.

Bean and Stampfle, 1971
Bean, Jacob, and Felice Stampfle. *Drawings from New York Collections. III: The Eighteenth Century in Italy.* Exhibition catalogue. New York, The Metropolitan Museum of Art and Pierpont Morgan Library, 1971. New York, 1971.

Beaucamp, 1928
Beaucamp, Fernand. "Un portrait inconnu de Robespierre au Musée de Lille." *La revue du nord* (February 1928), pp. 21–34.

Beaucamp, 1939
Beaucamp, Fernand. *Le peintre lillois Jean-Baptiste Wicar (1762–1834): son oeuvre et son temps.* 2 vols. Lille, 1939.

Beck, 1972–73
Beck, Hans-Ulrich. *Jan van Goyen 1596–1656: ein Oeuvreverzeichnis.* Amsterdam, 1972–73.

Béguin, 1982
Béguin, Sylvie. *Le XVIᵉ siècle florentin au Louvre.* Exhibition catalogue. Paris, Musée du Louvre, 1982. Paris, 1982.

Benisovitch, 1958
Benisovitch, Michel N. "Une autobiographie du peintre Louis Boilly." In *Essays in Honor of Hans Tietze*, edited by Ernst Gombrich, Julius S. Held, and Otto Kurz, pp. 365–72. New York, 1958.

Bennett and Wilkins, 1984
Bennett, Bonnie, and David Wilkins. *Donatello.* Oxford, 1984.

Benoit, 1909
Benoit, François. *La peinture au Musée de Lille.* 3 vols. Paris, 1909.

Benvignat, 1856
Benvignat, Charles. *Musée Wicar: catalogue des dessins et objets d'art légués par J. B. Wicar.* Lille, 1856.

Berenson, 1903
Berenson, Bernard. *The Drawings of the Florentine Painters.* 2 vols. New York, 1903.

Berenson, 1938
Berenson, Bernard. *The Drawings of the Florentine Painters.* 3 vols. Chicago, 1938.

Berenson, 1961
Berenson, Bernard. *I disegni dei pittori fiorentini.* 3 vols. Milan, 1961.

Berger, 1955
Berger, Klaus. *Géricault and His Work.* Lawrence, Kansas, 1955. Reprint. New York, 1978.

Bergström, 1956
Bergström, Ingvar. *Dutch Still-Life Painting in the Seventeenth Century.* London, 1956.

Bergström, 1963
Bergström, Ingvar. "Georg Hoefnagel, le dernier des grands miniaturistes flamands." *L'Oeil* 101 (May 1963), pp. 2–9, 66.

Bergström, 1982
Bergström, Ingvar. "Composition in Flower-Pieces of 1605–1609 by Ambrosius Bosschaert the Elder." *tableau* 5, no. 2 (November–December 1982), pp. 175–79.

Bergström, 1983
Bergström, Ingvar. "Baskets with Flowers by Ambrosius Bosschaert the Elder and Their Repercussions on the Art of Balthasar van der Ast." *tableau* 6, no. 3 (December 1983–January 1984), pp. 66–75.

Bergström, 1985
Bergström, Ingvar. "On Georg Hoefnagel's Manner of Working, with Notes on the Influence of the Archetypa Series of 1592." In *Netherlandish Mannerism: Papers Given at a Symposium in Nationalmuseum Stockholm,*

September 21–22, 1984, edited by Görel Cavallia-Björkman, pp. 177–87. Stockholm, 1985.

Berlin, 1964
Meisterwerke aus dem Museum in Lille. Exhibition catalogue. Berlin, Schloss Charlottenburg. Berlin, 1964.

Berlin–Amsterdam–London, 1991–92
Rembrandt, the Master and His Workshop: Paintings. Exhibition catalogue, by Christopher Brown, Jan Kelch, and Pieter van Thiel, with contributions by Jeroen Boomgaard, Josua Bruyn, A. Th. van Deursen, Sebastian Dudok van Heel, Volker Manuth, Robert Scheller, Bernhard Schnackenburg, and Ernst van de Wetering. Berlin, Altes Museum; Amsterdam, Rijksmuseum; and London, National Gallery, 1991–92. New Haven and London, 1991.

Berti, 1965
Berti, Luciano. *Pontormo: disegni*. Florence, 1965.

Berti, 1973
Berti, Luciano. *L'opera completa del Pontormo*. Milan, 1973.

Białostocki, 1964
Białostocki, Jan. "The Descent from the Cross in Works by Peter Paul Rubens and His Studio." *The Art Bulletin* 46 (December 1964), pp. 511–24.

de Bie, 1661
de Bie, Cornelis. *Het gulden cabinet van de edel vry schilder const*. Antwerp, 1661. Reprint. Soest, The Netherlands, 1971.

Bloch, 1955
Bloch, Vitale. "Addenda to Liss." *The Burlington Magazine* 97 (October 1955), pp. 323–24.

Bloch, 1966
Bloch, Vitale. "'German Painters and Draughtsmen of the Seventeenth Century' in Berlin." *The Burlington Magazine* 108 (October 1966), pp. 545–46.

Bloch, 1968
Bloch, Vitale. *Michael Sweerts*. The Hague, 1968.

Blunt, 1967
Blunt, Anthony. *Nicolas Poussin*. 2 vols. New York, 1967.

Blunt, 1970
Blunt, Anthony. *Art and Architecture in France, 1500 to 1700*. Harmondsworth, 1970.

Bocher, 1876
Bocher, Emmanuel. *Jean-Baptiste-Siméon Chardin*. Vol. 3 of *Les gravures françaises du XVIIIᵉ siècle. . . .* 3 vols. Paris, 1876.

Bodart, 1977
Bodart, Didier. *Rubens e l'incisione*. Rome, 1977.

Bode, 1920
von Bode, Wilhelm. "Johan Lys." *Velhagen und Klasing's Monatshefte* 35 (October 1920), pp. 163–77.

von Boehn, 1910
von Boehn, Max. *Guido Reni*. Bielefeld and Leipzig, 1910.

Boime, 1980
Boime, Albert. "Marmontel's 'Bélisaire' and the Pre-Revolutionary Progressivism of David." *Art History* 3 (March 1980), pp. 81–101.

Bol, 1960
Bol, Laurens J. *The Bosschaert Dynasty*. Leigh-on-Sea, England, 1960.

Borenius, 1909
Borenius, Tancred. *The Painters of Vicenza, 1480–1550*. London, 1909.

de Bosque, 1985
de Bosque, André. *Mythologie et maniérisme aux Pays-Bas*. Antwerp, 1985.

Bourin, 1907
Bourin, Henri. *Paul-Ponce-Antoine Robert (de Séry), peintre du cardinal de Rohan (1686–1733)*. Paris, 1907. Extract from *Revue historique ardennaise* 14 (1907), pp. 129–93.

Braham, 1979
Braham, Allan. "The Bed of Pierfrancesco Borgherini." *The Burlington Magazine* 121 (December 1979), pp. 754–65.

Braham, 1981
Braham, Helen. *The Princes Gate Collection*. London, 1981.

van den Branden, 1883
van den Branden, F. J. *Geschiedenis van de antwerpsche Schildersschool*. Antwerp, 1883.

Braunschweig, 1978
Die Sprache der Bilder: Realität und Bedeutung in der niederländischen Malerei des 17. Jahrhunderts. Exhibition catalogue, with introduction by E. de Jongh and contributions by Lothar Dittrich, Rüdiger Klessmann, Wolfgang J. Müller, and Konrad Renger. Braunschweig, Herzog Anton Ulrich-Museum, 1978. Braunschweig, 1978.

Braunschweig, 1979
Jan Lievens, ein Maler im Schatten Rembrandts. Exhibition catalogue, edited by Rüdiger Klessmann, with contributions by Jan Białostocki, Rudolf O. E. Ekkart, Sabine Jacob, and Rüdiger Klessmann. Braunschweig, Herzog Anton Ulrich-Museum, 1979. Braunschweig, 1979.

Bredius, 1913
Bredius, Abraham. "De bloemeschilders Bosschaert." *Oud Holland* 31 (1913), pp. 137–40.

Bredius, 1915–22
Bredius, Abraham. *Künstler-Inventare: Urkunden zur Geschichte der holländischen Kunst des XVIten, XVIIten und XVIIIten Jahrhunderts*. 8 vols. The Hague, 1915–22.

Brejon and Cuzin, 1974
Brejon de Lavergnée, Arnauld, and Jean-Pierre Cuzin. "À propos des caravagesques français." *La revue du Louvre et des musées de France* 24, no. 1 (1974), pp. 25–38.

Brejon and Scottez, 1991
Brejon de Lavergnée, Arnauld, and Annie Scottez-De Wambrechies. *La peinture française au XIXᵢᵉᵐᵉ siècle: le Musée des Beaux-Arts de Lille*. Exhibition catalogue. Yokohama, Sogo Museum of Art; Hokkaido, Hokkaido Obihiro Museum; Osaka, Museum of Art Kintetsu; and Yamaguchi, Yamaguchi Prefectural Museum of Art, 1991–92. Lille, 1991.

Brejon de Lavergnée, 1986
Brejon de Lavergnée, Arnauld. *L'inventaire Le Brun de 1683: la collection des tableaux de Louis XIV*. Paris, 1986.

Brejon de Lavergnée, 1987
Brejon de Lavergnée, Barbara. *Musée du Louvre, Cabinet des Dessins. Inventaire général des dessins: école française, dessins de Simon Vouet*. Paris, 1987.

Brejon de Lavergnée, 1989-1
Brejon de Lavergnée, Arnauld. "Pittori stranieri in Italia." In *La pittura in Italia: Il Seicento*, edited by Mina Gregori and Erich Schleier, pp. 531–58. Milan, 1989.

Brejon de Lavergnée, 1989-2
Brejon de Lavergnée, Barbara, with Dominique Cordellier, Catherine Goguel, and Frédérique Lemerle. *Renaissance et baroque: dessins italiens du Musée de Lille*. Exhibition catalogue. Lille, Musée des Beaux-Arts, 1989–90. Milan, 1989.

Brejon de Lavergnée, 1990-1
Brejon de Lavergnée, Arnauld. "Un Chardin pour le Musée de Lille." *Connaissance des arts*, no. 464 (October 1990), p. 96.

Brejon de Lavergnée, 1990-2
Brejon de Lavergnée, Arnauld. "Un tableau de Chardin pour le Musée des Beaux-Arts de Lille." *La revue du Louvre et des musées de France* 40, no. 5 (1990), pp. 353–55.

Brejon de Lavergnée, 1992
Brejon de Lavergnée, Arnauld. "A New Plan for the Restoration of the Musée des Beaux-Arts in Lille." In *The European Fine Art Fair: Handbook 1992*, pp. 28–33. Maastricht, The Netherlands, 1992.

Briels, 1987
Briels, Jan. *Peintres flamands en Hollande au début du siècle d'or.* Antwerp, 1987.

Briganti, 1962
Briganti, Giuliano. *Pietro da Cortona o della pittura barocca.* Florence, 1962.

Briganti, 1982
Briganti, Giuliano. *Pietro da Cortona o della pittura barocca.* 2nd ed. Florence, 1982.

Brown, 1976
Brown, Christopher. *Dutch Genre Painting.* Oxford and New York, 1976.

Brown, 1983-1
Brown, Christopher. "Jan Lievens in Leiden and London." *The Burlington Magazine* 125 (November 1983), pp. 663–71.

Brown, 1983-2
Brown, David A. *Raphael and America.* Exhibition catalogue. Washington, D.C., National Gallery of Art, 1983. Washington, D.C., 1983

Brussels, 1965
Le siècle de Rubens. Exhibition catalogue, with introduction by Leo van Puyvelde and contributions by S. Bergmans et al. Brussels, Musées Royaux des Beaux-Arts, 1965. Brussels, 1965.

Bruyn, 1982
Bruyn, Josua et al. *A Corpus of Rembrandt Paintings.* 3 vols. (vol. 1, 1982; vol. 2, 1986; vol. 3, 1989). The Hague, 1982, 1986, 1989.

Buijs and van Berge-Gerbaud, 1991
Buijs, Hans, and Maria van Berge-Gerbaud. *Tableaux flamands et hollandais du Musée des Beaux-Arts de Lyon.* Exhibition catalogue. Paris, Institut Néerlandais; and Lyons, Musée des Beaux-Arts, 1991. Paris and Zwolle, 1991.

Cantelli, 1983
Cantelli, Giuseppe. *Repertorio della pittura fiorentina del Seicento.* Fiesole, 1983.

Carlson, 1978
Carlson, Victor. *Hubert Robert: Drawings and Watercolors.* Exhibition catalogue. Washington, D.C., National Gallery of Art, 1978–79. Washington, D.C., 1978.

Carroll, 1990
Carroll, Stephanie. "Reciprocal Representations: David and Theater." *Art in America* (May 1990), pp. 198–207.

de Caso, 1992
de Caso, Jacques. *David d'Angers: Sculptural Communication in the Age of Romanticism.* Princeton, 1992.

Champfleury, 1973
Champfleury. "Le Salon de 1849." *La silhouette,* July 22, 1849. Reprinted in Geneviève and Jean Lacambre, eds. *Champfleury: le réalisme.* Paris, 1973.

Chapman, 1990
Chapman, H. Perry. *Rembrandt's Self-Portraits.* Princeton, 1990.

Châtelet, 1964
Châtelet, Albert. *Meisterwerke aus dem Museum in Lille.* Exhibition catalogue. Berlin, 1964.

Châtelet, 1967
Châtelet, Albert. *Dessins italiens du Musée de Lille.* Exhibition catalogue. Amsterdam, Rijksmuseum; Brussels, Bibliothèque Royale de Belgique; and Lille, Palais des Beaux-Arts. Amsterdam, 1967.

Châtelet, 1970-1
Châtelet, Albert. *Cent chefs-d'oeuvre du Musée de Lille* (special issue of *Bulletin de la Société des Amis du Musée de Lille*). Exhibition catalogue. Lille, Musée des Beaux-Arts, 1970. Lille, 1970.

Châtelet, 1970-2
Châtelet, Albert. *Disegni di Raffaello e di altri italiani del Museo di Lille.* Exhibition catalogue. Florence, Gabinetto Disegni e Stampe degli Uffizi, 1970. Florence, 1970.

Chetham, 1976
Chetham, Charles. *The Role of Vincent van Gogh's Copies in the Development of His Art.* New York and London, 1976.

Choix de dessins, 1926
Dessins et peintures des maîtres du XIXe siècle. I: Un choix de dessins de Jean-Dominique Ingres. Paris, Dornach, New York, and London, 1926.

Clapp, 1916
Clapp, Frederick Mortimer. *Jacopo Carucci da Pontormo: His Life and Work.* New Haven, London, and Oxford, 1916.

Clément, 1879-1
Clément, Charles. *Géricault: A Biographical and Critical Study with a Catalogue Raisonné of the Master's Works. Reprint of the Definitive Edition of 1879.* Introduction by Lorenz Eitner. New York, 1974.

Clément, 1879-2
Clément, Charles. *Géricault: étude biographique et critique avec le catalogue raisonné de l'oeuvre du maître.* 3rd ed. Paris, 1879.

Clément de Ris, 1859
Clément de Ris, Athanase Louis. *Les musées de province.* 2 vols. Paris, 1859.

Clément de Ris, 1872
Clément de Ris, Athanase Louis. *Les musées de province, histoire et description.* Paris, 1872.

Cologne, 1990-91
Raffael und die Zeichenkunst der italienischen Renaissance: Meisterzeichnungen aus dem Musée des Beaux-Arts in Lille und aus eigenem Bestand. Exhibition catalogue, by Barbara Brejon de Lavergnée, Dominique Cordellier, Frédérique Lemerle, and Uwe Westfehling. Cologne, Wallraf-Richartz-Museum, Graphische Sammlung, 1990–91. Cologne, 1990.

Cologne–Utrecht, 1985–86
Roelant Savery in seiner Zeit (1576–1639). Exhibition catalogue, by Anne-Caroline Buysschaert, Ekkehard Mai, Kurt J. Müllenmeister, Hans Joachim Raupp, and Sam Segal. Cologne, Wallraf-Richartz-Museum; and Utrecht, Centraal Museum, 1985–86. Cologne, 1985.

Cordellier, 1985
Cordellier, Dominique. "Un dessin de Raphael au Louvre: le visage de la poésie." *La revue du Louvre et des musées de France* 35, no. 2 (1985), pp. 96–104.

Cordellier, 1986
Cordellier, Dominique. *Hommage à Andrea del Sarto.* Exhibition catalogue. Musée du Louvre, Paris, 1986–87. Paris, 1986.

Correspondance
Joubin, André, ed. *Correspondance générale d'Eugène Delacroix. . . .* 5 vols. Paris, 1935–38.

Courthion and Cailler, 1947
Courthion, Pierre, and Pierre Cailler. *Géricault raconté par lui-même et par ses amis.* Geneva, 1947.

Courtrai. *See* Kortrijk

Cox-Rearick, 1964
Cox-Rearick, Janet. *The Drawings of Pontormo.* 2 vols. Cambridge, Massachusetts, 1964.

Cox-Rearick, 1981
Cox-Rearick, Janet. *The Drawings of Pontormo.* 2 vols. New York, 1981.

Crow, 1985
Crow, Thomas E. *Painters and Public Life in Eighteenth-Century Paris.* New Haven and London, 1985.

Cuzin, 1987
Cuzin, Jean-Pierre. "Un chef-d'oeuvre avorté de Simon Vouet: le *Saint Pierre et les malades* commandé pour Saint-Pierre de Rome." In *Il se rendit en Italie: études offertes à André Chastel,* pp. 359–70. Rome and Paris, 1987.

Davidson, 1985
Davidson, Bernice F. *Raphael's Bible: A Study of the Vatican Logge.* University Park, Pennsylvania, and London, 1985.

Dayot and Vaillat, 1907
Dayot, Armand, and Léandre Vaillat. *L'oeuvre de J.-B.-S. Chardin et J.-H. Fragonard.* Paris [1907].

De Bruyn, 1988
De Bruyn, Jean-Pierre. *Erasmus II Quellinus (1607–1678): de Schilderijen met Catalogue Raisonné.* Freren, Germany, 1988.

Delacre, 1931
Delacre, M. "Sur deux dessins de Pontormo." *Bulletin des musées de France* 3 (1931), pp. 139–40.

Delenda and Melnotte, 1985
Delenda, O., and C. Melnotte. *Iconographie de Sainte Madeleine.* Paris, 1985.

Delogu, 1958
Delogu, Giuseppe. *Pittura veneziana dal XIV al XVIII secolo.* Bergamo, 1958.

Descamps, 1753
Descamps, Jean-Baptiste. *La vie des peintres flamands, allemands et hollandois avec des portraits gravés en taille douce.* 2 vols. (vol. 1, 1753; vol. 2, 1754). Paris, 1753, 1754.

Descamps, 1769
Descamps, J.-B. *Voyage pittoresque de la Flandre et du Brabant.* Paris, 1769.

Detroit–Fort Worth, 1985–86
Italian Renaissance Sculpture in the Time of Donatello. Exhibition catalogue. Detroit, Detroit Institute of Arts; and Fort Worth, Kimbell Art Museum, 1985–86. Detroit, 1985.

Dézallier d'Argenville, 1745
Dézallier d'Argenville, Antoine-Joseph. *Abrégé de la vie des plus fameux peintres, avec leurs portraits gravés en taille douce. . . .* 3 vols. Paris, 1745–52.

Dézallier d'Argenville, 1749
Dézallier d'Argenville, Antoine-Joseph. *Voyage pittoresque de Paris; ou, indication de tout ce qu'il y a de plus beau dans cette grande ville. . . .* Paris, 1749. Reprint (4 vols. in 1). Geneva, 1972.

Diderot, 1957–67
Diderot, Denis. *Salons.* Edited by Jean Seznec and Jean Adhémar. 4 vols. Oxford, 1957–67.

Diderot, 1975–83
Diderot, Denis. *Salons.* Edited by Jean Seznec and Jean Adhémar. 2nd ed. 3 vols. Oxford, 1975–83.

Dinaux, 1847
Dinaux, Arthur-Martin. "Boilly." *Archives historiques et littéraires du Nord de la France et du Midi de la Belgique* 6 (1847), pp. 194–209.

Donzelli and Pilo, 1967
Donzelli, Carlo, and Giuseppe Maria Pilo. *I pittori del Seicento veneto.* Florence, 1967.

Dorival, 1976
Dorival, Bernard. *Philippe de Champaigne, 1602–1674: la vie, l'oeuvre et le catalogue raisonné de l'oeuvre.* 2 vols. Paris, 1976.

Driskel, 1991
Driskel, Michael Paul. "'Et la lumière fut': The Meanings of David d'Anger's Monument to Gutenberg." *The Art Bulletin* 73 (September 1991), pp. 359–80.

Ducourau and Sérullaz, 1979
Ducourau, Vincent, and Arlette Sérullaz. *Dessins français du XIXe siècle du Musée Bonnat à Bayonne.* Exhibition catalogue. Paris, Musée du Louvre, 1979. Paris, 1979.

Dulaure, 1786
Dulaure, Jacques-Antoine. *Nouvelle description des curiosités de Paris.* 4 vols. Paris, 1786.

Dussler, 1971
Dussler, Luitpold. *Raphael: A Critical Catalogue of His Pictures, Wall-Paintings, and Tapestries.* London and New York, 1971.

Edinburgh, 1991
The Stylish Image: Printmakers to the Court of Rudolf II. Exhibition catalogue, with essays by E. J. W. Evans and Eliška Fučíková and notes by Mungo Campbell. Edinburgh, National Gallery of Scotland, 1991. Edinburgh, 1991.

Eikemeier, 1984
Eikemeier, Peter. "Bücher in Bilder." In *De arte et libris: Festschrift für Erasmus, 1934–1984,* pp. 61–68. Amsterdam, 1984.

Eitner, 1959
Eitner, Lorenz. "The Sale of Géricault's Studio in 1824." *Gazette des Beaux-Arts* (February 1959), pp. 115–26.

Eitner, 1972
Eitner, Lorenz. *Géricault's Raft of the Medusa.* London and New York, 1972.

Eitner, 1983
Eitner, Lorenz. *Géricault: His Life and Work.* Ithaca, New York, 1983.

Ekelhart-Reinwetter, 1991
Ekelhart-Reinwetter, Christine. *J. A. D. Ingres: Zeichnungen und Ölstudien aus dem Musée Ingres, Montauban.* Exhibition catalogue. Innsbruck, Tiroler Landesmuseum Ferdinandeum; and Vienna, Graphische Sammlung Albertina, 1991.

Ekkart, 1979
Ekkart, Rudolf E. O. *Johannes Cornelisz. Verspronk.* Exhibition catalogue. Haarlem, Frans Halsmuseum, 1979. Haarlem, 1979.

Ekkart, 1991
Ekkart, Rudolf E. O. "The Portraits of 'The Vrijdags van Vollenhoven Family' by Jan Anthonisz. van Ravesteyn." *Hoogsteder Mercury* 12 (1991), pp. 3–16.

Emmens, 1963
Emmens, J. A. "Natuur, onderwijzing en oefening: bij een drieluik van Gerrit Dou." *Album discipulorum, aangeboden aan Professor Dr. J. G. van Gelder,* pp. 125–63. Utrecht, 1963.

Erasmus, 1908
Erasmus, Kurt. *Roelant Savery: sein Leben und seine Werke.* Halle, 1908.

Evans, 1973
Evans, R. J. W. *Rudolf II and His World: A Study in Intellectual History.* Oxford, 1973.

Ewald, 1967
Ewald, Gerhard. " 'Deutsche Maler und Zeichner des 17. Jahrhunderts,' Berlin, Orangerie des Charlottenburger Schlosses, 26. August bis 16. Oktober 1966." *Kunstchronik* 20 (January 1967), pp. 8–12.

Fahy, 1974
Fahy, Everett. "A 'Holy Family' by Fra Bartolommeo." *Los Angeles County Museum of Art Bulletin* 20, no. 2 (1974), pp. 8–17.

de la Faille, 1928
de la Faille, J.-B. *L'Oeuvre de Vincent van Gogh: catalogue raisonné.* 4 vols. Paris and Brussels, 1928.

de la Faille, 1939
de la Faille, J.-B. *Vincent van Gogh.* Translated by P. Montagu-Pollock. Paris, London, and New York, 1939.

de la Faille, 1970
de la Faille, J.-B. *The Works of Vincent van Gogh: His Paintings and Drawings.* Amsterdam, 1970.

Faranda, 1986
Faranda, Franco. *Ludovico Cardi detto il Cigoli.* Rome, 1986.

Félibien, 1688
Félibien, André. *Entretiens sur les vies et sur les ouvrages des plus excellens peintres anciens et modernes.* 4 vols. Paris, 1688.

Fermigier, 1971
Fermigier, André. *Courbet.* Geneva, 1971.

Fernier, 1949
Fernier, Robert. "Courbet au Salon de 1849." *Les amis de Gustave Courbet,* no. 5 (1949).

Fernier, 1977
Fernier, Robert. *La vie et l'oeuvre de Gustave Courbet: catalogue raisonné.* 2 vols. Paris, 1977.

Ficacci, 1989
Ficacci, Luigi. *Claude Mellan, gli anni romani: un incisore tra Vouet e Bernini.* Exhibition catalogue. Rome, Galleria Nazionale d'Arte Antica, 1989–90. Rome, 1989.

Filipczak, 1987
Filipczak, Zirka Z. *Picturing Art in Antwerp, 1550–1700.* Princeton, 1987.

Fiocco, 1929
Fiocco, Giuseppe. *Venetian Painting of the Seicento and Settecento.* Florence and New York, 1929.

Fischel, 1898
Fischel, Oskar. *Raphaels Zeichnungen: Versuch einer Kritisch der bischer veröffentlichen Blätter.* Strasbourg, 1898.

Fischel, 1913–45
Fischel, Oskar. *Raphaels Zeichnungen.* 8 vols. Berlin, 1913–45.

Fischer, 1975
Fischer, Pieter. *Music in Paintings of the Low Countries in the Sixteenth and Seventeenth Centuries.* Amsterdam, 1975.

Fischer, 1982
Fischer, Chris. "Remarques sur 'Le Mariage mystique de Sainte Catherine de Sienne' par Fra Bartolommeo." *La revue du Louvre et des musées de France* 31, no. 3 (1982), pp. 167–80.

Fischer, 1986
Fischer, Chris. *Disegni di Fra Bartolommeo e della sua scuola.* Exhibition catalogue. Florence, Gabinetto Disegni e Stampe degli Uffizi, 1986. Florence, 1986.

Fischer, 1990
Fischer, Chris. *Fra Bartolommeo: Master Draughtsman of the High Renais-sance.* Exhibition catalogue. Rotterdam, Museum Boymans-van Beuningen, 1990. Rotterdam, 1990

Florence, 1954
Mostra di disegni dei primi manieristi italiani. Exhibition catalogue, by Paola Barocchi, Maria Fossi, Luisa Marcucci, Bianca Maria Mori, and Giulia Sinibaldi. Florence, Gabinetto Disegni e Stampe degli Uffizi, 1954. Florence, 1954.

Florence, 1984
Raffaello a Firenze. Exhibition catalogue, by Sylvia Ferino-Pagden et al. Florence, Palazzo Pitti, 1984. Florence, 1984.

Florence, 1986–87
Il Seicento fiorentino: arte a Firenze da Ferdinando I a Cosimo III. Exhibition catalogue, by Anna Forlani Tempesti et al. 3 vols. Florence, Palazzo Strozzi, 1986–87. Florence, 1986.

Florent Le Comte, 1699–1700
Florent Le Comte. *Cabinet des singularitez d'architecture, peinture, sculpture et graveure.* 3 vols. Paris, 1699–1700.

de Forges, 1972
de Forges, Marie-Thérèse Lemoyne. "À propos de l'exposition 'Autoportraits de Courbet.' " *La revue du Louvre et des musées de France,* no. 6 (1972), pp. 451–56.

de Forges, 1973
de Forges, Marie-Thérèse Lemoyne et al. *Autoportraits de Courbet.* Paris, 1973.

Forlani Tempesti, 1970
Forlani Tempesti, Anna. *Disegni del Pontormo del Gabinetto di Disegni e Stampe degli Uffizi.* Exhibition catalogue. Milan, Pinacoteca di Brera, 1970. Florence, 1970.

Forster, 1966
Forster, Kurt W. *Pontormo: Monographie mit Kritischem Katalog.* Munich, 1966.

Fried, 1980
Fried, Michael. *Absorption and Theatricality: Painting and Beholder in the Age of Diderot.* Berkeley, Los Angeles, and London, 1980.

Fried, 1990
Fried, Michael. "Painter into Painting: On Courbet's *After Dinner at Ornans* and *Stonebreakers*." *Critical Inquiry,* no. 8 (Summer 1982), pp. 619–49. Reprinted in Michael Fried. *Courbet's Realism.* Chicago, 1990.

Furst, 1911
Furst, Herbert E. A. *Chardin.* London, 1911.

von der Gabelentz, 1922
von der Gabelentz, Hans. *Fra Bartolommeo und die florentiner Renaissance.* 2 vols. Leipzig, 1922.

Gachet, 1954-1
Gachet, Paul. *Paul van Ryssel, le Docteur Gachet, graveur.* Paris, 1954.

Gachet, 1954-2
Gachet, Paul. *Vincent à Auvers: "Les Vaches" de J. Jordaens.* Paris, 1954.

Galassi, 1991
Galassi, Peter. *Corot in Italy: Open-Air Painting and the Classical-Landscape Tradition.* New Haven and London, 1991.

Gaskell, 1989
Gaskell, Ivan. *The Thyssen-Bornemisza Collection: Seventeenth-Century Dutch and Flemish Painting.* London, 1990.

Gassier and Wilson, 1971
Gassier, Pierre, and Juliet Wilson. *The Life and Complete Work of Francisco Goya, with a Catalogue Raisonné of the Paintings, Drawings, and Engravings.* New York, 1971.

Gavelle and Turpin, 1920
Gavelle, Émile, and P. Turpin. *Cent tableaux du Musée de Lille*. Lille, 1920.

Geiger, 1986
Geiger, Gail L. *Filippino Lippi's Carafa Chapel*. Kirksville, Missouri, 1986.

van Gelder, 1950
van Gelder, J. G. *Catalogue of the Collection of Dutch and Flemish Still-Life Pictures Bequeathed by Daisy Linda Ward*. Oxford, 1950.

Gendre, 1981
Gendre, Catherine. *Dessins français: XVIIᵉ et XIXᵉ siècles du Musée Lambinet et de la Bibliothèque Municipale*. Exhibition catalogue. Versailles, Musée Lambinet, 1981. Versailles, 1981.

Gere and Turner, 1983
Gere, J. A., and Nicholas Turner. *Drawings by Raphael from the Royal Library, the Ashmolean, the British Museum, Chatsworth and Other English Collections*. Exhibition catalogue. London, British Museum, 1983. London, 1983.

Gerson and ter Kuile, 1960
Gerson, Horst, and E. H. ter Kuile. *Art and Architecture in Belgium, 1600 to 1800*. Harmondsworth, 1960.

Ghent, 1950
Quarante chefs-d'oeuvre du Musée de Lille. Exhibition catalogue. Ghent, Museum voor Schone Kunsten, 1950. Ghent, 1950.

Ghent, 1954
Roelandt Savery, 1576–1639. Exhibition catalogue, with introduction by Paul Eeckhout. Ghent, Museum voor Schone Kunsten, 1954. Ghent, 1954.

Giovannetti, 1991
Giovannetti, Alessandra. *Francesco Morandini detto il Poppi: i disegni, i dipinti di Poppi e Castiglion Fiorentino*. Exhibition catalogue. Poppi, Liceo Scientifico Statale "G. Galilei," 1991. Poppi, 1991.

Glen, 1977
Glen, Thomas L. *Rubens and the Counter Reformation: Studies in His Religious Paintings between 1609 and 1620*. New York, 1977.

Goldscheider, 1967
Goldscheider, Ludwig. *Michelangelo: Paintings, Sculptures, Architecture*. London, 1967.

de Goncourt, 1880–84
de Goncourt, Édmond and Jules. *L'art du XVIIIᵉ siècle*. 2 vols. Paris, 1880–84.

de Goncourt, 1909
de Goncourt, Édmond and Jules. *L'art du XVIIIᵉ siècle*. 3rd ed. Vol. 1. Paris, 1909.

Gonse, 1874
Gonse, Louis. "Musée de Lille: le musée de peinture, école française." *Gazette des Beaux-Arts* (February 1874), pp. 138–55; (April 1874), pp. 341–51.

Gonse, 1877
Gonse, Louis. "Le Musée Wicar." *Gazette des Beaux-Arts* (January 1877), pp. 80–95; (April 1877), pp. 386–401; (November 1877), pp. 393–409; (December 1877), pp. 551–60.

Gonse, 1878
Gonse, Louis. "Le Musée Wicar." *Gazette des Beaux-Arts* (January 1878), pp. 44–70; (March 1878), pp. 193–205.

Gonse, 1900
Gonse, Louis. *Les chefs-d'oeuvre des musées de France: la peinture*. Paris, 1900.

Gonse, 1904
Gonse, Louis. *Les chefs-d'oeuvre des musées de France: dessins, sculptures et objets d'art*. Paris, 1904.

Grassi, 1958
Grassi, Luigi. "Il disegno dal Rinascimento al XVIII secolo." *Enciclopedia universale dell'arte* 4 (1958).

Gregori, 1953
Gregori, Mina. "Una Madonna di Lelio Orsi." *Paragone* 43 (1953), pp. 55–56.

Gregori, 1987
Gregori, Mina. "Considerazioni su una mostra." *Atti del Congresso internazionale di studi*. Urbino and Florence, 1984. Reprint. *Studi su Raffaello*. Urbino, 1987.

Greindl, 1956
Greindl, Edith. *Les peintres flamands de nature morte au XVIIᵉ siècle*. Brussels, 1956.

Greindl, 1983
Greindl, Edith. *Les peintres flamands de nature morte au XVIIᵉ siècle*. Brussels, 1983.

Grimm, 1988
Grimm, Claus. *Stilleben: die niederländischen und deutschen Meister*. Stuttgart and Zurich, 1988.

Grunchec, 1978
Grunchec, Philippe. *L'opera completa di Géricault*. Milan, 1978.

Gruyer, 1886
Gruyer, G. *Fra Bartolommeo della Porta et Mariotto Albertinelli*. Paris, 1886.

Gudlaugsson, 1975
Gudlaugsson, S. J. *The Comedians in the Work of Jan Steen and His Contemporaries*. Soest, The Netherlands, 1975.

del Guercio, 1963
del Guercio, Antonio. *Géricault*. Milan, 1963.

Guiffrey, 1908
Guiffrey, Jean. *Jean-Baptiste-Siméon Chardin*. Paris, 1908.

Guillet de Saint-Georges, 1854
Guillet de Saint-Georges, Georges. *Mémoires inédits. . . .* 2 vols. Paris, 1854.

Guratzsch, 1980
Guratzsch, Herwig. *Die Auferweckung des Lazarus in der niederländischen Kunst von 1400 bis 1700*. 2 vols. Kortrijk, 1980.

Haak, 1984
Haak, Bob. *The Golden Age: Dutch Painters of the Seventeenth Century*. New York, 1984.

The Hague–San Francisco, 1990–91
Great Dutch Paintings from America. Exhibition catalogue, by Ben Broos, Edwin Buijsen, Susan Donahue Kuretsky, Walter Liedtke, and Peter C. Sutton. The Hague, Mauritshuis; and San Francisco, Fine Arts Museums of San Francisco, 1990–91. The Hague, 1990.

Hairs, 1965
Hairs, Marie-Louise. *Les peintres flamands de fleurs au XVIIᵉ siècle*. 2nd ed. Brussels, 1965.

Hairs, 1985
Hairs, Marie-Louise. *The Flemish Flower Painters in the Seventeenth Century*. Translated by Eva Grzelak. Brussels, 1985.

Halewood, 1982
Halewood, William H. *Six Subjects of Reformation Art: A Preface to Rembrandt*. Toronto, 1982.

Hallam, 1981
Hallam, John Stephen. "The Two Manners of Louis-Léopold Boilly and French Genre Painting in Transition." *The Art Bulletin* 63 (December 1981), pp. 618–33.

Hamburg, 1983
Luther und die Folgen für die Kunst. Exhibition catalogue, edited by Werner Hofmann, with contributions by Martin Dierker et al. Hamburg, Kunsthalle, 1983. Hamburg, 1983.

Hannover, 1980
Niedersächsisches Landesmuseum. *Verzeichnis der ausgestellten Gemälde.* Hannover, 1980.

Harrisse, 1898
Harrisse, Henry. *L. L. Boilly, peintre, dessinateur, et lithographe: sa vie et son oeuvre, 1761–1845.* Paris, 1898.

Hartt, 1958
Hartt, Frederick. *Giulio Romano.* 2 vols. New Haven, 1958.

Haskell, 1976
Haskell, Francis. *Rediscoveries in Art: Some Aspects of Taste, Fashion and Collecting in England and France.* London, 1976.

Haverkamp-Begemann, 1971
Haverkamp-Begemann, Egbert. "The Sketch." In Thomas Hess and John Ashbery, eds. *Painterly Painting (Art News Annual)* 37, pp. 57–74. New York, 1971.

Heckes, 1991
Heckes, Irving. "Goya's 'Les Jeunes' and 'Les Vieilles.'" *Gazette des Beaux-Arts* (February 1991), pp. 93–100.

Hedicke, 1913
Hedicke, Robert. *Cornelis Floris und die Florisdekoration.* Berlin, 1913.

Held, 1959
Held, Julius S. *Rubens: Selected Drawings.* London, 1959.

Held, 1967
Held, Julius S. "Review of 'Tekeningen von Jacob Jordaens.'" *Kunstchronik* 20 (1967), pp. 94–110.

Held, 1969
Held, Julius S. "Jordaens at Ottawa." *The Burlington Magazine* 3 (May 1969), pp. 265–72.

Held, 1980
Held, Julius S. *The Oil Sketches of Peter Paul Rubens.* 2 vols. Princeton, 1980.

Held, 1982
Held, Julius S. *The Collections of the Detroit Institute of Arts: Flemish and German Paintings of the Seventeenth Century.* Detroit, 1982.

Held, 1986
Held, Julius S. *Rubens: Selected Drawings.* 2nd ed. Oxford, 1986.

Hendy, 1974
Hendy, Philip. *European and American Paintings in the Isabella Stewart Gardner Museum.* Boston, 1974.

Henkel, 1930
Henkel, M. D. "Illustrierte Ausgaben von Ovids Metamorphosen im XV., XVI. und XVII. Jahrhundert." *Vorträge der Bibliothek Warburg* 6 (1930), pp. 58–144.

Hind, 1931
Hind, Arthur M. *Catalogue of Drawings by Dutch and Flemish Artists Preserved in the Department of Prints and Drawings in the British Museum.* London, 1931.

Hind, 1933
Hind, Arthur M. "Studies in English Engraving: Prince Rupert and the Beginnings of Mezzotint." *Connoisseur* 92 (July–December 1933), pp. 382–91.

Hirschmann, 1915
Hirschmann, Otto. "Beitrag zu einem Kommentar von Karel van Manders' 'Grondt der Edel Vry Schilder-Const.'" *Oud Holland* 33 (1915), pp. 81–86.

Hirst, 1961
Hirst, Michael. "The Chigi Chapel in S. Maria della Pace." *Journal of the Warburg and Courtauld Institutes* 24, nos. 3–4 (1961), pp. 161–85.

Hoffman, 1975
Hoffman, Joseph Robert. "Lelio Orsi da Novellara (1511–1587): A Stylistic Chronology." Ph.D. diss., University of Wisconsin, 1975.

Hofrichter, 1989
Hofrichter, Frima F. *Judith Leyster: A Woman Painter in Holland's Golden Age.* Doornspijk, The Netherlands, 1989.

von Holst, 1974
von Holst, Christian. "Fra Bartolomeo und Albertinelli: Beobachtungen zu ihrer Zusammenarbeit am Jüngsten Gericht aus Santa Maria Nuova und in der Werkstatt von San Marco." *Mitteilungen des Kunsthistorischen Institutes in Florenz* 18, no. 3 (1974), pp. 273–318.

Houbraken, 1718–21
Houbraken, Arnold. *De Groote Schouburgh der nederlantsche konstschilders en schilderessen.* 3 vols. Amsterdam, 1718–21.

Houdoy, 1877
Houdoy, Jules. "Les musées de province. I: études sur le Musée de Lille. III: Louis-Léopold Boilly." *L'art* 4 (1877), pp. 63–65, 81–84.

Huchard, 1985
Huchard, Viviane. *Galerie David d'Angers.* Angers, 1985.

Hulsker, 1980
Hulsker, Jan. *The Complete van Gogh: Paintings, Drawings, Sketches.* New York, 1980.

d'Hulst, 1956
d'Hulst, R.-A. *De tekeningen van Jacob Jordaens.* Brussels, 1956.

d'Hulst, 1974
d'Hulst, R.-A. *Jordaens Drawings.* 4 vols. London and New York, 1974.

d'Hulst, 1982
d'Hulst, R.-A. *Jacob Jordaens.* Ithaca, New York, 1982.

Huyghe, 1948
Huyghe, René. *Le dessin français au XIXe siècle.* Lausanne, 1948.

Illustrated Bartsch
Strauss, Walter L., ed. *The Illustrated Bartsch.* New York, 1978–.

Ingold, 1886
Ingold, Augustin-Marie-Pierre. *L'Église de l'Oratoire Saint-Honoré: étude historique et archéologique.* Paris, 1886.

Jaffé, 1968
Jaffé, Michael. *Jacob Jordaens, 1593–1678.* Exhibition catalogue. Ottawa, National Gallery of Canada, 1968. Ottawa, 1968.

Jaffé, 1977
Jaffé, Michael. *Rubens and Italy.* Oxford, 1977.

Janson, 1957
Janson, Horst W. *The Sculpture of Donatello.* 2 vols. Princeton, 1957.

Jantzen, 1910
Jantzen, Hans. *Das niederländische Architekturbild.* Leipzig, 1910.

Joannides, 1983
Joannides, Paul. *The Drawings of Raphael with a Complete Catalogue.* Berkeley and Los Angeles, 1983.

Johnson, 1981–89
Johnson, Lee. *The Paintings of Eugène Delacroix: A Critical Catalogue*. 6 vols. Oxford, 1981–89.

de Jongh, 1975–76
de Jongh, E. "Pearls of Virtue and Pearls of Vice." *Simiolus* 8, no. 2 (1975–76), pp. 69–97.

Jost, 1968
Jost, Ingrid. "Goltzius, Dürer et le collectionneur de coquillages Jan Govertsz." *La revue du Louvre et des musées de France* 18, no. 2 (1968), pp. 57–64.

Jouin, 1878
Jouin, Henri. *David d'Angers: sa vie, son oeuvre, ses contemporains*. 2 vols. Paris, 1878.

Journal
Joubin, André, ed. *Eugène Delacroix: Journal, 1822–1863*. Paris, 1931–32. Reprint. Paris, 1981.

Judson, 1959
Judson, J. Richard. *Gerrit van Honthorst: A Discussion of His Position in Dutch Art*. Utrecht, 1959.

Judson, 1970
Judson, J. Richard. *Dirck Barendsz., Excellent Painter from Amsterdam*. Amsterdam, 1970.

Kaufmann, 1988
Kaufmann, Thomas DaCosta. *The School of Prague: Painting at the Court of Rudolf II*. Chicago and London, 1988.

Kelch, 1986
Kelch, Jan et al. *Bilder im Blickpunkt: Der Mann mit dem Goldhelm*. (Eine Dokumentation der Gemäldegalerie in Zusammenarbeit mit dem Rathgen-Forschungslabor SMPK und dem Hahn-Meitner-Institut für Kernforschung Berlin.) Berlin, 1986.

Klessmann, 1970
Klessmann, Rüdiger. "Johann Liss: zum Werk der vorvenezianischen Zeit." *Kunstchronik* 23 (October 1970), pp. 292–93.

Klessmann, 1986
Klessmann, Rüdiger. "Addenda to Johann Liss." *The Burlington Magazine* 996 (March 1986), pp. 191–97.

Klinge, 1991
Klinge, Margret. *David Teniers the Younger*. Exhibition catalogue. Antwerp, Koninklijk Museum voor Schone Kunsten, 1991. Antwerp, 1991.

Knapp, 1903
Knapp, Fritz. *Fra Bartolommeo della Porta und die Schule von San Marco*. Halle, 1903.

Koevoets, 1976
Koevoets, Ben. *Oude tekeningen in het bezit van de Gemeentemusea van Amsterdam waaronder de collectie Fodor: Italië, 15e–18e eeuw*. Amsterdam, 1976.

Konečnỳ, 1983
Konečnỳ, Lubomìr. "Ueberlegungen zu einem Stilleben von Pieter Boel." *Artibus et historiae* 7 (1983), pp. 125–39.

Kortrijk, 1976
Roeland Savery. Exhibition catalogue, edited by P. Debrabandere. Kortrijk, Stedelijk Museum voor Schone Kunsten, 1976. Kortrijk, 1976.

Krempel, 1983
Krempel, U. *Jan van Kessel d. Ae., 1626–1679: die vier Erdteile*. Munich, 1983.

Kultzen, 1958
Kultzen, R., with Nolfo di Carpegna. *Michael Sweerts en Tijdgenoten*.

Exhibition catalogue. Rotterdam, Museum Boymans-van Beuningen, 1958. Rotterdam, 1958.

Kurz, 1937
Kurz, Otto. "Guido Reni." *Jahrbuch der kunsthistorischen Sammlungen in Wien* 11 (1937), pp. 189–220.

Kurz, 1937–38
Kurz, Otto. "Giorgio Vasari's 'Libro de' disegni.'" *Old Master Drawings* 12 (June 1937–March 1938), pp. 1–15, 32–44.

Laclotte, 1956
Laclotte, Michel. *De Giotto à Bellini: les primitifs italiens dans les musées de France*. Exhibition catalogue. Paris, Orangerie des Tuileries, 1956. Paris, 1956.

de La Monneraye, 1929
de La Monneraye, J. *Documents sur la vie du peintre Louis Boilly pendant la Révolution*. Paris, 1929.

Larsen, 1988
Larsen, Erik. *The Paintings of Anthony van Dyck*. 2 vols. Freren, Germany, 1988.

de Lastic, 1979
de Lastic, Georges. "Portraits d'artistes de Largillierre." *Connaissance des arts* 9 (1979), pp. 20–21.

Laveissière and Michel, 1991
Laveissière, Sylvain, and Régis Michel, with the assistance of Bruno Chenique. *Géricault*. Exhibition catalogue. Paris, Grand Palais, 1991–92. Paris, 1991.

Leblanc, 1932
Leblanc, Marie-Louise. *Le Musée de Lille: peintures*. Paris, 1932.

Léger, 1929
Léger, Charles. *Courbet*. Paris, 1929.

Legrand, 1963
Legrand, F.-C. *Les peintres flamands de genre au XVIIᵉ siècle*. Brussels, 1963.

Leiden, 1970
IJdelheid der ijdelheden: Hollandse Vanitas-voorstellingen uit de zeventiende eeuw. Exhibition catalogue, by Ingvar Bergström et al. Leiden, Stedelijk Museum "De Lakenhal," 1970. Leiden, 1970.

Lenglart, 1893
Lenglart, Jules. *Catalogue des tableaux du Musée de Lille*. Lille, 1893.

Lenoir, 1886
Lenoir, Albert. *Inventaire général des richesses d'art de la France, Archives du Musée des monuments français*. Vol. 2. Paris, 1886.

Levin, 1888
Levin, Theodor. "Handschriftliche Bemerkungen von Erasmus Quellinus." *Zeitschrift für bildende Kunst* 23 (1888), pp. 133–38, 171–76.

Liedtke, 1982
Liedtke, Walter A. *Architectural Painting in Delft*. Doornspijk, The Netherlands, 1982.

Liedtke, 1984
Liedtke, Walter A. *Flemish Paintings in The Metropolitan Museum of Art*. 2 vols. New York, 1984.

Liedtke, 1988
Liedtke, Walter A. "Toward a History of Dutch Genre Painting—II: The South Holland Tradition." In R. E. Fleischer and S. S. Munshower, eds. *The Age of Rembrandt: Studies in Seventeenth-Century Dutch Painting* (Papers in Art History from the Pennsylvania State University, vol. 3), pp. 92–131. University Park, Pennsylvania, 1988.

Liedtke, 1989
Liedtke, Walter A. "Reconstructing Rembrandt: Portraits from the

Early Years in Amsterdam (1631–34)." *Apollo* 129, no. 327 (May 1989), pp. 323–31, 371–72.

Liedtke, 1991
Liedtke, Walter A. "Pepys and the Pictorial Arts." *Apollo* 133, no. 350 (April 1991), pp. 227–37.

Liedtke, 1992
Liedtke, Walter A. "Rembrandt and the Rembrandt Style." *Apollo* 135, no. 361 (March 1992), pp. 140–45.

Lille, 1889
Exposition historique du Centenaire de 1789. Exhibition catalogue. Lille, Mairie de Lille, 1889. Lille, 1889.

Lille, 1968
Au temps du roi soleil: les peintres de Louis XIV (1660–1715). Exhibition catalogue, by Albert Châtelet, Jacques Thuillier, Antoine Schnapper, Sylvie de Langlade, Georges de Lastic, and Geneviève Becquart. Lille, Palais des Beaux-Arts, 1968. Lille, 1968.

Lille, 1981
Donation d'Antoine Brasseur (Grands noms, grandes figures du Musée de Lille, no. 2). Exhibition catalogue, by Hervé Oursel, M. P. Baudienville, Annie Castier, and Françoise Gaultier. Lille, Musée des Beaux-Arts, 1981. Lille, 1981.

Lille, 1983-1
Autour de David: dessins néo-classiques du Musée des Beaux-Arts de Lille. Exhibition catalogue, by Philippe Bordes, Maria-Vera Cresti, Jean-François Méjanès, Annie Scottez, and Arlette Sérullaz. Lille, Musée des Beaux-Arts, 1983. Lille, 1983.

Lille, 1984
Le Chevalier Wicar: peintre, dessinateur et collectionneur lillois. Exhibition catalogue, by Maria-Vera Cresti, Hervé Oursel, and Annie Scottez-De Wambrechies. Lille, Musée des Beaux-Arts, 1984. Lille, 1984.

Lille, 1988–89
Boilly, 1761–1845: un grand peintre français de la Révolution à la Restauration. Exhibition catalogue, by Arnauld Brejon de Lavergnée, Susan L. Siegfried, Sylvain Laveissière, and Annie Scottez-De Wambrechies. Lille, Musée des Beaux-Arts, 1988–89. Lille, 1988.

Lille–Arras–Dunkirk, 1972–73
Peinture hollandaise (Trésors des musées du Nord de la France, no. 1). Exhibition catalogue, by Jacques Foucart and Hervé Oursel, with Françoise Baligand and Françoise Maison. Lille, Musée des Beaux-Arts; Arras, Musée d'Arras; and Dunkirk, Musée des Beaux-Arts, 1972–73. Lille, 1972.

Lille–Calais–Arras, 1977
La peinture flamande au temps de Rubens (Trésors des musées du Nord de la France, no. 3). Exhibition catalogue, by Françoise Baligand, Philippe-Gérard Chabert, Jacques Foucart, Laurence Hardy-Marais, Jean Lacambre, Françoise Maison, Hervé Oursel, and Dominique Vieville. Lille, Musée des Beaux-Arts; Calais, Musée des Beaux-Arts; and Arras, Musée d'Arras, 1977. Lille, 1977.

Lille–Calais–Arras–Douai, 1975–76
Peinture française, 1770–1830 (Trésors des musées du Nord de la France, no. 2). Exhibition catalogue, by Hervé Oursel et al. Lille, Musée des Beaux-Arts; Calais, Musée des Beaux-Arts; Arras, Musée d'Arras; and Douai, Musée de Douai, La Chartreuse, 1975–76. Lille, 1975.

Lille–Dunkirk–Valenciennes, 1980
La peinture française des 17ᵉ et 18ᵉ siècles (Trésors des musées du Nord de la France, no. 4). Exhibition catalogue, by Hervé Oursel et al. Lille, Musée des Beaux-Arts; Dunkirk, Musée des Beaux-Arts; and Valenciennes, Musée des Beaux-Arts, 1980. Lille, 1980.

Lindeman, 1929
Lindeman, C. M. A. A. *Joachim Anthonisz. Wtewael*. Utrecht, 1929.

London, 1981
Wallerant Vaillant. Exhibition catalogue. London, Christopher Mendez, 1981. London, 1981.

López-Rey, 1964
López-Rey, José. "Goya's Cast of Characters from the Peninsular War." *Apollo* 79 (January 1964), pp. 54–61.

Lowenthal, 1986
Lowenthal, Anne W. *Joachim Wtewael and Dutch Mannerism*. Doornspijk, The Netherlands, 1986.

Lugano–Rome, 1989–90
Pier Francesco Mola: 1612–1666. Exhibition catalogue, by Manuela Kahn-Rossi. Lugano, Museo Cantonale d'Arte; and Rome, Musei Capitolini, 1989–90. Milan, 1989.

Lugt, 1956
Lugt, Frits. *Les marques de collections de dessins et d'estampes*. The Hague, 1956.

Mabille de Poncheville, André. *See* de Poncheville, André Mabille

Mabilleau, 1894
Mabilleau, Léopold. "Les dessins d'Ingres au Musée de Montauban." *Gazette des Beaux-Arts* (September 1894), pp. 177–201; (November 1894), pp. 371–90.

McCorquodale, 1977
McCorquodale, Charles. "Carlo Dolci's David with the Head of Goliath: A Rediscovered Masterpiece of the Florentine Baroque." *Connoisseur* 196, no. 787 (1977), pp. 54–59.

Macdonald, 1969
Macdonald, Bruce K. "The Quarry by Gustave Courbet." *Bulletin: Museum of Fine Arts, Boston* 67, no. 348 (1969), pp. 52–71.

Maclaren and Brown, 1991
Maclaren, Neil, and Christopher Brown. *The National Gallery Catalogues: The Dutch School, 1600–1900*. 2 vols. London, 1991.

Maffei, 1732
Maffei, S. *Verona illustrata*. Verona, 1732.

Manke, 1963
Manke, Ilse. *Emanuel de Witte, 1617–1692*. Amsterdam, 1963.

Mantua, 1989
Giulio Romano. Exhibition catalogue, by Ernest H. Gombrich, Manfredo Tafuri, Sylvia Ferino-Pagden, Christoph L. Frommel, Konrad Oberhuber, Amedeo Belluzzi, Kurt W. Forster, and Howard Burns. Mantua, Palazzo del Tè and Palazzo Ducale, 1989. Milan, 1989.

Marabottini, 1988
Marabottini, Alessandro. *Jacopo Chimenti da Empoli*. Rome, 1988.

Marmottan, 1889
Marmottan, Paul. *Notice historique et critique sur les peintres Louis et François Watteau dits: Watteau de Lille*. Lille, 1889.

Marmottan, 1913
Marmottan, Paul. *Le peintre Louis Boilly (1761–1845)*. Paris, 1913.

Martin, 1913
Martin, W. *Gerard Dou* (Klassiker der Kunst). Stuttgart and Berlin, 1913.

Martin, 1925
Martin, W. "Figuurstukken van Jan Davidszoon de Heem." *Oud Holland* 42 (1925), pp. 42–45.

Martin, 1969
Martin, John Rupert. *Rubens: The Antwerp Altarpieces*. New York, 1969.

Meaux, 1988–89
De Nicolò dell'Abate à Nicolas Poussin: aux sources du classicisme, 1550–1650.

Exhibition catalogue, by Sylvie Béguin et al. Meaux, Musée Bossuet, 1988–89. Meaux, 1988.

Meier-Graefe, 1922
Meier-Graefe, J. *Eugène Delacroix: Beiträge zu einer Analyse*. Munich, 1922.

Meijer, 1988
Meijer, Fred G. "Jan Davidsz. de Heem's Earliest Paintings, 1626–1628." *Mercury* 7 (1988), pp. 29–36.

Meijer, 1989
Meijer, Fred G. *Still Life Paintings from the Golden Age (Own Collection)*. Rotterdam, 1989.

Meltzoff, 1942
Meltzoff, Stanley. "The Revival of the Le Nains." *The Art Bulletin* 24 (September 1942), pp. 258–86.

Meyer, 1984
Meyer, Véronique. "Gilles Rousselet et la gravure d'interprétation en France au XVIIᵉ siècle." Thesis. Paris IV Sorbonne, 1984.

Michel, 1771
Michel, J. F. *Histoire de la vie de P. P. Rubens, chevalier et seigneur de Steen, illustrée d'anecdotes. . . .* Brussels, 1771.

Michel, 1900
Michel, Émile. *Rubens: sa vie, son oeuvre et son temps*. Paris, 1900.

Millar, 1967
Millar, Oliver. "An Exile in Paris: The Notebooks of Richard Symonds." In *Studies in Renaissance and Baroque Art Presented to Anthony Blunt*, pp. 157–64. London and New York, 1967.

Millier, 1955
Millier, Arthur. *The Drawings of Ingres*. Los Angeles and London, 1955.

Milman, 1982
Milman, Miriam. *Les illusions de la réalité: le trompe l'oeil*. Geneva, 1982.

de Mirimonde, 1964
de Mirimonde, A. P. "Les natures mortes à instruments de musique de Pieter Boel." In *Jaarboek van het Koninklijk Museum voor Schone Kunsten Antwerpen* (1964), pp. 107–43.

de Mirimonde, 1970
de Mirimonde, A. P. "Musique et symbolisme chez Jan-Davidszoon de Heem, Cornelis Janszoon et Jan II [sic] Janszoon de Heem." In *Jaarboek van het Koninklijk Museum voor Schone Kunsten Antwerpen* 10 (1970), pp. 241–95.

Monbeig-Goguel, 1972
Monbeig-Goguel, Catherine. *Inventaire général des dessins italiens. I: Vasari et son temps*. Paris, 1972.

Monbeig-Goguel, 1987
Monbeig-Goguel, Catherine. "Le tracé invisible des dessins de Raphaël." *Atti del Congresso internazionale di studi*. 2 vols. Urbino and Florence, 1984. Reprint. *Studi su Raffaello*. Urbino, 1987.

Morassi, 1973
Morassi, Antonio. *Guardi: Antonio e Francesco Guardi*. 2 vols. Venice [1973].

Morassi, 1975
Morassi, Antonio. *Guardi: tutti i disegni di Antonio, Francesco e Giacomo Guardi*. Venice, 1975.

Morelli, 1891–92
Morelli [Lermolieff], Giovanni. "Handzeichnungen italienischer Meister." *Kunstchronik* 3 (1891–92), no. 17, cols. 289–94; no. 22, cols. 373–78; no. 26, cols. 441–45.

Morford, 1991
Morford, Mark. *Stoics and Neostoics: Rubens and the Circle of Lipsius*. Princeton, 1991.

Morolli, 1989
Morolli, Gabriele. "Donatello e Alberti 'amicissimi.'" In *Donatello-Studien: italienische Forschungen herausgegeben vom Kunsthistorischen Institut in Florenz* 16, pp. 43–67. Munich, 1989.

Müllenmeister, 1988
Müllenmeister, Kurt J. *Roelant Savery*. Freren, Germany, 1988.

Muller, 1906
Muller, Samuel. "Arnoldus Buchelius, Traiecti Batavorum Descriptio." *Bijdragen en mededeelingen van het Historisch Genootschap (Gevestigd te Utrecht)* 27 (1906), pp. 131–268.

Munhall, 1976
Munhall, Edgar. *Jean-Baptiste Greuze: 1725–1805*. Exhibition catalogue. Hartford, Wadsworth Atheneum; San Francisco, California Palace of the Legion of Honor; and Dijon, Musée des Beaux-Arts, 1976–77. Hartford, 1976.

Münster–Baden-Baden, 1979–80
Stilleben in Europa. Exhibition catalogue, edited by Uta Bernsmeier, Christian Klemm, Joseph Lammers, Gerhard Langemeyer, and Gisela Luther. Münster, Westfälisches Landesmuseum für Kunst und Kulturgeschichte; and Baden-Baden, Staatliche Kunsthalle, 1979–80. Münster, 1979.

Müntz, 1888
Müntz, Eugène. *Les collections des Médicis au quinzième siècle*. Paris, 1888.

Murphy, 1972
Murphy, Anne S. "Riderless Race at Rome." *Bulletin: The Walters Art Gallery* 24, no. 6 (March 1972), n.p.

Naumann, 1978
Naumann, Otto. "Frans van Mieris as a Draughtsman." *Master Drawings* 16, no. 1 (1978), pp. 3–34.

Naumann, 1981-1
Naumann, Otto. *Frans van Mieris the Elder (1635–1681)*. 2 vols. Doornspijk, The Netherlands, 1981.

Naumann, 1981-2
Naumann, Otto. "Van Mieris as a 'Money Maker.'" *tableau* 3, no. 5 (April–May 1981), pp. 649–56.

New York, 1985
Liechtenstein: The Princely Collections. Exhibition catalogue. New York, The Metropolitan Museum of Art, 1985. New York, 1985.

Nochlin, 1971
Nochlin, Linda. *Realism*. New York, 1971.

Nochlin, 1976
Nochlin, Linda. *Gustave Courbet: A Study of Style and Society*. New York, 1976.

Le Normand-Romain, 1990
Le Normand-Romain, Antoinette. "Des archives impérissables: les monuments publics et funéraires." In Fondation Courbertin. *Aux grands hommes, David d'Angers*, pp. 43–50. Saint-Rémy-lès-Chevreuse, 1990.

Oberhuber, 1972
Oberhuber, Konrad. *Raphaels Zeichnungen*. Vol. 9. Berlin, 1972.

Oberhuber, 1983
Oberhuber, Konrad, Eckhart Knab, and Erwin Mitsch, with the assistance of Sylvia Ferino-Pagden. *Raphael: die Zeichnungen*. Stuttgart, 1983.

Oldenbourg, 1914
Oldenbourg, Rudolf. "Jan Lys." *Jahrbuch der Königlich Preussischen Kunstsammlungen* 35 (1914), pp. 136–67.

Oldenbourg, 1915
Oldenbourg, Rudolf. "An Unidentified Picture by Jan Lys." *Art in America* 4 (December 1915), p. 57.

Oldenbourg, 1921-1
Oldenbourg, Rudolf. *Jan Lys.* Rome, 1921.

Oldenbourg, 1921-2
Oldenbourg, Rudolf. *P. P. Rubens, des Meisters Gemälde* (Klassiker der Kunst). Stuttgart, 1921.

Olschki, 1960
Olschki, Leonardo. *Marco Polo's Asia.* Translated by John A. Scott. Berkeley and Los Angeles, 1960.

Oursel, 1974-1
Oursel, Hervé. *La collection d'Alexandre Leleux* (Grands noms, grandes figures du Musée de Lille, no. 1). Exhibition catalogue. Lille, Musée des Beaux-Arts, 1974. Lille, 1974.

Oursel, 1974-2
Oursel, Hervé. *From Poussin to Puvis de Chavannes: A Loan Exhibition of French Drawings from the Collections of the Musée des Beaux-Arts at Lille.* Exhibition catalogue. London, Heim Gallery; Cambridge, Fitzwilliam Museum; Birmingham, City Museum and Art Gallery; and Glasgow, Glasgow Art Gallery and Museum, 1974–75. London, 1974.

Oursel, 1976
Oursel, Hervé. "XIXᵉ siècle." *La revue du Louvre et des musées de France,* nos. 5–6 (1976), p. 388.

Oursel, 1984
Oursel, Hervé. *Le Musée des Beaux-Arts de Lille.* Paris, 1984.

Oursel and Scottez, 1979
Oursel, Hervé, and Annie Scottez-De Wambrechies. "Lille, Musée des Beaux-Arts: acquisitions de peintures, sculptures et objets d'art." *La revue du Louvre et des musées de France,* no. 29 (1979), pp. 380–83.

Oursel and Scottez, 1980
Oursel, Hervé, and Annie Scottez-De Wambrechies. "Lille, Musée des Beaux-Arts: deux portraits de Boilly et autres acquisitions." *La revue du Louvre et des musées de France,* nos. 5–6 (1980), pp. 309–10.

Ovid, 1944–46
Ovid. *Metamorphoses.* Translated by Frank Justus Miller. 2 vols. Cambridge, Massachusetts, and London, 1944–46.

Pallucchini, 1934
Pallucchini, Rodolfo. *L'arte di Giovanni Battista Piazzetta.* Bologna, 1934.

Pallucchini, 1950
Pallucchini, Rodolfo. "Opere del Museo di Lilla esposte a Gand." *Arte Veneta* 4 (1950), pp. 178–79.

Pallucchini, 1981
Pallucchini, Rodolfo. *La pittura veneziana del Seicento.* 2 vols. Milan, 1981.

Paris, 1965
Le décor de la vie privée en Hollande au XVIIᵉ siècle. Exhibition catalogue, with introduction by Sadi de Gorter. Paris, Institut Néerlandais, 1965. Paris, 1965.

Paris, 1965–66
Le XVIᵉ siècle européen: peintures et dessins dans les collections publiques françaises. Exhibition catalogue, by Roseline Bacou, Germaine Barnard, Jeannine Baticle, Sylvie Béguin, Victor Beyer, Arlette Calvet, Françoise Coulanges-Rosenberg, Jacques Foucart, Carlos van Hasselt, Michel Laclotte, Catherine Monbeig-Goguel, Pierre Rosenberg, and Jacques Thuillier. Paris, Musée du Petit Palais, 1965–66. Paris, 1965.

Paris, 1967
La vie en Hollande au XVIIᵉ siècle. Exhibition catalogue, with introduction by Paul Zumthor. Paris, Musée des Arts Décoratifs, 1967. Paris, 1967.

Paris, 1967–68
Ingres. Exhibition catalogue, by Lise Duclaux, Jacques Foucart, Hans Naef, Maurice Sérullaz, and Daniel Ternois. Paris, Musée du Petit Palais, 1967–68. Paris, 1967.

Paris, 1970–71
Le siècle de Rembrandt: tableaux hollandais des collections publiques françaises. Exhibition catalogue, by Arnauld Brejon de Lavergnée, Christian Cocault, Jean-Pierre Cuzin, Jacques Foucart, Jacques-Paul Foucart-Borville, Jean Lacambre, Jean-Hubert Martin, Véronique Noël-Bouton, Pierre-Henri Picou, Pierre Rosenberg, and Jacques Vilain. Paris, Musée du Petit Palais, 1970–71. Paris, 1970.

Paris, 1977–78
Le siècle de Rubens dans les collections publiques françaises. Exhibition catalogue, by Jean-Pierre De Bruyn, Philippe Durey, Jacques Foucart, Françoise Heilbrun, Jean Lacambre, Monique Nonne, Hervé Oursel, and Alain Roy. Paris, Grand Palais, 1977–78. Paris, 1977.

Paris, 1979
Réunion des musées nationaux. *Catalogue sommaire illustré des peintures du Musée du Louvre. I: Écoles flamande et hollandaise.* Inventory, by Arnauld Brejon de Lavergnée, Jacques Foucart, and Nicole Reynaud. Paris, 1979.

Paris, 1983–84
Hommage à Raphaël: Raphaël dans les collections françaises. Exhibition catalogue, by Sylvie Béguin, Jean-Pierre Cuzin, Philippe Costamagna, Odile Menegaux, Bernadette Py, Françoise Viatte, and Catherine Monbeig-Goguel, with Dominique Cordellier. Paris, Grand Palais, 1983–84. Paris, 1983.

Paris, 1990–91
Vouet. Exhibition catalogue, by Jacques Thuillier, with Jean-Pierre Cuzin, Barbara Brejon de Lavergnée, and Denis Lavalle. Paris, Grand Palais, 1990–91. Paris, 1990.

Paris, 1991
Dessins anciens des écoles du nord, françaises et italiennes. Exhibition catalogue. Paris, Bob P. Haboldt & Co., 1991. Paris, 1991.

Paris, 1991–92-1
Géricault. Exhibition catalogue, by Régis Michel, Bruno Chenique, and Sylvain Laveissière. Paris, Grand Palais, 1991–92. Paris, 1991.

Paris, 1991–92-2
Portrait de l'artiste: images des peintres, 1600–1890. Exhibition catalogue, with introductions by Elvire Perego, Evelyne Saez, and John Spike. Paris, Bob P. Haboldt & Co., 1991–92. Paris, 1991.

Paris–Detroit–New York, 1974–75
French Painting, 1774–1830: The Age of Revolution. Exhibition catalogue. Paris, Grand Palais; Detroit, Detroit Institute of Arts; and New York, The Metropolitan Museum of Art, 1974–75. Detroit and New York, 1975.

Paris–London, 1977–78
Gustave Courbet (1819–1877). Exhibition catalogue. Paris, Grand Palais; and London, Royal Academy of Arts, 1977–78. Paris and London, 1977.

Paris–Milan, 1988–89
Seicento: le siècle de Caravage dans les collections françaises. Exhibition catalogue, by Olivier Chevrillon, Arnauld Brejon, Natalie Volle, Giuliano Briganti, Yves Bonnefoy, Christel Haffner, Sabine Cotté, and Denis Lavalle. Paris, Grand Palais; and Milan, Palazzo Reale, 1988–89. Paris, 1988.

Paris–Ottawa, 1976–77
Puvis de Chavannes. Exhibition catalogue, by Louis d'Argencourt, Marie-Christine Boucher-Regnault, Douglas Druick, and Jacques Foucart. Paris, Grand Palais; and Ottawa, National Gallery of Canada, 1976–77. Paris, 1976.

Paris–Versailles, 1989–90
David, 1748–1825. Exhibition catalogue, by Antoine Schnapper, Arlette Sérullaz, Lina Propeck, and Élisabeth Agius-d'Yvoire. Paris, Musée du Louvre; and Versailles, Musée National du Château, 1989–90. Paris, 1989.

Parker, 1927
Parker, K. T. *North Italian Drawings of the Quattrocento*. London, 1927.

Parker, 1956
Parker, K. T. *Catalogue of the Collection of Drawings in the Ashmolean Museum. II: Italian Schools*. Oxford, 1956.

Pascal and Gaucheron, 1931
Pascal, André, and Roger Gaucheron. *Documents sur la vie et l'oeuvre de Chardin*. Paris, 1931.

Pepper, 1984
Pepper, Stephen. *Guido Reni: A Complete Catalogue of His Works with an Introductory Text*. New York, 1984.

Pepper, 1988
Pepper, Stephen. *Guido Reni: l'opera completa*. Novara, 1988.

Pérez-Sánchez and Sayre, 1989
Peréz-Sánchez, Alfonso E., and Eleanor A. Sayre. *Goya and the Spirit of Enlightenment*. Exhibition catalogue. Madrid, Museo del Prado; Boston, Museum of Fine Arts; and New York, The Metropolitan Museum of Art, 1988–89. Boston, 1989.

Pérez-Sánchez and Spinosa, 1978
Pérez-Sánchez, Alfonso, and Nicola Spinosa. *L'opera completa del Ribera*. Milan, 1978.

Perkins, 1864
Perkins, Charles C. *Tuscan Sculptors: Their Lives, Works, and Times*. 2 vols. London, 1864.

Petit Larousse
Petit Larousse de la peinture. 2 vols. Paris, 1979.

Petrioli Tofani, 1982
Petrioli Tofani, Annamaria. "Postille al 'Primato del Disegno.'" *Bollettino d'arte* 13 (1982), pp. 63–88.

Pevsner and Grautoff, 1928
Pevsner, Nikolaus, and Otto Grautoff. *Barockmalerei in den romanischen Ländern (Handbuch der Kunstwissenschaft)*. Wildpark-Potsdam, 1928.

Philadelphia–Berlin–London, 1984
Masters of Seventeenth-Century Dutch Genre Painting. Exhibition catalogue, by Peter C. Sutton, with contributions by Christopher Brown, Jan Kelch, Otto Naumann, William Robinson, and Cynthia von Bogendorf-Rupprath. Philadelphia, Philadelphia Museum of Art; Berlin, Staatliche Museen Preussischer Kulturbesitz, Gemäldegalerie; and London, Royal Academy of Arts, 1984. Philadelphia, 1984.

Phillips, 1894
Phillips, Claude. "The Ruston Collection: The Old Masters." *Magazine of Art* 17 (1894), pp. 19–26.

Piganiol de la Force, 1742
Piganiol de la Force, Jean Aimar. *Description de Paris, de Versailles, de Marly, de Meudon. . . .* 7 vols. Paris, 1742.

Pigler, 1974
Pigler, Andor. *Barockthemen*. 3 vols. Budapest, 1974.

Playter, 1972
Playter, Caroline B. "Willem Duyster and Pieter Codde: The 'Duystere Werelt' of Dutch Genre Painting, c. 1625–1635." Ph.D. diss., Harvard University, 1972.

Plietzsch, 1956
Plietzsch, Eduard. "Randbemerkungen zur holländischen Interieurmalerei am Beginn des 17. Jahrhunderts." *Wallraf-Richartz-Jahrbuch* 18 (1956), pp. 174–96.

Plietzsch, 1960
Plietzsch, Eduard. *Holländische und flämische Maler des 17. Jahrhunderts*. Leipzig, 1960.

Pluchart, 1889
Pluchart, Henry. *Ville de Lille, Musée de Lille, Musée Wicar. Notice des dessins, cartons, pastels, miniatures et grisailles exposés précédé d'une introduction et du résumé de l'inventaire général*. Lille, 1889.

de Poncheville, 1926
de Poncheville, André Mabille. "Les peintres Louis et François Watteau dits 'Watteau de Lille.'" *Gazette des Beaux-Arts* (April 1926), pp. 219–30.

de Poncheville, 1931
de Poncheville, André Mabille. *Boilly*. Paris, 1931.

de Poncheville, 1953
de Poncheville, André Mabille. *Philippe de Champaigne: sa vie et son oeuvre*. Paris, 1953.

Pope-Hennessy, 1986
Pope-Hennessy, John. "Donatello sconosciuto." *FMR* 42 (May 1986), pp. 68–69.

Pope-Hennessy, 1970
Pope-Hennessy, John. *Raphael*. New York, 1970.

Pope-Hennessy, 1985
Pope-Hennessy, John. *Italian High Renaissance and Baroque Sculpture*. New York, 1985.

Popham and Pouncey, 1950
Popham, A. E., and Philip Pouncey. *Italian Drawings in the Department of Prints and Drawings in the British Museum: The Fourteenth and Fifteenth Centuries*. 2 vols. London, 1950.

Popham and Wilde, 1949
Popham, A. E., and Johannes Wilde. *The Italian Drawings of the XV and XVI Centuries in the Collection of His Majesty the King at Windsor Castle*. London, 1949.

Posner, 1973
Posner, Donald. *Watteau: A Lady at Her Toilet*. New York, 1973.

Posse, 1925–26
Posse, Hans. "Ein unbekanntes Gemälde des deutsch-venetianischen Malers Johann Liss in der Dresdner Gemäldegalerie." *Zeitschrift für bildende Kunst*, n.s., 59 (1925–26), p. 27.

Pouncey, 1964
Pouncey, Philip. "Review of Bernard Berenson, *I disegni dei pittori fiorentini*." *Master Drawings* 2, no. 3 (1964), pp. 278–93.

dal Pozzo, 1718
dal Pozzo, B. *Le vite de' pittori . . . veronesi*. Verona, 1718.

Préaud, 1988
Préaud, Maxime. *L'oeil d'or—Claude Mellan*. Exhibition catalogue. Paris, Bibliothèque Nationale, Galerie Mazarine, 1988. Paris, 1988.

Providence, 1983
Old Master Drawings from the Museum of Art, Rhode Island School of Design. Exhibition catalogue, by Deborah Johnson et al. Providence, Rhode Island School of Design, Museum of Art, 1983. Providence, 1983.

Providence, 1984
Children of Mercury: The Education of Artists in the Sixteenth and Seventeenth Centuries. Exhibition catalogue, by Gabriele Bleeke-Byrne et al. Providence, Brown University, Department of Art, 1984. Providence, 1984.

Puppi, 1962
Puppi, Lionello. *Bartolomeo Montagna*. Venice, 1962.

van Puyvelde, 1953
van Puyvelde, Leo. *Jordaens*. Brussels and Paris, 1953.

Quintin, 1929
Quintin, Daniel. *Les Chardin de la collection H. de Rothschild*. Paris, 1929.

Ragghianti Collobi, 1974
Ragghianti Collobi, Licia. *Il libro de' disegni del Vasari.* 2 vols. Florence, 1974.

Rand, 1991
Rand, Richard, with a contribution by Joseph Fronek. *The Raising of Lazarus by Rembrandt.* Exhibition catalogue. Los Angeles, Los Angeles County Museum of Art, 1991–92. Los Angeles, 1991

Recklinghausen–Utrecht, 1962
Miracula Christi. Exhibition catalogue. Recklinghausen, Städtische Kunsthalle; and Utrecht, Aartsbisschoppelijk, 1962. Recklinghausen, 1962.

Reggio Emilia, 1987–88
Lelio Orsi, 1511–1587: dipinti e disegni. Exhibition catalogue, by Nora Clerici Bagozzi, Fiorella Frisoni, Elio Monducci, and Massimo Pirondini. Reggio Emilia, Teatro Valli, 1987–88. Milan, 1987.

dalli Regoli, 1966
dalli Regoli, Gigetta. *Lorenzo di Credi.* Pisa, 1966.

Reinach, 1897
Reinach, Salomon. *Répertoire de la statuaire grecque et romaine.* 6 vols. Paris, 1897–1931.

Renger, 1981
Renger, Konrad. "Sine Cerere et Baccho friget Venus: zu bacchischen Themen bei Rubens." In Zentralinstitut für Kunstgeschichte and Bayerischen Staatsgemäldesammlungen. *Peter Paul Rubens: Werk und Nachruhm,* pp. 105–35. Munich, 1981.

Reynart, 1856
Reynart, Édouard. *Notices des tableaux, bas-reliefs, et statues exposées dans les galeries du musée des tableaux.* Lille, 1856.

Reynart, 1875
Reynart, Édouard. *Notices des tableaux, bas-reliefs, et statues exposées dans les galeries du musée des tableaux.* Lille, 1875.

Reznicek, 1961
Reznicek, E. K. J. *Die Zeichnungen von Hendrick Goltzius.* 2 vols. Utrecht, 1961.

Riat, 1906
Riat, Georges. *Gustave Courbet.* Paris, 1906.

Robaut, 1885
Robaut, Alfred. *L'oeuvre complet d'Eugène Delacroix.* Paris, 1885.

Robaut, 1905
Robaut, Alfred. *L'oeuvre de Corot par Alfred Robaut, catalogue raisonné et illustré, précédé de l'histoire de Corot et de ses oeuvres par Étienne Moreau-Nélaton.* 5 vols. Paris, 1905.

Robaut, 1927
Paris, Bibliothèque Nationale, Cabinet des Estampes. *Don Moreau-Nélaton. Alfred Robaut. Croquis, calques, notes, photographies, coupures de journaux se rapportant aux oeuvres fausses ou douteuses de Corot.* Paris, 1927.

Robbin, 1990
Robbin, Carmen Roxanne. *Ottavio Leoni and Early Roman Baroque Portraiture.* Ann Arbor, 1990.

Robinson, 1979
Robinson, William W. "Family Portraits of the Golden Age." *Apollo* 110 (December 1979), pp. 490–97.

Rodee, 1967
Rodee, Howard D. "Rubens' Treatment of Antique Armor." *The Art Bulletin* 49 (September 1967), pp. 223–30.

Roelofsz, 1980
Roelofsz, Charles. "'Orpheus en de dieren' van Jacob Savery, of: wie leidde Roelant Savery tot het schilderen van vissen, vogelen en andere dieren?" *tableau* 2 (1980), pp. 312–16.

Roger-Marx, 1933
Roger-Marx, Claude. *Choix de cinquante dessins d'Eugène Delacroix.* Paris, 1933.

Roli, 1969
Roli, Renato. *I disegni italiani del Seicento: scuole emiliana, toscana, romana, marchigiana e umbra.* Treviso, 1969.

Romani, 1982
Romani, Vittoria. "Lelio Orsi e Roma: fra maniera raffaellesca e maniera michelangiolesca." *Prospettiva* 29 (1982), pp. 41–61.

Romani, 1984
Romani, Vittoria. *Lelio Orsi.* Modena, 1984.

Rome, 1975–76
Corot (1796–1875): dipinti e disegni di collezioni francesi. Exhibition catalogue, by Hélène Toussaint, Geneviève Monnier, and Martine Servot. Rome, Accademia di Francia in Roma (Villa Medici), 1975–76. Rome, 1975.

Rome, 1984
Raffaello architetto. Exhibition catalogue, by Christoph Luitpold Frommel et al. Rome, Palazzo dei Conservatori, 1984. Rome, 1984.

Rome, 1984–85
Raffaello in Vaticano. Exhibition catalogue. Vatican City, Braccio di Carlo Magno, 1984–85. Milan, 1984.

Rooses, 1886–92
Rooses, Max. *L'oeuvre de P. P. Rubens.* 5 vols. Antwerp, 1886–92.

Rosenberg, 1960
Rosenberg, Jakob. *Die Zeichnungen Lucas Cranachs d. Ä.* Berlin, 1960.

Rosenberg, 1972
Rosenberg, Pierre. "Un dessin de Simon Vouet au Musée de Berlin." *Berliner Museen* 1 (1972), pp. 30–33.

Rosenberg, 1979
Rosenberg, Pierre. *Chardin, 1699–1779.* Exhibition catalogue. Paris, Grand Palais; Cleveland, Cleveland Museum of Art; and Boston, Museum of Fine Arts. Paris, 1979.

Rosenberg, 1983
Rosenberg, Pierre. *Tout l'oeuvre peinte de Chardin.* Paris, 1983.

Rosenberg, 1990-1
Rosenberg, Pierre. *Masterful Studies: Three Centuries of French Drawings from the Prat Collection.* Exhibition catalogue. New York, National Academy of Design; Fort Worth, Kimbell Art Museum; and Ottawa, National Gallery of Canada, 1990–91. New York, 1990.

Rosenberg, 1990-2
Rosenberg, Pierre. "A Vouet Drawing from the Artist's Roman Period." *Master Drawings* 28, no. 2 (1990), pp. 310–14.

Rosenberg, Slive, and ter Kuile, 1966
Rosenberg, Jakob, Seymour Slive, and E. H. ter Kuile. *Dutch Art and Architecture, 1600–1800.* Harmondsworth, 1966.

Rosenberg and Thuillier, 1988
Rosenberg, Pierre, and Jacques Thuillier. *Laurent de La Hyre, 1606–1656: l'homme et l'oeuvre.* Exhibition catalogue. Grenoble, Musée de Grenoble; Rennes, Musée des Beaux-Arts et d'Archéologie; and Bordeaux, Musée des Beaux-Arts, 1988–89. Geneva and Grenoble, 1988.

Rosenblum, 1965
Rosenblum, Robert. "Letters: 'Jacques-Louis David at Toledo.'" *The Burlington Magazine* 107 (September 1965), pp. 473–75.

Rosenblum, 1990
Rosenblum, Robert. "Reconstructing David." *Art in America* (May 1990), pp. 188–97.

Rosenfeld, 1980
Rosenfeld, Myra Nan. *Largillierre and the Eighteenth-Century Portrait.* Exhibition catalogue. Montreal, Montreal Museum of Fine Arts, 1980. Montreal, 1980.

Rosenthal, 1905
Rosenthal, Léon. *Géricault.* Paris, 1905.

Rotterdam, 1991
Perspectives: Saenredam and the Architectural Painters of the Seventeenth Century. Exhibition catalogue, by Jeroen Giltaij and Guido Jansen, with essays by Jeroen Giltaij, Walter Liedtke, J. Michael Montias, and Rob Ruurs. Rotterdam, Museum Boymans-van Beuningen, 1991. Rotterdam, 1991.

Rotterdam–Braunschweig, 1983–84
Schilderkunst uit de eerste hand: olieverfschetsen van Tintoretto tot Goya. Exhibition catalogue. Rotterdam, Museum Boymans-van Beuningen; and Braunschweig, Herzog Anton Ulrich-Museum, 1983–84. Rotterdam, 1983.

Ruland, 1876
Ruland, C. *The Works of Raphael Santi da Urbino as Represented in the Raphael Collection in the Royal Library at Windsor Castle, Formed by H.R.H. the Prince Consort, 1853–1861, and Completed by Her Majesty the Queen Victoria.* Weimar, 1876.

de Salas, 1964
de Salas, Xavier. "Sur les tableaux de Goya qui appartinrent à son fils." *Gazette des Beaux-Arts* (February 1964), pp. 99–110.

Salerno, 1975
Salerno, Luigi. *L'opera completa di Salvator Rosa.* Milan, 1975.

Salvini, 1951
Salvini, Roberto. "Su Lelio Orsi e la mostra di Reggio Emilia." *Bollettino d'arte* 36, no. 1 (1951), pp. 79–84.

Salvini and Chiodi, 1950
Salvini, Roberto, and Alberto Mario Chiodi. *Mostra di Lelio Orsi.* Exhibition catalogue. Reggio Emilia, Civica Galleria Fontanesi, 1950. Reggio Emilia, 1950.

Sanderus, 1627
Sanderus, Antonius. *Gandavum sive Gandavensium Rerum Libri Sex.* Ghent, 1627.

Santi, 1985
Santi, Francesco. *Galleria Nazionale dell'Umbria: dipinti, sculture e oggetti dei secoli XV–XVI.* Rome, 1985.

Schama, 1988
Schama, Simon. *The Embarrassment of Riches: An Interpretation of Dutch Culture in the Golden Age.* Berkeley, 1988.

Schleier, 1972
Schleier, Erich. "Two New Modelli for Vouet's St. Peter Altarpiece." *The Burlington Magazine* 114 (February 1972), pp. 91–92.

Schneider and Ekkart, 1973
Schneider, H., with a supplement by R. E. O. Ekkart. *Jan Lievens: sein Leben und seine Werke.* Amsterdam, 1973.

Schulz, 1980
Schulz, Juergen. "Tintoretto and the First Competition for the Ducal Palace 'Paradise.'" *Arte Veneta* 34 (1980), pp. 112–26.

Schwartz, 1985
Schwartz, Gary. *Rembrandt: His Life, His Paintings.* Harmondsworth, 1985.

Scottez-De Wambrechies, 1988
Scottez-De Wambrechies, Annie. "Boilly et Houdon: Deux Amis." *Connaissance des arts* 441 (November 1988), pp. 128–33.

Seelig, 1990
Seelig, Lorenz. "Tableaux des néo-classicismes français et belge de la Résidence de Coblence." *Revue de l'art* 87 (1990), pp. 52–58.

Segal, 1982
Segal, Sam. "The Flower Pieces of Roelandt Savery." *Leids Kunsthistorisch Jaarboek* (1982), pp. 309–37.

Segal, 1983
Segal, Sam. *A Fruitful Past.* Exhibition catalogue. Amsterdam, Galerie P. de Boer; and Braunschweig, Herzog Anton Ulrich-Museum, 1983. Amsterdam, 1983.

Segal, 1991
Segal, Sam. *Jan Davidsz de Heem en zijn kring.* Exhibition catalogue. Utrecht, Centraal Museum, 1991. The Hague, 1991.

Sérullaz, 1963-1
Sérullaz, Maurice. *Eugène Delacroix (1798–1863): exposition du centenaire.* Paris, Musée du Louvre, 1963. Paris, 1963.

Sérullaz, 1963-2
Sérullaz, Maurice. *Les plus beaux dessins français du 19e siècle.* Paris, 1963.

Sérullaz, 1984
Sérullaz, Maurice, with the collaboration of Arlette Sérullaz, Louis-Antoine Prat, and Claudine Ganeval. *Musée du Louvre, Cabinet des dessins. Inventaire général des dessins: école française, dessins d'Eugène Delacroix.* 2 vols. Paris, 1984.

Sestan, Adriani, and Guidotti, 1982
Sestan, Ernesto, Maurilio Adriani, and Alessandro Guidotti. *La badia fiorentina.* Florence, 1982.

Shapley, 1979
Shapley, Fern Rusk. *National Gallery of Art, Washington: Catalogue of the Italian Paintings.* 2 vols. Washington, D.C., 1979.

Shearman, 1961
Shearman, John. "The Chigi Chapel in S. Maria del Popolo." *Journal of the Warburg and Courtauld Institutes* 24, nos. 3–4 (1961), pp. 129–60.

Shoemaker, 1977
Shoemaker, Innis Howe. *Filippino Lippi as a Draughtsman.* Ann Arbor, 1977.

Siegfried, 1992
Siegfried, Susan. "Louis-Léopold Boilly and the Frame-up of Trompe l'Oeil." *The Art Journal* (forthcoming).

Slive, 1970–74
Slive, Seymour. *Frans Hals.* 3 vols. London, 1970–74.

Sluijter, 1985
Sluijter, Eric Jan. "Some Observations on the Choice of Narrative Mythological Subjects in Late Mannerist Painting in the Northern Netherlands." In *Netherlandish Mannerism: Papers Given at a Symposium in Nationalmuseum Stockholm, September 21–22, 1984,* edited by Görel Cavalli-Björkman, pp. 61–72. Stockholm, 1985.

Sluijter, 1986
Sluijter, Eric Jan. *De 'Heydensche Fabulen' in de noordnederlandse schilderkunst circa 1590–1670.* Privately printed, 1986.

Smith, 1990
Smith, David. "Carel Fabritius and Portraiture in Delft." *Art History* 13, no. 2 (June 1990), pp. 151–74.

Soprani, 1768
Soprani, Raphael. *Vite de' pittori, scultori e architetti genovesi.* Genoa, 1674. Rev. ed. 1768.

Spear, 1965
Spear, Richard E. "The 'Raising of Lazarus': Caravaggio and the Sixteenth Century Tradition." *Gazette des Beaux-Arts* (February 1965), pp. 65–70.

Speth-Holterhoff, 1957
Speth-Holterhoff, S. *Les peintres flamands de cabinets d'amateurs au XVIIᵉ siècle*. Brussels, 1957.

Spicer, 1979
Spicer, Joaneath. "The Drawings of Roelandt Savery." Ph.D. diss., Yale University, 1979.

Spicer, 1983
Spicer, Joaneath. "'De koe voor d'aerde statt': The Origins of the Dutch Cattle Piece." In *Essays in Northern European Art Presented to Egbert Haverkamp-Begemann on His Sixtieth Birthday*, edited by Anne-Marie Logan, pp. 251–56. Doornspijk, The Netherlands, 1983.

Spike, 1984
Spike, John T. *Baroque Portraiture in Italy: Works from North American Collections*. Exhibition catalogue. Sarasota, John and Mable Ringling Museum of Art; and Hartford, Wadsworth Atheneum, 1984–85. Sarasota, 1984.

Spruyt, 1777
Spruyt, P. L. *Liste des tableaux appartenant à des mains mortes, qui se trouvent dans la ville de Gand . . . , 3 septembre 1777*. Printed in C. Piot. *Rapport à Mr le Ministre de l'Intérieur sur les tableaux enlevés à la Belgique en 1794 et restitués en 1815*, pp. 134–62. Brussels, 1883.

Spruyt, 1789
Duverger, E. "Filip Spruyt en zijn inventaris van kunstwerken in openbaar en privaat bezit te Gent (ca. 1789–91)." *Gentse bijdragen* 19 (1961–66), pp. 151–240. [Spruyt inventory.]

Stechow, 1968
Stechow, Wolfgang. *Rubens and the Classical Tradition*. Cambridge, Massachusetts, 1968.

Stechow, 1975
Stechow, Wolfgang. *Salomon van Ruysdael*. Berlin, 1975.

Stein, 1986
Stein, Susan Alyson, ed. *Van Gogh: A Retrospective*. New York, 1986.

Steinbart, 1940
Steinbart, Kurt. *Johann Liss, der Maler aus Holstein*. Berlin, 1940.

Sterling, 1933
Sterling, Charles. *Exposition Hubert Robert à l'occasion du deuxième centenaire de sa naissance*. Exhibition catalogue. Paris, Musée de l'Orangerie, 1933. Paris, 1933.

Sterling, 1937
Sterling, Charles. *Peinture française, XVIᵉ–XVIIᵉ siècles*. Paris, 1937.

Sterling, 1955
Sterling, Charles. *The Metropolitan Museum of Art: A Catalogue of French Paintings, XV–XVIII Centuries*. Cambridge, Massachusetts, 1955.

Strasbourg, 1987
L'amour de l'art: le goût de deux amateurs pour le baroque italien. Exhibition catalogue, by Alain Roy et al. Strasbourg, Musée des Beaux-Arts, 1987. Strasbourg, 1987.

Strauss, 1974
Strauss, Walter L. *The Complete Drawings of Albrecht Dürer*. New York, 1974.

Strauss, 1977
Strauss, Walter L., ed. *Hendrik Goltzius, 1558–1617: The Complete Engravings and Woodcuts*. 2 vols. New York, 1977.

Strauss and van der Meulen, 1979
Strauss, Walter L., and Marjon van der Meulen. *The Rembrandt Documents*. New York, 1979.

Sumowski, 1983
Sumowski, Werner. *Gemälde der Rembrandt-Schüler*. 6 vols. Landau (Pfalz), 1983.

Sutton, 1990
Sutton, Peter C. *Northern European Paintings in the Philadelphia Museum of Art*. Philadelphia, 1990.

Tapié, 1990
Tapié, Alain, with the collaboration of Jean-Marie Dautel and Philippe Rouillard. *Les vanités dans la peinture au XVIIᵉ siècle*. Exhibition catalogue. Caen, Musée des Beaux-Arts; and Paris, Musée du Petit Palais, 1990–91. Caen, 1990.

van Thiel, 1965
van Thiel, Pieter J. J. "Cornelis Cornelisz van Haarlem as a Draughtsman." *Master Drawings* 3, no. 2 (1965), pp. 123–54.

Thiem, 1977
Thiem, Christel. *Florentiner Zeichner des Frühbarock*. Munich, 1977.

Thieme-Becker
Thieme, U., and F. Becker. *Allgemeines Lexikon der bildenden Künstler*. 37 vols. Leipzig, 1907–50.

Thiery, 1787
Thiery, Luc Vincent. *Guide des amateurs et des étrangers voyageurs à Paris . . . .* 2 vols. Paris, 1787.

Thuillier, 1963
Thuillier, Jacques, with the assistance of Jennifer Montagu. *Charles Le Brun, 1619–1690: peintre et dessinateur*. Exhibition catalogue. Versailles, Château de Versailles, 1963. [Versailles], 1963.

Toledo, 1976
The Toledo Museum of Art: European Paintings. Toledo, Ohio, 1976.

Tomlinson, 1989
Tomlinson, Janis. *Francisco Goya: The Tapestry Cartoons and Early Career at the Court of Madrid*. Cambridge, England, 1989.

Torresan, 1975
Torresan, Paolo. "Per una rivalutazione di Pieter Codde." *Antichità viva* 14, no. 1 (1975), pp. 12–23.

Toschi, 1900
Toschi, Giovanni Battista. "Lelio Orsi da Novellara pittore ed architetto (1511–1587)." *L'arte* 3 (1900), pp. 1–31.

Toussaint and de Forges, 1977
Toussaint, Hélène, and Marie-Thérèse de Forges. *Gustave Courbet (1819–1877)*. Exhibition catalogue. Paris, Grand Palais, 1977. Paris, 1977.

Toussaint and de Forges, 1978
Toussaint, Hélène, and Marie-Thérèse de Forges. *Gustave Courbet: 1819–1877*. Exhibition catalogue. London, Royal Academy of Arts, 1978. London, 1978.

Trévise, 1924
Trévise, Duc de. "Géricault, peintre d'actualités." *Revue de l'art ancien et moderne* 45 (1924), pp. 297–308.

Trudzinski, 1986
Trudzinski, Meinolf. *Beobachtungen zu Donatellos Antikenrezeption*. Berlin, 1986.

Unger, 1954
Unger, W. S. *De geschiedenis van Middelburg in omtrek*. Middelburg, The Netherlands, 1954.

Utrecht–Braunschweig, 1986–87
Nieuw licht op de gouden eeuw: Hendrick ter Brugghen en tijdgenoten. Exhibition catalogue, by Albert Blankert and Leonard J. Slatkes, with contributions by Marten Jan Bok, Dirk E. A. Faber, Sabine Jacob, Guido Jansen, Paul Huys Janssen, J. Richard Judson, Rüdiger Klessmann, Cora Rooker, and Mieke Vermeer. Utrecht, Centraal Museum; and

Braunschweig, Herzog Anton Ulrich-Museum, 1986–87. Utrecht, 1986.

Valenciennes, 1918
Geborgene Kunstwerke aus dem besetzten Nordfrankreich. Exhibition catalogue. Valenciennes, Musée de Peinture et de Sculpture, 1918. Valenciennes, 1918.

Vandalle, 1937
Vandalle, Maurice. *Les frères Vaillant: artistes lillois du XVIIème siècle.* Lille, 1937.

Vasari-Milanesi, 1906
Le opere di Giorgio Vasari con nuove annotazioni e commenti di Gaetano Milanesi. 9 vols. Florence, 1906.

Venturi
Venturi, Adolfo. *Storia dell'arte italiana* 9, nos. 1–7. Milan, 1925–34.

Vergnet Ruiz and Laclotte, 1962
Vergnet Ruiz, Jean, and Michel Laclotte. *Petits et grands musées de France.* Paris, 1962.

Verzelloni, 1977–78
Verzelloni, S. "L'opera grafica di Lelio Orsi fino al soggiorno romano (c. 1535–1554)." Thesis, Università degli Studi di Bologna, 1977–78.

Viatte, 1963
Viatte, Françoise. "Catalogue raisonné des dessins florentins et siennois des XVe et XVIe siècles au Musée de Lille." Thesis, École du Louvre, 1963.

Viatte, 1967
Viatte, Françoise. "Two Drawings by Naldini for the 'Deposition' in S. Simone, Florence." *Master Drawings* 5, no. 4 (1967), pp. 384–86.

Viatte, 1969
Viatte, Françoise. "Italian Drawings at Lille." *Master Drawings* 7, no. 1 (1969), pp. 51–53. [Review of *Dessins italiens du Musée de Lille.*]

Viatte, 1988
Viatte, Françoise. *Inventaire général des dessins italiens. III: Dessins toscans XVIe–XVIIIe siècles. Tome I: 1560–1640.* Paris, 1988.

Viatte and Monbeig-Goguel, 1981
Viatte, Françoise, and Catherine Monbeig-Goguel. *Dessins baroques florentins du Musée du Louvre.* Exhibition catalogue. Paris, Musée du Louvre, 1981–82. Paris, 1981.

Vignau-Wilberg, 1986–87
Vignau-Wilberg, Thea. "Naturemblematik am Ende des 16. Jahrhunderts." *Jahrbuch der kunsthistorischen Sammlungen in Wien*, n.s., 46–47 (1986–87), pp. 146–56.

See also Wilberg Vignau-Schuurman

Villani, 1953–54
Villani, Maria Rosa. "Lelio Orsi." Thesis, Università degli Studi di Bologna, 1953–54.

Vlieghe, 1972
Vlieghe, Hans. *Saints I.* Part 8 of *Corpus Rubenianum Ludwig Burchard.* London, 1972.

Vlieghe, 1973
Vlieghe, Hans. *Saints II.* Part 8 of *Corpus Rubenianum Ludwig Burchard.* London, 1973.

Waddingham, 1976–77
Waddingham, Malcolm R. "Michael Sweerts, *Boy Copying the Head of a Roman Emperor.*" *Minneapolis Institute of Arts Bulletin* 63 (1976–77), pp. 56–65.

Washington, 1990–91
Anthony van Dyck. Exhibition catalogue, by Susan J. Barnes, Julius S. Held, and Arthur K. Wheelock, Jr., with essays by Christopher Brown, Carol Christensen, Zirka Zaremba Filipczak, Oliver Millar, Jeffrey M. Muller, and J. Douglas Stewart. Washington, D.C., National Gallery of Art, 1990–91. Washington, D.C., 1990.

Washington–Detroit–Amsterdam, 1980–81
Gods, Saints and Heroes: Dutch Painting in the Age of Rembrandt. Exhibition catalogue, by Albert Blankert, Beatrijs Brenninkmeyer-de Rooij, Christopher Brown, Susan Donahue Kuretsky, Eric J. Sluijter, D. P. Snoep, Pieter van Thiel, Astrid Tümpel, Christian Tümpel, and Arthur K. Wheelock, Jr. Washington, D.C., National Gallery of Art; Detroit, Detroit Institute of Arts; and Amsterdam, Rijksmuseum, 1980–81. Washington, D.C., 1980. 6 vols.

Washington–New York, 1986–87
The Age of Bruegel: Netherlandish Drawings in the Sixteenth Century. Exhibition catalogue, by John Oliver Hand, J. Richard Judson, William W. Robinson, and Martha Wolff. Washington, D.C., National Gallery of Art; and New York, Pierpont Morgan Library, 1986–87. Washington, D.C., 1986.

Weigert, 1939
Weigert, Roger-Armand, ed. *Bibliothèque Nationale. Inventaire du fonds français: graveurs du XVIIe siècle.* Vol. 1. Paris, 1939.

Weigert, 1961
Weigert, Roger-Armand. *Mazarin, 1602–1661.* Exhibition catalogue. Paris, Bibliothèque Nationale, 1961. Paris, 1961.

Welu, 1983
Welu, James A. *The Collector's Cabinet: Flemish Paintings from New England Private Collections.* Exhibition catalogue. Worcester, Massachusetts, Worcester Art Museum, 1983–84. Worcester, Massachusetts, 1983.

Wessely, 1865
Wessely, J. E. *Wallerant Vaillant: Verzeichnis seiner Kupferstiche und Schabkunstblätter beschrieben.* Vienna, 1865.

Wethey, 1969
Wethey, Harold E. *The Paintings of Titian.* Vol. 1, *The Religious Paintings.* London, 1969.

Wilberg Vignau-Schuurman, 1969
Wilberg Vignau-Schuurman, Th. A. G. *Die emblematischen Elemente im Werke Joris Hoefnagels.* 2 vols. Leiden, 1969.

See also Vignau-Wilberg

Wilde, 1953
Wilde, Johannes. *Italian Drawings in the Department of Prints and Drawings in the British Museum: Michelangelo and His Studio.* London, 1953.

Wildenstein, 1933
Wildenstein, Georges. *Chardin.* Paris, 1933.

Wildenstein, 1963
Wildenstein, Georges. *Chardin.* Zurich, 1963.

Wildenstein, 1973
Wildenstein, Daniel, and Guy Wildenstein. *Documents complémentaires au catalogue de l'oeuvre de Louis David.* Paris, 1973.

van der Wolk, 1987
van der Wolk, Johannes. *The Seven Sketchbooks of Vincent van Gogh: A Facsimile Edition.* Translated by Claudia Swan. New York, 1987.

Yamanaka, 1981
Yamanaka, Kimihito. *Old Master Drawings from Private Collections in Japan.* Exhibition catalogue. Kitakyushu, Municipal Museum of Art, 1981.

Index

Page references are in roman type. Catalogue entries are so designated. References to pages with figure illustrations are in *italic* type.

Photograph Credits

The works in the exhibition were photographed in color by Jacques Quecq d'Henripret, Lille. Black-and-white photographs are reproduced through the courtesy of the following institutions, photographic services, and photographers:

Alinari/Art Resource, New York: p. 193, fig. 1; p. 197, fig. 1; p. 199, fig. 1; p. 208, fig. 1; p. 212, fig. 1; p. 216, fig. 1; p. 219, fig. 1; p. 243, fig. 1; p. 257, fig. 1

Amiens Cathedral: p. 264, fig. 1

Amsterdams Historisch Museum, Amsterdam: p. 283, fig. 1

Art-Photo, G. Pivard, Vienne: p. 117, fig. 1

Bibliothèque Nationale, Cabinet des Estampes, Paris: p. 263, fig. 1

A. C. Cooper Ltd., Christies, London: p. 111, fig. 1

Deutsche Fotothek, Dresden: p. 99, fig. 1

Documentation photographique de la réunion des musées nationaux, Paris: p. 18, fig. 7

Fot. Soprintendenza per i Beni Artistici e Storici, Siena: p. 243, fig. 1

Galleria dell'Accademia, Florence: p. 202, fig. 1

B. P. Keiser, Herzog Anton Ulrich-Museum, Braunschweig: p. 69, fig. 1

Laboratoire et Studio Gérondal, Lomme-Lille: p. 42, fig. 3; p. 74, fig. 1

Lauros-Giraudon, Photographie Giraudon, Paris: p. 47, fig. 9; p. 52, fig. 13; p. 270, fig. 1

Los Angeles County Museum of Art: p. 93, fig. 1

The Metropolitan Museum of Art, Photograph Studio, New York: p. 87, fig. 1; p. 152, fig. 1; p. 277, fig. 1

Ministère de l'Instruction Publique & des Beaux-Arts, Direction des Beaux-Arts, Service Photographique & Cinématographique, Paris: p. 9, fig. 4

Minneapolis Institute of Arts: p. 77, fig. 2

Musée Thomas Henry, Cherbourg: p. 118, fig. 2

Musei Vaticani, Archivio Fotografico, Vatican City: p. 232, fig. 1

National Gallery, London: p. 227, fig. 1

National Gallery of Art, Washington, D.C.: p. 221, fig. 1

Norton Simon Art Foundation, Pasadena: p. 207, fig. 1

Jacques Quecq d'Henripret, Lille: p. 3, fig. 1; p. 29, fig. 1; p. 43, fig. 4; p. 48, fig. 10

Rijksmuseum-Stichting, Amsterdam: p. 77, fig. 1; p. 101, fig. 1

Studio Gérondal, Lomme-Marais (Nord): p. 20, fig. 9

Unusual Films, Bob Jones University, Greenville, South Carolina: p. 108, fig. 1

Victoria & Albert Picture Library, London: p. 93, fig. 2

Walters Art Gallery, Baltimore: p. 159, fig. 1